Freedom from
Obsessive-Compulsive
Disorder

W9-BLG-814

Freedom from Obsessive-Compulsive Disorder

A Personalized Recovery Program
for Living with Uncertainty

Jonathan Grayson, PhD

BERKLEY BOOKS
NEW YORK

9/2/14
LN
$17.00

THE BERKLEY PUBLISHING GROUP
Published by the Penguin Group
Penguin Group (USA) LLC
375 Hudson Street, New York, New York 10014

USA • Canada • UK • Ireland • Australia • New Zealand • India • South Africa • China

penguin.com

A Penguin Random House Company

Copyright © 2003, 2014 by Jonathan Grayson, PhD.
Penguin supports copyright. Copyright fuels creativity, encourages diverse voices, promotes free speech,
and creates a vibrant culture. Thank you for buying an authorized edition of this book and for complying
with copyright laws by not reproducing, scanning, or distributing any part of it in any form without
permission. You are supporting writers and allowing Penguin to continue to publish books for every reader.

BERKLEY® is a registered trademark of Penguin Group (USA) LLC.
The "B" design is a trademark of Penguin Group (USA) LLC.

Berkley trade paperback ISBN: 978-0-425-27389-0

The Library of Congress has catalogued the Jeremy P. Tarcher/Penguin hardcover edition as follows:

Grayson, Jonathan.
Freedom from obsessive-compulsive disorder : a personalized recovery
program for living with uncertainty / Jonathan B. Grayson.
p.   cm.
Includes index.
ISBN 1-58542-246-0 (alk. paper)
1. Obsessive-compulsive disorder—Treatment—Popular works.   I. Title.
RC533.G725   2003   2003050723
616.85'22706—dc21

PUBLISHING HISTORY
Jeremy P. Tarcher / Penguin hardcover edition / September 2003
Berkley trade paperback edition / September 2004
Updated Berkley trade paperback edition / May 2014

PRINTED IN THE UNITED STATES OF AMERICA

10   9   8   7   6   5   4   3   2   1

Cover design by Elaine Groh.
Interior text design by Tanya Maiboroda.

Every effort has been made to ensure that the information contained in this book is complete and accurate. However,
neither the publisher nor the author is engaged in rendering professional advice or services to the individual reader.
The ideas, procedures, and suggestions contained in this book are not intended as a substitute for consulting with your
physician. All matters regarding your health require medical supervision. Neither the author nor the publisher shall
be liable or responsible for any loss or damage allegedly arising from any information or suggestion in this book.

While the author has made every effort to provide accurate telephone numbers and Internet
addresses at the time of publication, neither the author nor the publisher is responsible for errors,
or for changes that occur after publication. Further, the publisher does not have any control over
and does not assume any responsibility for author or third-party websites or their content.

To Cathy, Josh, and Jane

Precious are our memories, joyous are our future hopes, and as for the present, our here and now, I couldn't ask for more.

Contents

PART 3

Personalizing Your Program:
Treatment Guidelines for Your Specific OCD Concerns

PART 4

Recovery and Beyond

Appendices

Acknowledgments

I am where I am today because of the contributions and efforts of many people. As one might expect, I have to start with my mother and father, Hal and Helen Grayson, who gave me the confidence to try anything, the courage to fail, and the humor to appreciate it all. Thanks to Tom Borkovec, my mentor in graduate school, whose wisdom, friendship, and curiosity about everything sharpened my thinking and whose extreme patience taught me to write, thus making this endeavor possible. To Edna Foa, whose work with OCD is still the cornerstone and core of our treatment. To Gayle Frankel, the members of GOAL, and everyone I have worked with, this is for you (I'm sorry there isn't enough space to name all of you): There is no way to measure what I have learned about life from witnessing the courage you have displayed in your quest for freedom. To my peers at my former center, the Anxiety and Agoraphobia Treatment Center, and my current center, the Anxiety and OCD Treatment Center of Philadelphia: Joanne Dobrowski, B. J. Foster, Lori Kasmen, Harold Kirby, Leslie Lenox, Kathy Rupertus, David Raush, Georgia Sloane, Linda Welsh, Lee Fitzgibbons, Karen Landsman, and Tejal Jakatdar; you are my second family, providing support and stimulation, never letting me get away with anything (well, not too much), and, in the words of Leslie, making work a fun place. I also have to thank my longtime colleagues and friends, Charles Mansueto and Alec Pollard. It's as if we were there at the beginning and I can't thank you enough for all of the inspiration, discussion, and unrestrained fun.

I also want to thank my agent, Jessica Lichtenstein. She found me and made this book possible. Her optimism and energy were a constant source of support. I can think of few tasks more painful than editing an author's first book. With the patience of a saint, Wendy Hubbert at Tarcher guided me through this ordeal, and my gratitude to her knows no bounds.

And, most of all, my family. My son, Josh, whose life has filled me with more love than I would have believed possible. Thank you for so cheerfully allowing me to make the vignettes of your trials and tribulations part of my clinical repertoire. To his wife, Jane, for completing his life and ours. I want to thank you in advance for your life stories that will undoubtedly become part of my clinical repertoire. Finally, to my wife, friend, and lifelong partner, Cathy—everything is from you and for you. What a long, strange trip it has been! For more than forty years, I have shared everything with you, and still you are the endless source of all that I could ever want: a dream come true. Without your patience, sacrifice, support, and help during this endeavor, this book wouldn't be.

Introduction

I was standing in an open field, looking back into the forest and brush, watching the others struggle their way out. It was raining. I had purposely taken everyone off trail through trees and undergrowth so densely packed that forward movement was a slow process of stepping over and through bushes and being on guard for branches snapping back from whoever was in front of you. Melanie, the fourth person to emerge into the freedom of the clearing, shouted, "I'm having a great time!" The photographer documenting our trip for *People* magazine snapped a picture. Seeing Melanie's joy, it was hard to connect this woman with the one I'd met seven months earlier at my former center, The Anxiety and Agoraphobia Treatment Center in Philadelphia.

When I met Melanie at our first session, she was an extreme suicide risk— all medications in her home, even aspirin, had to be locked in a safe. Her parents wouldn't permit her to carry more than two dollars at a time, fearing that access to more money would enable her to commit suicide with over-the-counter medications. She was an attractive and articulate twenty-nine-year-old with a fifteen-year history of both obsessive-compulsive disorder (OCD) and body dysmorphic disorder (BDD). Her OCD focused on issues of perfection. When taking notes during class, if there were any cross-outs, stray marks, folds, or creases in her notebook, she would feel compelled to discard the page. Similarly, she wouldn't tolerate any such marks in her textbooks and would cope with such "imperfections" by not using the text. Though she found school a nightmare of anxiety, Melanie did well in the courses she managed to complete. But many of her attempts to go to school resulted in anxiety and depression severe enough to require psychiatric hospitalization.

Melanie also felt as though she was horribly ugly—so repulsive that she believed it was a burden for those around her to tolerate her presence. This is what it feels like to have BDD, a form of OCD in which sufferers can't stand their own appearance. She spent endless hours agonizing over her hair and makeup, trying to get ready to go out, but often wouldn't be able to leave the house. For more than fifteen years, she had no memory of ever being free from her anxiety and despair.

Yet here she was on a camping trip. And not just any trip, but one that I've been running almost every year for more than two decades as a therapeutic journey for OCD sufferers. Even non-sufferers might find it difficult to spend a weekend sleeping in tents, using latrines without the benefit of running water, and taking torturous hikes through the mud and muck. For the OCD sufferers I treat, especially those with contamination fears, the accomplishment of making it through such an experience is often nothing less than a tremendous breakthrough in their recovery.

This camping trip is just one of the approaches I've found to be of use in working with OCD sufferers during the last twenty-five years. Earlier in my career, as a faculty member in the Department of Psychiatry at Temple University's School of Medicine, I was part of a research team studying the treatment of OCD. Though our research excelled at delineating the mechanics of treatment— our results and findings regarding the behavioral techniques known as *exposure and response prevention* are still the core of today's treatment for OCD—I felt the need to go beyond the actual treatment process.

I wanted to address issues our research was ignoring, such as relapse prevention. So in 1981, with an OCD sufferer named Gayle Frankel (who was then the current president of the Philadelphia Affiliate of the Obsessive-Compulsive Foundation), I started the first OCD support group in the country. Called GOAL (**G**iving **O**bsessive-compulsives **A**nother **L**ifestyle), our group was more than a place for sufferers to share their stories. Its purpose from the beginning was to help sufferers *understand* their OCD and to make and maintain treatment gains.

Helping people understand their OCD is the key to my treatment approach. One of the greatest problems for those of you who suffer from this disorder is the disparity between your inner world and the outside. For all of us, the person we show the world is not exactly who we are; we all have our private thoughts, opinions, and secrets. But, for you, the gulf between your private and public selves is greater. No matter which aspects of your OCD everyone else sees, you and I know it is only the tip of the iceberg. You understand the pain and frustration of being locked in a strange world in which you know that your thoughts and behaviors make no sense. It is as if you have simultaneously lost your mind and, at the same time, are so sane that you are a witness to the loss. You are an expert at knowing what OCD feels like, but fully understanding your plight is another story.

You may have heard many explanations for your OCD—it's a chemical imbalance, it's a learned behavior. These are explanations, but they are no better than saying a car works because it has an engine. Knowing that a car has an engine doesn't tell you how to fix a car that's not running. For you to fully understand your OCD, a meaningful explanation needs to be more than logical and scientific. It must address your feelings and experience and answer questions such as: *I'm staring at the stove and can see that it is off. Why don't I know that it is off?* If an explanation touches you, and you can't help exclaiming, "That's me!" then you understand.

If you suffer from OCD, you have probably seen many different professionals, tried numerous medications, and read any number of books dealing with anxiety and OCD. This book, however, is different. It is not simply a cookbook explaining how to recover from OCD, because overcoming OCD requires more than simply following instructions. Treatment without understanding is like painting by numbers; there will be some improvement and symptom reduction, but you want more.

To go beyond symptom reduction and stop OCD from controlling your life, I believe you'll do better as a master artist. The "master artist" has the understanding to create and fashion his or her own work. This book offers the self-guided version of the treatment program used at my center, where helping sufferers understand their OCD is the crucial first step to recovery, because they can't truly agree to therapy if they don't understand their OCD and the treatment process.

Your success depends upon your becoming an equal partner in designing your recovery program. As you'll find in this book, with understanding you won't follow a treatment protocol, you'll design your own. Copies of the forms, worksheets, and other materials found in this book are also available for free download from www.FreedomFromOCD.com.

Part 1 of this book, Understanding Obsessive-Compulsive Disorder, will help you to truly understand your OCD experience. You will begin to answer the questions that plague you—for example: *How can I not know what I know? Why can't I stop ritualizing?* In making sense of your OCD, you will begin to realize that this disorder doesn't set you apart from the rest of humanity. You will come to recognize that the difference between you and non-sufferers is a matter of degree, not unlike the differences between social and problem drinkers. In the case of drinking, getting drunk isn't the problem; it is how often and how much it interferes with your life. For OCD, it is not rituals, seemingly irrational thoughts, or anxiety that differentiates the sufferer from the non-sufferer, but how much these interfere with your daily life. This section will also address the role of medication in recovery and the cognitive behavioral techniques that you will use in your OCD program.

In Part 2, The Foundation of Your Program, I will demystify the process of OCD assessment and treatment, allowing you to design a recovery program for yourself that you can understand and believe in. Then I will guide you through the initial steps of assessing your OCD.

Your newfound understanding will be transformed into practical knowledge as you use the tools and instructions I provide to further assess your OCD and prepare the materials you will need in your self-guided recovery program. The most important of these will be the "scripts" you will be creating to keep up your motivation, fight discouragement, and overcome difficult hurdles. These scripts will help you address one of the greatest difficulties in carrying out a self-guided OCD treatment program: the absence of a therapist to provide you with support specifically targeted and appropriate to your needs of the moment. Although a book can't replace an experienced therapist, sample therapist scripts are provided, along with directions that will enable you to adapt them to your own needs or to create your own. These scripts will appear throughout the book. Ideally, your recovery program should be a collaboration between you and an experienced OCD therapist. This book is meant to be used as an adjunct to therapy or at times when you can't find a therapist.

Part 3, Personalizing Your Program: Treatment Guidelines for Your Specific

OCD Concerns, is the heart of this book and focuses upon the different manifestations of OCD. Each poses special challenges that need to be addressed when designing a recovery program, particularly if most of your OCD symptoms seem to fall into a single category, such as obsessions focusing on contamination or violent thoughts. The chapters in Part 3 will provide guidance for modifying and individualizing your recovery program through examples, adjusted treatment guidelines, and scripts.

Even when your obsessive concerns seem to have a single focus, they may affect your life in more ways than you realize. For example, if you have contamination concerns, you may find that, in addition to washing your hands, you check the environment for contaminants and mentally ruminate about what you have or have not touched. Or if violent thoughts are your focus, you may spend your time both trying to figure out what it means that you have such thoughts and trying to find ways to prevent the thoughts from coming into your mind. Because of this, you will discover advice throughout Part 3 that you will want to incorporate into your recovery program.

Part 4, Recovery and Beyond, will help you complete your recovery. Working alone on your recovery can be hard. I provide you with guidelines for using family and/or friends as helpful supports during treatment. However, sometimes you will want help from someone who knows exactly how you feel. For this purpose, I also provide instructions for setting up an effective GOAL support group.

Your recovery program doesn't end when you feel you have overcome your symptoms. Maintaining your gains is a process that requires continued effort. In the last chapter, you will discover why "slips" are normal and how, when you prepare for them, they don't have to lead to a complete relapse.

The good news is that, while OCD can be a devastating and debilitating psychological disorder, surprisingly it is one of the most treatable. Current research holds that 70 percent of those suffering from OCD will significantly benefit from a treatment involving exposure and response prevention (the treatment of choice for OCD). This should be a time of hope and optimism for finding treatment.

The key, though, is finding therapists who are truly experienced in treating OCD, who know how to properly use exposure and response prevention instead of offering traditional talk therapies or nothing more than medication.

When Melanie, my camping trip client, first came to me, I found that her psychiatrist had been underprescribing the SSRI (Selective Serotonin Reuptake Inhibitor) antidepressant she had been taking. When this was rectified, she went from being an extreme suicide risk to a moderate one. Her OCD and BDD, though identified early in her previous therapies, had never been properly treated. Her course of treatment with me included exposure and response prevention, and seven months later she was camping and having a great time. One year after that trip, Melanie was no longer controlled by OCD, BDD, and depression; had completed two semesters of school with ease; had spoken at the annual national conference of the Obsessive-Compulsive Foundation about her recovery; and had gone on her second OCD camping trip.

Too often I am faced with seeing another Melanie—someone who has needlessly suffered for years. *Freedom from Obsessive-Compulsive Disorder* is my solution. I believe that OCD, when properly understood, is not a disorder of hopeless torment but one that can be overcome. Conquering OCD is hard work, but not as hard as what OCD sufferers already go through every day. So, I invite you, like my campers, to find the hope and courage to journey with me to a better place.

PART **1**

Understanding
Obsessive-Compulsive
Disorder

Chapter 1

Uncertainty: The Core of OCD

A few years ago, I was in a doughnut shop, waiting to be served. A well-dressed woman was sitting at the counter next to me. When her server—Jared, according to his name tag—brought her doughnuts, she had a special request. "Would it be okay if I pay you after I eat?" she asked. "I'm not going to run out or anything, but I just washed my hands, and if I go into my purse to touch money, they will be dirty and I'll have to wash them again."

"Do you realize how dirty money is?" she continued. "Money is handled by so many people that anything could be on it. That's why they don't allow cashiers to both handle money and serve food. In fact . . ." She went on for quite some time, ignoring or pretending not to notice Jared's expression, which silently said, *What is wrong with you? Fine, pay later—just let me get back to work.*

The answer to Jared's unspoken question was *obsessive-compulsive disorder (OCD).* And the woman in the doughnut shop—to my trained eye, an OCD sufferer—is not alone. I am often struck by how many people I pass on any given day—driving my car on the highway, walking through a mall, sitting in a movie theater—who likely have OCD as well. Statistically, for every forty of the thousands of faces I see, one is suffering or will suffer from OCD. When I was in graduate school in the late seventies, I was taught that OCD was a rare and hopeless disorder that only affected about .05 percent of the population (1 in 2,000). However, in the early eighties, I quickly realized that these figures had to be wrong. At that time, I was working at Temple University's School of

Medicine with Dr. Edna Foa, who was on the first of her many National Institute of Mental Health (NIMH) grants that researched and pioneered today's treatment of OCD. Everyone I discussed my work with seemed to know of someone who exhibited OCD symptoms (significant symptoms, like those of the woman in the doughnut shop, not the little habits and rituals all of humanity engages in on a daily basis). I wondered, *How could OCD be simultaneously rare and yet so common that everyone knows someone with it?* Since then, worldwide studies have found lifetime prevalence rates for OCD to vary between 2 and 3 percent—about one in every forty people.

For the most part, OCD sufferers are able to remain invisible. There are exceptions, of course: those of you who make no effort to hide your compulsions, whose suffering is obvious, if in nothing else, in your inability to function. The billionaire Howard Hughes, for example, suffered from OCD so severely that his life was reduced to a tortured and limited existence. His seemingly bizarre habits and lifestyle, coupled with his wealth and fame, attracted the media like a magnet.

The way OCD looks to outsiders is a far cry from what OCD really is. To outsiders, the disorder is what the press shows us—extreme cases of people who claim they have to do things that make no sense to themselves or others. But the truth is that when you have OCD, something is happening to you, you are *not* crazy, and there *is* something you can do about it.

Why doesn't the outside world have a better understanding of OCD? One problem is that many of you are experts at hiding all or almost all of your rituals, so you appear to have, at worst, a minor problem. Colleagues at work just think of you as a neat freak, or as that man with the odd but harmless habit of circling his car a few times in the parking lot after locking it. You function in the world, and you don't appear to be in obvious distress. Unlike the extreme cases publicized in the press and on talk shows, your OCD doesn't seem to be much of a difficulty to live with. There are a number of reasons you may strive to hide your fears and rituals. For many of you, concealing your problem is necessary to keep your job and preserve your relationships. Another reason you may try to hide OCD is that you simply want to avoid the humiliation of being labeled "crazy." So even if you engage in a few small rituals—enough to have others label you a neat freak—you make sure no one sees how anxious you are underneath that "neatness." This ability of yours to successfully function under stress has a special name: *competence.*

Anyone who is successful in the world has this ability. Imagine coming to me for treatment. If, during your first session, you found me shaking, stuttering, and discussing a terrible problem I was having at home, you'd quickly decide you were in the wrong place. You'd expect that whatever problems I might have, I would pull myself together and do my job. There is only one difference between me and you: I don't rely on using this competence as often as you do.

Competence works both for and against you. On the one hand, it allows you to function in the world. There are many accomplished individuals whose OCD we'd never know about if they hadn't admitted to the problem publically. Actor-director Billy Bob Thornton, as well as former host of Nickelodeon's *Double Dare* show, Marc Summers, are both very forthright about their OCD and have managed to find ways to have successful careers. It is important for you to recognize this strength in yourself. Some of what I will be asking you to do later will seem very hard, but what you are doing now is also very hard. How many of your colleagues and friends who don't suffer from OCD could function as well as you if they were under the same constant level of anxiety and stress? Bravery is not a feeling; bravery is how you behave when you are scared. You are among the bravest people I know. The strength and competence you are accustomed to using in order to get through your daily life can help you succeed in treatment.

But competence can also work against you. It has led many of you to delay seeking treatment. After all, if you are trying to hide your problem, seeking treatment might be a flag to others that something is wrong. If your OCD started when you were a child or an adolescent, you may have felt especially afraid that adults, if they discovered your secrets, would confirm that you were going crazy. Jessica, for example, came to my center at age sixteen after having hidden her OCD for five years. During the previous school year, she had begun to obsess about harm coming to her family and felt the need to protect them with numerous rituals involving movement and symmetry. Every time she went through a doorway, she felt she had to touch the left and right sides of the doorway to protect her family. She would continue to do this until it "felt right." Her OCD only became evident to her teachers and family when her anxiety became so intolerable that she no longer felt capable of hiding her pain and rituals. In "crashing," she was one of the lucky ones. She worked very hard in treatment and was able to overcome her OCD. I have worked with sufferers who successfully hid their OCD for twenty years or longer.

Where does this leave you? Trapped with anxiety, painful thoughts, rituals you feel you can't control, and the frustrating knowledge that you logically know your fears and compulsive actions make no sense. You don't understand what is happening, and you are surrounded by people who understand even less about it than you do. Often your friends and family are aware of your OCD and will try to offer helpful advice: "You don't have to wash your hands again— they are clean." "The door is locked, we can leave now." "Yes, for the fiftieth time, I'm sure you didn't hit anyone on the way home; you can stop asking."

Most of the time, you don't listen to the advice. Others tell you not to worry, because your fears make no sense. You already know this. Their exhortations merely confirm your suspicions that you must be losing your mind. So you desperately try to hide your symptoms, because who wants to be thought of as crazy? Though you may succeed in appearing "normal" to the outside world, you know something that non-sufferers don't: You know how anxious you feel.

Your family would like you to stop ritualizing, but you know they have no idea what stopping will do to you. Indeed, there have likely been occasions in which you tried to resist ritualizing. Even though your most feared disaster didn't occur, your anxiety probably increased. In the end, you may have gone on a binge of ritualizing that lasted far longer than usual. And as anyone with OCD knows, five hours of handwashing isn't simply washing your hands over and over. It is a hell in which every repetition is accompanied by mounting frustration and anxiety: *Why can't I stop? Why don't I know my hands are clean when I know they must be? How long is this going to last?* On such occasions, you didn't stop ritualizing because you finally felt you got it right; you stopped because of exhaustion. The whole process felt crazy and out of control.

No matter what disaster you may fear with your OCD—illness, death, or whatever—usually the feeling that "I can't take another second" or "I will lose control or go crazy" is almost certainly present. In the previous *Diagnostic and Statistical Manual of Mental Disorders-IV*, the psychiatric handbook for diagnosing mental disorders, OCD was listed as an anxiety disorder. This probably comes as no surprise to you. Although OCD has been given its own category in the *DSM-V*, we know that anxiety is the driving force behind OCD: an anxiety that feels overwhelming and endless, an anxiety that spirals out of control as attempts to reassure and neutralize fail over and over again. So, even if your obsessions and compulsions are literally attempts to avoid potential disaster, they are also attempts to *make your anxiety stop*. In order to avoid intolerable out-of-control feelings, to avoid going crazy, you ritualize. Ritualizing may not make sense to your friends and family members, but they don't know what will happen to you emotionally if you stop. Given all they don't know about OCD, listening to their advice *really* would be crazy!

Despite its crucial role in OCD, anxiety is not the defining feature of OCD. OCD has many different faces—contamination concerns and handwashing; repetitious checking of doors, stoves, and locks; concern about violent or sexual thoughts. How can so many different manifestations all stem from the same problem? What ties them together? What is the core of OCD and the source of the painful anxiety it evokes? In preparing to write this book, I created a survey questionnaire that asked sufferers and their families to describe their experiences with OCD. It was disseminated at my center and over the Internet.

Ira, a forty-eight-year-old man, has suffered from OCD since he was nineteen years old. The following excerpt from his survey response provides us with an answer:

> *I work in the city, and it's such a filthy place. If I could have my way, I wouldn't go there, that way I wouldn't have to go near so many dirty people— people sneezing, coughing, touching everything—but that's where my law firm is. During the day, I'm not too bad. I have dirty clothes for wearing outside and decontaminated clothes for home. I make sure to keep my hands away from my mouth during the day, and I'll only go out to lunch at certain clean restaurants.*
>
> *But when I get home, that's when the ordeal begins. I make everyone in the family come into the house through the laundry room. That way they can take their clothes off down there, go straight to the downstairs shower to wash, and then put on house clothes. I have everyone keep house clothes separate from going-out clothes. The going-out clothes have to be washed three times before I feel they are clean. After I'm done with them, I run the empty washer two more times to get it clean enough to wash the house clothes.*
>
> *My laundry procedure is as follows: I take a shower and put on gloves to take the going-out clothes to the washer. I carefully put them in and then put the detergent in and turn the machine on. I then take the gloves off, throw*

them away, and wash my hands. When the cycle is finished, I get another pair of gloves, put the detergent in, and start the machine. Then I throw away those gloves and wash my hands. Then I do this one more time. When the final load of the night is done, I clean the outside of the machine with ammonia during each of the two cleansing cycles.

We go food shopping on Saturday. All cans and packages that can be washed are. For boxed goods, I put on gloves and carefully open the top of the box and peel it away, so that nothing inside could possibly touch the outside. Then I put the contents in decontaminated Tupperware containers. The kids' school books and papers used to be a problem—I didn't want to let them into the house, but I knew I couldn't do that, so we have a special homework room and homework clothes for them. I hate this problem and what it's done to me. I have a great family; they put up with me, even though I put them through hell. I know none of it makes sense, but you don't know what it feels like, trying to be so perfect to get things clean that you know don't really have to be. No one else does this, but then I think about getting AIDS or my family getting it. And what if I was the unlucky one to somehow get it from something someone with AIDS touched. What if . . .   —IRA

In Ira's description, you can see all of the many defining features of OCD: anxiety, painful thoughts, rituals he feels he can't control, and the frustrating knowledge that his fears and compulsive actions make no sense. But it is in the last line of the excerpt that he provides us with the answer to our question about the source of anxiety in OCD: "What if?" The intellectual and emotional uncertainty of "what if" is, I believe, the root of most OCD symptoms. By *intellectual,* I am referring to our ability to question any aspect of our lives, for example, wondering if the door is locked or how you will do on tomorrow's test. *Emotional* uncertainty refers to our feelings about unpredictable events, usually things that in some way threaten us or the people or things that are important to us.

The core of OCD is trying to get rid of uncertainty in our lives in an attempt to be 100 percent certain. Everyone, sufferer and non-sufferer alike, knows what certainty feels like. There are numerous aspects of our lives for which we take this feeling for granted: My car is in the driveway; I am sitting on a sofa at this moment, reading a book; the sun will rise tomorrow. However, while all of us feel certain about many things, the truth is that the absolute certainty we feel is an illusion. An event may be probable or improbable, but neither is an absolute. The inability to feel or be certain is reasonable. My car *may* have been stolen and *may* no longer be in the driveway. Rather than reading a book on the sofa, perhaps I'm actually in a state mental institution experiencing a very realistic and remarkable hallucination. Do I have any evidence to the contrary? No, after all, by definition if I'm delusional and hallucinating, my senses are not to be trusted. Certainly no one around me can answer the question—my wife might be part of my delusional system, merely saying what I am making her say. As for the sun rising, some cataclysmic cosmic event might destroy the sun tonight, in which case there will be no dawn tomorrow. Improbable is not impossible.

To better grasp the deceptive nature of certainty, take a moment to imagine someone you love who is not in the room with you right now. Is this individual alive? If you answered yes, how do you know? Even if the two of you spoke to each other ten minutes ago, isn't it possible that he or she has had an accident, or a heart attack, or has been physically attacked in those ten minutes? And yet, if this isn't the focus of your OCD concerns, you still *feel* certain that your loved one is alive. Despite the fact that your feeling is based on probability, not truth, despite the effect the loss of this person would have on you, you have no urge to rush to the phone to make sure your loved one is alive. You are coping in a "normal" way: regarding your *feeling* of certainty as truth and not planning to act otherwise unless you receive a horrible phone call informing you of disaster. With your OCD symptoms, you do the reverse—rather than waiting for disaster to occur, you want immediate answers to your obsessive questions.

Having OCD doesn't mean that you are consumed by a driven, all-pervasive pursuit of certainty in every aspect of your life. That urge to be certain is restricted to your OCD fears and concerns. Some might suggest that OCD concerns are unreasonable as opposed to reasonable concerns. They would argue that washing your hands for two hours to avoid contamination or driving around the block fifteen times to make sure you haven't hit someone is not as reasonable as worrying about a terrorist attack in the city you live in. My response to this is, "How could anyone argue that concerns about death, disease, or causing an accident are unreasonable?" Reasonable vs. unreasonable is not the issue. Non-sufferers might also argue that the issue is not only the type of event but also the likelihood that it will occur—that non-sufferers can live with uncertainty without anxiety for what we would identify as *low-probability events,* that is, events not likely to occur.

But this isn't true: Everyone becomes concerned with low-probability events at times in their lives. Imagine being the parent of a teenage girl who is going out on her first date with a boy you don't know who has only had his driver's license for five months. The odds are heavily in favor of her safely returning home, but how many parents would be unconcerned? How would they feel if she was late? Consider the anthrax scare that followed the destruction of the World Trade Center on September 11, 2001. Although very few people contracted anthrax and even fewer died, many people were terrified about opening their mail. From a statistical point of view, it was more likely that they would be maimed or killed in a car crash than contract anthrax, but they were still anxious. Why? After all, you don't hear people asking, "Do I really need to risk being injured in a car crash just to go shopping at the mall?"

The fact is that we all live with risk. We drive cars to and from work. We cross streets. We go to sleep secure in our belief that if a fire starts, our smoke detector will wake us in time. And we all take precautions that are unnecessary or don't make sense. Parents of newborn babies will often look in on their baby before going to bed. If asked why, they would tell you how much they just love looking at their baby, sleeping so peacefully, but they would also admit that they would feel uncomfortable going to bed without checking. Let's look at this objectively. If you put your baby to sleep at 8:00 p.m., there are about three hours between then and your bedtime for something terrible to happen. At 11:00 p.m., when you go to bed, you check the baby, and now there is a whole night during which tragedy could occur. In reality, this is a ritual check that may make the new parents feel better, but it doesn't protect their baby.

If this concern were the focus of your OCD, you'd frequently check your baby throughout the night. Your OCD wants you to be 100 percent certain (who wouldn't want this?). But there is a problem: Uncertainty is making you feel anxious, and because of this you make the mistake—from literally not knowing any better—of trying to alleviate your anxiety by obtaining absolute certainty. You try to use logic to change your feelings, and that doesn't work.

The reason we try to use logic to change feelings is that we are used to believing what our feelings tell us—some things *feel* so obvious that questioning their veracity seems unnecessary (e.g., your certainty that your loved ones are alive). You experience feelings of certainty for the non-OCD parts of your life. Because of this, when confronted by OCD fears, you seek to feel the comforting illusion of certainty you feel in those unaffected parts of your life. You desperately try to use what you logically know to change these feelings—it seems as though experiencing certainty should be easy and within reach. Armed with logic, you pursue the feeling of certainty, sending yourself round and round in endless circles: *I know I don't want to hurt my wife, but if I don't want to hurt her, then why did the thought of hurting her pop into my head? Maybe I have a secret urge to hurt her that I don't know about. So maybe I will hurt her. But why would I want to do that? I love her. Everyone knows I wouldn't hurt a fly. I've never hurt anyone. . . .* It's an endless circle, a vicious spiral of frustration and anxiety. As you have discovered, for every logical answer there is a what-if.

What you need to learn is that logic doesn't change feelings. For example, imagine that pizza is one of your favorite foods. Think about how wonderful it tastes. Now suppose you discover it is no longer safe for you to eat this food, that your cholesterol is very high, so you can't have any more cheese in your diet. Would knowing that cheese is dangerous for you make cheese taste bad? Unlikely.

Logic doesn't change your feelings. It provides you with reasons to listen or not to listen to your feelings. I may deprive myself of cheese because of my cholesterol problem, but I will still love pizza. What most people don't realize is that what they experience as a certainty is not a fact, but a feeling. Frequently, our feeling of certainty correlates with reality; that is, most of the time our car isn't stolen, the sun rises, our loved ones have not been shot, along with so many of our other expectations, that we come to believe that this certainty emotion is a fact. If this were true, then how can Democrats and Republicans both have certainty about their beliefs. Similarly, how can two people who are devoutly dedicated to different religions both be certain? In both of these cases at least one group has to be wrong. And although the odds of the sun not rising are slim, cars do get stolen and people do get shot. Rather than representing a factual reality, the feeling of certainty, at most, represents a probability and not necessarily a high one. Despite this, we cling to trying to feel certain, not only because it is so often reinforced by the environment, but because we are wired to pursue this feeling.

So logic fails as it must. For some of you, the failure of logic and the resulting vicious circle of endless questioning and anxiety have left you feeling that you are no longer able to discern whether or not something is safe: that not washing your hands really may harm your family, that you did run over someone on the way to the office, or that you don't know whether or not the door you are staring at is locked. You know what you are feeling, but you don't understand why. The words you use in an attempt to capture your emotional experience haven't been accurate with regard to what is actually happening. You tell yourself and others that rituals can't be resisted, so you can't stop washing your hands, or that your judgment is impaired, because you can't tell whether or not your hands are clean after two hours of washing. It is hard to separate how you feel from what you know, when you don't have the language to communicate what is happening inside. As a result, both you and therapists inexperienced with the treatment of OCD can end up focusing on the wrong goals.

So, are your perceptions accurate? Do you know anything for certain? Can you get better without knowing? The answer to the last is yes. Knowing is too difficult. Therefore, let's focus not on what you "know," but on what you *guess*. Throughout this book, I will be asking you to make your best guess about different situations. Coming up with a best guess means you don't have to be sure of your answer. This can be very hard, because you want to *feel* that your guess is right. If it were right, it wouldn't be a guess. To help you guess, you can use a method that I call the *Gun Test*.

The next time you are having trouble making a decision, think of the following scenario. Imagine I have a gun pointed at you and your loved ones, and I am going to give you a single guess about your concern (for example, Will this particular contamination kill your children? Is the front door open?). You will only have one guess, and if you guess wrong, you and they will be killed. You don't have to be confident in your guess, but you do have to guess, because if you don't, everyone will be killed. What is your guess?

To date, everyone makes the "right" guess. I put right in quotes to denote that it is not so much right as it is merely the same guess that those who aren't suffering from OCD would make. The Gun Test is an aid to help you distinguish between what you intellectually and logically know from the emotional feeling of certainty you want. It won't, however, make your guess feel right—if it did, you would be done with OCD. Learning to guess and to live with the consequences of guessing will play an important part in your self-guided program.

Obviously, the program you will be designing for yourself in the coming chapters will be built on more than just guesses. In thinking about your program, ask yourself if the ideas in this chapter have begun to change your thoughts about recovery. You probably started with the general goal of wanting to overcome OCD, wishing your thoughts and rituals would stop and your anxiety would go away. It seemed that getting better would put an end to painful doubting. You may have even heard of OCD referred to as the "doubting disease." But I hope that after reading this chapter you have come to realize that this is wrong—doubt is normal. OCD is the problem in which you try to eradicate all doubt—and that is impossible. As near as we can tell the only people to possess absolute certainty are stupid—something that you are not! Non-sufferers may tell you that they are definitely certain about some things. The truth is that they *feel* certain when the odds are not absolute (either 100% or 0%). Technically, they are comfortable with uncertainty just as you are in the parts of your life unaffected by OCD. To achieve your desire of overcoming OCD, you now know that learning to live with uncertainty needs to be one of your goals.

Can you do this? I think you can. You've seen how you have already successfully lived with many uncertainties every moment of your life. The idea is to learn how to cope with your *OCD uncertainties* the same way you cope with life's other uncertainties. To achieve this, you need to understand why you have greater difficulty with uncertainty than non-sufferers; in other words, why do you have OCD? To answer this question, in the next chapter we will look at the factors that gave rise to your OCD.

Chapter 2

Causes of OCD: Biology and Learning, Not Biology vs. Learning

o one likes uncertainty, but why is coping with it harder for you than for non-sufferers? Is there something different about your biology? Did you somehow "learn" to have OCD? The answer to these questions is yes: OCD is both a learned and a biological disorder, and these two factors interact with each other. The experience of one of my clients, Mary, is a good example of the interplay between biology and learning. Mary had an eight-year history of severe contamination rituals. She was afraid of germs and illness, particularly hepatitis, and was fearful of making herself and her family sick. Simply leaving the house was an ordeal. Her husband did all the food shopping, because she didn't want to touch anything at the supermarket. Doctors and nurses, who may have had contact with hepatitis, may have been there touching everything. For the same reason, she had not bought new clothes for years. Her husband and children had to engage in cleaning rituals when they came home from work or school. In discussing history of suffering, Mary said she felt like "absolute hell" during some of those years. There were other years in which she wasn't functioning, but they somehow didn't feel as bad.

After going through an intensive treatment program, Mary became basically symptom-free. During the year that followed treatment, she would periodically call me when she found herself slipping. We'd make an appointment, but Mary always canceled it, because in the week between her phone call and our scheduled appointment, she did everything I would have suggested she do, and her symptoms abated. Then, a year after her treatment, she finally came to an appointment. Although using the techniques she had learned in treatment helped her to keep functioning, she continued to be plagued by painful urges. After a few weeks, her psychiatrist and I decided to put her back on an SSRI antidepressant, and shortly thereafter, her OCD urges ceased.

I believe the dysfunctional years that felt like absolute hell to Mary before her treatment represented times when her OCD was a function of both biology and learning. For the other pretreatment years when she felt unable to function even though she didn't feel as bad, I believe her OCD was being maintained purely on the basis of learned responses. After treatment, she experienced two kinds of slips: slips based on learned factors that were overcome with techniques she had learned in therapy, and slips resulting from a shift in her biology, which necessitated the use of medication to return to symptom-free functioning.

Though we may never agree on whether the chicken or the egg came first, when it comes to OCD we do know that biology precedes learning. Research suggests that a person will not develop OCD without having a biological vulnerability to it. This means that people don't cause their own OCD. It is not the result of some character weakness on your part or something that your parents did to you.

Let's look briefly at the biology underlying OCD before turning to the learned factors. What you most need to know about the biology of OCD is not the nitty-gritty biochemistry and neuroanatomy, but how the underlying biology is related to your emotional experience of OCD.

OCD and Neurobiology: It's Not All Learned

OCD is a neurobiological disorder—that is, the differences between you and non-sufferers are reflected in the biology of your brain. Many of you find these words comforting: They are proof that you have a real problem—you aren't just being willfully difficult or controlling. At the same time, it's terrifying to think that something really is wrong with you. However, it would be wrong to accept the neurobiological aspect of OCD as a complete explanation of the disorder. Unfortunately, many people, including professionals, make this mistake. When treatment decisions are based on this misunderstanding, the result is incomplete treatment. To understand the underlying neurobiology of OCD is to only partially understand OCD.

At present, scientific evidence suggests that OCD is genetically transmitted. This means that the biology you were born with made you more vulnerable to developing OCD. Some of you may protest and say your OCD started not in childhood but later in life. But because the control our genes have over our lives is very complicated, developing OCD later in life is not evidence that genes don't have a role in OCD. Encoded in our genes is what age we will hit puberty, when our hair will turn gray, and how susceptible we may be to heart disease.

The biological component of OCD is not always active. As Mary's history illustrates, OCD sufferers can experience periods during which symptoms are less severe or even absent, even without treatment. Some of you may experience symptom-free years followed by a return of old or new OCD symptoms, while others may experience a predictable cycle of symptoms increasing and decreasing in severity. Still others may have symptoms that are ever-present. These kinds of variations can also be seen in other psychiatric problems, such as depression, and in part can be accounted for by an activation and deactivation of the neurobiological components of OCD.

At this point in time, the factors that cause the "OCD genes" to turn on are unknown. Scientists assume that stress and learning, as well as biological mechanisms, play a role in activating the genes. Again, we see this kind of phenomenon in other health problems. Individuals with a predisposition to migraine headaches will develop them in response to a variety of triggers. These include external stressors, as well as internal ones, such as hormonal changes. For individuals without the genetic vulnerability, there are no triggers that will cause a migraine headache.

Upon reading that there is a genetic component to OCD, some of you may be concerned about having children. I hope no one would use this information as a reason not to have children. If you have OCD, there is a one in four chance that your child will have it. Important results from OCD twin studies find that there is not a 100 percent concordance for OCD in identical twins, that is, for a sizable number of the twin pairs, only one member had OCD. Having a genetic vulnerability for OCD is not the same as saying you will develop OCD.

Knowing that OCD has a genetic component tells you nothing more than there is a reason you have OCD. But how does this component lead to your experience of OCD? The next step would be to explain that genes and other factors lead to a chemical imbalance in your brain. The most studied theory of this sort regarding OCD is called the *serotonergic theory.* Brain cells communicate with one another through neurotransmitters, and serotonin is one of many chemicals that the brain uses as a neurotransmitter. This theory does not suggest, as many mistakenly believe, that OCD sufferers do not have enough serotonin in the brain. The research indicates that they have enough serotonin but that it is not as available as it needs to be for certain brain communications to take place.

How does this lead to OCD feelings and urges? The brain is not a simple organ; it has many different parts, each with its own special tasks and functions. For those suffering from OCD, the problem isn't simply the unavailability of serotonin throughout the brain; instead, it is the unavailability of serotonin in specific parts of the brain. The structures of the brain that are affected by OCD— the orbital cortex, basal ganglia, striatum, caudate nucleus, and thalamus—are interconnected and form a circuit where, researchers suspect, OCD symptoms originate. Messages that are ignored by non-sufferers keep intruding on consciousness and require conscious effort to be suppressed by those suffering from OCD.

At this level of explanation, the theories begin to evoke your experience; you know the feeling of intrusive thoughts all too well. A clearer explanation of the role these brain structures may play in your experience of OCD has been offered by William Hewlett, a researcher from Vanderbilt University. What appears here is a simplified version of his ideas. He suggests that one of the functions of the brain structures involved in OCD is responding to uncertainty with discomfort. From an evolutionary point of view, this makes perfect sense. Imagine primitive man walking through a jungle and hearing a noise behind him. His chances of survival will be enhanced if he feels nervous enough to turn around and check the jungle behind him for danger. Being uncomfortable with uncertainty is normal and can be healthy.

Another function of the brain structures involved in OCD suggested by Hewlett is responding to task completion with satisfaction—parts of our brain drive us to complete what we start. Again, this is normal and healthy. From an evolutionary point of view, you don't build a complex civilization like ours if there is no motivation to complete anything. This is the deficit that you've come to fear and hate, this is the biology underlying your experience of, "I know I did 'x' (check the locks, wash my hands, etc.), so why don't I know that I did 'x.'" Again, the logical facts we are aware of and the emotional feeling of certainty are two different events. And just as you can't instantly make yourself happy, sad, or mad, you can't make yourself experience emotional certainty on command.

Having OCD may mean that you have a lower threshold for these responses, so you feel more anxious in response to less uncertainty, and when an action is completed, you don't experience the feeling of completion. It's not that you're overwhelmed by every potential uncertainty in your life. For example, you may have a moment like many of us do: *Did I set the clock? What was that bump in the road? Look how cute and helpless that baby is—it would be so easy to hurt.* Most people respond to such thoughts by checking the clock, looking in the rearview mirror, and turning their thoughts away from what they could do to the baby. But the brains of OCD sufferers, Hewlett suggests, are better at learning avoidance responses. The very fact that you so strongly avoid the discomfort elicited by uncertainty makes you more likely in future confrontations with similar situations to experience anxiety and a desire to escape that situation.

In this model, biology sets the stage for learning. You feel greater anxiety in response to uncertainty and try to avoid it. However, for every logical solution you put forth, you find a way to question it. Obtaining absolute certainty is impossible: *I touched the faucet knobs after washing my hands—maybe they are recontaminated. And what about the doorknob? Maybe the last person who touched it didn't wash their hands. What am I going to do?* This is further exacerbated by not feeling the normal satisfaction of completing an act. If you have OCD, you know the frustration of engaging in a ritual and knowing you have done it, but at the same time feeling like you haven't—more agonizing uncertainty: *I've been checking the stove for an hour; I can see it is off, but it doesn't feel like it is off.*

What this tells us is that the different presentations of OCD are the result of biology setting the stage for learning OCD responses. Your specific checking rituals or violent obsessions are the result of a complex mix of your cultural background, personal history, environment, and state of mind at the onset of your OCD symptoms. Thus, the range of OCD symptoms is the result of the disorder's learned component.

OCD and Learning: It's Not All Biology

Learned emotions, as we know, can be very powerful, very resistant to change, and, most important, are not altered by medication. After all, when you take medication, you don't forget how to add, where you live, your feelings of love for your family, or, unfortunately, your OCD concerns.

When we think about learning, we usually think about choosing something we are interested in and then making an effort to learn it. Given this, why would anyone choose to learn obsessive-compulsive behavior? The answer is simple: by accident. You didn't and couldn't know that what you were doing at a given point was going to lead to OCD. At some moment when your biological vulnerability to OCD was active, your brain was more sensitive to uncertainty. Compared to non-sufferers, you would have felt more anxiety in response to less uncertainty. You may have been confronted by something that triggered your anxiety—perhaps a violent thought, a dirty bathroom, or a homework assignment you wanted to do a good job on. Your initial response to this anxiety was to try to remedy the situation—by avoidance, perhaps, or reassurance. You would likely repeat the behavior that worked in that situation the next time you found yourself in that same anxiety-provoking situation.

As an example, imagine that I'm afraid of cats, and I know I won't feel anxious if I can successfully avoid them. One of my coping techniques might be to have my cat-owning friends lock up their pets when I visit. This would work, except you know how cat owners are—they don't take your fears as seriously as you do. So every now and then, the cat might escape and run across the room. There is that horrible startle when I first see the cat, and then I'll feel terrible anxiety until the animal is put away. Eventually I'll come up with a new strategy: My cat-owning friends can come to my house, or they can meet me in a public place, but as long as they have a cat, I'm not going to their house. And while I'm on the subject, what about those people who live three blocks from me, who let their cats run loose? Whenever I walk by their house, I have to cross the street. But then one day I think to myself, *Why walk down that street at all?* If I keep progressing along this path of avoidance, I will get to the point where walking out of my front door is difficult, because a cat might be close by. My descent might be in small gradual steps—so small that it is not noticeable. Similarly, OCD does not usually occur suddenly; that is, an individual isn't washing their hands normally one day and then washing them for five hours the next.

According to psychologists, there are two kinds of learning: *classical conditioning* and *operant conditioning*. Classical conditioning is the association of emotions or feelings with cues and stimuli. Take eating, for example. Besides wanting food when your body needs nourishment, you may feel hunger at other times: at noon, because this is your regular lunchtime, or when someone brings a box of doughnuts or chocolates to work. You have learned to feel hunger in conjunction with these nonbiological stimuli. This kind of learning has little to do with what is rational or what you know. With OCD, this simple conditioning accounts for much of the nightmare and seemingly irrational frustration of OCD fears, when a sufferer feels anxious about a situation or thought that seemingly has no rational connection.

Imagine, for example, that I attach an electrode to your hand, and every time I ring a bell, I administer a shock. After a number of trials, you would begin to jump at the sound of the bell before the actual shock came. Now imagine that I remove the electrode. Logic tells you that nothing will happen when the bell rings. But when I ring the bell, you'll still jump. This is what has happened with your OCD—you have accidentally conditioned yourself to respond to certain situations with anxiety. When you are confronted with these situations, it doesn't matter what you logically know; your body still "jumps." Until you go through treatment, your body will continue to respond with fear— whether or not it makes sense.

While classical conditioning explains how our feelings come to be associated with different stimuli and situations, operant conditioning accounts for how we will behave in response to different stimuli and situations. Through operant conditioning, we learn to pursue whatever is reinforcing—that is, works—in the short run, whether it be going after something positive and pleasurable like food or avoiding something negative like anxiety.

So operant conditioning won't explain why you feel hunger, but instead it reinforces any action that alleviates hunger. That action is likely to be repeated in future situations involving hunger. But eating doughnuts is also reinforcing, because they taste good. Given this, operant conditioning suggests that when doughnuts are available in future mornings, you will be more likely to eat them just for the taste—even if you aren't hungry.

Operant conditioning also explains avoidance behavior. Let's return to the bell-and-shock example, except this time, rather than take the shock electrode off, I'm going to give you a button that prevents the shock if you press it as soon as you hear the bell. It isn't difficult to predict that you will soon be pressing the button every time you hear the bell. Avoiding shock is reinforcing. In the early stages of developing OCD avoidance, you probably felt less anxious after engaging in a ritual or avoidance: the ritual worked. Operant conditioning does not tell us how you will feel in a situation; it tells us how you will act.

These two kinds of learning work together. Imagine a sufferer-to-be whose OCD will focus on contamination. Perhaps he is in a public restroom, looking at a disgustingly filthy urinal, when thoughts about AIDS arise. Because of his underlying biological vulnerability, he feels more anxious about this compared to someone with less vulnerability. He washes his hands the way he usually does, but is still thinking about AIDS when it occurs to him: *Some people don't use soap when they wash their hands; some people don't even wash their hands, so the restroom door might be contaminated, and maybe I could get AIDS. I'm going to use my elbow to open the door, just in case.* The avoidance works, and he feels less anxious. He may continue to have some discomfort with thoughts of the bathroom and AIDS throughout the day, but that probably won't be enough to foster new rituals. The next time he is in a public restroom, he is likely to feel anxious (classical conditioning) and, because it worked before, he will want to use the same avoidance technique when he leaves (operant conditioning).

Through classical conditioning, this sufferer's fear of contracting AIDS has begun to be associated with bathrooms. When he needs to go to a public restroom, he will feel some anxiety and will be a little more careful than he used to be. He will become conscious of other places in the bathroom that might be too "dangerous" to touch. He will continue to use his elbow to open the door. Why not? It isn't a big deal, it doesn't take much time, and this way, he won't have to worry about his hands becoming contaminated. Without realizing it, though, his problem is getting worse. *Over time he is conditioning himself to feel more anxiety and to find more ways to avoid his fears.*

It is important to remember what is driving the behavior of our sufferer: the *fear* of the *possibility* of contracting AIDS. Fear, not the practical threat of contracting AIDS, is the sensation that drives behavior. Fear is upsetting in its own right; you engage in rituals in an attempt to alleviate your anxiety as much as to avoid the feared consequence itself (for example, *I might contract AIDS*). If you think about the differences between your good days and bad days, it is not that the world was safer on good days (the public restroom isn't any less contaminated on good days). On good days, you felt less fearful about your OCD concerns.

Possibility—the possibility of a feared consequence happening—is merely another word reflecting uncertainty. As your OCD grows in severity, the intensity of your anxiety will increase and your tolerance for your particular uncertainty will decrease. Finding a way to know, to be absolutely certain your fear won't be realized, seems like the only possible escape from fear. But there is always another what-if. More and more stimuli—people, places, and situations—become frightening, as classical conditioning associates these stimuli with fear. Through operant conditioning, the ways you choose to avoid anxiety will also multiply. Over time, using your elbows to open the door in a public restroom may lead you to completely avoid public restrooms and engage in special cleaning rituals once you're home. The list of places and people to be avoided and rituals to be engaged in grows.

To make matters more complicated, behavior is not only driven by reward but also by the possibility of reward. The result of this is like gambling— engaging in behaviors that are unlikely to pay off. In other words, people pursue hope, even false hope.

Imagine playing the slot machines at a casino. Like everyone else, you know the slots are there to make money for the casino. You already know that if you start playing, you will probably lose money. But what happens when you are standing in front of a slot machine? You think about how incredible it would be to hit the jackpot. You have wonderful fantasies about how to spend your winnings. It could happen; some people do win. You want this so badly, it is as if it wouldn't be fair if you lost. So you put a quarter in—three if you are really serious—pull the lever, and then . . . shock! Exactly what you would have predicted happened: You lost. You stand there in disbelief; it feels wrong, as if you deserved to win. Do you walk away? No, you put in another quarter. Every now and then you do win—not enough to offset your losses, but enough to keep you playing. If you have a gambling problem, you won't stop until you run out of money.

You do the same thing with your OCD. Your rituals often don't work, you say, but once you get started, you feel unable to stop. And, like the gambler, when faced with an accidental exposure, you are faced with a choice: You can walk away and suffer all day, or if you can just get this ritual right, you'll be free for the rest of the day. So you gamble on the ritual. And, as with the gambler, your prediction comes true—either you get lost in endless rituals, stopping only when you give up out of exhaustion, or, just as bad, the rituals work, but just enough to keep you hooked on chasing them.

These two types of conditioning form the basis of our understanding of the learned components of OCD. Do learning and biology combine to make your fears and rituals irresistible? Many of you have come to believe this. But it isn't true: *You don't have to ritualize.* Saying you don't have to ritualize is not the same as saying the choice is simple and painless. The decision is a difficult one in which you are weighing the pain of engaging in or resisting rituals against your expectations of the possible consequences and how you will *feel* afterward. Before treatment, you feel like the choice is between painful rituals that might work and anxiety and obsessions that feel as though they will never end. Before treatment, you may believe this is no choice at all.

There is another version of the Gun Test that can help you realize that ritualizing is a choice. Imagine I'm holding a gun to your head or to the heads of your loved ones. I tell you that if you ritualize, I'll shoot. I'm not leaving, so this is not a matter of waiting. Under these circumstances, will you engage in your rituals? If the answer is no, that you would resist, then you are admitting it is a choice. Again, it may be a very difficult choice, but it is a choice nonetheless. Now suppose I asked you to float three feet in the air under your own power for thirty seconds to prevent me from shooting. Outside of a miracle, you won't float, because you can't, even when threatened by death. This is an example of having no choice. You may argue that all of this is a contrived scenario and that in real life there is no weapon pointed at your head, but you are wrong. There is one: It's called OCD, and every time you give in to your rituals, you and your family lose another piece of your life.

We all make choices depending on the rewards and punishments we expect to receive. Since you don't make decisions to ritualize with guns pointed at your head, is there any proof or real-life evidence you can point to that demonstrates how ritualizing is a choice? Yes. Many OCD sufferers ritualize more in private than in public. Recently I met a new client, Jane, at my center. I held out my hand for her to shake and, for the briefest of moments, she hesitated before taking it. I was not surprised to find out that her OCD focused on contamination. But she made the choice to touch my hand despite her fear of physical contact with others. At that moment, the discomfort of embarrassment was greater than her fear. If rituals were truly irresistible, this couldn't happen.

All of our behavior takes place within a context—a complex set of cues and stimuli determining what we are likely to feel and how we are likely to respond at any given moment. These are learned through complex interactions between operant and classical conditioning. For Jane, part of the context included the fear stimulus of my extended hand with its many possible contaminants. Her taking my hand wasn't a function of her feeling safe. Her contextual environment also included being in my center's waiting room and, perhaps more important on this occasion, the presence of an unknown person and how this person might judge her. For many of you, the fear of public humiliation in response to your rituals is worse than the fears driving your urges to ritualize. For the rituals you do perform in public, you may often believe that no one will notice or that they don't look too bad. Or the obsessive fear driving your urge may be greater than your fear of embarrassment.

Broadly defined, *context* is simply a description of anything and everything associated with the performance of a behavior. This concept is very powerful in its ability to predict behavior. A rat, for example, can be trained to press a lever to obtain food. Suppose there is a red light and a green light in the rat's cage. When the green light is on, if the rat presses the lever, he will be reinforced with food, but when the red light is on, food won't be available and pressing the lever won't do anything. The rat will quickly learn not to waste his time with pressing the lever while the red light is on. The green light, though, becomes part of the rat's context for lever pressing.

How does this relate to OCD? Many of you may have discovered that your OCD isn't as severe when you are away from your normal work and home life—perhaps on a vacation, despite the fact that you may still be confronted with triggers that usually result in ritualizing. For those of you for whom this is true, the vacation environment is not part of your contextual environment for ritualizing, and as a result you feel less anxious. I have met some sufferers who have made the mistake of deciding that the best way to cope with their OCD was to move to a new place. If this really did work, it would be an ideal treatment. Unfortunately, without treatment, the problems that sufferers have will inevitably gradually reassert themselves in the new location.

Does everyone initially experience relief when he or she goes on vacation or moves to a new area? Of course not. Everyone is an individual. Just as the range of OCD fears and rituals is limitless, so too are the myriad ways context will play a role in a sufferer's behavior. For some of you, your OCD is so "portable" that you never have any relief. For others, you will feel as though different environments vary in safety.

Context is more than simply your environment. Your own behavior is a part of the context that controls your emotions and behaviors. Your rituals are both a response to your OCD fears and a part of the context that triggers further rituals. You have probably found that as your OCD progresses, rituals that used to work for you begin to fail to alleviate your anxiety and discomfort. When this happens, you repeat the ritual with the same disappointing outcome. What is happening?

Consider the thoughts you have when you worry about ritualizing: *I hope this isn't one of those times when my rituals get out of hand.* This is not a comforting thought. Your emotional response to it will likely be an increase in anxiety, which makes your ritual less likely to work, since a main goal of the ritual is to decrease anxiety. If you do repeat the ritual, your anxiety will further increase: *Oh no, is it happening? Is this going to be one of those times when I lose control?* With each repetition, your anxiety rises—the opposite of your goal. Your suffering, anxiety, and frustration mount. Your rituals have become a part of your context for failing. You stop performing them, not because they worked but because you gave up out of exhaustion. On such occasions, ritualizing feels like being in a hole and trying to dig your way out—unfortunately, you are going in the wrong direction.

Like behavior, our emotions are not only responses to triggers and context, but can themselves be triggers for other emotions and behavior. Responding to your internal environment is called *state-dependent learning.* Consider the example of a rat placed in a T-maze, a long alley at the end of which the rat must go right or left. Prior to being placed in the alley, the rat is given an injection of either a stimulating drug or a saline solution that has no effect. For the rat injected with the active drug, food will be placed at the end of the path leading to the left. When the rat is injected with the saline solution, it will find that the food has been placed on the right. The rat quickly learns to go left when injected with the active drug and to go right when injected with the saline solution. Obviously, it is not the drug that makes the rat turn left, since we could reverse the contingencies and put the food on the right when it is given the drug. The rat has learned where food will be, depending on its internal physical state.

In people, an example of state-dependent learning can be seen in a student who drinks a great deal of coffee when studying for a test. This student will do better on the test if he drinks coffee before taking it. The material was learned in a "caffeinated" state, and the individual will best recall that learning in the same state. The implication is that how we are feeling physically and emotionally is not only a response to what is happening to us. Our feelings also play a role in determining how we are likely to respond in a given situation and will serve as a trigger for other feelings, thoughts, and memories.

How does this apply to you? Perhaps you have found that your OCD gets worse when you are exposed to stressors that have nothing to do with OCD (for example, arguments with a spouse, problems at work, getting married, or moving to a new house). This makes perfect sense. During your worst OCD episodes, what were you feeling? Overwhelming stress, perhaps, accompanied by depression? Whatever feelings were present during your worst OCD trials will become triggers for your OCD. From this point of view, the following chain of events would be typical. You are stressed by a non-OCD situation, such as problems at work. These feelings of stress will trigger your body to respond with an increase in OCD feelings, which may be experienced as any or all of the following: heightened anxiety that gets your guard up in case you come into contact with stimuli and situations that you fear; greater anxiety when you're accidentally exposed to things you fear; increased urges to ritualize, making compulsions harder to resist; or rituals that don't "feel right" when performed, causing you to repeat them over and over. If your initial stressor was OCD-related, then your anxiety and urges to ritualize would be further exacerbated, because the context more closely matches the original learning situation that caused you to ritualize in the first place.

In viewing emotions as part of the context that will increase or decrease the likelihood of OCD responses, we begin to tie together our picture of OCD as both biological and learned. Our feelings are a mixture of what is happening in both our internal and external environments. We are all aware of how the external world affects us. Internal events affect your mood and your behavior as well. If you are very sick with the flu, are suffering from PMS, had a poor night's sleep, or have a hangover, your emotional and behavioral responses to your environment are likely to be different. A change in your internal environment changes your experience of the world and your reactions to it. When your OCD neurobiology is turned on, the world and how you perceive it is changed in a way that facilitates OCD learning, and the stage is set for you to learn OCD responses.

How does this mix of biology and learning determine which fears and rituals will characterize your OCD? At this point in time, we can only make guesses. Learning is probably more important than biology, since members of the same family with OCD will often have very different symptoms. For some of you, there may be a traumatic triggering event that makes the focus of your OCD easy to understand. For others, personal history may play a role, but there are so many ways this could take place that we wouldn't be able to predict your form of OCD from your life history alone. For many of you, the best predictor of the form your OCD will take may simply have to do with what thoughts captured your mind when you were most vulnerable to its emergence. Though we aren't able to predict the form someone's OCD will take, we are increasingly able to understand the process of how OCD is learned and acquired, which is the key to structuring an effective treatment program.

At this point, I hope your new understanding of where your OCD feelings, urges, and behaviors come from will help make what you are experiencing less mysterious. Your OCD follows rules—it's not some uncontrollable beast. You are not crazy. Biology and learning have brought you to this point. But you don't yet know enough to design your recovery program, because knowing about the factors that gave rise to your OCD is just the beginning of understanding OCD itself. What are obsessions and compulsions? What is the connection between them? This is our focus in the next chapter.

Chapter 3

Obsessions and Compulsions:
What Sufferers Fear and What Sufferers Do

Up to this point, my focus has been on the whys of OCD—helping you make sense of the forces that have given rise to the obsessive-compulsive feelings and urges that drive your behavior. Hopefully you have come to realize that, however extreme, severe, and even disabling your symptoms might be, they are still on the continuum of experiences that everyone in the world has.

Now let's shift from the whys of OCD to the whats and hows—the core OCD experiences and how they interact with one another. This will provide the building blocks for you to analyze and evaluate your own obsessive-compulsive behavior in preparation for designing your own self-guided treatment program.

What Sufferers Fear

There are two aspects of the OCD experience: your fears and how you respond to them. Let's first consider the range of OCD fears. Your OCD focuses on a limited number of uncertainties that have become your source (or sources) of anxiety. The frightening and uncomfortable thoughts and feelings arising from these uncertainties are called *obsessions*. The word *obsession* is generally used in many different ways. Sometimes it is used to refer to the process of thinking the same thoughts over and over again or endlessly trying to analyze something. It's also used to describe something we like, love, or are addicted to. In this book, I'm using the word *obsession* to describe what it is that you fear.

What do sufferers fear? What are their obsessions? A better question is: What can people be uncertain about? The content of obsessions is limited only by human imagination, which is to say their variety is limitless. Your obsessions can focus on the external world (for example, being contaminated by germs or causing hit-and-run accidents) or the internal world (for example, experiencing unwanted violent or blasphemous thoughts).

Most obsessions have consequences that you are afraid of. You might think identifying your obsession would make it easy for you to predict the consequences you fear. For example, if you tell me you have contamination fears that focus on bodily fluids—such as saliva, sweat, and blood—the obvious prediction would be that you are afraid of contracting or infecting others with some disease. Can you think of any other possible consequences arising from an obsession focused on bodily fluids? From sufferers I have seen at my center, I have identified four different feared consequences that can appear singly or in any combination: (1) harm to oneself; (2) harm to others; (3) finding the idea of contact with bodily fluids overwhelmingly disgusting; and/or (4) feeling that having thoughts of contamination is too awful to tolerate. An individual can have many different obsessions and many different feared consequences.

Just as the list of obsessions can be limitless, so too is the list of feared consequences. However, there are several that tend to come up again and again. Below is a list of the feared consequences most often seen in my center. If you don't find yours on the list, don't worry. This doesn't mean your OCD is more difficult to overcome; having a less common feared consequence simply means it is less common.

FEARED CONSEQUENCES OF OBSESSIONS

1. Fear of harm to oneself and/or to others
2. Fear of what a thought or action might mean
3. Fear of forgetting and/or loss
4. Fear of misperceptions and/or misunderstandings
5. Fear of anxiety or other uncomfortable feelings resulting from the obsession and/or not experiencing feelings the "right way"
6. Fear of constant attention to thoughts or images and/or constant perception of bodily sensations
7. Fear of imperfection

For some of you, the above items may serve as an obsession (what you fear) as opposed to a feared consequence. When this is the case, a different item on the list can act as the feared consequence. Or, to make matters more complicated, some fears on the list can function as both obsession and feared consequence at the same time. I know this is confusing, but try to keep in mind that I am elaborating on two different facets of your obsessions: what you are afraid of (the obsession) and what you fear will happen if you don't ritualize (the feared consequence). Two common treatment mistakes I want you to avoid are failing to identify all your obsessions and, for any obsession, focusing only on its most apparent feared consequences while ignoring ones that may be more critical to your treatment progress. Let's look closely at each of the feared consequences on the list to help you make critical distinctions among them.

Fear of Harm to Oneself and/or to Others

Fear of harm to oneself or others is perhaps the most common obsessive concern. It can be a consequence of almost any obsessive fear. The harm to yourself or others could be: illness resulting from contamination; injury caused by carelessness, such as leaving the stove on or the front door unlocked; death because you gave in to thoughts of violence; or eternal damnation of the soul due to blasphemous thoughts or actions.

Fear of What a Thought or Action Might Mean

For many of you, the terror of your obsession focuses on what having the obsession may or may not mean about who you are. Steve, a young man treated at my center for violent obsessive thoughts, provides us with an example.

Last night, I was lying in bed next to Sharon. I was feeling calm and enjoying being together. Then, out of the blue, the thought about how easy it would be to stab her with a knife just popped into my head. Why does this happen to me? I'm a good person; I love her and don't want to hurt her. We weren't fighting or anything, not that I would want to hurt her if we were fighting—I mean an argument, nothing physical—so why should I have a thought like

that? Do I have some secret urge to hurt her, or am I some kind of monster? I
don't want to be that way, but what if that's who I really am? How do I know
I won't really do it?   —STEVE

Steve's OCD had three feared consequences: (1) that his thoughts may mean he is "some kind of monster"; (2) that his thoughts may be indicative of some real underlying urge to hurt Sharon; and (3) that he might act on the thought and hurt her. This did not have to be the case. There are those of you who would feel sure you wouldn't act on the urge, but simply feel that having such a thought is unacceptable.

An obsession like Steve's might also have consequences that have nothing to do with his potential for violence or the unacceptability of violent thoughts. Instead, he could have worried that his violent thoughts meant he didn't really love Sharon. Knowing your obsession isn't synonymous with knowing your feared consequence.

Fear of Forgetting and/or Loss

Forgetting and loss differ in their source of anxiety. For forgetting, your concern is about remembering information about the past, present, or future. When your anxiety is about misplaced or lost material possessions, loss is the concern. This can be a primary consequence, in which the disaster is simply the actual or possible forgetting or loss, or it can have secondary disasters associated with it: *I'll get fired from my job if I forget my supervisor's instructions; If I misplaced my keys, I won't be able to drive my car home.*

Fear of Misperceptions and/or Misunderstandings

Misperception involves a focus on your senses (sight, touch, hearing, smell, or taste), leading you to ask questions like *Did I see "x" or not? Did I touch that spot on the wall?* or *Did I hear the lock click shut?* Misunderstanding refers to questioning of language-based material: *What did my boss say?* or *What did that sentence mean?*

A common obsessive-compulsive problem associated with this feared consequence is difficulty with reading. If you find yourself frequently reading a sentence again and again, then you know the pain of trying to be sure you understand what you are reading. I have seen sufferers at my center whose reading difficulties were so severe that they had dropped out of school and had completely given up reading.

Fears about misunderstanding and misperceiving can also play an intermediary role between your main obsession and main feared consequence. For example, one of my patients, Jack, was forty-eight years old when he came to treatment. His OCD symptoms focused entirely on his driving. His main obsession and feared consequence were the same: that he might have hit someone with his car without realizing it and could possibly have left the victim alone and injured in the street.

> *My OCD is hit-and-run. I dread having to go anywhere if I have to drive. Anytime I go over a bump, drive near someone, or see something in my rearview mirror, I'm afraid it was a person I hit.*   —JACK

For Jack, anything he might see or feel on or near the road served to activate his misperception fears *(Was that a bump or did I hit someone? Did I hit that woman who was waiting for the bus?)*, his ultimate feared consequence being that he possibly harmed someone.

Fear of Anxiety or Other Uncomfortable Feelings Resulting from the Obsession and/or Not Experiencing Feelings the "Right Way"

Imagine how you would feel if the consequences you fear actually came true. How would this affect the steps you then took to escape or avoid your obsession? One consequence that materializes for all OCD sufferers is that of experiencing anxiety. Once it is triggered—whether by touching dirt, walking by a stove, or having a violent thought—you are overwhelmed by anxiety and the terror that you will suffer forever or will be unable to continue coping. This fear is often masked by feared consequences that are more directly related to your obsession (for example, you may think the fear of contracting an illness is the only feared consequence of your contamination obsessions). Often, anxiety as a consequence is so secondary to the others that it doesn't need direct attention in treatment. However, there are those among you for whom the possibility of never-ending anxiety is of equal or greater importance compared to the easily apparent consequences.

But the feared feeling resulting from the obsession doesn't have to be anxiety. For example, for some sufferers with contamination obsessions, the feared consequence is simply feeling disgust when they feel contaminated. Note that this feared consequence feels like it comes true—you fear feelings of disgust from contamination, and you actually feel them when you touch something dirty.

A common but usually overlooked feared obsession consequence is the concern that OCD itself is altering your feelings so you aren't feeling what you believe you *should* be feeling: *If it wasn't for this obsession, I would be enjoying this movie. I wouldn't be so stressed out by work if it weren't for my obsessions.* This is often subtle and hard to identify, because the triggering fear for this is usually another obsession that you are responding to.

Identification of feared consequences like these can mean the difference between success and failure in treatment. Elise came to me for treatment at age twenty, after being unsuccessfully treated elsewhere. She had severe obsessive thoughts of having told terrible lies about her loved ones in the past, which led to her dropping out of college during her junior year. Her previous treatment had focused on the obvious consequences: that the lies might result in harm to her loved ones. She showed no apparent improvement, however, because an equally important consequence had been missed. Whenever Elise obsessed, she reported not feeling "like herself." Feeling like herself meant she felt "natural, clear about my emotions, and connected to the environment." Not feeling like herself was not only elicited by her obsessions about telling lies but also by situations in which she felt uncomfortable, such as being nervous at social gatherings. She assumed that these feelings were somehow caused by the fact that she had OCD, not because she was uneasy in certain situations. In response to this, she would begin to obsess about her possible lying in hopes of reassuring herself that the lies hadn't harmed her loved ones. She assumed that resolving this would allow her to feel natural. Of course, this never happened; instead, she would endlessly ritualize and suffer increasing anxiety. There were two feared consequences we focused upon in treatment. The first was coping with the possibility of having harmed loved ones. The second was learning to live with the fact that we don't always feel the way we wish we would.

Fear of Constant Attention to Thoughts or Images and/or Constant Perception of Bodily Sensations

The disaster feared here is that your life will be ruined because a particular thought or image will get "caught" in your mind and never leave you alone. You imagine it will constantly intrude upon your thinking, demanding your attention to the exclusion of all else. You may also fear an obsession with a bodily sensation, one that you will constantly notice and that will be so intense and uncompromising as to prevent you from having a life. These additional consequences almost all of you have felt at some time. Combined with your anxiety, this feeling of never-ending obsessions results in hopelessness and despair.

Most of the time, this feared consequence is secondary to your main consequences, so it doesn't need to be addressed in your treatment. However, there are those of you for whom this consequence is of equal or greater importance than any other consequence. It often appears in combination with fears of anxiety. Because of this, it is often not identified, which results in partial treatment success at best. The triggers for this consequence can be as simple as a thought or image, even a neutral one—you only have to feel like the thought or image is threatening to stay forever. A perfect example of this is provided by Ellen, a thirty-four-year-old single woman for whom anything in the environment could become an obsession. She was always afraid that anything she saw might stay (or in her words, "stick") in her mind and never leave.

> *I never know what's going to stick; I just know something will. I try all kinds of things to make sure nothing will—I must be trying to punish myself, because something always does. I once saw this stupid billboard on the highway; it meant nothing to me, but it stuck for two years. It was horrible. I couldn't make it go away, and it drove me crazy.*   —ELLEN

Ellen's obsession with neutral stimuli—the billboard—had no consequence other than her anxiety that the obsession (the image of the billboard) would always be with her.

Other neutral stimuli that sufferers have focused on include advertising jingles, songs, or bodily sensations such as breathing or tinnitus (ringing in the ears). Sufferers not only fear being forever stuck with these thoughts, images, and feelings, but they also fear how these thoughts or perceptions will interfere with everything they do. Because of the obsession, it feels like they won't be able to enjoy anything, so why bother trying? Even worse, it seems as if their worst nightmare is coming true—for two years, Ellen was in misery, trapped with the image of a billboard.

The triggering obsession for this feared consequence doesn't have to be neutral. For example, I have seen a number of clients who were constantly plagued by feelings and memories about thoughts of past events. If you suffer from this fear, you are usually unhappy with your own behavior, the behavior of others, or the outcome of those past events. The relentless ever-presence of your memories seems to drain the present of all joy and pleasure.

Fear of Imperfection

Perfectionism in its many forms is an attempt to achieve a kind of certainty that frequently is a part of many people's OCD symptoms. Perfectionism can be pursued in the service of avoiding other consequences, such as perfectly washing one's hands in a specified fashion to ensure that they are clean and devoid of contamination. It can also be pursued for its own sake. Sometimes a sufferer's definition of perfection is almost achievable (for example, spacing hangers in the closet exactly a half inch apart). I say almost, because the attempt to be 100 percent perfect is unlikely. Other kinds of perfection are obviously unachievable, no matter how much one desires it. This is particularly true when perfection is defined by getting a "just right" feeling. Most of you have experienced the agony of knowing a ritual is completed but feeling the need to continue because you didn't feel that elusive "just right" feeling.

What Sufferers Do

As you have seen, to truly understand the countless number of obsessions that can plague you, you need to identify the consequences that you fear. You don't just have obsessions with feared consequences; you try to find a way to neutralize your fears by engaging in *compulsions,* which can also be referred to as *neutralizing rituals,* or simply *rituals.* Like obsessions, the forms that compulsions can take are as limitless as your imagination. The defining characteristic of all compulsions is the goal of neutralizing the potential consequences of your obsessions with 100 percent certainty.

When your OCD was just beginning, neutralizing may have been possible, for example, you could feel certain that the front door was locked with less than a minute spent worrying about it. However, as your OCD progressed in severity, successful neutralizing became harder and harder to achieve, and certainty became further out of your reach. For most OCD sufferers, the inability to achieve certainty eventually leads to the development of more rituals and the frustrating endless repetition of rituals.

The ways in which compulsions attempt to neutralize fears can range from the obvious to the almost magical. Consider contamination and some of its possible feared consequences: harm to oneself or others, or feelings of disgust. To alleviate the first two, a handwashing compulsion seems to make sense, since washing could get rid of the source of the contamination and thus the "danger." However, if your feared consequence is feelings of disgust, is there an obvious solution? You could wash your hands, but a feeling of disgust might continue after washing if you are still thinking about the contamination that was on your hands. Perhaps trying to think "clean" thoughts and repeatedly saying "I am clean" instead of washing your hands would work. Or you could try to convince yourself that what you touched wasn't really dirty in the first place. These are three different compulsions to cope with the same feared consequence. Handwashing attempts to neutralize disgust by undoing the contamination. Saying "I am clean" is neutralizing by trying to control your feelings. And arguing with yourself that whatever you touched wasn't dirty in the first place is an attempt to neutralize by analyzing the situation.

In the above example, the different rituals for trying to neutralize feelings of disgust associated with contamination were all logically connected to the obsessive fear and its consequences. As many of you know, this doesn't have to be the case. Jessica, the high school student who feared harm coming to her loved ones, would tap her left foot three times and then her right foot to ensure her mother's safety. The form of her ritual had no obvious connection to her fears other than that it seemed to work for her.

While the connection between your compulsions and obsessions may or may not make logical sense, you can learn to understand their relationship by knowing the actual function of each neutralizing ritual and the consequences the ritual is helping you avoid or escape. Below is a general list of functions that rituals might fulfill. As with the list of feared consequences, this list is not exhaustive. More important, many compulsions serve multiple functions, and in evaluating your OCD you need to focus on more than the obvious.

FUNCTIONS OF NEUTRALIZING RITUALS

1. Preventing and restoring
2. Analyzing and "figuring out"
3. Controlling or stopping feelings
4. Controlling or stopping thoughts
5. Wishing

Preventing and Restoring

Preventive and restorative rituals share the ultimate goal of trying to avoid harm coming to you or others. The difference between the two is whether safety is being maintained or reestablished. Ira, who felt compelled to follow extensive cleaning and washing rituals, feared that his clothes were terribly contaminated by the end of the day. His numerous rituals for decontamination were ways for him to return his clothing to a safe "clean" state. Thus, his rituals were restorative. Compare these to Claire's checking rituals:

> *Half the time, going out isn't worth the trouble. I have to check all the doors and windows to make sure they are locked, the lights and stove to make sure they are off, and it's not a simple 1, 2, 3—I get anxious just thinking about the system, so I'm not going into it. But, you know we only have one house, and I'm not going anyplace if my house isn't safe. And trust me, it takes a long time for me to be sure.*
> —CLAIRE

Claire, a fifty-year-old married woman who responded to my Internet survey, is concerned about fires and break-ins in her house. The goal of her rituals is to maintain the integrity of her house; thus, they are preventative. A preventative ritual for Ira would be using tissues to touch doorknobs whenever he went out; in so doing, he would avoid contamination and wouldn't have to wash later. There are times when these categories can be hard to tell apart. Jessica's foot tapping in connection to thoughts about harm coming to her mother could be preventative; however, it is actually a restorative ritual, because she perceives her thoughts about harm coming to her mother as the source of potential harm.

Analyzing and "Figuring Out"

Analyzing and "figuring out" are rituals in which the focus tends to be on fears of what a thought or action might mean. If we look at Steve's description of his thoughts of stabbing his girlfriend, Sharon, you see him trying to convince himself that his thoughts don't mean he is a bad person. Analyzing and "figuring out" can also play a role for obsessions that aren't mental. To try to neutralize his hit-and-run fears, the first thing Jack would do as soon as he came home was sit in a chair and try to convince himself that he hadn't hit anyone. On a bad day, this could take a half hour, during which he would try to visualize his drive home, laying out all of the reasons he shouldn't worry, including the countless checks he'd made in the rearview mirror to see if someone was lying in the street and the many times he had circled the block to make sure there was no one lying hurt in the street.

Almost all of you have used analyzing when your main rituals seem to be failing (*My hands must be clean after two hours, but* . . .). Unfortunately, the desire for absolute certainty, the impossible goal, undermines all your analytic attempts. No matter what evidence you present yourself with, there is always a what-if to undermine your confidence.

Controlling or Stopping Feelings

Almost all rituals involve the attempt to control or stop feelings, with anxiety being the most common feeling. This is frequently overlooked, because a sufferer's rituals are often also attempts to avoid some disaster (for example, Jack driving around the block to make sure he didn't run over anyone). However, most of the time the power of the urge to ritualize is not purely a function of the content of your feared consequence. Instead, it is directly related to how anxious you are feeling at that moment—the greater your anxiety, the greater your urge to ritualize.

You may have noticed that you have good days, when obsessions don't seem to hit you as hard, and bad days, during which all your obsessions seem worse than usual. Many times, you can't figure out why something that did or didn't bother you yesterday bothers you so much today. The difference is often the result of how much anxiety was generated by your obsessions: For contamination fears, a good day doesn't mean you have decided your contaminants are less dangerous; instead, you feel less anxiety around your contaminants.

Controlling or stopping feelings can also be the prime function of a ritual. When this is true, the sufferer's goal is to avoid feeling out of control or experiencing extreme anxiety or other negative emotional states.

Controlling feelings through rituals does not always mean trying to lessen the intensity of negative emotions like anxiety. Your attempts to control feelings can focus on maintaining or inducing a feeling. Seeking the "just right" feeling is an example of a common motivation underlying some rituals. For example, the function of Claire's checking was preventative, but her decision of when she had checked sufficiently was partially determined by a "just right" feeling that she had followed her procedures. Without this feeling, she would start the checking process over from the beginning. For some of you, pursuing the "just right" feeling is primary. Some of the "just right" feelings I have seen people pursue include: wanting to feel connected to other people, wanting to feel natural, and wanting emotions to appropriately match their present situation.

Controlling or Stopping Thoughts

Controlling or stopping thoughts is closely related to controlling or stopping feelings, since the purpose of both is to avoid feelings of anxiety. Ellen's attempts to stop thinking about a particular billboard provide a painfully eloquent description of this kind of neutralizing.

> *Toward the end, I stopped working because any sign I saw—stop signs, street signs, you name it—reminded me of the billboard. TV was out, because you never know what they'll show, and besides, they could show the commercial for it and then I'd be done. I spent days in bed, crying, full of anxiety. I couldn't stand it. It took everything away from me. I couldn't go out of the house, because every sign I saw made the billboard thoughts stronger. Every day,*

I spent hours lying in bed, saying "stop" over and over to make the pain go away.
—ELLEN

Wishing

Everyone has dreams, hopes, and wishes; these lie at the core of our creativity and humanity's greatest achievements. However, when we pursue an impossible wish, it can lead to our downfall. Almost all neutralizing rituals include an attempt to achieve the impossible—at the very least, in the pursuit of an absolute certainty or perfection that can withstand all questioning. Because of the logical impossibility of neutralizing by wishing, it is often overlooked in treatment evaluations. Mike, a thirty-five-year-old, had obsessions about his junior year of college. That year, a severe bout of OCD resulted in his dropping out of school mid-semester. Although he returned to school in the fall and completed his education, he always felt that his life was never the same after that semester. He constantly obsessed about the events of that year and how much better his life would have been if he hadn't dropped out. In other words, he was constantly wishing he could undo his negative experience. When a definition of recovery requires achieving the impossible, the hopeless depression experienced by so many of you will be inevitable. How wishing is handled can determine the success or failure of treatment.

Now THAT YOU have gained a deeper understanding of how OCD develops and the relationship between obsessions and compulsions, take a moment to consider your own obsessions and your feared consequences. What kinds of rituals do you use to cope with your fears? Do all your rituals neutralize your obsessions the same way?

Your answers may give you some new ideas of what your recovery goals will be and what kinds of changes you will have to make in your life. But before you can go further in planning your program, you will have to decide upon what role medication will or won't play in your treatment. The next chapter will focus on what you can and can't expect from medication.

Chapter 4

Understanding the Role of Medication

If you were coming to me for treatment, medication would likely be on your list of concerns to discuss. You may already be taking medication and hope to use cognitive behavioral therapy (CBT) as a way to overcome OCD without medication. Alternatively, you may be wondering if a combination of medication and CBT is the best way to free yourself from OCD's hold on you. The main focus of this book is what *you* can do to overcome your OCD, and deciding what to do about medication is one of your tasks. This decision needs to be made in collaboration with a physician. To help you be a partner in this decision, this chapter will help you understand what medication can and cannot add to your self-guided program.

Because there is a neurobiological component to OCD, medication may need to play a role in your recovery. But what if you don't like the idea of medication and are determined not to take it? There is nothing wrong with this mindset. Using medication is an idea that takes getting used to. In an effort to encourage acceptance of medication, my colleagues and I offer the following diabetes analogy to almost every medication-reluctant sufferer: "If you were a diabetic and your body needed insulin to function properly, wouldn't you take it?" This analogy is wonderful—for anyone who isn't suffering from diabetes. We all act as if diabetics are happy to take their insulin. I remember working with Liz, a diabetic in her mid-twenties, who exercised regularly and watched her diet like a hawk, determined to manage her diabetes without insulin. But her body didn't care what she wanted. Her diabetes couldn't be controlled without injections of insulin. It took some time for her anger about giving up the wish to be insulin-free to abate. Most people don't like the idea of medication, but our biology doesn't care about our wishes.

For Liz, the use of insulin was not a "crutch," as many medication-reluctant people feel. It was a necessity. It was also not a panacea: Even with insulin, Liz still had to watch what she ate. Similarly, for OCD sufferers, medication is not a crutch. When medication is needed, it is because something is biologically wrong that no amount of strength and fortitude will change. And it is not a panacea, because it will only affect the biological components of your OCD. Medication doesn't make you forget how to add, or whom you feel love for, and it doesn't undo all the OCD learning that has taken place. Medication alone, on the average, leads to a 30 to 50 percent reduction in symptoms—better than nothing, but leaving most of you with symptoms that would still interfere with your life.

To try to understand how medication can help with biological urges but still not be enough, you could look at one of the side effects that some people experience on Prozac: loss of appetite and weight loss. When people who are depressed and overweight come to our center and are prescribed Prozac, they are wonderfully pleased. They think they will be able to get rid of both depression and unwanted pounds. But to date, the only people I have seen lose weight on Prozac are skinny people. And this makes perfect sense—skinny people only eat when they are hungry, so if you remove their hunger, they stop eating. The rest of us not only eat because we are hungry but also because someone brought doughnuts to work, because we are happy, or because we are sad. Reducing a biological urge is helpful, but it is not enough to make everyone lose weight.

You can think of medication doing three things for you: (1) reducing your sensitivity to uncertainty; (2) increasing your feelings of completion; and (3) making it easier to "let go" of thoughts. Without medication, your sensitivity to obsessive triggers is greater. CBT alone can help you cope with your responses to obsessions, but it won't reduce your biological sensitivity, so increased anxiety and urges are still likely to be triggered whenever you are confronted by your obsessive concerns.

When medication is working, your responses to obsessive triggers are purely the result of learning, not biology. This is the ideal foundation for CBT, which can help you stop responding to learned obsessive cues so that you become symptom-free over time.

When deciding to use or not use medication, think of an alcoholic trying to stop drinking. Fighting your OCD without medication, when it is necessary, is like trying to stop drinking while you are in a bar with all your drinking buddies. Being in the bar makes drinking very hard to resist, so learning to be alcohol-free in the bar is, at best, very difficult. When medication is working, fighting your OCD is like trying to stop drinking when you are at home with no alcohol in the house. At home, resisting temptation and learning to live without alcohol is easier. You would still need to work at it, though, because you could easily leave your home to go to a bar.

Must you go on medication if you have OCD? No. Remember, the biological component of OCD may not be active at all times. When it is inactive, medication isn't necessary. How do professionals determine whether or not you need to be on medication? Are there special medical tests? At the time of this writing, there are no medical tests, from brain scans to blood screens, for OCD. The truth is that medication is prescribed as an educated guess. Professionals are experienced at recognizing signs that suggest medication may be necessary. For me, the presence of depression is a major indicator that a patient needs medication.

Although depression, like your OCD, can have both environmental and biological elements, its biological components seem more responsive to medication and are less likely to be masked by environmental components. Because the learned component of OCD can mask the positive effects of medication, I look to a reduction in depressive symptoms—not OCD symptoms—to determine if the medication is working. If there is improvement in depression, then it is probable that the medication is also helping with your OCD.

For OCD sufferers who aren't depressed, I have seen some do well without medication and others who found medication helpful. Doing well without medication doesn't mean you will never need it. It may be that your OCD biology isn't active, but it could become so in the future. It could also mean that your OCD biology is active but not very strong.

Greg, a sufferer in his mid-twenties, had severe OCD symptoms that ultimately appeared not to be biologically driven. Though he had mental obsessions of a sexual nature that tortured him throughout the day, he was a successful graduate student who went through treatment without medication and was able to overcome his OCD. Afterward, he decided to try medication to see if it would provide any additional benefits. Here is what he had to say:

> *I started to wonder, could I feel any better? Part of me thought I might just be doing my perfectionist thing, but I wanted to know. So I started Paxil, very slowly. I didn't know life was supposed to feel this good. Without the meds, I was doing okay with my OCD. Every day I might have a thought or two, and I'd just do my exposure homework and it would be gone. If that was the best I could do, that would have been fine, because I was free. But with the meds, it's easier. A thought might pop in, and it's just easier to let go of it.* —GREG

Greg's biological component was active but presumably not very strong. Deciding whether or not to use medication was a choice. For those whose biological response is very strong, living under its power without medication is not really a viable option.

If medication turns out to be right for you, deciding how long you'll need to stay on it is another question that can only be answered with a guess and an experiment: You try discontinuing your medication. I wouldn't suggest doing this the minute you start feeling better; you need to remember that medication is part of the reason you are feeling better. Your physician can guide you toward a reasonable time to try to discontinue your medication. You should do this very slowly, even though it may be medically safe to discontinue it quickly. By going slowly, the return of symptoms will be gradual if your guess was wrong and you still need to be on the medication. This way, you will be able to rapidly go back to your therapeutic dose. If you were on a high dose and abruptly stopped taking your medication, the return of symptoms could be severe and painful. This would leave you suffering, possibly for weeks, while you built back up to a therapeutic dose.

Some of you will always need to be on medication, some of you will never need to take medication, and some of you may have a cycle that permits you to discontinue or reduce medication for months, years, or forever. Such cycles are often discovered by accident.

Jessica, the patient you met in Chapter 1, reported that her OCD had intensified around Christmas during her junior year in high school. She was treated without medication in the summer and was symptom-free by autumn. Around Christmastime, though, she reported a return of urges and depression. She found herself becoming increasingly more depressed, and when she came to see me, I asked her physician to put her on an SSRI. Not only did her symptoms disappear, but she also discovered she had been mildly depressed for years. The greater depression she was feeling disappeared, and she realized that what she had called "normal" was really mild depression. As a result, she decided to stay on the medication.

The following Christmas, she again returned to treatment, because her depression had come back, even though she was on medication. What was happening? I made the following guess in conjunction with her physician. Jessica is always biologically depressed and biologically obsessive-compulsive, but in early winter, both problems worsen. The year before, when she was put on medication for the first time, she was near the end of her more intense cycle. Thus, by the time medication kicked in, she was back to her "normal" level of biological OCD and depression. To test our idea, we raised her medication to help with her current suffering and lowered it in early spring. As we expected, her symptoms abated in the winter and didn't return when we lowered her dose in the spring. Then, the following November, a time that seemed to precede the biological intensification of Jessica's depression and OCD, we raised her medication. Her symptoms didn't return. Now her medication is raised every November and decreased in February. It took three years to learn her cycle, which may change over time. As you can see, there are many factors that you will need to consider in conjunction with your physician when you are deciding the role that medication will play in your recovery.

If you and your physician decide that medication would be helpful, you probably want to know which medication is the best. In the table that follows, I have provided a list of medications commonly used to treat OCD and their usual maximum dosages. Your physician may feel you need a higher dosage. Under the guidance of an experienced physician, this is acceptable.

This list is not exhaustive. At present, the medications that work best are the SSRI (selective serotonin reuptake inhibitor) medications. My clinical impression is that the different SSRIs are equal in effectiveness, but this isn't to say that they are interchangeable. We have sufferers who will respond to all of them, to only one of them, or who may only be able to tolerate the side effects of one of

MEDICATIONS AND MAXIMUM DOSAGES COMMONLY USED FOR OCD

TRICYCLICS

Anafranil	250 mg

SELECTIVE SEROTONIN REUPTAKE INHIBITORS (SSRIs)

Celexa	40 mg
Lexapro	20 mg
Luvox	300 mg
Paxil	60 mg
Prozac	80 mg
Zoloft	200 mg

UNCLASSIFIED ANTIDEPRESSANTS

Effexor	375 mg
Cymbalta	60 mg
Remeron	45 mg
Serzone	600 mg

ANTIPSYCHOTICS

Risperidal	16 mg
Zyprexia	20 mg

them at a therapeutic dose. Prescribing medication is not all science—a great deal of trial and error is involved.

For most people, an SSRI is tried first, and if it doesn't work or can't be tolerated because of side effects, another SSRI is often tried. Even if you have had the same side effect in response to Prozac, Luvox, Paxil, Lexapro and Zoloft, you might not have it when taking Celexa. There are a host of other issues that exist with medications that won't be detailed here and are best discussed with your physician—ideally, a psychiatrist or psychopharmacologist who is experienced in working with OCD.

What if medication is necessary but none seems to work either alone or in combination? It may be that the drug that would work best for you hasn't been developed or approved yet. You can contact the International Obsessive-Compulsive Disorder Foundation (see page 347) and/or the National Institute of Mental Health (see page 348) to find out if any experimental medication studies are being carried out in your area. Also, some medications that are not currently available in the United States are available in Canada and Europe. These can be legally obtained if you have them shipped to your prescribing physician to dispense to you.

Although medication may play an important role in your treatment, the key to your recovery will be understanding how to design and implement a program of cognitive behavioral therapy specifically tailored to your needs. Exposure and response prevention, the behavioral part of your cognitive behavioral recovery program, is the core of all OCD programs.

In the next section, I will be taking you through the process of creating your own self-guided program of exposure and response prevention. I will help you properly evaluate your OCD. Then, I'll show you how to evaluate the results of your assessment, choose your treatment goals, and then design your program and implement it.

But the very first step of your program will be to understand the goals of treatment and accepting them. After all, you can't accept goals that you can't understand, and how can treatment succeed if you don't accept the goals of that treatment? These issues are at the heart of the next chapter, Accepting Uncertainty: Your First Step.

PART 2

The Foundation of Your Program

Chapter 5

Accepting Uncertainty: Your First Step

Any change you make in your life involves choosing goals and then breaking them down into smaller sub-goals that will determine the actions you will have to take to achieve your major goals. Thus, the process of treatment for your OCD, whether self or professionally directed, involves choosing specific goals and finding the best way to achieve them. And the definition of "best" is, quite simply, what is most likely to work. The self-guided program you will be designing in the pages to come won't work if you don't embrace its goals.

Your major goal is overcoming OCD—you wouldn't be reading this book if you didn't want to escape this monster. But wanting to overcome OCD isn't enough. The first step you will take to conquer your OCD is both the easiest and the hardest. It is the easiest because you aren't required to change any of your behaviors—you merely have to answer a question. It is the hardest because your answer will change the way you view your life and your future.

The question is simple, but its answer is critical. I believe the success or failure of treatment depends on your response. The goal of this chapter is to guide you to the answer that will bring freedom.

The question: *Are you willing to learn to live with uncertainty?*

Don't say yes without thinking about it. There are reasons for you to be afraid of answering yes, because "yes" means wanting to live in a world where harm might come to your loved ones—and it could be your fault. You might kill someone you love. Maybe you're evil. Maybe you've committed sins. Maybe some thought will always be with you. Maybe tomorrow you realize you are gay. Maybe. Is it possible to live comfortably and be aware of such possibilities in a world where anything can happen?

Can you live with the possibility of your greatest fears coming true? Yes— you already successfully live with a multitude of non-OCD uncertainties every day. Just to see a movie, you risk injury and death by driving your car to the movie theater. And when your loved ones are out of sight, you don't know if they are okay, even though you may feel they are. Even so, most of you feel able to go to the movies. Most of you don't call home every fifteen minutes to prove to yourself that your loved ones are still alive.

It is quite likely that you agree with the premise that you can never be certain. Indeed, the persistence of your OCD symptoms and its constant attendant doubt have shown you that certainty is unattainable. Yet you persist in trying to achieve the impossible. Why? Why won't you accept what you know?

Answering the question with a "yes" means choosing acceptance of what you already know instead of denial. But what do these two words, *acceptance* and *denial,* really mean? On the surface, their definitions are simple. Denial is rejecting reality, and acceptance is living with reality. Often these are applied to someone who has lost a loved one to death. Again, what do these concepts mean? Suppose I ask someone who has just suffered a loss, "Do you accept Ann's death, or are you in denial?"

"What do you mean denial? I know she's dead," this person would likely reply. How can you be in denial of a death?

The answer is fantasy and wishing. In the case of death, denial is not a delusional fantasy of believing the dead are alive; it is comparing the present with how much better life would be if the deceased were still alive. Life might be better with your loved one still alive. Or perhaps something more terrible might have happened in the future. Of course, something more terrible in the future isn't part of the fantasy comparison. You don't put problems in fantasies, so in comparisons between real life and fantasy, fantasy always wins.

However, when we compare reality with fantasy, we also destroy and demean the moment. Imagine being with your lover at a beach by a small lake at sunset. And suppose you think to yourself, *If we were rich, we could be at a fabulous Caribbean resort by the ocean, watching a brilliant sunset with waiters bringing tropical drinks at the snap of our fingers.* It's a nice thought, but if you allow yourself to be consumed by such fantasy wishes, the beauty of your very real lakeside sunset will be tarnished.

We see other instances of denial in life. A woman in a bad relationship may know all her lover's faults, but she will say she can't leave him because she loves him. She'll describe how wonderful he can be at times, and she'll wish he were that way all of the time. What she is really saying is that she loves this man 20 percent of the time and wishes the other 80 percent would change. If he changed, though, he would be someone else. Does she, in fact, love him? I would say she doesn't. Or, to be more accurate, she does love 20 percent of him, and what she needs to do is find someone with more of the qualities she loves and less that she wants to change. Perhaps no one will be perfect, but she could do better than 20 percent.

Acceptance of her true feelings for her lover would involve loss. Her friends will tell her it is great that she finally left him. But what about her fantasy relationship—the 20 percent that she clung to, wishing it were more? With her fantasy lover gone, she will be left with nothing but emptiness.

Imagine a gambler who has stopped gambling. Everyone around him congratulates him. Finally, he will get out of debt. His family life will come back together. He won't lose his house. It is a time of triumph. But he is sad. Why? Because he will never be rich. He'll spend the rest of his life being just like everyone else. Again, this is his fantasy, because in reality he probably would never get rich by gambling.

Even in mourning, in the short run denial can feel better than acceptance. You can feel this difference in the words of denial vs. acceptance. In denial, a person says, "Life would be better if my wife were still here." In acceptance, this becomes, "My wife is gone." The sadness of the denial statement doesn't come close to the stark reality of moving toward acceptance. Mourning is the process of moving from fantasy to acceptance. You may always miss your loved one, but you can also relearn to enjoy life in the present. Mourning is not easy to go through, but avoiding the pain of mourning means trapping yourself in a fantasy that can never become reality. Just like the gambler, the lover, and perhaps just like you with your OCD.

Imagine that you've lost your arm in an accident. Obviously, you would rather have both arms, and there would be times when you miss your arm, but how would you want the many years ahead of you to be? Do you want to compare every moment to how much better it would be if you had two arms and, in so doing, ruin every moment of your life? Or do you want to find a way to live the best one-armed life you can? I suggest choosing the second option, because what you really want—two arms—is no longer an option.

Much of what you will gain from overcoming OCD is obvious, but you also need to be aware of what you will lose. Some of the losses are obvious. Some may transcend OCD. Some may be difficult to accept. For example, let's look at what losses Donna, a patient of mine, had to accept in order to overcome her OCD. When Donna first came to me, she was fifty-three years old and divorced. Her daughter, Margie, age twenty-five, still lived at home. Donna's obsessions focused on Margie's well-being.

> *I drive my daughter, Margie, crazy. She's a good kid, but I worry about her. When she goes out at night, I make her call me whenever she gets to where she is going and again when she leaves to come home. I can't stand not knowing whether or not she's okay. If I start to worry, I'll call her. Even though she hates this and it makes her angry, she always answers, because she knows how nuts I get. And if she gets the sniffles, you'd think she had cancer by how much I hover.*
>
> —DONNA

Since Margie's birth, Donna had been in a state of almost constant vigilance—listening, watching and inspecting her, concerned that anything she noticed might be a sign of illness. She frequently called Margie's pediatrician for reassurance or appointments. She barely let Margie out of her sight for fear of what might happen to her, and when she was forced to, she would constantly question anyone with her about their thoughts concerning Margie's current safety. Her behavior was, in part, responsible for her husband divorcing her when Margie was five. Although at age twenty-five, Margie didn't give in to all Donna's demands to be examined, to see her physician, or to stay in rather than go out, she gave in to many. Just to appease Donna, Margie still lived at home.

Donna desperately wanted to change for both her sake and Margie's, but to answer the question "yes" and overcome her OCD, she had two losses to accept. The first was learning to live with the uncertainty of her daughter's safety whenever she was out of sight. The second, even harder for her, was living with the fear faced by every parent: Your children can die, and there is nothing you can do to prevent it.

The first time I suggested this to Donna, our conversation went something like this:

DR. GRAYSON: For you to get better, you have to decide that you want to learn to be happy in a world where you or your loved ones could die at any time.

DONNA: No, I don't want that. Who would?

DR. GRAYSON: Okay, but can you tell me what the alternative is? Because if you have one, I'm coming to your world.

You can see the bind Donna was in. Intellectually, she knew I was correct, but emotionally she didn't want to accept that idea. So she continued to spend her time worrying about her daughter, even when they were together. She was comparing the real present, in which Margie seemed okay, to an imaginary one, in which Margie would be okay forever.

The goal of Donna's treatment was *not* to convince herself that Margie was always going to be safe. That would be a lie. The goal wasn't to teach her that Margie's premature demise was a low-probability event, because she knows this, but wants better. The goal was to help her accept the possibility of Margie's death. So rather than focusing on low probabilities, I helped her focus on the impossibility of absolute safety. One of her treatment goals was to have the truth of what I was saying overwhelm her fantasy, so that she would give it up and accept her helplessness and her daughter's mortality. In so doing, Donna would come to accept the futility of her rituals—that for all of the effort she put into them, they don't work. They never make Margie 100 percent safe.

Is knowing that she can never truly protect her daughter good for Donna? Yes. In treatment, Donna learned that the only time she "has" Margie is when she is with her. The past is a memory, and the future is no more than a hope. We make plans for tomorrow not because it will come, but because it might, and if we make no plans, tomorrow will be beset with a host of problems. Before treatment, when Donna was with Margie, her thoughts were always elsewhere, worrying about what catastrophe might happen to her daughter next. If Margie is to have a full life, Donna would miss it because mentally she would be consumed by her worries in OCD-land, not Margie. And if for some reason, Margie only had another two years to live, Donna would miss those precious few years for the same reason. Because of her fears, Donna had already missed most of Margie's childhood. Because of her OCD, Donna lost the only thing any of us can count on having: the present. With the acceptance she gained through treatment, she was now able to live in and treasure the present.

The decision to live with acceptance and uncertainty is critical if treatment is to succeed. But it is only the first step. If accepting uncertainty were nothing more than a decision, treatment would be a wonderfully short process. But acceptance involves a number of stages for which there are no shortcuts. Even if you know all the stages and where you're supposed to be at the end, you still have to go through the process. It is not unlike being in Philadelphia and deciding to go to New York. Making the decision to go to New York doesn't get you there; you still have to make the journey. Without the decision, though, you may never get there.

Many people feel that treatment should be easier. Sometimes they argue or try to bargain about what their treatment should be. I remind clients like these that I don't have two different treatments in my repertoire—one easy and one difficult—and for some reason, I have decided to make their lives miserable by assigning them the difficult treatment. I don't have a choice; I can only offer the treatment that I know works. If I am wrong, then perhaps someday there will be an easier treatment. But how long will it be until that day arrives?

No matter how much better life would be if our wishes came true, we are all trapped in the real world. Figuring out whether to pursue dreams or give them up is difficult. For myself, I believe the only dreams worth pursuing are those for which I am willing to pay the price of pursuit and, if worse comes to worse, for failure. Are you willing to spend your life suffering with OCD and hoping for an easier treatment? If the answer is no, then you aren't willing to pay the price of waiting. Will treatment definitely work for you? If you believe the answer is no, you will still be faced with deciding between definite suffering and the possibility of getting better.

Which of these two outcomes is the right one for you to choose? Can you, in fact, make a "right" decision? No. All decisions are guesses. I'm not suggesting that they are wild guesses or that we might as well flip a coin for every choice we are confronted with. However, an educated guess is not certainty. For some choices, the evidence of our feelings seems so overwhelmingly obvious that guessing which choice to make is easy. But even when a guess is easy, that doesn't mean the decision is right. To know whether or not a decision is right, we have to know what will happen after we make that decision. So, when do

we find out whether we've made the right decision? When it is too late to reverse it.

For example, imagine your wedding day. Most people getting married expect to have a good marriage. If, after fifty blissful years, your marriage is still
going, you will know you made a good choice fifty years ago. But if your marriage ends in a messy divorce after eight months, you will know you made a bad
choice. And what do we call it if you have ten good years of marriage followed
by three bad years and a divorce? I don't know. No matter what the outcome,
the answer to your guess came too late, long after your wedding day, when you
were full of hope.

If you are making this book a part of your recovery, then I am asking you to
take your first step. Take the risk of choosing to learn how to live with risk.
Answer *the question* with a yes. Make your guess even if you are uncomfortable
that the outcome isn't guaranteed. Even feeling sure about an outcome is not a
guarantee. You may find that there are times when a decision that seemed wrong
turns out to be right. I am where I am today because of three decisions that
didn't go the way I thought I wanted them to go. The first occurred when I was
starting graduate school. I had applied to a number of good schools and chose
the University of Iowa as my "safety school"—a school I thought I could count
on getting into as a last resort, because, being young and full of East Coast
biases, I assumed there was nothing of value in the Midwest. I was accepted
there, and my undergraduate professors told me I had accidentally applied to a
good school. If I had known the University of Iowa was good, I wouldn't have
applied there as my safety school.

Going to Iowa led directly to my internship at Brown University School of
Medicine four years later. As an intern at Brown, I had a number of rotations to
choose from. The one rotation I did not want was the one that involved working with alcoholics, so of course that's the one I got stuck with. A few years after
my internship, much of what I learned in that rotation became the foundation
of the GOAL OCD support group I established. Most of my early reputation
was built on the success of GOAL.

Finally, after my internship, when it came time to look for a job, my wife
and I decided that we wanted to stay in the Northeast. I didn't particularly want
to return to Philadelphia, but I had decided not to eliminate it from my choices.
The best job offer I had ended up being in Philadelphia. It was working with

Dr. Edna Foa on the first of her NIMH grants exploring the treatment of OCD—a job where I discovered my passion for working with those who suffer from OCD. This led directly to my becoming an OCD expert.

On each of these occasions, my impulse was to choose a course that would have placed me somewhere else today. I like to think that the alternative life I might have had would have been a good one. It is, however, merely a fantasy, and I am enjoying the way this life has turned out.

Fantasies are a fun distraction, a way to express your creativity, and perhaps a way to make some dreams come true. But pursuing fantasy not only detracts from living in the present—it can also interfere with pursuing achievable goals. The woman in a bad relationship spends no time finding a better mate. The gambler spends no time finding a fulfilling job. Wishing for a fantasy life is easier than the pursuit of real goals. There may be no guarantee that you will achieve real goals, but the odds of maybe are better than the fruitless pursuit of fantasy.

In the film *Fiddler on the Roof*, residents of a small Jewish ghetto in Russia in 1910 are told they have twenty-four hours to leave their village at the film's end. They would lose everything: their homes, possessions, traditions—their community. It was the greatest catastrophe of their lives. Do you know where most of them went? To America.

They would miss further pogroms and beatings by Cossacks. They would miss the Russian Revolution. They would miss Stalin's purges, Gulags, and religious persecution. They would miss Hitler's march into Russia and mass exterminations of Jewish people.

And the journey to America must have been a nightmare for them— peasants from a landlocked country, who have never been more than twenty miles from their village, spending weeks in the middle of an ocean in cramped quarters.

When you suffer from OCD, you are like those peasants. You know the world you are suffering in all too well. But what I am describing—living with uncertainty and risks—sounds terrifying, impossible, and unimaginable. But look where you are—you're in Russia, and I'm asking you to come to America to start anew.

Uncertainty is an inescapable part of our daily lives. To overcome your OCD, deciding you want to learn how to live with uncertainty is the bedrock of your recovery program. Without this foundation, you aren't likely to attain the freedom you want. After all, why would you expect a treatment to work if you don't accept its goals?

Decide now to accept the goals of treatment, so that your recovery can begin. In the chapters that follow, you will start to learn how to use the cognitive and behavioral tools that will turn your choice into a reality.

So now I'm asking you *the question*: Are you willing to learn to live with uncertainty? What is your answer?

Chapter 6

Exposure and Response Prevention:
The B in Cognitive Behavioral Therapy

E xposure and response prevention is the core treatment for OCD, and it will be the core of your self-guided plan. These two techniques are part of the cognitive behavioral therapy (CBT) armamentarium. Exposure and response prevention will help you confront your fears and stop your rituals. If you were to examine the research on the treatment of OCD, you would find that there are no conclusive studies of successful OCD programs that don't also include exposure and response prevention in some form. Or to put it another way, both the American Psychological Association and the American Psychiatric Association recommend exposure and response prevention as a critical component of treatment. Exposure and response prevention is a very powerful intervention—even a poorly designed treatment program using exposure and response prevention will provide some benefit to the majority of OCD sufferers.

Probably the best way to begin to understand exposure and response prevention is to start with what treatment looks like, stripped of all its sophistication, what is referred to at my center as "CBT's dirty little secret": If x frightens you, then we'll help you overcome your fear by confronting and never avoiding x.

This kind of direct approach to treatment is quite different from the public's view of what therapy with a psychologist should look like. In that view, shaped through movies, television, and the popular press, therapy seems to be a process of talking and getting to the root of your problems. It doesn't look like exposure and response prevention, the action-oriented behavioral component of cognitive behavioral therapy for OCD. The focus of this chapter is to help you understand why exposure and response prevention needs to be the center of your recovery program. This means clearing away any misconceptions you may have about the recovery process that would interfere with accepting the critical role of this intervention. With the path cleared, I'll help you understand the mechanics of exposure and response prevention, so that you will be able to use it as the framework for your self-guided recovery program. You will then start collecting the information you will need to create the foundation of your program.

The idea that "real" treatment uncovers and resolves the "true" underlying causes of your problems rather than simply targeting the "superficial" symptoms of OCD is a popular idea that you may subscribe to. You may feel that an exposure-and-response-prevention-based recovery program can't work, because you won't be addressing your underlying issues. Indeed, there are still a number of therapists who are not OCD experts, who still believe that OCD is the result of underlying psychological conflicts and that discovery and resolution of these will make your OCD evaporate. This is especially true for such therapists if you clearly do have issues and problems besides OCD. At my center, we have a more complicated view of human behavior: Only the problems that are treated will get better. If we only work on your OCD and other issues exist, those other issues won't resolve themselves. Similarly, if I focus exclusively on those other issues, they may be helped, but your OCD will remain. The fact that some problems are exacerbated or get worse in the presence of OCD (or vice versa) should not be confused with the idea that one set of problems is causing the other.

Some of you may still feel that the focus of your treatment needs to be on the past, because you believe there was an initial cause for your OCD—perhaps you are even aware of what it was. Even if this is true, that does not mean it must be addressed to overcome your OCD. Research has found that the conditions that lead to a behavior are not necessarily the same conditions that maintain that same behavior. For example, imagine that I was unassertive at age seventeen and began to smoke because all my friends did. Thirty years later, my unassertiveness doesn't explain why I am still smoking. And, as you might expect, treating my assertiveness problems may be very helpful to me, but it is not likely to stop my smoking. I will need a more direct approach to try to stop smoking. Similarly, whatever biological, environmental, and psychological variables contributed to the onset of your OCD, the variables maintaining it today are not likely to be exactly the same. As you have probably discovered for yourself, over time your OCD has developed a life of its own.

The other source of misconceptions about exposure and response prevention for OCD comes from some practitioners who claim to practice cognitive behavioral therapy (CBT). In theory, a therapist who practices CBT is one who uses cognitive and behavioral techniques that have been researched and have been found to be effective for the problems they are being used for. Many sufferers know that OCD is treated with CBT, but they don't realize that CBT comprises many cognitive and behavioral techniques besides exposure and response prevention. Thus, they seek out a therapist who claims to practice CBT but treats their OCD with a CBT technique such as relaxation, which is not the best CBT treatment for OCD. These sufferers mistakenly conclude that CBT doesn't work for them without realizing that they didn't receive the CBT treatment of choice for OCD.

But what about those among you who have received treatment of which exposure and response prevention was a part and your personal results were disappointing? Your skepticism feels justified to you. This reminds me of what I love most about medication: knowing. You can tell me you were given x medication at x dose and were maintained on that dose for x amount of time, and I'll know exactly what has happened. But if you tell me you've had CBT, I'll have no idea what has taken place. Knowing that exposure and response prevention was a part of your treatment doesn't tell me if your program was properly designed and implemented or whether you were properly prepared for it. Were you asked *the question:* Are you willing to learn to live with uncertainty? Were the goals of treatment different from the ones I have been describing? There may have been flaws in your treatment that you will now be able to address.

Exposure

The "exposure" part of exposure and response prevention is simply confronting whatever you fear. Earlier, using a fear of cats as an example, I discussed how fear grows when you try to cope with it through avoidance. If you had a fear of cats, the goal of CBT would be to help you overcome your fear by exposing you to them and to ultimately put a cat in your lap. What would happen if we did this? You would hit the ceiling—after all, you haven't been within five blocks of a cat for years, and now we want to put one in your lap? At this point, you make one of two very important choices. One, you throw the cat off your lap and run screaming from my office. Or two, you sit and suffer. Does your fear start to diminish if you choose to stay and suffer? No! It will get worse. That's what happens when you confront a fear. If fear began to diminish as soon as it was confronted, no one would have OCD. Most people try to confront their fear at some point, and if that lessened the fear right away, everyone would do exposure and would quickly recover. *The fact is, fear increases when you confront it.* If you tried to do exposure without knowing this, you would give up and conclude that there was no point to an intervention in which the outcome was ever-increasing fear.

Fortunately, this isn't the case. After twenty-four hours of suffering with a cat in your lap, you may still not like cats, but you'll know that the thing in your lap is just a cat. You will have gotten past the point of increasing fear, which is when healing can begin. This may sound scary, but consider how much fear and anxiety you are already living with on a daily basis right now. Exposure is hard work, but consider all the hard work your ritualizing takes. *Remembering how much you are constantly losing to OCD will help you stay with difficult exposures while you are waiting for your fear to diminish.*

Understanding that exposure is difficult and takes time to work will help you to have accurate expectations about what you will experience when you start treatment. Accurate expectations can mean the difference between a successful treatment outcome and giving up in frustration. Knowing why exposure works tells you what to expect and what not to expect from successful exposure. Many people have the mistaken idea that the goal of exposure is to prove that their feared consequences won't take place (for example, "I touched a toilet seat and didn't get sick"). They assume that anxiety goes down as a result of this proof. This is wrong. Exposure helps to facilitate a process known as *habituation.*

Simply speaking, if you repeatedly expose yourself to a feared situation, the level of fear gradually reduces as the body "gets used to" the fear. Habituation is a process that takes place for any kind of repeated stimulus. For example, earlier I told you that by ringing a bell every time I shocked you, eventually the bell would make you jump, even after the shock electrode was removed. If you allowed me to ring the bell over and over again without shocking you, your body would habituate to the bell, so that you would no longer jump when it rang. But for this to work, you would have to agree to put yourself in that situation. If you ran away every time the bell was rung, habituation couldn't occur. With fear-producing stimuli, running away interferes with the reduction of fear in two ways. The first is that habituation doesn't have a chance to occur. The second is that when you run away before habituation has occurred you probably did so while your fear was rising, so that your memory of how awful you were feeling will provide you with additional motivation to avoid the situation the next time you are confronted with it.

However, your own experience with OCD has probably shown you that there must be more to exposure and habituation than simply staying in the situation. You probably have been in situations in which the exposure seemed constant but your fear didn't go down. The reason for this is that the rituals you use to try to neutralize fear can be both behavioral and mental. You may think you are aware of all of the rituals you use, but it is quite likely that you are wrong.

For example, expecting exposure to prove you are safe or trying to convince yourself that an exposure is safe is actually counter-therapeutic and dilutes the effectiveness of exposure. In my work with OCD, I have found that some sufferers inadvertently try to reassure themselves during exposure with internal dialogues such as: *The therapist wouldn't let me do anything really dangerous* or *I'm not responsible, because the therapist told me to do this.* The first statement is an attempt to establish the absolute safety of the exposure. Remember, in doing an exposure, such as touching a toilet seat to confront fears of contamination, one of your goals is to try to get used to uncertainty. Trying to reassure yourself that the exposure is safe is an attempt to avoid that uncertainty and its accompanying anxiety. In the second statement, the sufferer is trying to evade responsibility for his actions. Presumably, responsibility for causing harm was a part of the sufferer's feared consequences. Such mental ritualizing is often so automatic that you don't have the choice of not thinking these things.

There is another kind of exposure, however, that you will use to help you combat these internal attempts to neutralize: It is called *imaginal exposure.* Up until now, all the exposures I have been discussing are called *exposure in vivo—* that is, exposure to stimuli in the real world. During imaginal exposure, you imagine being exposed to your obsessions, as well as imagining the possibility of your feared consequences coming true.

Imaginal exposure becomes a critical part of treatment for those of you whose obsessions are primarily mental in nature. Examples of these include: violent obsessions (*I had the thought of stabbing my wife. I know I don't want to do this, but if I don't want to do this, then why did I have the thought? Do I have a secret urge to kill her?*); sexual obsessions (*Am I gay? Will I molest that child over there?*); or religious obsessions (*Have I committed a sin?*).

Identifying Your Obsessive Fears and Avoidances

For exposure to work, the target of the exposure has to be correct. You will need to carry out an extensive evaluation of your OCD. The quality of your assessment will determine how much your recovery program truly reflects your situation and needs. Gathering all of the information you need will take a few days.

You will begin by completing two rating scales: the Obsessive Concerns Checklist and the Compulsive Activities Checklist. Their purpose is not to provide you with an overall severity rating for your OCD. You know your symptoms are severe enough to cause you or your loved ones enough discomfort to read this book. Rather, these two checklists will help you identify and specify the different kinds of situations you fear and the kinds of rituals you engage in.

Turn to page 74 of this book (all forms in this book are available for free download at www.FreedomFromOCD.com). Now, even if you feel you already know what your OCD symptoms are, complete the checklists. Although you may be very aware of your main concerns, in working through these checklists you may discover that other habits or behaviors that you didn't recognize as OCD symptoms are actually a part of your OCD. If you feel that you don't need to attend to these other symptoms because they are not out of control, you are wrong. These other manifestations of OCD are additional ways that you allow the fear of uncertainty to rule your life; identifying them and addressing them is vital. If they really are of lesser importance and give you less difficulty, then they should be easier to confront and may be the ideal place for you to start your treatment.

Take the time to complete the two checklists now. Don't spend hours agonizing over your answers. If there are items you don't understand, that probably means that they don't apply to you. The checklists are only the first step, and although you should answer all of the items, your program won't succeed or fail because you missed an item or accidentally marked one symptom as a 5 when it really is a 3. Also, if you are willing, don't fill in the circles perfectly.

After you complete the two checklists, look at the items you rated with 4's and 5's. These represent the obsessive concerns and rituals that give you the greatest difficulty. Write these down on another piece of paper. Depending on your test-taking style, 3's may represent areas of minor difficulty that either need little attention or, because they provoke less anxiety, they may point to the ideal feared situations for you to confront early in your program.

After completing the two checklists, the next step is to complete the Daily Self-Monitoring Log, also found at the end of this chapter. Turn to page 93. Note that the log is made up of six columns: date, time, event, ritual, time spent, and anxiety level. Let's start with the third column: the event. Over the course of a day, record in the event column anything that triggers your obsessions and leads you to engage in either rituals or avoidance. Make sure to include in your monitoring any new situations that you identified as problems in the checklists (the items rated 5's and 4's, and, for some of you, 3's).

When you record an event, you don't have to write a book—after all, this is for your use only. Some examples of events you might record are: using a public restroom, locking the front door, seeing violence on the TV news, seeing a red spot on the pavement, or driving by a school when it was letting out. Record the date and time the event occurred in the first two columns. In the ritual column, record your response to the event. Your response may have been behavioral (washed my hands, checked to see if the door was locked, changed the TV station, looked in my rearview mirror, or repeated a prayer) or mental (analyzed my thoughts, mentally recounted or prayed, or reviewed the event). Record how much time you spent ritualizing.

Finally, record your level of anxiety using the SUDs (subjective units of discomfort) scale. This is simply a 0 to 100 scale, with 0 reflecting perfect calm and 100 being the most intense anxiety possible. When using 100, try to re-member that this means there is no greater anxiety you can feel—or, in other words, don't use ratings of 110. With regard to the accuracy of your SUDs rat-ing, don't worry. The ratings are meant to generally measure what feels mildly distressing to severely distressing. Record the highest SUDs you experienced during the event or while ritualizing.

Keep the log for three days—you don't need to do more for the purpose of evaluation. Although this can be tedious, I have found keeping a log to be use-ful in a number of ways. First, it allows you to see when, where, and how much difficulty you are having on a daily basis. You may believe that you already know this, and you may be right. On the other hand, I can't tell you how often my clients with OCD were shocked to see how much of their day was lost due to ritualizing. It is also possible that the log will reveal some patterns that you weren't aware of.

You will not be able to self-monitor perfectly, so don't try. If you don't feel comfortable pulling out your log while at work or in conversation with others, that's okay. Make a mental note of some of the problems you run into or sur-reptitiously make periodic notes during the day to capture them.

Some of you may be so successful at avoiding everything that might lead to a ritual that your daily log is almost empty. This kind of avoidance is referred to as *passive avoidance,* because you are not engaging in a ritual to neutralize an obsessive fear. The term *passive* doesn't communicate how truly destructive this kind of avoidance is. Your passive avoidance is a reflection of how much of your life has been sacrificed to OCD. Avoiding public restrooms, driving, public places, or reading, or never leaving your house are all ways in which the circle of your life has shrunk and become less fulfilling. The next step of your self-assess-ment will capture your passive avoidances and anything else you may have missed.

Creating Your Fear Hierarchy

Now, gather all the information you've collected thus far through your list of checklist 4's and 5's and your daily logs. On a separate sheet of paper, create a new list of all the situations you fear, whether you cope with them through ritu-alizing or avoidance. Because the checklists and Daily Self-Monitoring Log may not have captured everything, make sure you include any situations that you avoid or that lead you to ritualize. Also, if you are aware of obsessive fears that haven't yet been identified, be sure to add these to your list. If you have different kinds of obsessions, such as contamination fears of illness or checking for fire hazards, you should put these on separate lists.

After completing this list or lists, it is time to create your *fear hierarchy*. A fear hierarchy is a ranked order of the situations that cause you anxiety, ranked from most to least anxiety provoking. This hierarchy will be the blueprint for your exposure-and-response-prevention program, guiding your decisions about what to expose yourself to and when. To create your fear hierarchy, take your list and rewrite it, but this time put the items in order, from those causing the most fear to those causing the least fear. If you have more than one list, then make a hierarchy for each. To make this ordering process easier, you may find it helpful to put a SUDs rating beside each item, or you can mark them as mild, moderate, or severe. Use whatever system is most comfortable for you. If everything that triggers your obsessions seems equally terrifying, ask yourself the question: *If I were forced to confront one of these two, which would I choose?* If you can choose one, then the two items aren't equal, and the one you chose is easier.

Now examine your hierarchy. Do you have any items that would be easier to start with (items in a SUDs range of 25 to 50 or moderately labeled items that are almost mild)? If not, go back to the checklists, look at items in your problem areas marked with 1's and 2's, and decide which of these would be useful to add to your hierarchy. Later, these easy items will provide the ideal place to start exposure.

The next question to ask yourself is: *Are my worst exposures included in my hierarchy?* Don't exclude something just because you feel you would never do it. For example, if you have contamination fears, you may be tempted to leave hospitals or public restrooms off your hierarchy, because you don't want going into a hospital or using a public restroom to be part of your plan. Writing down a difficult exposure isn't the same as doing it; therefore, to do so is safe, giving you no reason to avoid this step. As you go through recovery, I will keep urging you to always follow through with the easy *safe steps*, regardless of how adamant your feelings are that you won't ever do that step. To refuse doing the safe steps ensures that you will never get to the hard ones. Writing down fearful exposures that you are sure you won't do is safe. So examine your data and see if you need to add anything.

Some of you may worry about putting down something that is "over the top"—an exposure that really would be too dangerous to do. Of course, you can never be entirely sure, but there are some guidelines for you to use. Rather than going by what you believe non-sufferers say about what they will or won't do, ask yourself the following: *Are there ways in which non-sufferers accidentally do the exposure I'm concerned about without realizing it?* For example, do non-sufferers touch hospital walls without washing their hands? Not on purpose, perhaps, but surely they unconsciously walk down hospital halls with no awareness of whether or not they are touching railings or leaning against walls when they stop to talk to someone. And in hospital waiting rooms or patient rooms, they have no idea what they have come in contact with. They probably pay no attention to the floor as they walk through a hospital—they might even touch their contaminated shoes when sitting down. By this reasoning, you could plan to do such things on purpose. "Normal" people might even brush by the bio-hazard container, so touching the biohazard container could go on your list. On the other hand, people don't accidentally open biohazard containers and play with the contents, so you can exclude that one. Remember, putting an item on your fear hierarchy is safe, so there is no reason to exclude it.

Response Prevention

Your hierarchy/ies will help you determine what you will expose yourself to and when you will do so. By fostering habituation to your obsessional anxiety and fear of uncertainty, your exposures will decrease the intensity of your urges to ritualize. But what happens when you have done your exposure homework for the day? Suppose you suffer from "hit-and-run" checking, in which you fear you might have unknowingly hit someone with your car . After driving by schools during their dismissal time, you might want to examine your car to see if there are any new and unexplained dents in the bumper. If you worked very hard during your exposure session, will this checking interfere with the beneficial effects of your exposure work? The answer is yes; such checking would undermine your progress.

Clinical observation and OCD treatment research have noted that many of you are accustomed to enduring exposures while in public and are able to delay your ritualizing until you are home. As long as you can engage in your rituals at some point in time, your fear won't habituate and your OCD symptoms will continue to be maintained. This is why response prevention is a necessary addition to exposure. Simply defined, *response prevention* is the complete cessation of all rituals. For example, if you had contamination obsessions and handwashing rituals, then the response prevention part of your program would be the complete elimination of all handwashing. By instituting this, exposure changes from being a temporary intervention to a permanent way of life. In this way, your recovery is like coming to America from Russia: There is no turning back once the boat is in the middle of the ocean.

The idea of completely stopping your rituals may seem very difficult. You may feel sure that you can't do it: In the past, you have always given in to your urges to ritualize, so why try? This reminds me of an experience I had with my son when he was ten years old. As we were riding our bikes up a big hill in Valley Forge National Historical Park, Josh expressed his very sincere belief that he needed to stop and rest. Now, I knew he could make it up the hill without resting, and I also knew that if I didn't stop, he would keep riding. So being the pain in the neck that I am, I kept riding—cheerfully saying things like "You can make it! No problem!" Josh did make it to the top of the hill—with epithets flowing from his mouth that sounded mature beyond his years.

"So, Josh," I said when we were driving home, "I hate to say this, but I was right—you made it to the top of the hill. How do you feel about that?"

Of course he was proud of himself, but I continued, "When you asked me to stop, you really were tired, right?" Josh had no trouble agreeing with me.

"And going all the way to the top without stopping took a lot of extra effort, didn't it?" Again, he agreed.

"But if you had stopped when you wanted to," I said, "you wouldn't have known you could make it to the top. You would have thought that whenever you got that tired, you'd have to stop, because that's what you always do. The real lesson of the hill is that when you think you have reached your limit, you are underestimating yourself."

Similarly, if you have OCD and believe you can't fight it, you are underestimating yourself. Not giving in can be very hard, but hard is not impossible. Your problem with resisting rituals in the past is a common problem resulting from your learning history. Whenever you or anyone else engages in a particular action in response to a stimulus, you are deprived of the opportunity to try an alternative response. For example, imagine an alcoholic who drinks whenever he and his spouse begin to have an argument. Drinking not only gets him away from fighting, but it also prevents the possibility of learning other ways to cope with the marital conflict and the emotional distress it causes.

You know from experience that ritualizing feels inevitable and necessary. The anxiety and the urge to ritualize are the results of conditioning that took place at some point in your life when ritualizing worked to reduce your anxiety. A conditioned response, which you experience as an urge to ritualize, is automatic and feels like a natural and irresistible way to deal with something you fear. Giving in to these urges not only interferes with habituation and prevents you from learning new ways to cope with your obsessions; it also increases the power of your urges, making them feel more necessary and more irresistible. By examining the cycle of being confronted by obsessive fears, followed by giving in to the urge to escape such fears by ritualizing, you will be able to see how this occurs.

Every time you perform a ritual, you are reinforcing the idea that the best way to cope with an obsessive fear is to avoid it. It is as if you are on that hill and gave in to the urge to stop and rest halfway up the hill. The next time you are on the hill, you won't even consider trying to go to the top without resting, because you "know" you can't. By giving in to the urge to ritualize, you weaken your resolve to resist OCD urges. Then, on those occasions when your attempts to neutralize your anxiety by using rituals don't work and you are caught in a vicious cycle of endless ritualizing and ever-increasing anxiety and frustration, the agony convinces you that the best way to survive is to somehow get it right the first time or to just avoid feared situations. Slowly your world shrinks as you begin to avoid more and more situations. Giving up so much of your life in response to fear makes that fear seem dangerous, as if it were the fear and not the avoidance of that fear that was stealing your life away. All of these have combined to make you feel helpless and hopeless in the face of your obsessions.

Exposure and response prevention helps you with this problem by teaching you to respond to fears in a new way: by confronting and overcoming them. As treatment begins to take hold, exposure becomes a response to not only fight

OCD, but one that inspires hope and competence. Treatment is a process in which exposure, a new response to a situation, is trying to compete with rituals and avoidance (your old response). The strongest response, the one that will become automatic for you, will be the one you practice most.

Think of this situation in a different way. If you type, the keyboard you currently use is known as a QWERTY keyboard, named for the top left-hand row of letters. But there is an alternative to the QWERTY keyboard known as a Dvorak keyboard. On the Dvorak keyboard, the letters are arranged in such a way as to make typing in English much easier. Imagine that I replace your QWERTY keyboard with the Dvorak. Could you learn to type on the Dvorak? Initially, it would feel very unnatural and difficult. For a while, you would probably keep slipping into your old QWERTY habits. But eventually you would be able to type on the Dvorak. Exposure and response prevention is learning the new keyboard.

To be most effective, exposure and response prevention needs to become a part of your life. It is not just something you engage in for an hour or two a day. You may be wondering how you can start with the easy items on your hierarchy and simultaneously achieve the total immersion I'm suggesting. What about the higher-level item you are avoiding at the beginning of treatment? Fortunately, total immersion is not a matter of which exposures you are currently working on and which you are avoiding. Immersion is a function of how you implement exposure and response prevention. Suppose your problem is contamination, and you are afraid to touch doorknobs. A poorly designed program of exposure and response prevention would be touching a doorknob with two fingers and nothing else. This would be a wonderful beginning to an exposure session but a terrible end. Why? If this is all you do, you would constantly focus on those two contaminated fingers and spend the rest of the day avoiding touching anything "important" with those fingers. In addition, washing two fingers is easy, so the temptation to return them to a "clean state" would be difficult to resist.

Instead, a good program might begin with your touching a doorknob with two fingers and then working up to holding the knob with your whole hand. This would be followed by having you touch your clothing, body, face, head, lips, and tongue with your contaminated hand. You would then completely contaminate your home by touching the beds, all the towels and sheets in your linen closet, the dishes, and all your family members and their belongings. You would be totally immersed in the contamination of the doorknob.

The more total and inescapable you make your exposure, the more effective it will be. Sufferers with contamination obsessions have the greatest success in treatment, because making their contamination exposures total and inescapable is relatively easy. Contrast the above contamination exposure scenario with exposure for the obsessive fear that maybe you've hit someone while driving. For the hit-and-run sufferer, exposure and response prevention would probably involve the sufferer spending a few hours driving while simultaneously listening to an imaginal exposure script emphasizing that he may never know whether or not he's hit anyone.

At the day's end, both of you go to sleep. The next morning, with your house totally contaminated, you have three choices: (1) take a shower and stand naked in the middle of your room, since all your towels, chairs, dishes, and clothing have been contaminated; (2) engage in a massive cleaning, knowing full well how long it takes to decontaminate just a small area; or (3) allow the contamination to stay, and give up the fantasy of safety. The choice of avoidance or ritualizing is so difficult that there is less temptation to violate your response prevention. The hit-and-run individual, in contrast, has to decide anew whether or not to get in the car, drive, and potentially cause more deaths.

Designing and implementing a totally immersive program of exposure and response prevention is your best path to recovery. The hierarchy/ies you've created will be the framework at the center of your recovery program and will guide you as you implement exposure and response prevention.

But you know that it isn't so easy. There have been times in the past when, with the best intentions, you decided you were going to stand up to your OCD. And perhaps you had some success until the voice of OCD filled you with doubt and anxiety. You wanted to fight back, but its voice was louder than yours—so loud that ritualizing and giving up seemed the only way to escape your rising dread. One of my most important roles as a therapist is knowing how to be the voice of encouragement at those difficult times, while helping you to find your own. In the next chapter, you'll learn how to properly use cognitive techniques to become your own voice of encouragement.

OBSESSIVE CONCERNS CHECKLIST*

For some people certain thoughts may seem to occur against their will, and they cannot get rid of them. Only endorse thoughts that: you perform excessively, are undesirable to you, you attempt to resist doing, and have interfered with your functioning in some way.

Instructions: Rate the thoughts listed below from 1 to 5, according to the degree of disturbance during the past week:

① This thought does not trouble me at all.
② This thought rarely troubles me (once a week or less).
③ This thought often troubles me (several times weekly).
④ This thought troubles me very often (daily).
⑤ This thought troubles me continually (all waking hours).

1. AGGRESSIVE OBSESSIONS

① ② ③ ④ ⑤   1. Actively harming others intentionally

① ② ③ ④ ⑤   2. Harming yourself intentionally

① ② ③ ④ ⑤   3. Going crazy and harming others

① ② ③ ④ ⑤   4. Violent or repulsive images, thoughts, or words

① ② ③ ④ ⑤   5. Blurting out obscenities or insults

① ② ③ ④ ⑤   6. Making embarrassing or obscene gestures

① ② ③ ④ ⑤   7. Writing obscenities

① ② ③ ④ ⑤   8. Acting out in antisocial ways in public

① ② ③ ④ ⑤   9. Having insulted or offended others

① ② ③ ④ ⑤ 10. Acting on impulses to rob, steal from, take advantage of, or cheat others

① ② ③ ④ ⑤ 11. Rejecting, divorcing, or being unfaithful to a loved one

① ② ③ ④ ⑤ 12. Deliberately hoping that others will have accidents, become ill, or die

① ② ③ ④ ⑤ 13. Other:_____

* Adapted and modified from Fred Penzel, Ph.D., *Obsessive-Compulsive Disorders: A Complete Guide to Getting Well and Staying Well* (New York: Oxford University Press, 2000).

2. SEXUAL OBSESSIONS

① ② ③ ④ ⑤   1. Forbidden or perverse thoughts, images, or impulses

① ② ③ ④ ⑤   2. Sex with children

① ② ③ ④ ⑤   3. Sex with animals

① ② ③ ④ ⑤   4. Incest

① ② ③ ④ ⑤   5. Being homosexual or acting homosexually

① ② ③ ④ ⑤   6. Doubt about your sexual identity

① ② ③ ④ ⑤   7. Sex with religious figures or celebrities

① ② ③ ④ ⑤   8. Acting sexually toward others

① ② ③ ④ ⑤   9. Doubt about possibly having acted sexually toward others

① ② ③ ④ ⑤   10. Doubt about possibly having been acted upon sexually by others

① ② ③ ④ ⑤   11. Other: _____

3. CONTAMINATION OBSESSIONS

① ② ③ ④ ⑤   1. Bodily waste or secretions (feces, urine, saliva, perspiration, blood, semen, etc.)

① ② ③ ④ ⑤   2. Dirt or grime

① ② ③ ④ ⑤   3. Germs, bacteria, or viruses

① ② ③ ④ ⑤   4. Environmental contaminants (asbestos, lead, radiation, toxic waste, etc.)

① ② ③ ④ ⑤   5. Household chemicals (cleansers, solvents, drain openers, insecticides, etc.)

① ② ③ ④ ⑤   6. Auto exhaust or other poisonous gases

① ② ③ ④ ⑤   7. Garbage, refuse, or their containers

① ② ③ ④ ⑤   8. Grease or greasy items

① ② ③ ④ ⑤   9. Sticky substances

① ② ③ ④ ⑤   10. Medication, or the effects of having ingested medication in the past

① ② ③ ④ ⑤   11. Your food or drink having been tampered with by others

① ② ③ ④ ⑤   12. Broken glass

① ② ③ ④ ⑤   13. Poisonous plants

① ② ③ ④ ⑤   14. Contact with live animals

① ② ③ ④ ⑤   15. Contact with dead animals

① ② ③ ④ ⑤   16. Contact with insects

① ② ③ ④ ⑤   17. Contact with other people

① ② ③ ④ ⑤   18. Contact with unclean or shabby-looking people

① ② ③ ④ ⑤   19. Contracting an unspecified illness

① ② ③ ④ ⑤   20. Contracting a specific illness: _____

① ② ③ ④ ⑤   21. Spreading illness to or contaminating others

① ② ③ ④ ⑤   22. Hospitals, doctor's offices, and health care workers

① ② ③ ④ ⑤   23. Leaving or spreading an essence or trace of yourself behind on objects or others

① ② ③ ④ ⑤   24. Being contaminated by thoughts of harm happening to yourself or others

① ② ③ ④ ⑤   25. A specific person or place felt to be contaminated in some nonspecific way

① ② ③ ④ ⑤   26. Being contaminated by certain words:

_____

① ② ③ ④ ⑤   27. Being contaminated by the names of certain illnesses

① ② ③ ④ ⑤   28. Being contaminated by seeing an ill or disabled person

① ② ③ ④ ⑤   29. Being contaminated by the memory of a person who has died

① ② ③ ④ ⑤   30. Being contaminated by certain numbers or their multiples

① ② ③ ④ ⑤   31. Being contaminated by certain colors

① ② ③ ④ ⑤   32. Your belongings being contaminated by having been present or used when something unpleasant was occurring

① ② ③ ④ ⑤   33. Being contaminated by evil or the devil

① ② ③ ④ ⑤   34. Other: _____

4. RELIGIOUS OBSESSIONS

① ② ③ ④ ⑤   1. Being deliberately sinful or blasphemous

① ② ③ ④ ⑤   2. Doubtful thoughts as to whether you have acted sinfully or blasphemously in the past

① ② ③ ④ ⑤   3. Fears of having acted sinfully or unethically

① ② ③ ④ ⑤   4. Doubting your faith or beliefs

① ② ③ ④ ⑤   5. Unacceptable thoughts about religious figures, religion, or deities

① ② ③ ④ ⑤   6. Thoughts of being possessed

① ② ③ ④ ⑤   7. Thoughts of having to be perfectly religious

① ② ③ ④ ⑤   8. Other: _____

5. OBSESSIONS OF HARM, DANGER, LOSS, OR EMBARRASSMENT

① ② ③ ④ ⑤   1. Having an accident or illness, or being injured

① ② ③ ④ ⑤   2. An accident, illness, or injury happening to someone else

① ② ③ ④ ⑤   3. Accidentally losing control and harming others

① ② ③ ④ ⑤   4. Accidentally losing control and harming yourself

① ② ③ ④ ⑤   5. Causing harm to others through your own negligence or carelessness

① ② ③ ④ ⑤   6. Causing harm to others through your thoughts

① ② ③ ④ ⑤   7. Causing harm to yourself through your own negligence or carelessness

① ② ③ ④ ⑤   8. Causing harm to yourself through your thoughts

① ② ③ ④ ⑤   9. Never being able to be happy, or never being able to get what you want in life

① ② ③ ④ ⑤   10. Doubt about whether you have somehow harmed or injured others in the past

① ② ③ ④ ⑤   11. Being deliberately harmed by others

① ② ③ ④ ⑤   12. Being rejected by a loved one

① ② ③ ④ ⑤   13. Being cheated or taken advantage of by others

① ② ③ ④ ⑤   14. Having somehow cheated or taken advantage of others

① ② ③ ④ ⑤   15. Having insulted or offended others

① ② ③ ④ ⑤   16. Objects in your environment having been moved or changed in unexplainable ways

① ② ③ ④ ⑤   17. Damage or theft of your property

① ② ③ ④ ⑤   18. Losing or misplacing your property

① ② ③ ④ ⑤   19. Forgetting information (memories, facts, appointments, etc.)

① ② ③ ④ ⑤   20. Being trapped in an unsatisfactory life or relationship

① ② ③ ④ ⑤   21. Being looked at or noticed by others in a critical way

① ② ③ ④ ⑤   22. Acting inappropriately in public

① ② ③ ④ ⑤   23. Your own mortality

① ② ③ ④ ⑤   24. The mortality of your family and friends

① ② ③ ④ ⑤   25. Your children not being your own

① ② ③ ④ ⑤   26. Other: _____

6. SUPERSTITIOUS OR MAGICAL OBSESSIONS

① ② ③ ④ ⑤   1. Having bad luck

① ② ③ ④ ⑤   2. Bad luck happening to someone else

① ② ③ ④ ⑤   3. Lucky or unlucky numbers or their multiples

① ② ③ ④ ⑤   4. Lucky or unlucky colors

① ② ③ ④ ⑤   5. Lucky or unlucky objects or possessions

① ② ③ ④ ⑤   6. The possibility that thinking or hearing about bad events can make them occur to yourself or others

① ② ③ ④ ⑤   7. Certain words, names, or images being able to cause bad luck

① ② ③ ④ ⑤   8. Certain actions or behaviors being able to cause bad luck

① ② ③ ④ ⑤   9. Being possessed

① ② ③ ④ ⑤   10. Places, objects, or people associated with unlucky occasions causing bad luck by contact

① ② ③ ④ ⑤   11. The need to perform certain activities a special number of times

① ② ③ ④ ⑤   12. Lucky or unlucky mental arrangements of things

① ② ③ ④ ⑤   13. Other: _____

7. HEALTH AND BODY-FOCUSED OBSESSIONS

① ② ③ ④ ⑤   1. Parts of your body are ugly or disfigured in some way

① ② ③ ④ ⑤   2. Your body gives off a bad odor (e.g., breath, armpits, genitals, etc.)

① ② ③ ④ ⑤   3. Your body has scars or marks

① ② ③ ④ ⑤   4. Questioning how certain parts of your body work or function

① ② ③ ④ ⑤   5. A part of your body does not work properly or functions differently than it used to

① ② ③ ④ ⑤   6. Parts of your body are asymmetrical

① ② ③ ④ ⑤   7. Part(s) of your body is (are) too large or too small

① ② ③ ④ ⑤   8. You are overweight or underweight

① ② ③ ④ ⑤   9. You will choke or vomit accidentally

① ② ③ ④ ⑤   10. You are going bald or have thinning hair

① ② ③ ④ ⑤   11. Part(s) of your body is (are) aging prematurely

① ② ③ ④ ⑤   12. Clothing does not fit certain parts of your body correctly (too loose or too tight)

① ② ③ ④ ⑤   13. You have brain damage or your mental faculties are impaired

① ② ③ ④ ⑤   14. You have undiagnosed serious illnesses. Which ones?

_____

① ② ③ ④ ⑤   15. Other: _____

8. PERFECTIONISTIC OBSESSIONS

① ② ③ ④ ⑤   1. Questioning whether you have said, done, or thought certain things perfectly

① ② ③ ④ ⑤   2. Questioning whether others perfectly understand what you have said

① ② ③ ④ ⑤   3. Wanting to do, think, or say everything (or certain things) perfectly

① ② ③ ④ ⑤   4. Wanting to have a perfect appearance

① ② ③ ④ ⑤   5. Wanting your clothes to fit perfectly

① ② ③ ④ ⑤   6. Questioning whether you have told the truth perfectly

① ② ③ ④ ⑤   7. Making or keeping your home or possessions perfectly clean or pristine

① ② ③ ④ ⑤   8. Keeping your possessions in perfect order

① ② ③ ④ ⑤   9. Ordering things or making them symmetrical

① ② ③ ④ ⑤   10. Wanting to know everything about a specific subject or topic

① ② ③ ④ ⑤   11. Perfectly understanding what you have read

① ② ③ ④ ⑤   12. Perfectly communicating your thoughts through writing

① ② ③ ④ ⑤   13. Other: _____

9. NEUTRAL OBSESSIONS

① ② ③ ④ ⑤   1. Sounds, words, or music

① ② ③ ④ ⑤   2. Nonsense or trivial images

① ② ③ ④ ⑤   3. Counting for no special reason

① ② ③ ④ ⑤   4. Repetitive questions which are unimportant or for which there are no answers

① ② ③ ④ ⑤   5. Excessive awareness of your own thought processes

① ② ③ ④ ⑤   6. Awareness of specific things in your environment (sounds, colors, objects, people, etc.)

① ② ③ ④ ⑤   7. Excessive awareness of normal body functioning (breathing, eyes blinking, heartbeat, etc.)

① ② ③ ④ ⑤   8. Excessive awareness of abnormal body functioning (ringing in ears, aches, stiffness, pains, etc.)

① ② ③ ④ ⑤   9. Other: _____

COMPULSIVE ACTIVITIES CHECKLIST*

Instructions: Rate each activity on the scale below from 1 to 5, according to how much impairment is present due to obsessive-compulsive symptoms. Impairment can be the result of how long it takes to complete an activity, how often you repeat the activity, or how much you avoid the activity.

① I have no problem with this activity: It takes me about the same amount of time as most people; there's no need to repeat it and/or avoid it.

② I have minor problems with this activity: It takes me a little longer than most people; I may repeat it a few times and/or sometimes avoid it.

③ I have moderate problems with this activity: It takes me moderately longer than most people; I often repeat it numerous times and/or often avoid it.

④ I have problems with this activity very often: It takes me much longer than most people; I frequently repeat it many times and/or frequently avoid it.

⑤ I have almost constant problems with this activity: It takes me very long compared to most people, or I'm unable to complete it; I almost always repeat it an extreme number of times or almost always avoid it.

1. DECONTAMINATION COMPULSIONS

① ② ③ ④ ⑤   1. Washing your hands ritually and/or excessively

① ② ③ ④ ⑤   2. Bathing or showering ritually and/or excessively

① ② ③ ④ ⑤   3. Disinfecting yourself

① ② ③ ④ ⑤   4. Brushing your teeth to remove contamination

① ② ③ ④ ⑤   5. Disinfecting others or having them disinfect themselves

① ② ③ ④ ⑤   6. Disinfecting and/or cleaning your environment or your possessions

---

* Adapted and modified from Fred Penzel, Ph.D., *Obsessive-Compulsive Disorders: A Complete Guide to Getting Well and Staying Well* (New York: Oxford University Press, 2000).

① ② ③ ④ ⑤   7. Washing or cleaning items before they can be used or allowed in the house

① ② ③ ④ ⑤   8. Changing or having others change clothing frequently to avoid contamination

① ② ③ ④ ⑤   9. Discarding or destroying potentially contaminated items

① ② ③ ④ ⑤   10. Wiping, blowing on, or shaking out items before using them

① ② ③ ④ ⑤   11. Avoiding certain foods that may be contaminated

① ② ③ ④ ⑤   12. Avoiding specific people, places, or objects that may be contaminated

① ② ③ ④ ⑤   13. Using gloves, paper, etc., as a barrier when touching things

① ② ③ ④ ⑤   14. Having family or friends perform any of the above on your behalf

① ② ③ ④ ⑤   15. Performing, reciting, or thinking ritually to avoid or remove contamination

① ② ③ ④ ⑤   16. Excessively questioning others about contamination

① ② ③ ④ ⑤   17. Using public telephones

① ② ③ ④ ⑤   18. Touching door handles in public places

① ② ③ ④ ⑤   19. Handling or cooking food

① ② ③ ④ ⑤   20. Washing dishes

① ② ③ ④ ⑤   21. Washing clothing

① ② ③ ④ ⑤   22. Handling money

① ② ③ ④ ⑤   23. Handling garbage or wastebaskets

① ② ③ ④ ⑤   24. Traveling on public transportation (buses, trains, taxis, etc.)

① ② ③ ④ ⑤   25. Using the toilet to urinate

① ② ③ ④ ⑤   26. Using the toilet to defecate

① ② ③ ④ ⑤   27. Using public restrooms

① ② ③ ④ ⑤   28. Visiting a hospital

① ② ③ ④ ⑤   29. Eating in restaurants

① ② ③ ④ ⑤   30. Going to the movies

① ② ③ ④ ⑤   31. Other: _____

2. CHECKING COMPULSIONS

① ② ③ ④ ⑤   1. Doors and windows

① ② ③ ④ ⑤   2. Water taps

① ② ③ ④ ⑤   3. Electrical appliances

① ② ③ ④ ⑤   4. Stoves

① ② ③ ④ ⑤   5. Light switches

① ② ③ ④ ⑤   6. Car doors, windows, headlights, etc.

① ② ③ ④ ⑤   7. Items to be mailed or mailboxes

① ② ③ ④ ⑤   8. Whereabouts of sharp objects

① ② ③ ④ ⑤   9. Extinguished cigarettes or matches

① ② ③ ④ ⑤   10. The arrangement of objects for symmetry or perfection

① ② ③ ④ ⑤   11. Surfaces or objects for marks or damage

① ② ③ ④ ⑤   12. Objects, surfaces, or your own body parts for contamination

① ② ③ ④ ⑤   13. Repetitive praying or crossing yourself

① ② ③ ④ ⑤   14. What you have read

① ② ③ ④ ⑤   15. Your paperwork or writing for errors

① ② ③ ④ ⑤   16. Your writing for obscenities or errors

① ② ③ ④ ⑤   17. Filling out forms

① ② ③ ④ ⑤   18. Doing arithmetic

① ② ③ ④ ⑤   19. Counting money and/or making change

① ② ③ ④ ⑤   20. Driving situations (to verify that you did not hit someone or something with a vehicle)

① ② ③ ④ ⑤   21. Your own or another's vital signs or body (for signs of illness)

① ② ③ ④ ⑤   22. For possible hazards to children

① ② ③ ④ ⑤   23. The possibility that unspecified harm will occur to yourself or others

① ② ③ ④ ⑤   24. Frequent phone calls to family and loved ones to ensure that they are safe

① ② ③ ④ ⑤   25. The possibility that you may have harmed yourself or others accidentally or through negligence

① ② ③ ④ ⑤   26. Whether or not someone has acted sexually toward you

① ② ③ ④ ⑤ 27. Whether or not you have acted sexually toward someone else

① ② ③ ④ ⑤ 28. For prowlers (in closets, under the bed, etc.)

① ② ③ ④ ⑤ 29. For objects dropped accidentally

① ② ③ ④ ⑤ 30. That valuable items were not accidentally thrown away

① ② ③ ④ ⑤ 31. That you haven't left anything behind when you leave a place

① ② ③ ④ ⑤ 32. Container tops or lids for closure

① ② ③ ④ ⑤ 33. That you did not injure another through negligence

① ② ③ ④ ⑤ 34. Your own words or actions (to verify that you did not act inappropriately)

① ② ③ ④ ⑤ 35. Your own memory (by asking yourself or others)

① ② ③ ④ ⑤ 36. That you have made the perfect decision

① ② ③ ④ ⑤ 37. Repetitively apologizing or asking for forgiveness

① ② ③ ④ ⑤ 38. That you have not touched something hazardous or contaminated

① ② ③ ④ ⑤ 39. Yourself or your environment for signs of contamination

① ② ③ ④ ⑤ 40. For sources of dangerous gases or fumes

① ② ③ ④ ⑤ 41. That you have not ingested foods that are unhealthy or forbidden

① ② ③ ④ ⑤ 42. Your food or drink for drugs or chemicals put there by others or by accident

① ② ③ ④ ⑤ 43. Your phone for eavesdroppers

① ② ③ ④ ⑤ 44. Following your spouse or lover to make sure they are being faithful

① ② ③ ④ ⑤ 45. The mail, e-mail, or phone usage of your spouse or lover to make sure they are being faithful

① ② ③ ④ ⑤ 46. Questioning the whereabouts of your spouse or lover to make sure they are being faithful

① ② ③ ④ ⑤ 47. Watching who your spouse or lover looks at (in public or in movies, TV, and magazines) to make sure they are not being unfaithful

① ② ③ ④ ⑤ 48. Other: _____

3. MAGICAL/UNDOING COMPULSIONS

① ② ③ ④ ⑤   1. Reciting or thinking of certain words, names, sounds, phrases, numbers, or images

① ② ③ ④ ⑤   2. Moving your body or gesturing in a special way

① ② ③ ④ ⑤   3. Having to mentally arrange certain images, numbers, words, names, etc.

① ② ③ ④ ⑤   4. Having to physically arrange objects in your environment in special ways

① ② ③ ④ ⑤   5. Stepping in special ways or on special spots when walking

① ② ③ ④ ⑤   6. Repeating an activity with a good thought or image in mind

① ② ③ ④ ⑤   7. Performing actions or movements in reverse

① ② ③ ④ ⑤   8. "Washing off" ideas or thoughts

① ② ③ ④ ⑤   9. Rethinking thoughts

① ② ③ ④ ⑤   10. Thinking thoughts in reverse

① ② ③ ④ ⑤   11. Having to eat or not eat certain foods

① ② ③ ④ ⑤   12. Gazing at or thinking of certain numbers or words to cancel others out

① ② ③ ④ ⑤   13. Gazing at objects in a special way

① ② ③ ④ ⑤   14. Touching certain things in a special way

① ② ③ ④ ⑤   15. Other: _____

4. PERFECTIONISTIC COMPULSIONS

① ② ③ ④ ⑤   1. Arranging objects or possessions in special or symmetrical ways

① ② ③ ④ ⑤   2. Keeping new possessions unused and in perfect condition

① ② ③ ④ ⑤   3. Only buying items that are perfect

① ② ③ ④ ⑤   4. Returning items with minor flaws

① ② ③ ④ ⑤   5. Keeping your home or living space perfectly clean and orderly

① ② ③ ④ ⑤   6. Putting laundry away

① ② ③ ④ ⑤   7. Avoiding the use of rooms, closets, drawers, etc., once they have been arranged perfectly

① ② ③ ④ ⑤   8. Keeping your possessions perfectly neat and clean

① ② ③ ④ ⑤   9. Perfectly and neatly arranging items in drawers, closets, or cabinets

① ② ③ ④ ⑤ 10. Saying things perfectly

① ② ③ ④ ⑤ 11. Remembering or memorizing things perfectly or in a special order

① ② ③ ④ ⑤ 12. Reading or rereading every word in a document to avoid missing anything

① ② ③ ④ ⑤ 13. Knowing or learning everything about a particular subject

① ② ③ ④ ⑤ 14. Remaking decisions to ensure picking the perfect one

① ② ③ ④ ⑤ 15. Rewriting or writing over numbers or letters to make them perfect

① ② ③ ④ ⑤ 16. Performing ordinary activities extra slowly to get them done perfectly

① ② ③ ④ ⑤ 17. Thinking of certain things perfectly or exactly

① ② ③ ④ ⑤ 18. Being perfectly religious

① ② ③ ④ ⑤ 19. Punishing or penalizing yourself when you do not behave perfectly

① ② ③ ④ ⑤ 20. Being perfectly self-denying

① ② ③ ④ ⑤ 21. Looking at certain things in the environment in a special or perfect way (visually tracing or lining things up, etc.)

① ② ③ ④ ⑤ 22. Being perfectly aware of everything that's going on around you in your environment

① ② ③ ④ ⑤ 23. Telling the truth or being perfectly honest

① ② ③ ④ ⑤ 24. Perfectly confessing all your thoughts or behaviors to others

① ② ③ ④ ⑤ 25. Confessing to having done wrongful things, whether you have done them or not

① ② ③ ④ ⑤ 26. Making your appearance perfect (for example, hair, nails, clothes, makeup, etc.)

① ② ③ ④ ⑤ 27. Cutting your hair (to make it perfect or symmetrical)

① ② ③ ④ ⑤ 28. Performing activities until they feel just right

① ② ③ ④ ⑤ 29. Keeping extensive lists or records of certain
                things

① ② ③ ④ ⑤ 30. Only performing certain activities at perfect
                times

① ② ③ ④ ⑤ 31. Other: _____

5. COUNTING COMPULSIONS

① ② ③ ④ ⑤ 1. While performing certain activities

① ② ③ ④ ⑤ 2. Repeating behaviors a special number of times

① ② ③ ④ ⑤ 3. Performing behaviors an odd or even number of
              times

① ② ③ ④ ⑤ 4. To ensure that an activity has been done a
              certain number of times or for a long enough
              duration

① ② ③ ④ ⑤ 5. To ensure that an activity has been done an odd or
              even number of times

① ② ③ ④ ⑤ 6. The numbers of objects or occurrences of certain
              things in your environment

① ② ③ ④ ⑤ 7. Up to or beyond certain numbers

① ② ③ ④ ⑤ 8. Simply to count (unconnected with any special idea
              or activity)

① ② ③ ④ ⑤ 9. The occurrences of certain body functions (for
              example, breathing, stepping, etc.)

① ② ③ ④ ⑤ 10. Other: _____

6. TOUCHING OR MOVEMENT COMPULSIONS

① ② ③ ④ ⑤ 1. Gesturing or posing in a special way

① ② ③ ④ ⑤ 2. Looking or glancing at something in a special
              way

① ② ③ ④ ⑤ 3. Moving in symmetrical or special ways

① ② ③ ④ ⑤ 4. Having to step in special ways or on special spots
              when walking

① ② ③ ④ ⑤ 5. Ticking, twitching, or grimacing in a special way

① ② ③ ④ ⑤ 6. Moving in special ways while carrying out certain
              activities

① ② ③ ④ ⑤ 7. Reversing movements you have just made

① ② ③ ④ ⑤ 8. Repeating certain activities (for example, sitting down, getting up, passing through doorways or by certain locations) a special number of times, or until they feel right

① ② ③ ④ ⑤ 9. Touching furniture before sitting down or standing up

① ② ③ ④ ⑤ 10. Touching doors or drawers before opening or closing them

① ② ③ ④ ⑤ 11. Touching the edges or certain parts of things

① ② ③ ④ ⑤ 12. Touching doorways before walking through them

① ② ③ ④ ⑤ 13. Touching things a certain number of times

① ② ③ ④ ⑤ 14. Touching things in special patterns

① ② ③ ④ ⑤ 15. Touching, moving, or handling possessions a certain way before using them

① ② ③ ④ ⑤ 16. Other: _____

7. MENTAL COMPULSIONS

① ② ③ ④ ⑤ 1. Making mental maps of places

① ② ③ ④ ⑤ 2. Memorizing facts or information

① ② ③ ④ ⑤ 3. Making mental lists or arrangements

① ② ③ ④ ⑤ 4. Knowing or learning everything about a particular subject

① ② ③ ④ ⑤ 5. Repeatedly reviewing past situations to try to remember or understand them

① ② ③ ④ ⑤ 6. Thinking specific thoughts in special ways

① ② ③ ④ ⑤ 7. Thinking about specific topics

① ② ③ ④ ⑤ 8. Creating specific mental images or pictures

① ② ③ ④ ⑤ 9. Repeating your own or someone else's words in your mind

① ② ③ ④ ⑤ 10. Thinking of sequences of special numbers or words

① ② ③ ④ ⑤ 11. Rethinking specific thoughts

① ② ③ ④ ⑤ 12. Thinking certain thoughts in reverse

① ② ③ ④ ⑤   13. Analyzing your thoughts to determine if they are (or were) appropriate

① ② ③ ④ ⑤   14. Analyzing your thoughts to determine if they are really obsessions or not

① ② ③ ④ ⑤   15. Checking your own memory to determine if you came to harm in the past

① ② ③ ④ ⑤   16. Analyzing whether your own thoughts or reactions indicate that you are sexually attracted to others in ways that are inappropriate to you

① ② ③ ④ ⑤   17. Other: _____

8. PROTECTIVE COMPULSIONS

① ② ③ ④ ⑤   1. Questioning others, or your own memory, to determine if you have harmed or insulted someone (recently or in the past)

① ② ③ ④ ⑤   2. Recording and collecting information about past events to help determine if harm has occurred to yourself or others

① ② ③ ④ ⑤   3. Collecting and removing objects from the environment that could harm others (for example, tacks, razor blades, nails, matches, lit cigarettes, glass, etc.)

① ② ③ ④ ⑤   4. Having difficulty using sharp instruments (for example, knives, scissors, etc.)

① ② ③ ④ ⑤   5. Checking on the whereabouts of others to be certain that harm has not come to them

① ② ③ ④ ⑤   6. Trying to limit the activities of others to prevent harm from happening to them

① ② ③ ④ ⑤   7. Repeatedly warning others of potential harm or danger

① ② ③ ④ ⑤   8. Asking others if you will be safe or if things will turn out well for you

① ② ③ ④ ⑤   9. Asking others if they will be safe or if things will turn out well for them

① ② ③ ④ ⑤   10. Confessing to having done things you believe may have harmed others

① ② ③ ④ ⑤   11. Making lists

① ② ③ ④ ⑤   12. Other: _____

9. BODY-FOCUSED COMPULSIONS

① ② ③ ④ ⑤   1. Checking your appearance in the mirror for problems/imperfections

① ② ③ ④ ⑤   2. Checking your appearance or physical reaction to assure yourself about your sexual identity

① ② ③ ④ ⑤   3. Choosing what clothes to wear

① ② ③ ④ ⑤   4. Questioning others directly or indirectly about your appearance

① ② ③ ④ ⑤   5. Seeking frequent medical consultations to check your appearance

① ② ③ ④ ⑤   6. Feeling like you have to have your appearance improved surgically

① ② ③ ④ ⑤   7. Checking your body for symmetry or perfection

① ② ③ ④ ⑤   8. Checking your appearance or grooming for symmetry or perfection

① ② ③ ④ ⑤   9. Cutting your hair to excess or for long periods of time to make it perfect

① ② ③ ④ ⑤   10. Washing your hair to make it perfect

① ② ③ ④ ⑤   11. Checking your body for a bad odor (e.g. breath, genital, armpits, etc.)

① ② ③ ④ ⑤   12. Picking or squeezing pimples or blemishes to make your skin perfect

① ② ③ ④ ⑤   13. Checking the way your body works

① ② ③ ④ ⑤   14. Seeking medical consultations for possible illnesses

① ② ③ ④ ⑤   15. Reading about illnesses in books or on the Internet

① ② ③ ④ ⑤   16. Self-examination of your body for lumps or marks that could mean you have an illness

① ② ③ ④ ⑤   17. Frequent examination for current symptoms of possible illness

① ② ③ ④ ⑤   18. Having family examine you for signs of possible illness

① ② ③ ④ ⑤   19. Discussing symptoms of possible illness with family and/or friends

① ② ③ ④ ⑤   20. Taking your temperature

① ② ③ ④ ⑤   21. Other: _____

10. HOARDING/COLLECTING COMPULSIONS/IMPULSIONS

① ② ③ ④ ⑤   1. Saving broken, irreparable, or useless items

① ② ③ ④ ⑤   2. Buying excessive quantities of items beyond an amount needed for reasonable usage

① ② ③ ④ ⑤   3. Retrieving from or searching through your own or other people's trash

① ② ③ ④ ⑤   4. Having an inability to throw things away due to fear of accidentally throwing important items away

① ② ③ ④ ⑤   5. Going to excessive lengths (including extreme self-denial) to save money

① ② ③ ④ ⑤   6. Saving excessive quantities of informational matter (newspapers, old lists, magazines, junk mail, etc.)

① ② ③ ④ ⑤   7. Saving items simply because they belong to you or your loved ones

① ② ③ ④ ⑤   8. Having to own complete collections of certain things, even if they're not important

① ② ③ ④ ⑤   9. Keeping extensive lists or records of certain things

① ② ③ ④ ⑤   10. Other: _____

11. GROOMING IMPULSIONS

① ② ③ ④ ⑤   1. Hair pulling (from head, eyebrows, eyelashes, pubic area, body, etc.)

① ② ③ ④ ⑤   2. Skin picking or biting

① ② ③ ④ ⑤   3. Nail or cuticle biting, picking, or cutting

① ② ③ ④ ⑤   4. Picking or squeezing pimples or blemishes for the sensation of it

① ② ③ ④ ⑤   5. Picking or squeezing pimples or blemishes to "fix" them or "help" to heal more quickly

① ② ③ ④ ⑤   6. Other: _____

12. SELF-MUTILATIVE IMPULSIONS

① ② ③ ④ ⑤   1. Cutting or scratching yourself

① ② ③ ④ ⑤   2. Burning yourself

① ② ③ ④ ⑤   3. Poking yourself (eyes, ears, etc.)

① ② ③ ④ ⑤   4. Biting yourself (e.g., insides of cheeks)

① ② ③ ④ ⑤   5. Other: _____

DAILY SELF-MONITORING LOG: DAY 1

DATE	TIME	EVENT	RITUAL	TIME SPENT	ANXIETY LEVEL

DAILY SELF-MONITORING LOG: DAY 2

DATE	TIME	EVENT	RITUAL	TIME SPENT	ANXIETY LEVEL

DAILY SELF-MONITORING LOG: DAY 3

DATE	TIME	EVENT	RITUAL	TIME SPENT	ANXIETY LEVEL

Chapter 7

Tools to Counter the Voice of OCD:
The C in Cognitive Behavioral Therapy

There will be times when you are in the midst of working your program that the voice of fear will stand in
your way. It will tell you not to risk doing an exposure
or to immediately ritualize following an exposure, thereby undermining your
exposure-and-response-prevention treatment. Or the pressure of your fear may
be so great that you will want to give up treatment altogether. If you were in
treatment with me or one of my colleagues, we would use what we know about
you and your OCD to help you through these difficult times. In your self-guided
program, the job of coming up with the right words will be yours. By using and
adapting the sample scripts I've provided and applying the techniques of cognitive therapy to analyze your beliefs and cognitive distortions, you will be able to
create scripts that will help you to maintain the motivation you need to overcome your OCD.

The assumption underlying the techniques of cognitive therapy is that how
you appraise the world determines how you feel about yourself and the world
around you, which, in turn, influences the ways in which you choose to respond
to the world. Cognitive therapy works by helping you identify patterns of
thinking, known as *cognitive distortions,* that lead you to have irrational beliefs
about the world. It then works on challenging and changing your beliefs, which
should improve how you feel about yourself and should lead to better life decisions. For example, consider a young man with low self-esteem walking into an
important meeting. He is anxious and worried about how he will do at the

meeting. To him, it feels as though everyone can see how nervous he is. Based on this, he concludes that they will all think he is incompetent and won't want to associate with him. Cognitive therapy would help him see that he has no way of knowing whether anyone, let alone everyone, notices his nervousness. Furthermore, his assumptions that he will be judged as incompetent or will be disliked simply for being nervous will also be identified as beliefs for which he has little evidence.

Having identified what he believes, cognitive therapy would help him to further understand how irrational his beliefs are by helping him recognize that there are systematic flaws, his cognitive distortions, in the reasoning he used to conclude that no one would want to associate with him. Identifying the specific cognitive distortions he uses will help him understand the kind of mistakes he is making and what he needs to do about it.

Of the many distortions identified by cognitive therapy, the six discussed below are relevant to your OCD. There are others that you may use, but these play a role in non-OCD problems that are outside the scope of this book. Because cognitive therapy relies on the use of logic to facilitate change, it is easy to misuse these techniques in the service of your rituals. To help you avoid this, I explain how not to use these techniques, as well as how to appropriately use them. Go through the list and consider the possible role each distortion might be playing in your OCD thinking. You may find that your thinking is characterized by more than one distortion.

Common OCD Cognitive Distortions

1. Intolerance of uncertainty
2. Black-and-white thinking (also known as all-or-none thinking)
3. Mind reading
4. Overimportance of thoughts, also known as thought-action fusion (TAF)
5. Excessive concern about the importance of controlling your thoughts
6. Inflated sense of responsibility

Intolerance of Uncertainty

By now you recognize that intolerance of uncertainty is the core distortion of almost all manifestations of OCD. To conquer your OCD, you have learned that you must accept the impossibility of ever being 100 percent certain. You may find that some of the other cognitive distortions below are also a part of your OCD. However, for OCD problems, intolerance of uncertainty will almost always play a central role in how you cope with the other distortions. For each of them, only the establishment of absolute certainty would satisfy the demands imposed by the distortion.

Recall that deciding to live with uncertainty means having to accept a loss. Identifying the role that distortions play in your OCD thinking will help you better understand what you will have to give up to overcome OCD. As you read through the description of cognitive distortions, have a paper and pen within reach. After each description, think about your OCD and consider whether or not that distortion characterizes your thinking. If it does, write it down so you will be able to incorporate that information into the scripts you will be creating for your program. If you don't have paper and a pen with you now, then get them before continuing.

Black-and-White Thinking (Also Known as All-or-None Thinking)

Black-and-white thinking is a cognitive distortion common to a great deal of OCD issues. With black-and-white thinking, every decision or judgment you make is dichotomous, with no shades of gray. This is the distortion that plays a role in all forms of perfectionism. For example, if the focus of your OCD is being scrupulously honest, then to you, all lies are equally wrong. A single lie of any magnitude would make you a liar, as damnable as a person who lies every day of his life.

When coupled with intolerance of uncertainty, perfectionism is transformed from barely achievable to impossible, since you can never be sure that there isn't a fatal flaw in what you would like to achieve, whether it is never telling a lie or folding your shirts perfectly.

Traditional cognitive therapy tries to help patients adopt a different and more "reasonable" standard of making judgments, so that their self-judgments won't be so harsh. In the treatment of OCD, where intolerance of uncertainty has to be taken into account, the goal is modified. Behaviorally, you are asked to stop using the rule of black and white to guide your actions. However, you aren't expected to change your standard of self-judgment, which would only lead to endless mental ritualizing as you try to prove your "innocence" and doubt yourself. The goal is to accept your judgment. So if you were scrupulously honest, your behavioral task might be to tell white lies throughout the day—such as complimenting a coworker's clothing—when in fact you really think your colleague's taste is terrible. As for your judgment, rather than trying to convince you that this isn't lying, instead your goal would be learning to live with being as much of a liar as those around you. Take the time to examine your fear hierarchy and think about your feared consequences and the rituals you use to neutralize them. Does black-and-white thinking play a role? If so, write this down.

Mind Reading

In this distortion, you not only worry about what others are thinking, you also assume that they are thinking something negative about you. One young man I worked with was afraid that people would think he was gay if he looked at a man the "wrong" way. This resulted in a great deal of anxiety, which further complicated his situation, because he was sure that the discomfort he felt in the presence of men showed on his face. He believed that his anxious expression would be misconstrued by others as further evidence that he was gay.

Cognitive therapists help individuals who rely on the cognitive distortion of mind reading to assume what others are thinking to generate other possible interpretations—both good and bad—that others might have of your behavior. The therapeutic goal of this is to learn how to live comfortably not knowing what others think, even if they are thinking something awful. Used this way, labeling mind reading becomes part of your exposure to both uncertainty and your greatest feared consequence.

Does mind reading play a role in your OCD? If so, add this to your written list of the cognitive distortions that characterize your thinking.

Overimportance of Thoughts, Also Known as Thought-Action Fusion (TAF)

If this distortion is part of your OCD, then you tend to consider thoughts equivalent to action. You spend your time trying to figure out why you are having such an awful thought and whether or not it means something terrible about you. For example, if you have a thought about killing someone, you may fear that you are, in reality, a violent or evil person and on the same level as someone who has committed murder. This is a common distortion experienced by sufferers of the primary mental obsessions (for example, obsessions focused on violence, sexuality, and/or religion).

If this describes you, you probably have made the mistake that many other sufferers in your situation have made: thinking that the goal of treatment is either to stop the thoughts or to know that they mean nothing of importance. As your ritualizing has demonstrated, knowing what a thought means is impossible—for you and for all of us. Behind our every thought are a number of conflicting feelings and meanings—not just one single meaning. The goal of treatment is to learn to accept the possibility of all these meanings—even the possibilities of the worst ones. Add this to your list if TAF is one of your distortions.

Excessive Concern About the Importance of Controlling Your Thoughts

This is very similar to thought-action fusion. The difference is that here the emphasis is not on the meaning of your thoughts, but on the belief that you should be able to control your thoughts or avoid having certain thoughts. To fail at this is interpreted as having terrible consequences ranging from your being evil and possibly liable to act on your thoughts to simply fearing that your inability to control your thoughts means that they will plague you forever. Such thought control is not possible for anyone to achieve. Any and all thoughts that come into your mind, no matter how evil, twisted, or perverse they may seem, are normal. This is another distortion that is commonly exhibited by those suffering from the primary mental obsessions.

For this distortion, the goal of treatment is not to stop these thoughts, but to learn to allow them to be on your mind without being upset about them. However, if you try to accomplish this by emphasizing the normality, and thus the harmlessness, of your thoughts, then you are neutralizing and sinking deeper into your OCD. Instead, your purpose in identifying this distortion and adding it to your list is to remind yourself that your attempts to control your thinking are impossible, which makes exposure the most viable alternative for coping.

Inflated Sense of Responsibility

With inflated responsibility, you believe you are responsible for preventing any possible harm from coming to yourself or others. The cause of the harm will depend on the nature of your OCD. The potential harm could be due to actions on your part (for example, hit-and-run obsessions), dangers that you note in your environment (for example, a possible piece of glass on a supermarket floor that might harm a child), or having intrusive thoughts that you might act on (for example, violent, obsessive thoughts of murder). Failure either to prevent or to try to prevent such harm is experienced as guilt that's very much the same as if you had actually caused the harm.

As with all the cognitive distortions, on the surface the concern seems reasonable—shouldn't you be careful not to harm others through negligence? Shouldn't you be concerned and responsible for warning others of danger or taking care of any dangers that you notice? As with all types of OCD, the problem is establishing the line where your responsibility ends. In the fantasy resolution of this problem, you can be successfully responsible in any situation you can imagine. As you have discovered, you can always come up with ways that you might be failing. Your exposure/acceptance goal that will become a part of your scripts will be to learn to live with the "sins" of irresponsibility that all of us are guilty of.

Using Tools of CBT

Traditional cognitive therapy holds that identifying your distortions will provide you with a more rational interpretation of your feelings, which will result in a reduction of the negative feelings elicited by problem situations. In the case of the young man with low self-esteem, identifying his cognitive distortion of mind reading should help reduce his anxiety in public situations, because he will now realize that it isn't true that everyone notices his behavior or has a negative opinion about it. The reduction in anxiety that is expected to take place would make it easier for him to expose himself to public situations, which would facilitate further reductions in anxiety.

But there are two problems with this approach. The first is cognitive therapy's assumption that logic can change feelings. Remember, logic alone doesn't change feelings. You are not likely to start hating the taste of pizza because your cholesterol is high and you know the pizza is bad for your heart, nor are you likely to stop being afraid of cats because you are told that cats aren't dangerous. On the other hand, you can use logic to decide whether or not you will listen to your feelings (for example, *I want to eat pizza, but I'd better not, because my cholesterol level is high; I'm afraid of cats, but if I hold the cat long enough, my level of fear will eventually go down*). In these examples, logic suggests going against your feelings, but the emotional response is not changed upon the immediate application of logic.

For our young man, identifying mind reading alone may not alleviate his anxiety, but he may now realize that there is a difference between how he feels about a situation and what is actually happening. Before identifying the distortion, he felt that the result of exposure—going to the meeting—would be social rejection by everyone. Now he realizes that some people might feel this way, but not everyone—the situation is logically less dangerous, so he is more willing to risk exposure in spite of his anxiety.

A second problem with cognitive therapy is specific to its use in the treatment of OCD. Cognitive therapy insists that a rational analysis of a situation will produce logical answers—that you can know a thought is irrational and thus reject it. If you suffer from OCD, the implication of this is that you can live with a kind of certainty. The promise of establishing certainty through rational thought makes cognitive therapy very attractive to you.

Trying to establish certainty with cognitive therapy turns these techniques into rituals that attempt to neutralize your obsessive fears through analyzing and figuring out. They take the all-too-familiar form: "I know 'x' can't be true. But what if I'm wrong and 'x' is true?" Fortunately, cognitive techniques can be adapted to treat OCD. The guiding principle for deciding which techniques to use and how to use them is deceptively simple: Is the technique supporting exposure or neutralizing?

Using this simple question, a cognitive technique is a neutralizing ritual if its use: (1) is an attempt to convince you that your feared consequences aren't likely; or (2) provides you with a reason why you shouldn't be concerned about your obsessions or your anxiety. To support exposure, a cognitive technique must simultaneously encourage you to confront your fears and risk the consequences of doing so.

This means that the goal of identifying cognitive distortions is *not* to ultimately dismiss them as irrational, to change your feelings, or to make you feel certain in any way. All of these are examples of neutralizing. If you use CBT in this way, you would be adding a new ritual to your repertoire. Instead, the goal of knowing which cognitive distortions you use is to clarify which losses you will have to accept to overcome OCD. The young man in our example not only has to accept living with uncertainty but also the possibility that some people will notice his behavior and that the result of their noticing might be rejection.

Cognitive therapy includes a number of techniques that will help you identify your distortions and then use the results to support your recovery. Because of cognitive therapy's reliance on logic, you need to be careful how you use the techniques. It would be very easy for you to mistakenly use them in the service of your neutralizing compulsions instead of supporting exposure. Many therapists make this mistake, and some even use cognitive therapy techniques that aren't suitable for treating OCD.

For example, the Experimental Method is a technique that you may read about elsewhere, but it shouldn't be used to treat OCD. At first glance, the Experimental Method would seem to be an ideal marriage between your exposure work and cognitive techniques. To use this tool, you would be asked to expose yourself to something that triggers your obsessive fears. So if your fears involve hit-and-run obsessions, you would be asked to drive. The problem is the next step. You would be asked to think of exposures as experiments in which you are testing a hypothesis or guess about what will happen following the exposure. In this model, the failure of a disaster to take place is supposed to reassure you that your fears are unfounded. Essentially, the lack of disaster should neutralize your fear and take away your uncertainty. But you know better— nothing can ever be 100 percent certain. Many of you have probably already found the flaws in this approach. First, you know that escaping negative consequences this time may just have been luck, so you'll feel that further exposures will simply increase your chances of disaster. Second, this tool can't be applied to consequences that wouldn't immediately be evident following an exposure (for example, *If I touch that spot, I may get AIDS and it may not show up for six months; if that causes cancer, it will be years before it shows up*). Finally, there are real risks we must all live with, and the experiment isn't really proof that disaster won't occur. No one can guarantee that you will never have a car accident, never burn down a house, or never hurt someone's feelings.

Remember, the purpose of exposure is not to create reassurance or safety, but to help you learn to live with the uncertainty arising from your fears in the same way you live with all the uncertainties that are not the focus of your OCD. The Experimental Method has no place in any OCD treatment program.

Although the Experimental Method is not a good treatment for OCD, there are other CBT techniques you will find helpful. You will be using the techniques that follow both in designing and implementing your recovery program. They will be the tools that will help you develop your own therapeutic voice, so that you will be able to provide yourself with the motivation and determination to work your recovery program. Because each of them can be countertherapeutic if used improperly, attention is given to both their use and misuse.

The Downward Arrow (Also Known as Vertical Arrow and What-If Technique)

The success of your recovery program depends on your understanding the feared consequences and cognitive distortions underlying your obsessive fears. The more you know about these, the more you will be able to:

1. Refine your version of *the question*. Remember, some sufferers were unsuccessful in treatment because they never understood that the goal was to learn to live with uncertainty. By clarifying *the question*, you'll better understand what you have to accept and what your recovery program is going to accomplish. Without doing this, you may be working on a program with goals that you haven't yet decided to accept.

Cognitive Techniques for OCD and Their Proper Use

1 *Downward Arrow/Vertical Arrow/What-If Technique*
Use: Identifying feared consequences of exposure to obsessive fears. This can be incorporated into imaginal exposure scripts as well as your Cost-Benefit Analysis.

2 *Survey Method*
Use: Identifying rituals for response prevention when you have lost touch with what is ritual versus "normal."

3 *The Double-Standard Method*
Use: Identifying cognitive distortions and rituals for response prevention when you have lost touch with what is ritual versus "normal."

4 *Socratic Questioning*
Use: Supports exposure and response prevention by fostering acceptance of cognitive distortions and the futility of response prevention.

5 *Cost-Benefit Analysis*
Use: Supports exposure and response prevention by keeping in mind what you have to gain from treatment and to lose from giving up.

6 *Externalization of Voices*
Use: Supports exposure and response prevention by teaching you to talk back to your OCD.

7 *Distraction and Refocusing*
Use: Supports exposure and response prevention by delaying urges to violate response prevention.

2. Create imaginal exposure scripts with more details that reflect your true concerns. The more details your scripts contain, the more effective they will be in fostering acceptance and habituation of your fears.

All this information can be found within your obsessive fears, rituals, and passive avoidances through the use of Downward Arrow. To use this technique, imagine you're in an anxiety-provoking situation. Think what might happen if you didn't ritualize. What feared consequences would come true? Now imagine how you would try to cope with the disaster and what would happen if that also

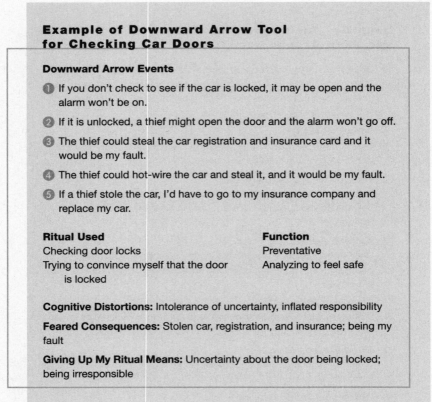

**Example of Downward Arrow Tool
for Checking Car Doors**

Downward Arrow Events

1. If you don't check to see if the car is locked, it may be open and the alarm won't be on.

2. If it is unlocked, a thief might open the door and the alarm won't go off.

3. The thief could steal the car registration and insurance card and it would be my fault.

4. The thief could hot-wire the car and steal it, and it would be my fault.

5. If a thief stole the car, I'd have to go to my insurance company and replace my car.

Ritual Used	**Function**
Checking door locks	Preventative
Trying to convince myself that the door is locked	Analyzing to feel safe

Cognitive Distortions: Intolerance of uncertainty, inflated responsibility

Feared Consequences: Stolen car, registration, and insurance; being my fault

Giving Up My Ritual Means: Uncertainty about the door being locked; being irresponsible

turned out badly. Continue with this process until it can go no further. The last disaster is your worst-feared consequence.

In traditional cognitive therapy, you are also asked to guess the odds of each disaster occurring at every step along the way to demonstrate how unlikely it would be for your worst-feared consequence to occur. You won't be doing this, because you may be tempted to try to reassure yourself with the odds, which would start an endless cycle of *It probably won't happen, but it might happen, but it probably won't. . . .* With this modification, Downward Arrow provides no neutralizing.

To help you use Downward Arrow (also called the Vertical Arrow or What-If Technique), examine Alice's Downward Arrow analysis for her car-door-checking rituals. In public parking lots, she would spend five minutes to a half hour staring at her car to make sure the doors were properly locked. When she would finally leave to go to her destination, she would spend another ten to twenty minutes trying to remember that she saw that the doors were locked. Look at the chart on the previous page and notice the steps she has taken. First she imagined the worst consequence that might take place as a result of not locking her car. Next she looked at the rituals she used and how they functioned. Finally, using the data she generated, she identified her cognitive distortions, feared consequences, and what she would have to live with by giving up her rituals.

Now use the Downward Arrow Technique to examine your own hierarchy, starting with the most difficult items. Think about the different rituals you use for each situation and when you use them. Ask yourself the following questions about these items and write down your answers. Imagine being confronted with an item on your list and not ritualizing. Which consequences do you fear? What might happen to you? Would you become sick? Would your house burn down? Would you do something horrible? Would life be miserable forever?

Don't stop here. What would happen next? You would be sick and then what? What would you do the day after your house has burned down? How would you continue if your life was miserable, and in exactly which ways would it become miserable? Continue this process until you can go no further. Your last sentence could look like any of the following: "I would die from AIDS"; "I would be responsible for causing the fire that killed my family, everyone would know it, and I'd spend the rest of my life in prison"; "I would commit a sin, go to prison, and be condemned to hell"; or "These thoughts will always be with me and interfere with my enjoyment of everything, and I will never be at my best." After identifying your primary feared consequences, you still have more work to do. Often your primary feared consequences concern events that *might* happen. There are lesser consequences that will take place when you institute exposure and response prevention, and you need to be ready for them. To uncover these consequences, examine all the rituals you use in response to the item and determine how each functions to neutralize your obsession. When you institute response prevention, these functions won't be fulfilled. Is it a restorative ritual, such as cleaning your house to decontaminate it, or is its goal to analyze a situation to determine whether or not it is safe? If your cleaning rituals are meant to decontaminate the environment to prevent illness, then

DOWNWARD ARROW CHARTING FORM

DOWNWARD ARROW EVENTS
1.
2.
3.
4.
5.
6.
7.
8.
9.

RITUAL USED	FUNCTIONS
1.	
2.	
3.	

COGNITIVE DISTORTIONS:

FEARED CONSEQUENCES:

GIVING UP MY RITUAL MEANS:

RITUALS AND THEIR FUNCTIONS CHART

RITUAL	FUNCTION	COGNITIVE DISTORTION	LOSS I MUST ACCEPT TO OVERCOME OCD

exposure and response prevention not only means that everyone might get sick, it also means that your environment will be contaminated—forever. Are you trying to stop your thoughts? Then response prevention means that your thoughts will never stop. Consider what you will have to live with if you do exposure and response prevention and your worst fear doesn't materialize. These are the uncertainties and losses you have to decide to live with if you want to overcome OCD. Record this information on the Rituals and Their Functions Chart provided on page 109. These losses are the consequence of answering *the question* with a yes.

Go back over what you have written and see if you rely on any of the other cognitive distortions besides intolerance of uncertainty. These represent themes that probably appear over and over again in your obsessions.

The more your answer reflects a true understanding of what *the question* means to you, the more your decision to accept uncertainty will mean. To increase your understanding, ask yourself which cognitive distortions you can detect in your thinking when you look at your core fears. Black-and-white thinking? Thought-Action Fusion? Inflated Responsibility? Each represents a set of impossible demands that you have been pursuing in an effort to appease your OCD fears. Your future freedom and happiness can't depend on attaining the impossible. Record any of the distortions you have identified. One of the ways you will support yourself during treatment will be working to constantly recognize and accept the impossibility of achieving OCD goals, such as being 100 percent certain or being able to control your thoughts.

The Survey Method

You may have found that you have been engaging in OCD rituals for so long that you no longer feel you know what "normal" behavior is. The Survey Method is a tool that can be used to help you find a partial solution to this issue. To use the Survey Method, simply compare your thinking and behavior to that of others. The idea behind this is that the majority can serve as a guide to how you might cope with obsessional trigger situations.

Used properly in an OCD recovery program, the Survey Method can help you identify which behavioral rituals need to be suppressed, because others don't engage in them (for example, non-sufferers don't walk around their car five times before leaving it). However, if you use the Survey Method to seek reassurance (for example, thinking, *This must be safe, because everyone else does it*), then the technique becomes another neutralizing ritual.

The Survey Method can be harmful to your recovery if you use it as a reason to reject exposure-and-response-prevention exercises (for example, *No one touches bathroom toilets* or *Everyone washes their hands after using the bathroom*).

If you do this, you are making three mistakes. The first is your selective use of the Survey Method—that is, using it as a reason to avoid exposure and response prevention, but not as a reason to stop your rituals (for example, washing your hands for twenty minutes). Second, you may not realize it, but "normal" people lie. For example, most people would tell you that they wouldn't touch a Dumpster and then eat. If you have contamination fears, you hear this and then, when I ask you to touch a Dumpster, you'll tell me, "Even normal people wouldn't do this." However, those same "normal" people will take out the garbage as they leave the house to go to work and then stop for breakfast on the way without washing their hands. Because they don't have OCD, they don't notice what they are doing and they don't care. Finally, you are forgetting that recovery is like a diet: You don't start by going from overeating to normal eating—you start by eating less.

Think about your rituals. Do you believe any of them are "normal" and shouldn't be changed? If so, use the Survey Method to determine if your way of doing this activity is the same as that of non-sufferers, or if it is somehow more extensive. If it is the latter, then including this behavior in your response prevention will help you in the long run.

The Double-Standard Method

The Double-Standard Method is a tool that you will use to examine your behavior and determine if you are holding yourself to a higher standard than everyone else (for example, thinking, *Others can be forgiven for a mistake, but I cannot*). If the cognitive distortion of inflated responsibility is one of yours, then the Double-Standard Method will uncover it. Like the Survey Method, the Double-Standard Method can become a part of the logic for confronting or giving in to OCD symptoms. In standard cognitive therapy, the Double-Standard Method is used to challenge negative self-evaluations. Suppose, for example, that you made a mistake at work and would normally castigate yourself for the entire day. The Double-Standard Method could help you recognize that you feel others at work who made the same mistake should not torture themselves. With this in mind, you would try to convince yourself that your mistake wasn't so bad and that you should forgive yourself.

For non-OCD issues, this is a reasonable beginning to altering your thoughts (for example, thinking, *If I think others can be forgiven for mistakes, then I'm not being reasonable for failing to forgive myself*). If such thoughts are part of your obsessive fears, using the Double-Standard Method this way would be neutralizing. However, with a small modification, it can be used to support exposure. Imagine you had the thought, *I might be evil because I didn't check my stove, and if a fire started, everyone in my apartment building could die.* Using the Double-Standard Method the classic way, you might think, *I don't think anyone else is evil if they don't check the stove when they leave their apartment, so I can't be evil.* This statement is neutralizing and would eventually result in endless what-if circles. To support exposure, you would modify your statement to the following: *To fight this OCD, I have to live like everyone else and not check the stove, even though this means I might be evil.* In the modified statement, you will change your behavior based on the standards you expect of others, but, at the same time, you will also expose yourself to the possibility that you may be evil.

Examine your Rituals and Their Functions chart on page 109. Using the Double-Standard Method, you may discover that inflated responsibility is one of your distortions. If this is true, what will you have to accept to overcome your OCD? Record this on your chart.

Socratic Questioning

Socratic Questioning is simply using logic to question the validity of your beliefs. In traditional cognitive therapy, after identifying your cognitive distortions and beliefs, Socratic Questioning focuses on the truth of your beliefs and the lack of evidence supporting them.

Many of you would find this approach very seductive, since Socratic Questioning used this way has the goal of reassuring you that your beliefs and fears aren't reasonable. In classic cognitive therapy, such questioning was supposed to lead to a reduction of your fears. When used this way, Socratic Questioning is neutralizing and is a form of analyzing and figuring out.

Socratic Questioning can be used in the service of exposure. For example, if, by this point in this book, I have convinced you that part of your recovery depends on accepting uncertainty, then you have experienced the power of Socratic Questioning in my writing. It can be used to support exposure by reinforcing the impossibility of achieving OCD goals. For example, I was working with a woman with contamination rituals, who was afraid of one of the doorknobs in her house. She avoided touching it, and if she did, she immediately washed her hands to avoid spreading the contamination. Using Socratic Questioning, I uncovered inconsistencies in her ritualizing through a dialogue that sounded like the following:

DR. GRAYSON: So you avoid touching the doorknob and anything that may have touched the doorknob so that you won't spread the contamination?

PATIENT: Yes. I don't want to make anyone sick.

DR. GRAYSON: Do you monitor whether or not your family touches the knob?

PATIENT: Oh, yes. If I know they touched it, they have to wash immediately.

DR. GRAYSON: What if you aren't home?

(THE PATIENT DOESN'T ANSWER, BUT INDICATES THAT SHE DOESN'T KNOW WHAT HAPPENS.)

DR. GRAYSON: And if you are upstairs, might they touch that knob without your knowing?

PATIENT: Yes.

DR. GRAYSON: Do you think this has happened, and if so, do you think they wash when they don't have to?

PATIENT: I'm pretty sure that happens. And no, I'll bet they don't wash when they don't have to.

DR. GRAYSON: So that means that they have contaminated the house, and because you touch other things that they have touched, you also spread it. Basically, the things I'm asking you to do—to completely contaminate your house—have already been done. The only difference is that you will be aware of it.

PATIENT: Well, yes, but at least I wasn't responsible for the initial contamination.

DR. GRAYSON: Of course you are. You admitted that they probably touch the doorknob when you are upstairs and you do nothing, because you didn't hear them. If you are protecting them, then they should always be protected. You could put a buzzer on the door so that you would hear it. The fact is, you are inconsistent.

In this dialogue, you can see how we established through logical questioning that the patient's house is actually already completely contaminated. Note that there was no suggestion that this somehow makes her home safe, because that would be neutralizing through reassurance. The purpose was to help her see that what seemed like a terrible exposure is already a part of her life.

Socratic Questioning put her in the position of recognizing that if she is going to give in to her fears, she isn't ritualizing enough. If she were to suggest further refinements to her rituals to make the house "safer," I would use Socratic Questioning to find the holes in her reasoning. Ultimately, she would be left acknowledging the futility of her rituals. She can never ritualize enough to truly protect her family, which leaves her deciding to start learning how to live with risk rather than trying to avoid it.

The second point concerns her inconsistency. Many of you have probably realized that you are inconsistent in your own precautions. This is not unusual. The fact is, people without OCD are terribly inconsistent and, without realizing it, are constantly violating the rules they would tell you they follow. The difference between you and "normal" people is the degree of consistency. When talking about OCD, *consistency is the measure of severity.* The more consistent you are, the more severe your OCD will be, which translates to more rituals, more anxiety, and more dysfunction.

Examine your rituals again, but this time try to find ways in which you are often inconsistent and your rituals don't really accomplish what you want. You will often find that you aren't concerned about your inconsistencies. This is fine, but recognize that this means your rituals don't accomplish what you want and that this can become another reason to risk doing exposure. You should write down your Socratic Questioning, because it is easier to work through it that way. In addition, you will be able to incorporate what you write into the scripts you create.

If you haven't yet decided to learn to live with uncertainty, then skip using this tool for now. Because you aren't ready for treatment, Socratic Questioning is likely to be more upsetting than useful.

Cost-Benefit Analysis

Often, when you are considering giving up on treatment, you act as if the choice is between some hellish treatment and your otherwise comfortable life. Cost-Benefit Analysis is a tool that you can use to stay motivated with the program. It reminds you that the alternative to recovery is also hell. And even worse, for all your work and agony, your rituals often don't make you feel safe.

In the end, both treatment and rituals can be equally difficult to go through; the major difference is that refusing treatment leads to endless pain and rituals, while treatment leads to an end of pain and rituals.

The first step in creating your Cost-Benefit Analysis is to examine what you have lost to OCD. On pages 117 and 118 are two forms—Exposure and Response Prevention Motivators. The first focuses upon what you have lost to OCD. Most of the time when you think about your OCD, you think about your pain and all of the reasons that it feels necessary to give in to the demands of the OCDemon. The purpose of this form is to examine the ways in which you have been hurt by OCD. ***Do not include ways in which your OCD has hurt others***—there is another form for this. In considering what you have lost to OCD, it is important to be detailed about the painful parts of this loss. For example, rather than stating that OCD has kept you from having more money, be specific and remind yourself that your OCD kept you from pursuing career and employment opportunities that would have led to an increase in salary and how you felt about not making more money. It is very important to be detailed—even if this upsets you. In the next chapter you will use these facts and detailed scenarios to create scripts to motivate yourself to continue with your self-guided program of exposure and response prevention.

The second Exposure and Response Prevention Motivator form is very similar to the first, but now the focus is upon how your OCD behavior has hurt your loved ones. I know that hurting others wasn't your intention, but it is an unintended consequence of your obsessive and compulsive actions—even if your rituals and avoidances ultimately had the goal of trying to "protect" them. Again, provide as many details as possible so that you can have a full picture of how OCD has impacted your life and that of those around you.

For example one of my clients shared one occasion when he had locked himself in the bathroom. When his seven-year-old son knocked on the door, the sufferer told him he was using the toilet. His little son began banging on the door, crying and whimpering that he knew his daddy was ritualizing. My client allowed this to go on for twenty painful minutes and the memory is still a terrible shame to him. And when he is in the middle of being tempted by rituals, this is the story I encourage him to recall and rely on, as this is a reason to fight OCD.

Now you have the information you need to create a Cost-Benefit Analysis. Examine the sample Cost-Benefit Analysis on page 119. Then gather your assessment materials and fill out the chart on page 120.

Next, consider the advantages and disadvantages of rejecting treatment and holding on to your OCD. Some of the disadvantages have been captured by the work you have done thus far: for example, the time you have lost to ritualizing, what you have lost through the passive avoidances that you have identified, and your chart of rituals and their functions. Try to come up with additional disadvantages. For example, do any of your rituals actually increase the odds of your feared consequences coming true? Some sufferers try so hard to make no mistakes on the job that they end up losing their jobs because they work too slowly. Hit-and-run sufferers will often check their rearview mirror so much that they are actually at greater risk of being involved in an accident. Is your house a mess because perfect cleaning is too difficult? On the flip side, do your rituals significantly decrease the odds of your feared consequences coming true? Besides these disadvantages, there is the painful knowledge that your friends and family may lose respect for you and discuss your behavior with others. What other disadvantages can you think of?

Next, address and record the advantages of rejecting treatment. Look back at your Downward Arrow analysis, and think about the fantasies you might have to give up. Does going through treatment make you worry that you will always feel irresponsible or that your house will always be dirty? At the very least, one advantage of rejecting treatment is avoiding the pain of exposure and response prevention.

Now write down the advantages and disadvantages of overcoming OCD. If having less anxiety and more free time is one of your advantages, consider what you will do with more free time. If you don't have an answer for this, you need to start thinking about the possibilities. After all, one of the main reasons to recover is to make life more fun and fulfilling. If this isn't the case, then why get better?

ERP MOTIVATOR I: WHAT HAVE I LOST TO OCD

INSTRUCTIONS: Most of the time when you think about your OCD, you think about your pain and all of the reasons that it feels necessary to give in to the demands of the OCDemon. The purpose of this form is to examine ways in which you've been hurt by OCD. **Do not include ways in which your OCD has hurt others**, there is another form for this. In considering what you have lost to OCD it is important to be detailed about the painful parts of the loss. For example, rather than saying you could have more money, remind yourself of employment opportunities that you lost to OCD and how you lost them. The categories below are just suggestions. Feel free to come up with your own. If you need to, use the back of this form or additional paper.

LOST/WASTED TIME:

BECAUSE OF OCD, I'VE MISSED:

HUMILIATING EXPERIENCES:

BECAUSE OF OCD, I'VE BEEN LATE TO:

FINANCIAL/EMPLOYMENT LOSSES:

DAMAGED OR LOST RELATIONSHIPS:

GUILT:

OTHER OCD LOSSES:

ERP MOTIVATOR II: HOW GIVING IN
TO OCD HAS HURT MY LOVED ONES

INSTRUCTIONS: Most of the time when you think about your OCD, you think about your pain and all of the reasons that it feels necessary to give in to the demands of the OCDemon. The purpose of this form is to examine how you have hurt the ones you love by giving into OCD. In considering what you have lost to OCD it is important to be detailed about the painful parts of this loss. For example, rather than saying you have missed events, try to think about specific events and how your loved ones must have felt (e.g., the disappointment a child would feel because your actions made them late to an event). The categories below are just suggestions. Feel free to come up with your own. If you need to, use the back of this form or additional paper.

FORCING THEM TO RITUALIZE:

HURT THEM WITH MY OCD RIGIDITY:

MAKING THEM LATE OR MISSING EVENTS:

IGNORING THEM BECAUSE OF OCD THOUGHTS:

HURT THEM WITH MY OTHER OCD DEMANDS:

IGNORING THEM BY WITHDRAWING:

HURT THEM WITH MY OCD ANGER:

OTHER:

Cost-Benefit Analysis of Accepting vs. Refusing Treatment

ACCEPTING TREATMENT

Advantages
1. I'll have freedom from anxiety.
2. I'll have more free time to do the things I like.
3. I'll have no more agonizing rituals.
4. I won't have to lie about my OCD symptoms.
5. I'll be able to go out in public and not have to ritualize when I get home.
6. I won't have to avoid going to certain places.
7. I'll be able to use public restrooms rather than holding it.
8. My children won't be forced to do rituals for me.
9. My children and my spouse will respect me.

Disadvantages
1. Treatment is hard work.
2. My worst fears might come true, and everyone will get AIDS.
3. Treatment might not work.
4. Treatment costs a great deal of money.

REFUSING TREATMENT

Advantages
1. I won't have to do the hard work of treatment.
2. I won't have to pay for treatment.
3. My worst fears are less likely to come true.

Disadvantages
1. I'll have to continue doing rituals and wasting time.
2. I'll continue to have an adverse effect on my family.
3. I'll continue to waste money on extra soap, alcohol, paper towels, and cleaning bills.
4. I'll continue to suffer from anxiety.
5. Since I'm often not convinced that my rituals have been done correctly, my worst fears might come true, and everyone might get AIDS.

Downward Arrow can also be used to generate entries here. Alice's worst consequence in her Downward Arrow analysis was having her car stolen and then replaced by insurance. In her Cost-Benefit Analysis, she decided that a

COST-BENEFIT ANALYSIS OF ACCEPTING
VS. REFUSING TREATMENT

ACCEPTING TREATMENT	REFUSING TREATMENT
ADVANTAGES	ADVANTAGES
1.	1.
2.	2.
3.	3.
4.	4.
5.	5.
6.	6.
7.	7.
8.	8.
9.	9.
DISADVANTAGES	DISADVANTAGES
1.	1.
2.	2.
3.	3.
4.	4.
5.	5.
6.	6.
7.	7.
8.	8.
9.	9.

stolen car was not as frightening as lifelong OCD. This comforting thought became one of her reasons to embrace the goals of recovery. Just because it is comforting does not mean it is neutralizing. For comfort to be neutralizing, there would need to be some reassurance that the worst disasters won't happen.

Externalization of Voices: Answering the Voice of OCD

The main goal of cognitive therapy is to help you to stop responding to the automatic self-defeating thoughts that arise from distortions. You can use Externalization of Voices as a tool to rally your motivation and to fight negative thoughts by turning them into the enemy. Deborah, one of my clients, used the Externalization of Voices tool to address low self-esteem, a non-OCD issue, although one shared by many OCD sufferers.

> *I've always thought of self-esteem as something I had to earn. And there was always this critic inside me, tearing down everything I do. But this past week I had two different thoughts—that maybe the critic is my enemy. And second, that I've been making a mistake all these years, that self-esteem, rather than being something you have to earn, is something that needs to be nurtured and protected from the enemy, the same way you would protect your child from an overly critical adult.*   —DEBORAH

Deborah had avoided advancing her career because of her low self-esteem. By transforming her negative self-evaluations into an enemy—the internal critic—Deborah changed her view of taking risks. Rather than accepting herself as a failure who shouldn't even attempt advancing her career, opportunities to advance became challenges—part of a battle with a voice that she no longer wanted to listen to. Note how this supports exposure: Transforming these negative self-evaluations into an enemy didn't ensure that she would be successful in her attempts to advance her career. Instead, it motivated her, because listening to the advice of an enemy doesn't make sense.

Many of you often experience your OCD as another part of yourself, a monster within. In the scripts you'll make to support yourself, you'll take the data from your Cost-Benefit Analysis to turn OCD into the enemy who has taken too much from you and whose goal is to keep you as a slave to its demands.

By doing this you remind yourself that OCD is not who you are, but a problem you have.

Distraction and Refocusing

Distraction and Refocusing is a tool of action. Overwhelming urges to ritualize and avoid tell you that you must give in, because you will not be able to tolerate another minute of anxiety. Often if you can find a way to delay giving in, an urge to ritualize can be transformed from an overwhelming desire to something you can cope with.

The goal of Distraction and Refocusing is twofold. Urge reduction is one goal, but the less important of the two. The primary goal is to delay ritualizing and to practice functioning while facing anxiety and urges to ritualize. If you don't have a significant fear that your obsessive thoughts or feelings will stay forever, then it's okay for those thoughts to periodically drift from your awareness during other activities. But if one of your major feared consequences is that your thoughts or feelings will stay forever, or if you find yourself accidentally measuring the success of Distraction and Refocusing by how much it reduces your urges to ritualize rather than the fact that you delayed ritualizing, you'll need to modify this tool to prevent it from happening. While engaging in activities that delay ritualizing, create a simple recording with a single word that can be relevant to your fear. For example, if you struggle with obsessions concerning violent thoughts, you can use *murder*. The word can be anything, even simply *it*, since you'll know what *it* means. In making the recording, follow these steps:

SCRIPT

Single Word Exposure Script

1. *Say the word.*
2. *Wait for 30–40 seconds.*
3. *Repeat the word.*
4. *Wait 50–70 seconds.*
5. *Repeat the word.*
6. *Wait 20–40 seconds.*

Listening to this recording while you are delaying your urges to ritualize provides you with an exposure-and-response-prevention exercise that undermines the possibility of forgetting your thoughts or feelings by keeping them in the foreground, which helps you to not turn the delay into a new neutralizing ritual. The Single Word Exposure Script can be an important tool in attaining the "ten-minute frame of mind" discussed in Mindfulness on page 129.

Note that many sufferers who try to use this tool do so with the mistaken belief that one of its goals is to take your mind off your concerns—to help you control your thoughts. Such a goal would be in the service of neutralizing, especially if one of your feared consequences is that your feelings or thoughts will never end.

Acceptance and Commitment Therapy (ACT)

Acceptance and Commitment Therapy or ACT is a set of cognitive behavioral techniques based upon Relational Frames Theory. ACT could easily have its own chapter, but I am including it here to make a point. You have learned that cognitive therapy is composed of many techniques, but not all of them are suitable for using with OCD and others need modification; the same is true for ACT. However, with modifications to account for the cognitive distortions that characterize OCD, ACT can add to our armamentarium to fight OCD.

ACT was developed by Steven Hayes and its core idea is very simple: Our lives are not always happy and in everyone's life there will be suffering. With this in mind, the goal of any treatment cannot be constant unending happiness. On the other hand, how we cope with life and our thoughts can make our suffering worse or better, so the focus becomes upon accepting what you can't change and learning how to live *mindfully* in the present. To help people do this, ACT focuses upon six processes: acceptance, defusion, values, committed action, self as context, and mindfulness. As we go through each of these processes, it will become clear that ACT is consistent with our program. However, there is a but! Although ACT is a part of cognitive behavioral therapy and a good ACT therapist will include exposure and response prevention in his treatment, ACT is a top-down approach; that is, ACT therapists want to help you change your entire view of everything and then assume that this will make the process of exposure and response prevention easier and perhaps more natural to go through. Changing the way you look at the world is one of our goals, but we believe that we have to start from the bottom up; we believe that your OCD interferes with your life too much to start anywhere else. Imagine trying to help an alcoholic with his life problems while he is drunk—it makes more sense to help him become sober before working on other issues. In this respect, OCD is no different.

With this in mind, you may be beginning to wonder why am I discussing ACT at all. The answer is twofold. First, including ACT principles in a bottom-up approach adds to treatment effectiveness, and once your OCD is under control, you may want to continue pursuing ACT to make further improvements in your life. Second, many cognitive behavioral therapists include ACT in their repertoire and it's important for you to know whether they are modifying ACT for you or are trying to fit you into a treatment protocol. Now let's turn to the six processes of ACT and see how to tailor them to your needs as opposed to trying to make you fit in a treatment protocol.

ACCEPTANCE: In ACT, acceptance is based on the idea that trying to avoid or to get rid of pain will make that pain worse. That's not to say that acceptance means giving up and living a life of misery. Instead, ACT has you identify the myriad ways in which you have difficulty with acceptance, whether it be your OCD, your relationships, your self-esteem, or anything else. Certainly when I'm working with a client, I do want to obtain all of this information, because, as noted earlier, therapy will start with the problems that are giving the client the greatest difficulty. For OCD sufferers it is usually their OCD. Since you are reading this book, OCD is obviously a major problem for you. It makes sense to focus upon acceptance more narrowly and as it relates to your condition. Of course, after you have your OCD under control, you may want to continue to pursue ACT.

I'm asking you to start by accepting the idea that uncertainty is the rule of life. This is not just for you because you have OCD, this is true for everyone. In accepting uncertainty, you will also be accepting the possibility that your feared consequences may occur—that you might kill your spouse, that you might contract cancer, and that your house may burn down. Sufferers and non-sufferers alike shudder when I say things like this. Obviously you don't want them to come true, but one of our goals is to explore ways to cope with the worst as opposed to planning to give up if it happens. Part 3 will show you how to do this for all of your feared consequences. At this point you may be wondering if you can actually do this.

I know that you can. Allow me to make a guess about you, even though we haven't met: I believe that you don't want to be maimed, paralyzed, and disfigured. Assuming I'm correct (I'm almost, but not 100 percent, sure that I am), I have another question: How do you get from place to place? Do you drive? Or are you driven? Either way, once in a car you are at risk for another driver ramming your car. And while we are on this subject, if you are the driver, do you use your cell phone when driving? Do you drink or eat? Do you talk to others? If you answered yes to any of these, you actually increase your risk of being maimed, paralyzed, and disfigured. Whether or not you are the driver, have you carefully checked the vehicle to make sure it is in top operating condition—the air pressure in the tires, brake fluid, brake pads, tire tread. . . . Unless driving is one of your OCD problem areas, your brilliant plan for coping with a car accident is the "normal" one—you are going to do nothing until you are crushed under the metal. In fact, you even risk death just in going to see a movie. That's crazy! No, that's life. In non-OCD life we cope with most disasters after they occur and we live with uncertainty and risk. In the OCD part of your life, you try to eliminate risk immediately. The goal of treatment is to accept your OCD fears the same way you accept living with potential non-OCD disasters.

Exposure will be the method you will use to do this. Exposure will not only focus on your obsessions and feared consequences, but also how you would try to cope if the worst happens—no matter what that is.

DEFUSION: Defusion is a word created by ACT to describe detaching our thoughts from the meanings and importance we give to them. They correctly note that our thoughts are not necessarily accurate reflections of reality, and that we have many beliefs and make many judgments. We make judgments concerning everything—from how we think others should treat us to what we believe about the nature of God to our ability to cope with feelings like anxiety. ACT's goal is to help you to think without such judgments. For example, consider your feelings of anxiety. Technically, you are worried about a feared consequence and your body is having physiological responses that feel terrible but are harmless. You may say you can't endure another minute of living this way, but in fact, you have done so many times.

It is here that ACT therapists run into trouble with OCD. They like to say that a thought is just a thought. To a non-OCD sufferer this is not a judgmental statement. For you, how often have you had this wish? The traditional ACT therapist would like you to turn your attention away from your thoughts to your present experience (e.g., *At this moment I'm not killing anyone, my heart is pounding, I'm in my room, there are thoughts in my head, but they are just thoughts*). Such advice may be reminiscent of that you often get from family, when they tell you, "don't worry." Such comments are infuriating and frustrating; as if this were an idea or hope that you never had before and all you had to do was stop. If only it could be so simple.

For someone with OCD, the idea that a thought is just a thought is a judgment. Although this is not what ACT therapists are trying to convey, there is the promise that perceiving a thought as just a thought will take power away from it. In your mind, this is interpreted as there is no reality basis to the thought, so you don't have to worry. The ACT therapist is falling into the same trap as earlier cognitive therapists who wanted to argue about the probability of an event happening. You will obsess about whether the current thought is really just a thought or a real concern. The truth is: A thought is a thought and its probability of occurring is a maybe. Remember the Gun Test—it doesn't tell you if you are absolutely safe, but it helps you guess; the same way you get into a car and repeatedly make the guess you will survive. A good guess isn't a guarantee. Deciding to live with uncertainty is the beginning of defusion. As you come to accept this, you'll realize that the time you've lost ritualizing is particularly tragic, since you never get the prize—absolute certainty. For all of the rituals you engage in, your feared consequences may still occur. Exposure is acceptance, and as you go through it, you will learn and will become comfortable with guessing.

This does involve considering disasters—feared consequences that haven't yet occurred. Some might argue that concern over a possible future event that might not happen doesn't make sense, but the reality is that it might happen. I believe that thinking about coping with a potential negative consequence rather than obsessing about one makes sense. Everyone would agree that if you have just lost a loved one, mourning that loss and working on adjusting to a new life is necessary. Equally important would be thinking about mourning the coming loss of a loved one, who is terminally ill with only six months to live. Attempting to not think about the impending loss will only serve to make those thoughts more present and will make enjoying those last few months impossible. I would further argue that thinking about the potential loss of a loved one who isn't sick or dying is adaptive. After all, isn't that one of the reasons there are so many medical series on TV, that we all wonder about the loss of ourselves and loved ones? Coping with potential consequences is a creative and adaptive process that is very different from ritualizing. Obsessing and ritualizing are generally attempts to deny possible realities that upset you. Being able to think any thought without fear is defusion, since the thought has now become a thought with many possibilities and not one absolute outcome.

VALUES: Exposure and response prevention is a difficult treatment and much of this book is written not only to help you design your self-guided program, but also to help you be motivated enough to follow through with the hard work. ACT urges you to think about what you value in life and what you have been avoiding, and it suggests that these values, rather than your OCD, should guide your decisions. Again, we will start from the bottom up and look at how OCD has interfered with your values. If you haven't filled out the ERP Motivator Forms, do so now. By examining what you have lost to OCD and how you have hurt your loved ones, you will see the ways that giving in to OCD has led you to go against your own values. Consider the dialogue below that I had with Lily, a young mother at a workshop at the annual convention of the International OCD Foundation, a convention for both OCD sufferers and professionals. I was working with her to help her carry out a contamination exposure.

DR. GRAYSON: Do you love your children?

LILY: Of course I do.

DR. GRAYSON: And you would do anything for them?

LILY: Absolutely.

DR. GRAYSON: I'm sorry, but you are lying. I believe that you would like to be that way, but right now, you put your OCD fears in front of your child's welfare. How often have you made your child late, because you were ritualizing? Or forced them to ritualize? Or yelled at them because they weren't making your rituals easier for you? I believe you love your children and that you have a lot to offer, but at this moment you are risking having a thirteen-year-old who tells his/her friends what a crazy joke you are. Or worse, your child has a one-in-four chance of having OCD; do you want them to be able to cope with it or to handle it the way you do?

LILY: (At this point there are tears in her eyes.) Not like me.

DR. GRAYSON: Your child will learn by what you do, not what you say. If you continue to handle your OCD this way, you will teach them that they will be helpless in the face of OCD. I know that you feel like you are trying to protect your child, but as we have discussed, your efforts to prevent your child from contamination are doomed if you plan to allow your child to go to school and have friends. And if you were to actually deprive them of friends, then what are you allowing your OCD to do to their future? The reality is that your child will be exposed to all of the horrors you fear and, like all parents, all you have in the end is luck. Most of the time the worst disasters don't happen.

The only time you ever have your children is when you are with them. At this moment with me, they are memories of good times past and a hope they will be there when you get home. Except, you don't even get to have the present, because rather than being with them, you are in OCD-land.

I know what I'm saying is scary, but what I'm suggesting is that you can make your earlier statement true, that your children come first and you will make your love for them greater than your OCD fears.

Lily thought of herself as a good mother because she loved her children and because she only wanted what was best for them. This interaction made her realize that in giving in to her OCD, she was behaving like a bad mother. Now her reasons for doing the exposure were not only to overcome OCD, but to be the mother she wanted to be. The act of exposure now was an act of love for her children. As you look over what you have lost to OCD and how you have hurt your family, think about what values these losses may represent. Go back to your Cost-Benefit sheet and include these in your reasons for choosing to go through with your self-guided program.

COMMITTED ACTION: Committed action is simply living your values. Like so many ideas and techniques, simple is not the same as easy. ACT urges you to stop delaying your life and to work toward being the person you choose to be. An ACT therapist would claim that having identified your desire to be a good mother will, with therapeutic guidance, lead you to naturally stop forcing your children to ritualize for you and that you will simply stop washing your hands in front of them. Furthermore, you will start to engage in previously avoided activities that would have been fulfilling. Exposure will be taking place because you are living again. Although ACT, like exposure and response prevention, argues that avoidance will make your problems worse, the failure of ACT therapists to specifically target your OCD obsessions and feared consequences constitutes incomplete treatment. Hoping that exposure will be a natural consequence of living your values is no different from saying stop worrying about your OCD because it is irrational. The path to regaining your life is starting with your OCD and working your way up. Does this mean I'm saying don't start living your life until you've conquered your OCD? Of course not. But on your way to living the values-driven life that ACT urges, I'm saying start by using your values to help you follow through with your own self-guided recovery program.

SELF AS CONTEXT: ACT describes three aspects of the self: the conceptualized self, self as a process of ongoing awareness, and the observing self. Briefly, the conceptualized self is made up of the beliefs and evaluations that we use to define ourselves. It is part of our life's work to try to understand the flaws in our definition and where our thoughts about ourselves are fused to our beliefs—for example defining oneself as a failure for not being the best at something doesn't represent fact, but a belief system. Self as an ongoing process refers to our awareness of the present moment—it is critical for negotiating our way in the world, but judging and categorizing may get in the way of living. Finally, the observing self concerns the goal of living and experiencing the present without fused thoughts. This is an overarching goal we all strive for. The goal of deciding to live with uncertainty sets the groundwork for you to continue down this path after your OCD is under control. Living with uncertainty is the beginning of not accepting thoughts and feelings as truths. Because OCD can be such a severely disabling disorder, overcoming it is a life-changing experience. "Crazy thinking" suddenly makes sense, "irresistible urges" are found to be resistible. Fused language is constantly challenged. "Can't" becomes "I choose not to" and successful therapy means that just because I'm afraid to choose doesn't mean that I have to allow fear to make my choices. Overcoming OCD provides fertile ground for ACT. Living with uncertainty will teach you that all you ever have is the moment and running from potential fear is impossible.

MINDFULNESS: In the public's eye, mindfulness is an oft-misunderstood concept, confused with the idea of being in a relaxed Zen-like state, in which bliss replaces all problems and negative feelings. Perhaps this may be possible for the ninety-year-old Zen master who has meditated for a lifetime. In a sense, mindfulness is being in the state of the observing self. Life with all of its diversity is a part of our experience. Mindfulness exercises can be very useful in learning to sit with negative feelings, because cognitive defusion from our feelings allows us to experience them, to feel the pain, but to not increase the suffering with judgments of "I can't take this for another second," or "why am I so sick and weak."

For many OCD sufferers, working on exposure to your feared consequences makes the teaching of mindfulness superfluous in the short run, because being able to cope with them relieves your overwhelming anxiety. There is a subgroup of sufferers, whose anxiety is intense and a part of their feared consequence network. A modified version of mindfulness can help them learn to sit with anxiety feelings. Our first task is convincing them that there is a cognitive component to their anxiety. As you read the dialogue below, think about your own answers to my questions.

DR. GRAYSON: I'm curious. If in the middle of your worst anxiety, I could, by some means, assure you that it would be over, forever, in ten minutes, would that change anything? Would you be able to put up with it?

OCD SUFFERER: (Most sufferers will say yes, because knowing it will end seems to make it easier.)

DR. GRAYSON: That's interesting. That means that something is different about your thinking, because for the first ten minutes, the pain of the anxiety is exactly the same, whether it is going to be over or continue forever. We know it's not the sensations of anxiety, because if I subject you to the worst physical torture imaginable, ten minutes may be better than ten hours, but it isn't tolerable. I know you are saying that the fact that it will be over is the reason, but cognitively, there is something different you are doing as a result of this reason. Do you have any idea what it is?

OCD SUFFERER: (Usually sufferers cannot identify what would be different.)

DR. GRAYSON: Let me describe a different situation. Imagine that your spouse died three weeks ago and now you are back to work. Thoughts of your spouse will pop into your mind and will probably interfere with what you are doing. Are these obsessions? And if you say no, the answer is not because mourning is normal. The difference in both situations is that you decide to allow the thoughts or feelings to be there rather than trying to stop them. Our goal is to help you get into, what we will call "the ten-minute frame of mind."

Mindfulness training to cope with the sensations of anxiety would follow its normal course, with the caveat that during this practice, uncertainty and its feared consequences won't be addressed. Mindfulness training usually begins with deep breathing, but the goal is not for you to be relaxed, but for you to learn to focus on body sensations and environmental sensations (sounds, odors, etc.) without judgments. As this skill improves with practice, you will start to focus on the physiological components of your anxiety when you are in the middle of it. Again your OCD concerns will not be your mind's main focus. This doesn't mean stop thinking those thoughts—if this were possible you wouldn't need this book. Instead, I'm suggesting that you focus the bulk of your attention back onto physical sensations. In doing this, you are learning to defuse your thoughts from your anxiety sensations. The sensations are still unpleasant, but you are learning/practicing to be in the ten-minute frame of mind. This still leaves you needing to cope with the feared consequences. When not engaging in this targeted practice, you can practice exposure and response prevention normally while simultaneously using what was learned during mindfulness training for anxiety. Note, in so doing, we are also defusing experiencing anxiety sensations from the other feared consequences of OCD. You may want to explore some other books about mindfulness. For example, Steven Hayes's book *Get Out of Your Mind and Into Your Life* discusses ACT and provides steps to practice mindfulness. Remember that his book is a general book about ACT and you will need to adapt it for your OCD.

In the beginning of Chapter 5, you were asked an important question: *Are you willing to learn to live with uncertainty?* Hopefully you have answered yes, because you know that treatment can't succeed if you reject this goal. You've also learned about the tools that will help you during your treatment. The tools for designing your program are powerful. Exposure and response prevention, the core of your recovery program, has been tremendously successful in helping sufferers like you to overcome OCD. But it is a difficult treatment, and oftentimes people fail because they give up on treatment, not because the treatment is not working.

In the next chapter, you will put together what you have learned and begin working on your recovery program. This will include preparing many of the scripts you will be using throughout your recovery and following the guidelines I'll provide to help you design your program of exposure and response prevention. The final touches and implementation of your program will take place in Part 3, Personalizing Your Program: Treatment Guidelines for Your Specific OCD Concerns.

Chapter 8

Designing Your Recovery Program

For many of you, seeing the amount of work you will need to do and the uncertainties you will have to face may seem insurmountable. At this same point in therapy, many of my clients report feeling as though it's too much to do and that maybe others can succeed, but not them. If you are feeling this way, I would tell you the same thing I tell them: You are wrong—you are underestimating yourself. You are feeling scared, but remember, courage isn't a feeling, it's what you do when you are scared. But during your treatment program, you will rely on more than courage. To go through a self-guided program, you and any helpers you have will have to act as therapists—finding the words of encouragement to keep you going when you feel you can go no further. These words won't often come to you in the midst of stress, so your task will be to come up with therapist-like scripts beforehand to keep you motivated.

Using these scripts will be necessary in all phases of your program, because exposure and response prevention is not easy to go through. This is especially true if you don't have the support of a friend or a family member. Becoming discouraged and slipping into your old ways of thinking will be all too easy. You already have a well-developed repertoire of reasons to avoid and ritualize, which you repeat over and over again in your mind without realizing it. Imagine for a moment that your recovery thoughts and your OCD thoughts are two competing advertising campaigns. The OCD campaign would have the glitter and polish of a huge and abundantly funded Pepsi campaign, while the campaign for recovery would be minuscule, like one for NoBrand Cola. Your recovery campaign needs the help that the scripts will provide.

Your scripts have to fulfill a number of requirements. They have to be words you can believe, as opposed to simple, empty statements that you wish you could believe. They have to be detailed. Details make your scripts come to life. The details you will need are in the assessment data you have been gathering. Finally and most important, the scripts need to support exposure, not neutralizing. It may very well be true that your fears are unlikely, but focusing on this tends to be detrimental, because when you say "unlikely," you are really trying to force unlikely into certainty. There are better truths to include in your scripts that will support exposure.

Coming up with scripts can be very difficult when you have no experience creating them. Throughout this book, there may be a number of ideas that you have found very useful or encouraging. If they speak to you, use them as they are or modify them as you see fit. When creating your own scripts, you will find that writing them down will make the process easier. You may have to go through two or three versions before a script meets your needs. But don't try for perfection if perfectionism is one of your problems. Perfect scripts don't exist, and the imperfections in your scripts will actually be a useful addition to your exposure work.

After writing down the scripts, record them on a portable player that will allow you to play them on loop and work on recovery anywhere you go, whenever you want.

In addition to recording scripts, create script cards that you can carry, so you will be able to use them if you aren't in a position to listen to the recording. End script cards with a line reminding yourself to think of and consider three or more reasons you want to fight OCD, and then take the time to actually come up with those three or more reasons whenever you read the script.

You will be able to prepare some of your scripts while going through the rest of this chapter. For others, the sample scripts in this chapter may only provide you with a template that you will later need to modify with guidelines and suggestions from the chapters that focus on specific obsessive-compulsive presentations. Finally, once you implement your program, you may run into some difficulties that necessitate returning to this book to work on scripts that you hadn't realized you would need.

Your recovery program planning is now going to shift to exposure and response prevention. The remainder of this chapter will focus on the general guidelines to follow for designing your program of exposure and response prevention. Included in these will be sample scripts for you to adapt to your own needs and suggestions for how and when you should use them. The details of what your exposure-and-response-prevention program will entail and how you will actually implement it will be the focus of Part 3: Personalizing Your Program: Treatment Guidelines for Your Specific OCD Concerns.

Exposure is the heart of your exposure-and-response-prevention program. In a sense, the main purpose of everything in this book is to support exposure to your hierarchy. Following through with your exposures is more than a matter of "just do it." How you approach exposure and what you do during exposure are important variables that can greatly affect your motivation to continue treatment.

The first issue for you to decide is when you are going to do your exposure. You should plan to spend an hour or two every day consciously doing *active* exposure. For example, if you had contamination concerns, touching everything in your home during your exposure time would be active; whereas, simply not washing your hands and going about your business, contaminating whatever you happen to touch, would be passive. The latter is also important, but the active exposure is critical. If every day you have times set aside for exposure, you will be more likely to complete your homework than if your plan is to get to it in your free time. This may seem like a huge commitment, but think about how much time you lose to rituals on a daily basis. In the long run, an hour or two of daily exposure homework will take less time than engaging in your rituals.

At my center, treatment is carried out over a three- to five-week period. We have found that such intensive treatment is easier to carry out in the long run. If you are willing, try to follow such a schedule. However, there is a reason therapists are useful, and you may find such a pace too difficult to follow in your self-guided program. Exposure isn't easy, and there will be challenges that will threaten your progress. There will be times when you won't want to continue with an exposure because it feels too hard. There may be other times when you won't even want to start because you will feel certain that you will never follow through with your assignment.

Exposure and Response Prevention Guidelines

- Prepare support materials, including therapy scripts, script cards, red-dot labels (small quarter-inch self-sticking labels that you can use as reminders and prompts).

- Put aside at least an hour a day to do your exposure work.

- When you start doing exposure, start with something you will do, rather than trying to do something you might fail at.

- Always follow through with the safe steps!

- Use all your allotted exposure time.

- Listen to imaginal exposure scripts as constantly as you can.

- When urges to ritualize following exposure feel overwhelming, consider doing more exposure. If this feels too difficult, consider using Distraction and Refocusing to delay your ritualizing.

Now reexamine your fear hierarchy. You should have items on it that cover situations both in and out of the home and at various levels of difficulty. Choose your starting point. The absolutely most critical factor in choosing a starting point is that it must be one that you are willing to do. No matter how trivially easy it may seem to you and no matter how much more work you have left in your recovery, initial success is one of the most important steps. After all, wherever you start is the beginning you will build on.

If you find yourself having difficulty with an exposure, do not end your active exposure session early. Always use your entire allotted time—there will always be tasks you can carry out that won't increase your anxiety. I call these "safe steps." For example, if you feel unable to do an exposure, a safe step would be using your allotted time writing or listening to scripts that remind you why you want to follow through with the exposure. If you do this, go to where your exposure was to take place, or at least as close as feels safe. If your fear is hit-and-run driving, you should be in the car. You don't have to drive, just turn it on. If this is too much, then just sit in it. If you have contamination concerns and you were to touch a doorknob, then listen to your script while standing near the door. Again, these are the safe steps, so there is no excuse for not fol-

lowing through with these suggestions. Go as far as you can during your exposure time. If you have hit-and-run fears, perhaps you will get no further than
sitting in the car with the motor turned on. Or maybe you will decide to drive
around the block. That's okay. You are beginning.

It is true that one of the disadvantages of moving slowly is that your recovery will take longer and you will probably feel discouraged at some point. Such
feelings are normal, but it is extremely important not to give in to them by
quitting. No matter how quickly or slowly you proceed through your hierarchy,
your most powerful weapon against OCD is setting aside at least an hour a day
for exposure. Listen to your scripts while doing so. Reinforcing your success is
also important. You are probably in the habit of berating yourself for your difficulties, constantly noticing your failures and calling yourself silly or stupid.
OCD is a real problem, and learning to congratulate yourself for every step you
take will help you keep up your motivation to continue. Remember, any progress is progress.

If paying attention to your progress is hard, then consider keeping a success
log. You can use the Daily Self-Monitoring Log of Success on page 140. This is
similar to the log you kept when you were assessing your OCD. In the events
column, record any events you successfully coped with. This should include
scheduled exposure sessions. In the next column, record the kind of exposure
and/or response prevention you used to cope. All of the other columns are the
same as before. Then, anytime that you complete an exposure or resist the urge
to ritualize, record your success. Include your exposure session time, even if
your only success was listening to your scripts. At this point, success is not mea-
sured by how calm or anxious you feel, but by your behavior—what did you
do? If necessary, create a "Noticing My Successes" script card, like the following
example, to look at whenever you have made progress but were disappointed
with the amount.

SCRIPT

> *Today I succeeded by doing "x." If I'm not feeling like this is much of a step,
> I'm forgetting to follow through with one of the important rules for beating
> OCD—congratulating myself. No matter what else happened today, I was
> being successful when I did "x." My big goal is to build on this, so that I am
> doing more—doing bigger exposures and more response prevention. What I
> did today puts me on the road to where I want to go.*

There is one difficulty that you need to be warned of in attempting to keep such a log. As you improve, your behavior will become more like that of non-sufferers—you will be less aware of what you are doing, and often you won't realize that you were exposed to your fears because you didn't care at the time. In the early stages of recovery, it can be disconcerting to have touched something that used to feel dangerous and not to have realized it. Remember, this is the feeling you want to get used to. Your ultimate goal is to be less conscious of your environment so you can be free to enjoy the flow of life, to take all your creative and imaginative energy and have your thoughts dominated by things that you actually want to think about.

On the other hand, you may find that you are very anxious immediately following your exposure. One way to cope with overwhelming anxiety from an exposure is to continue active exposure. I don't mean that you have to go further up your hierarchy; just continue repeating all the steps that you did earlier. Continue to do this until your anxiety has dropped to a level that you feel you can cope with, whether this takes fifteen minutes or eight hours. This may feel like the last thing you want to do when you are overwhelmed, but it is actually one of the most effective ways to battle your anxiety. At such times, you will find it very helpful to externalize your OCD and try to turn your anxiety into anger at your OCD with an "I'm Not Going to Let You Win" script. If you have named your OCD or have envisioned it as some person or creature, incorporate this into your script.

SCRIPT

I'm sick of what you have been doing to my life. You are there at every turn, trying to ruin everything that I do. Look what listening to you has done to my life! I'm sitting here an anxious wreck. I've lost too much to you already, and I'm not letting you take any more from me. You can do your worst, but I'm not going to listen. I've been running from your threats, but look where that has gotten me. No more! I'm not giving in to you. I'm not going to decontaminate. In fact, I'm going to do more exposure. Maybe I'll get sick from it, but so what? At least I'll be free from you. Being sick in peace is better than the living hell you try to keep me in. Just watch me do exposure. You think you can make my anxiety worse? Then do it, because I'm not going to let that work. You think making my family sick will stop me? Then do it, because I'm not listening to threats anymore. At least I'll be able to enjoy *my family, however long I'll have them. I will beat you, and I'll learn to cope with whatever life throws at me, because after living with you, I know what hell is like. And after beating you, I'll know that I'll be able to handle anything life throws at me. Watch me touch this, you #$%*!*

In making this script, you may have to record it a few times, because it will work best if you can sound as angry as you can be. After all, you really do hate your OCD and all that it has done to you. When you are modifying the above script for your own use, think about what OCD has done to you and what it has taken from you. Remember, you are not only trying to free yourself from OCD, but you are working toward being the kind of person you want to be— to live up to your values, whether that means being a good mother, a man of honor, or simply someone who is able to appreciate life. Refer to your Cost-Benefit Analysis and your ERP Motivators for details you can add regarding all that OCD has cost you. Feel free to call your OCD names and to curse at it freely. Your goal is to rant and rave at your OCD and to turn your anxiety into a determined anger—one that focuses the anger on OCD rather than yourself. By doing this, you can turn your anxious energy into grim determination to battle your OCD with exposure.

Up to now the exposures I have been talking about are active exposures. During these, your time, attention, and behavior are fully devoted to confronting your fears. Besides your hour or two of active exposure, you will also need to do passive exposures. In passive exposure, you are engaging in other activities while an exposure is taking place. This allows you to be immersed in treatment throughout your day, as opposed to just during your allotted homework time. Examples of what this looks like will depend on the form your OCD takes. For some problems, such as contamination, passive exposure means that you continue to function throughout the day while contaminated, making no effort to avoid spreading the contamination further. For other presentations, passive exposure may be a little less than passive. For hit-and-run fears, your passive exposure when not driving may be interfering with the automatic mental ritualizing that takes place after a difficult drive. One way to achieve this is through listening to *imaginal exposure scripts*.

Imaginal exposure scripts need to be a part of your program, and using them can be both an active and passive procedure. Active imaginal exposure

DAILY SELF-MONITORING LOG OF SUCCESS

DATE	TIME	EVENT *Note if scheduled homework or part of daily living*	EXPOSURE AND/OR RESPONSE PREVENTION	TIME SPENT	ANXIETY LEVEL

means devoting your full attention to the content of the exposure scripts. In passive imaginal exposure, you listen to your scripts while engaged in other activities. Do this as often as possible. For example, play your scripts while you are going to and coming home from work. At home, have them constantly playing in the background. There are many places you can wear headphones and play the scripts at a low volume while engaging in other activities. Friends and family who know about your OCD won't mind the headphones; they will be happy that you are putting an effort into getting better. After all, seeing you with headphones on is preferable to watching you suffer or having you force them to engage in your rituals. I would also suggest playing the scripts throughout the night. Again, the volume can be low enough to allow you to fall asleep.

You should engage in this intensive imaginal exposure to try to strengthen your anti-OCD thinking. Again, think of the advertising campaign metaphor. Up until now, the pro-OCD campaign has had a lot of airtime, and those terrifying OCD thoughts come to you automatically, especially in times of stress. You are trying to strengthen thoughts of exposure and overcoming OCD by increasing the airtime of your recovery campaign.

The content of your imaginal exposure will consist of scripts that focus on the possibility of your feared consequences coming true. For example, for many of you, harm or death of loved ones is a prime feared consequence. Besides not wanting any harm to come to them, you may also have the additional pressure of feeling responsible for protecting others and/or of not being the one who does the harm. For these concerns, the uncertainty you will want to learn to live with is the possibility that your loved ones can be harmed and that you could be the cause of it. The "I Can't Truly Protect Anyone" script below is written for concerns about causing death or harm to come to loved ones. It easily can be modified to address the fear of being the one responsible for yourself or others contracting nonfatal or fatal illnesses.

SCRIPT

Knowing that my loved ones could die from "x" is very painful, and I hope it doesn't happen. However, I realize that death is not completely in my control. In fact, this fear—that they could die from "x"—is really covering up a more pervasive fear and truth: I can't really protect my loved ones, and there are many ways they might come to harm. There are even other ways I could make myself responsible for their well-being that aren't related to contamination. Do I have our cars perfectly maintained? Do I check them thoroughly before driving them anywhere? Have I done everything possible to protect my family from fire? And although I make sure I don't contaminate them, do I really do everything possible, or are there ways I could protect them more? For example, why shouldn't I be responsible for making sure they don't come into contact with anything potentially dangerous in the environment when I'm not around?

The fact is, I only try to protect them from harm related to my OCD fears, and even then, I don't do everything possible. I am inconsistent, and that's good, because the more consistent I am, the worse my OCD is. In learning to accept that they could come to harm from my exposures, I am also trying to cope with the fact that I can't protect them as much as I would like to. I need to do these exposures until I accept that the only time I can have my family is when I am with them. When they aren't with me, they are just fond memories of the past and a hope to see them in the future. With my OCD, I don't even get to have them in the present, because I'm lost in OCD-land. I need to try to learn to accept the possibility of losing them if I am ever to enjoy them while I can. That's why I have to choose to put everyone at risk with these exposures.

Response prevention is the other way you will support exposure and give more airtime to your recovery program. Response prevention begins as soon as you have decided to start your program. Ideally, all rituals should stop. It may seem overwhelmingly sudden to institute this so completely, but this is what I do with the sufferers I treat, because this is what works. You are probably tempted to do less, because it seems either too difficult, too extreme, or just too unusual. Try not to give in to this temptation. In fighting your OCD, you are trying to develop and strengthen new learning (for example, responding to OCD triggers with exposure, so that habituation of your fears can occur) and weaken old learning (for example, ritualizing in response to your fears, thereby maintaining your anxiety and misery). Whichever you practice most will be strongest. Think about trying to switch from your QWERTY keyboard to a Dvorak keyboard. It wouldn't be easy, but how much harder would it be if, every fifteen minutes, you switched the keyboards? Incomplete response prevention is like going on half a diet—you'll benefit from such a diet, but you won't reach your goal.

Even if you don't want to implement a complete program of response prevention, design one. There are two reasons to do so. First, it is a safe step—you lose nothing by taking the time to do this, and as you progress in your self-guided program, you may reach a point when you will be ready to switch from half a diet to a complete diet. You might as well be ready with the plan. The second reason is that if you are going to institute response prevention in a partial manner, there are ways to do so that will still benefit you and ways that won't. Having the proper template to work with will allow you to plan a partial implementation of response prevention rather than doing it in a haphazard fashion.

A partial implementation of response prevention will be a gradual planned process. Your exposure hierarchy will be your guide. This means that what you do and don't do will not be determined by your mood of the moment but by your own rating of how fearful giving up a particular ritual would be and in what circumstances. For example, if you have contamination fears and handwashing is your ritual, in an ideal program you will cease all handwashing. In the modified program, handwashing will only take place in response to exposures that are more fearful than the ones you have already worked on. Thus, if you are now able to touch doorknobs in public places, you will no longer wash your hands following any contamination by a public doorknob. However, because you haven't yet worked on public toilet seats, you will still wash in response to touching one.

Whether your response prevention is complete or modified, periodically you will feel overwhelmed by anxiety or an accidental exposure—and the urge to ritualize will seem irresistible. You will think of numerous reasons that make breaking your response prevention seem like a necessity. These will include such excuses as: "This situation is different," "I have something very important to do and have to be calm," or simply, "I can't stand another second of this." Continued exposure is one way to cope with such urges. Another way is using Distraction and Refocusing, which is actually a version of Alcoholics Anonymous' advice of taking things "one day at a time." What is the longest delay you are sure you can tolerate before giving in? Two hours? One hour? Five minutes? Choose a delay that you are sure you can tolerate. Obviously, the ultimate goal will be to follow the first delay with a second delay, and so on, until you have successfully fought off the urge. However, your focus needs to be only on the delay that you are currently working on. You are making no promises to yourself that you will continue delaying after the time is up. Decide this only when the designated time has passed, not before.

During your delay, you may not feel in the mood to do anything, but don't let that stop you. If you weren't anxious and didn't have any OCD concerns, what would you like to be doing at this moment? If it is something active, do it. Remember, the object of this activity isn't to distract you from your anxiety, although that might happen. The goal is to increase your ability to function during exposure. Being active makes resisting urges to ritualize easier than when you're doing nothing. If possible, listen to your scripts while engaged in another activity. For example, if you are watching TV, listen to your therapy script with the volume low enough for you to be able to pay attention to the TV but loud enough so that you will sometimes have your attention drawn to it. If you aren't in a place where you can play your therapy scripts, look over your script cards.

A "Supporting Response Prevention" script could look like this:

> *I can make myself hold out for just a few minutes, no matter how hard it is. There have been other times when I was forced to delay by circumstances, so even though this is hard, I can make myself do it. It doesn't matter if I have always ended up ritualizing in the past, because any practice in delaying will build up my ability to delay in the future. As for what I do after this delay, I will put off deciding either way until this delay is over. And the other reasons I'm going to do this are . . .*

The other reasons you can add are those listed in your Cost-Benefit Analysis and ERP Motivators. Make sure these are included—they are part of the recovery campaign airtime. Again, you are fighting to be the person you want to be.

Any successful delay in ritualizing is progress, so congratulate yourself. If you found you didn't last as long as you thought you could—for example, if you wanted to delay for an hour but only lasted fifteen minutes—there are two rules you should implement. The first rule is to congratulate yourself for however long you lasted. The second is to pick a shorter delay period in the future. Choosing fifteen minutes as your delay and succeeding is better than deciding on a half hour and lasting only fifteen minutes. The reason for this is simple: The first feels like success.

The other reasons you will add will be the reasons you want to overcome OCD. Look back to the Cost-Benefit Analysis you created on page 120 and ERP Motivators on pages 117 and 118. If possible, be active during your delay and engage in other activities. The goal of this isn't to distract you from your anxiety, but to build on your ability to function with anxiety, which will strengthen your ability to resist ritualizing in the future. If you do engage in other activities, don't expect to function or to enjoy the activity as you would at your best. You can add "Living with Reduced Satisfaction" to your script-supporting response prevention. Follow the example below.

> *Maybe I'm not going to totally enjoy doing "x." Maybe I will only get 60 percent of the enjoyment I could get if I were anxiety-free. By delaying and continuing response prevention, I am fighting my OCD and working toward a time when I won't have to worry about ritualizing. Rather than focusing on what I might miss now, I need to remember how much more I will miss in the future if I don't fight my OCD.*

Sometimes overwhelming urges will be the result of unexpected situations, and you may not be able to listen to your script. Have your script cards handy at all times so you can read them for support. At home you can also put these script cards in any place where you will notice them, and particularly in areas where you might ritualize, such as the sink you wash your hands in if you have contamination fears, or by the stove if you frequently check to see if it is on or off. It is true that these cards alone won't stop you from ritualizing, but you can at least make an agreement with yourself that you will always read them aloud a few times before carrying out your compulsions.

When you follow these instructions, you change response prevention from a simple passive act of trying not to do something to an active way to fight rituals. Both time spent and effort exerted will strengthen your recovery campaign. If you go back to the advertising campaign metaphor, time and effort translate to more airtime and better ads.

Advertising campaigns usually have two goals: to change your mind about something and to help you remember their product. Forgetting is one problem you may run into with response prevention; that is, sometimes you may accidentally engage in rituals not because you were driven to, but because they are so ingrained in your mind that they are automatic. To prevent this, you can expand your recovery campaign with script cards—my equivalent of billboards. The script cards should be put in high-risk areas to serve as reminders to interfere with accidental ritualizing. If you are too embarrassed to use the cards, there are substitutes you can use. In most office supply stores, you can find round color-coding labels in both ¼- and ¾-inch sizes. These small round dot labels can serve as useful reminders that can be stuck unobtrusively in public environments without raising embarrassing questions. For myself, I'm partial to the small red-dot labels.

Sometimes this may not be enough, because you may not notice your reminders. Try to come up with other ways to make the reminders more obvious. Remember that the advertising campaigns that work best are the ones you notice. One sufferer I worked with would unthinkingly wash his hands whenever he went by his kitchen sink. He came up with an ingenious reminder to overcome his automatic handwashing. Using masking tape, he attached toothpicks to the faucet handle. Whenever he reached for the handle, the lumpy feel of the toothpicks under the masking tape caught his attention and reminded him not to wash, which allowed him to be more successful with his response prevention.

You are now armed with understanding and the basics of your exposure-and-response-prevention recovery program. In the chapters to follow, the focus will shift to the special issues that can arise from different obsessions and compulsions, and the program modifications you will need to make. Does this mean that after reading this chapter, you should jump to the chapter that seems most relevant to your problems? No. I would urge you to read all the chapters. Each chapter will focus on issues that may not be common to everyone; however, it is unlikely that all your needs will be found in a single chapter. For example, if you have contamination fears, handwashing may be your primary method of neutralizing your fears. But you also might rely on checking rituals to make sure you weren't contaminated and analyzing rituals to convince yourself that you are clean. Guidelines and advice for these rituals will be found in the chapters on checking and primary obsessions, respectively. Similarly, if your obsessive concerns focus on violent thoughts—a primary mental obsession—you may also be concerned about harming others. Much of the advice that's relevant to you will come from the chapter on primary obsessions, but you will likely also find useful information in other chapters that deal with issues surrounding harming others, such as chapters about contamination and checking.

Another reason to read all the chapters is that you may discover that you have obsessive concerns that you hadn't previously identified. Perhaps they are secondary concerns to those that you consider your main obsessional fears. This may mean that getting control of them would be easier than your primary concerns, and you may want to consider working on them first, especially if the idea of exposure overwhelms you. Easier tasks often lead to success, and success is a great way to start a program.

Some of you may fear reading about other problems because you fear that you might make them your own. Remember, this is a book about learning to live with risk. Your recovery can't depend on successfully hiding from information and ideas. But if this isn't one of the uncertainties you have chosen to face, then you aren't ready to go on, and the chapters that follow will be frightening. At this point, your task is to find the courage to answer *the question* with a yes so that you too can come to America. Every day, you need to devote an hour or two to going through all the reasons you want to overcome OCD, from the impossibility of appeasing the demands of your OCD to what your OCD-free life would be like.

Some of you may worry that treatment will make your OCD worse. In general, this doesn't happen. But there is one exception. If you begin treatment, but the answer to your version of *the question*—Am I willing to learn to live with uncertainty?—is no, in treatment you are likely to reach a point at which you will want to quit. But what about the exposures you have already performed? Undoing them can be very difficult. Once you have entirely contaminated your house, how can you decontaminate it? This is why asking yourself *the question* to determine your readiness for recovery is critical. When you get on the boat going to America, you need to have truly made that choice. Getting off is very difficult, and, if you want to get better, that is a blessing.

Many OCD sufferers who have gone before you and recovered will admit to having temporarily lost faith during treatment, but in the end they persevered rather than turn back to a life of misery with OCD. When you are doing exposure and response prevention, you may go through some uncomfortable emotions (see page 152). These feelings should be viewed as a natural and helpful part of your recovery and are *never* a reason to give up. By allowing them, they will pass and you will get stronger.

However, simply saying "don't give up" is not enough. The chapters that follow will help you take the data you've collected and turn it into a recovery program. But even that is not enough. Experience tells us that you will face many temptations to sabotage your own program. My good friend Dr. Alec Pollard at Saint Louis Behavioral Medicine Institute calls these TIBs (Treatment Interfering Behaviors). In his words, a TIB is "any behavior that is incompatible or directly interferes with a person's ability to participate in treatment directly. TIBs are important to address because they can prevent people from overcoming problems. TIBs are not defined by a person's intentions, but by the outcome of the behavior."

This may seem like a simple notion, but embedded within it are three very important concepts you need to use to become your own therapist. The first is the very idea of identifying TIBs. Up to this point when you've attempted to cope with OCD, you probably have felt that there were behaviors that you simply couldn't do and these feelings guided your behavior; or in other words, you gave up. Now you are in the midst of reading this book and designing your own self-help program. The steps you are taking are enabling you to understand and evaluate your OCD and to come up with a treatment plan with well-defined steps to follow. A part of that plan also needs to include the steps you will take when you deviate from your plan.

These are the three concepts embedded in TIBs:

1. identification and understanding
2. designing anti-TIB procedures
3. implementing anti-TIB procedures

Without identification and understanding you are helpless. Think about how mysterious and overwhelming OCD was before you began reading this book. Prior to this, your OCD made you feel like you were losing your mind or were at war with some part of yourself. Although your OCD is still hurting, hopefully your new understanding has given you hope and helped you feel less out of control. Simply put, anytime you find yourself deviating from designing an effective program or deviating from your recovery plan, I want you to recognize the TIB as a flaw in your program to be addressed.

I've already mentioned the most common TIB, avoiding a key part of your program, probably an exposure or following through with response prevention. However, there are other kinds of TIBs. On page 150 is a form for identifying TIBs. This form is a modified version of Dr. Pollard's work. His forms were made for therapists to fill out about sufferers they were treating. These have been modified to be filled out by you. Not only does this allow you to identify Treatment Interfering Behaviors, but it also helps you to identify your potential reasons for choosing to not follow the program you designed. These explanations will assist you in designing anti-TIB strategies. Rather than simply saying you will or won't do something, you need to identify the behavior or reason you are being tempted to slip. Obviously, the list is not exhaustive, but it will provide you with a good start.

The implementation of your anti-TIB plans should be clear and well defined. If you plan to do something, it isn't sufficient to say you will do it when you have time; specify exactly when and where you will follow through. You won't be able to fill out the TIB Identification Form until you have designed your program and have begun to implement it. It is not a failure to have TIBs. Imperfection is part of being human and your goal is to be able to enjoy your humanity. Having and recognizing your TIBs is simply taking control of your life. In the chapters that follow, TIBs and what to do about them will be discussed in greater detail.

Look at the list on page 152 and consider what may be keeping you from following your program. Return to it whenever you find yourself feeling discouraged or you have given up. Keep in mind that implementing your program can be scary, and you might find it helpful to think of it as an adventure. When my son was nine years old, we went on a father-son camping trip with two of my friends and their sons. During one of our hikes, we were stuck on a hill that was too steep, rocky, and slippery for the boys to climb—and there was no way to go back. To get them up the hill, we had to form a short human chain of dads to help the boys make it from one point to the other. In this very gradual manner, we eventually made it to the top. The boys had been very scared, and the fathers—well, let's just say we had been worried. When we arrived at the top, the boys were still shaken, and the dads were elated. My friend Glenn explained to the boys that now they knew what an adventure was: something that can be awful to go through but wonderful to talk about afterward. It's time for your adventure.

Identifying Treatment Interfering Behaviors (TIBs)*

What are TIBs? *A TIB is any behavior that is incompatible or directly interferes with a person's ability to participate in treatment successfully. TIBs are important to address, because they can prevent people from overcoming problems. TIBs are primarily defined by a person's behavior (or lack of), not their intentions. For example, a person not engaging in daily exposure exercises because they are caring for a sick parent does not have the intention of disrupting treatment. However, the behavior is still a TIB and it is important to address. Some reasons may be useful to identify for the purposes of designing anti-TIB measures. TIBs are ongoing behaviors; a single instance of disrupted treatment is not a TIB. Finally it's okay if you don't have a reason for your TIB. Identifying the behavior is the most important step.*

If you are having any difficulty with your recovery program, please check any of the items below that may apply.

Exposure Issues:

____ ① Not engaging in daily exposure.

____ a. It makes me too anxious.

____ b. I don't seem to have time.

____ c. I don't want to take the risk.

____ d. Other: _____

____ ② Lying to helpers about your doing exposures or any aspect of treatment.

____ ③ Other: _____

Response Prevention Issues:

____ ① Not using response prevention.

____ a. It makes me too anxious.

____ b. I don't want to take the risk.

____ c. Other: _____

*Adapted from Pollard, C.A. (2006). Treatment readiness, ambivalence, and resistance. In M.M. Antony, C. Purdon, & L. Summerfeldt, *Psychological treatment of OCD: Fundamentals and Beyond,* (pp. 61-75). Washington D.C.: APA Books

_____ ② Ritualizing following exposure.

    _____ a. It makes me too anxious.

    _____ b. I don't want to take the risk.

    _____ c. My mind won't let me rest until I ritualize.

    _____ d. Other: _____

_____ ③ Other: _____

Script Issues:

_____ ① Not listening to scripts as often as possible.

    _____ a. It's too much work.

    _____ b. I don't want to take the risk.

    _____ c. Other: _____

_____ ② Not writing or listening to scripts at all.

    _____ a. It's too much work.

    _____ b. I don't have an MP3/IPod player.

    _____ c. I can't write or don't know what to write.

    _____ d. I don't like the sound of my voice.

    _____ e. Other: _____

Treatment Preparation Issues:

_____ ① Not filling out forms to assist in designing treatment.

    _____ a. I don't think they are necessary.

    _____ b. It's too much work.

    _____ c. Other: _____

Feelings Commonly Experienced During Exposure and Response Prevention

Anger (Go ahead and have a tantrum, just continue your work when done.)

Sadness (Cry if you need to.)

Discouragement (Remember, people with OCD are recovering every day.)

Shame (OCD is a disorder, not a character flaw.)

Fear (Trust the strength of the program and your ability to get well.)

Distrust of your helper(s) and/or therapist(s), feeling that they are crazy (Your proof of this is the crazy, extreme things they are asking you to do as part of treatment!)

Resentment at your helper(s) and/or therapist(s) for "mistreating you" and "making you suffer" (Remember, you gave them permission to support you in recovery.)

Feeling trapped "between a rock and a hard place" (You worry that you can't do what is required to get better, but you also can't bear to live with OCD anymore.)

Self-pity (What could be worse than having this disorder and going through this miserable treatment? Having OCD and *not having a cure*.)

PART 3

Personalizing Your Program:
Treatment Guidelines for Your
Specific OCD Concerns

Chapter 9

Contamination: The Obsession That Spreads

I n the world of OCD suffering, contamination is probably the most common form of OCD. It is also the ideal symptom presentation to begin this section, because designing a recovery program for contamination is the most straightforward application of exposure and response prevention. As such, it will provide the clearest picture of what an ideal program should look like.

In general, the problem for those of you with contamination fears is that they spread, so your concern is not only with the primary source—for example, dog feces, AIDS-infected blood, etc.—but also secondary and tertiary sources. For example, you may avoid shopping in food stores, because doctors and nurses also probably shop there. What if any of them had come into direct contact with an AIDS patient, or someone or something else in the hospital that was exposed to a patient? Afterward, while shopping, they could have picked up a can or some produce, thereby contaminating it, and then returned it to the shelf where you could unknowingly touch it. Contamination obsessions have the potential to leave you with no safe places to go and no way to function outside your home. By avoiding direct and indirect contact with contaminants and potential contacts, your world can contract into a very small, safe place with little room for living.

Diseases and potential poisons are most often the focus of contamination obsessions. However, as you have learned in the contamination section of the Obsessive Concerns Checklist, innumerable other sources of contamination exist. The most common feared consequence of contamination is the potential harm that may come to you or others through infection or poisoning. Of course the feared consequences need not involve harm. Some individuals desperately want to avoid unpleasant feelings of disgust. Others fear any place that they feel is contaminated by certain kinds of people or individuals, because it leads to them "feeling under the influence" of those people. The possibilities are endless.

If you have completed all the self-assessment steps from the last chapter, you will have identified your personal recovery goals, made the decision to learn to live with the uncertainties plaguing you, completed your Cost-Benefit Analysis, and identified your TIBs that will help you to develop strategies for creating a more effective recovery program. With this in mind, you can turn your attention to further examining the blueprint of your exposure-and-response-prevention recovery program—your hierarchy.

It is very important for your hierarchy to contain items that cover the full range—from exposures that would be easy to face to exposures that would be most difficult for you. The easier exposures need to be represented, because these will be the exposures you will do first. The difficult ones are also necessary, because they will help you identify your feared consequences and because overcoming them will free you from OCD.

Sometimes sufferers with contamination obsessions have difficulty finding easier items to put on their hierarchy—everything seems bad. Ira, whose contamination fears were of becoming infected by or infecting his family with AIDS and other diseases, had this problem. Examine his hierarchy, on page 157, to see how he solved this problem. Rather than using SUD scores, he chose to rate items as low, moderate, high, and very high. Within these groupings, the items are still arranged from hardest to easiest.

To help him come up with easier items, I used the fact that items that have touched contaminated items were not as bad as the original contaminated items. So he used his spouse's shirt, which he felt might be contaminated by her hands but was not as likely to have had direct contact with outside items. He used a clean tissue to touch her shirt. He thought this would be contaminated enough to cause him anxiety, but the anxiety would be low enough that he wouldn't be overwhelmed by it. In this way, we were able to create lower items.

Ira's Hierarchy

Item	Rating
Suspicious marks on hospital walls	Very high
Biohazard containers	Very high
Doors marked with biohazard signs	Very high
Toilets in hospital restrooms	Very high
Faucet knobs in hospital restrooms	Very high
Hospital doorknobs and elevator buttons	Very high
Toilets in public restrooms	High
Faucet knobs in public restrooms	High
Door handles in public restrooms	High
Toilets in office restroom	High
Door handles to any public building	High
Seats on train	High
Sidewalk in the city	High
Groceries from the food store	High
Toilet in my house	High
Sidewalk in the suburbs	Moderate
My clothes	Moderate
My spouse's shirt	Moderate
Front door (outside)	Moderate
Front door (inside)	Moderate
Tissue that touched toilet in the house	Low
Tissue that touched my spouse's shirt	Low
Tissue that touched the inside of the front door	Low

He also had some difficulty coming up with his true worst fears. Initially, his top fear had been the public restroom at his office. He hadn't included any public restrooms outside the office, because he wouldn't imagine himself ever using one. He also didn't list hospitals, because he couldn't imagine a worse place and saw no reason he would go to one if he didn't have to. Remember, always do the safe steps. It was the idea of actually exposing himself to hospitals and public restrooms that was terrifying to Ira. Because he had no fear of merely adding them to his list, he added them to his hierarchy.

With your hierarchy in place, choose the exposure that you are willing to start your program with. By "exposure," I mean more than simply touching the item. Immersing yourself in exposure is the secret of success, so your starting exposure should be one in which you are willing to go through the anxiety of total immersion, the instructions for which are provided below. Part of learning to cope with your uncertainties is learning to recognize the impossibility of certainty and the ultimate inescapability of your concerns—your world is never really 100 percent decontaminated. By playing an active role in creating inescapable immersion, you will speed up your recovery. At this point, you may be feeling that total immersion seems overwhelming. This is normal. It is for this reason that you start with easier items on your hierarchy rather than at the top. And each exposure can be broken down into smaller steps. If the beginning steps below are too easy for you, skip to the most difficult step you are willing to do.

STEPS FOR COMPLETING CONTAMINATION EXPOSURES

1. For the briefest of moments, lightly touch the contaminant with one finger. Repeat this brief touching until you are ready for step 2.
2. Keep your finger on the contaminant and gradually add your other fingers until you are ready to place your entire hand on the contaminant.
3. Add your other hand.
4. Contaminate your clothes, hair, face, and lips with one of your hands. If necessary, start by briefly touching your finger to each of these until you are ready to maintain contact. Always focus on what you are willing to do rather than stopping because you are sure you won't complete the entire exposure.
5. Lick your lips. This seems very difficult. For this reason, you should be playing your scripts for encouragement. Remind yourself that during the course of the day, non-sufferers, who might not do what you are doing on purpose, quite likely have done the same thing by accident. This step is very important, because without this step, you will find eating very difficult.
6. Lick your contaminated finger. Again, start with a brief touch of your tongue if necessary.
7. If possible, touch the actual contaminant to your face, body, and hands. At my center, my staff and I have done this with trash taken out of the Dumpsters or cigarette butts found on the ground. If this feels too diffi-

cult, approach it in a gradual fashion, repeating your own version of steps 1 through 5.

8. Next you need to contaminate your belongings. If you aren't at home, take a piece of the contaminant home with you. If this isn't possible, you can wipe the contaminant with a paper towel and bring the towel home. For example, wipe a Dumpster completely with a paper towel. Don't study it, looking for the cleaner spots! (You might also include this advice in your therapy scripts.)

9. At home, touch everything that is not a higher-level contaminant (if the toilet in your house is worse than what you are currently working on, then you need not contaminate it—yet). This means you will contaminate all towels, dishes, silverware, clothing (including underwear), pillows, linens, and the inside of the dryer (so that everything you wash will also be contaminated). If you use liquid soap, open the bottle and put some of the contaminant inside. This is to be done to all your and your family's belongings. If you are at work, you can surreptitiously contaminate the work environment. At my center, my therapists and I are constantly contaminating one another's offices, the staff room, and, when no one is looking, items in public areas, such as the paper cups by the water cooler.

If you come to an exposure that you feel you can't do, use your allotted time and follow through with the safe steps. For contamination, this involves instituting a number of pre-exposure steps. For example, suppose you were planning to touch a trash can, but you set aside an hour for active exposure and now you feel you can't do it. Rather than giving up, spend an hour doing the following. First, go as close to the trash can as you are willing to go, whether it be six feet or one foot. Stay there and listen to your therapy scripts. When and if you are willing, go a little closer. Get to the point where you can hold your hand as close as you are willing—whether twelve inches or three inches. Once you are at this point, do not remove your hand under any circumstances until your allotted exposure time is up. If your hand gets tired, hold it there anyway, because, after all, there is no reason you can't do this part. The fact that you are trying to encourage yourself to go further doesn't mean that you have to. Ask yourself this question: *If the choice came down to touching this and being free of OCD or having my painful OCD forever, which would I choose?* This is actually the choice you will have to make bit by bit to fight your way out.

If your finger is three inches from the contaminant, keep asking yourself if you are willing to move it two inches from the contaminant. And once it is there, try to move it one inch from the contaminant. And finally, do the briefest and lightest of touches. Now you have made it to step 1. If you don't make it to the last step of total immersion by the end of your session, then try to make an effort to repeat the last step you completed throughout the day, whether it was a brief touch with one finger or holding your hand one foot away from the contaminant. The more often you do this, the better. At your next full session, you will probably get to this step more quickly. If necessary, use the same gradual procedure to complete each new step. Continue this process daily until you have completed the exposure rather than attempting to move on to a more difficult item.

The scripts you use to support exposure will need to include the feared consequences you have identified. You might think this means creating horrific scenes of contamination resulting in your family's death, assuming that this is one of your worst fears. You are partially correct; such material helps to prevent you from mentally diluting the exposures you carry out with thoughts like *No one will be hurt from this* or *This exposure is safe* or by simply trying not to think about your feared consequences. All these are neutralizing and will therefore interfere with your recovery.

However, this doesn't mean that scripts focusing on your feared consequences can't include positive statements—they just can't include any statements supporting neutralization. Below is a sample script in which a mother's obsessive fear was that she would cause the family to contract hepatitis. Note how frightening material is interspersed with positive material in this Imaginal Exposure Script for Feared Consequences.

SCRIPT

I need to contaminate my entire house, even if my family contracts hepatitis and everyone blames me and asks how I could have followed advice from this stupid book. I don't want this to happen, because if it did, I can see myself standing over the open caskets of my family, looking at my husband and knowing it was my fault he died, and seeing my innocent little ones, knowing that I robbed them of their life and knowing that everyone in the church is staring at me and accusing me. But I still need to do this, because even though all of the above might happen, if I don't follow through with exposure, I won't have any family life, because I can't function this way. As my children grow older, I will lose their respect and will have to live with the thought that they may be telling their friends how crazy their mother is. And that assumes that my husband stays with me. What if he leaves? And worse, the way they live, they could still get hepatitis if they left, and all my rituals would have accomplished was losing both their respect and their company.

Could you find the positive material? If you couldn't, it is probably because you were looking for comforting content. In the above example, the positive does not comfort; instead, it provides you reasons for continuing exposure. In this case, the possible disaster of her family's death is juxtaposed against the likely losses she will suffer from continuing to give in to the demands of her OCD, such as losing the respect of her children, not being able to function, and not really protecting them from hepatitis.

Did you notice how her feared consequences were included? She didn't say her children would contract hepatitis. Instead, she said they might get hepatitis, and if they did, all the consequences that might follow were listed. Saying this "might happen" is a better exposure than saying it "will happen" for the following reasons: First, you are trying to learn to live with uncertainty, so saying it might happen makes exposure to uncertainty part of the script. Second, it is more accurate. She is afraid of the possibility, not the inevitability, of her children dying from hepatitis. Remember to follow this form in constructing your feared consequences scripts.

Reexamine your Cost-Benefit Analysis and your ERP Motivators. What else do you have to lose and gain from overcoming OCD? Besides not being controlled by OCD, in what other ways can you make your life better once you free yourself from OCD? Look at the negative consequences of overcoming OCD; are any of them less awful than having OCD? For example, if one of the reasons you avoid contamination is to avoid nonfatal illnesses, wouldn't spending two to four weeks in the hospital be better than living a lifetime with OCD? And what if some of your rituals are performed merely to avoid catching a cold? Wouldn't you prefer a few colds a year to living with OCD?

One of the most common feared consequences shared by those of you with contamination obsessions is the permanent contamination of your home environment that will be the ultimate result of carrying out exposure and response prevention. This is one of the goals of your recovery—it is part of creating an environment that makes decontamination unnecessary, because it is no longer possible to achieve. To many of you, this seems like an unimaginable nightmare. However, if you closely examine your rituals and look for the flaws in how they are carried out, you will probably discover that your home is already contaminated—unless you are one of the very rare sufferers who are so completely consistent in their rituals that you barely function at any level. You can use the "My Rituals Are Useless Anyway" script below to encourage yourself to follow through with your exposure and response prevention.

If I look at my rituals, do they accomplish what I want? Am I 100 percent consistent, or are there areas that I allow to slide, just like non-sufferers do? And what about my family members? I can't watch them twenty-four hours a day, so I don't know if they carry out the rituals that I ask when I'm not around. Even if I try to fall back and claim that I'm not responsible for things that they might bring into the house, why aren't I? Couldn't I be more observant? Couldn't I do a better job of cleaning up after them? The fact is, the contaminants I fear are probably already in the house, so I would actually have to engage in more rituals than I currently do to be safe and sure. And that's too much, even for me. Besides, I can never be 100 percent certain, so doing exposures to get used to the current level of contamination and risk is my only real option, because the saddest thing of all is that for all the time and pain I spend ritualizing, I don't even get the safety I crave.

Instituting response prevention for your contamination issues tends to be a straightforward process. Like exposure, the goal of response prevention is to help create an environment of total immersion, so that exposure never really stops. The following is a list of guidelines for implementing your response prevention.

GUIDELINES FOR RESPONSE PREVENTION FOR CONTAMINATION

1. Completely cease handwashing. This means no handwashing before eating, before food preparation, or after going to the bathroom.

2. Your family members no longer have to follow any rituals you have imposed. If they choose to be supportive by following the response prevention rules in this list, that would be wonderful.

3. Do not decontaminate objects that come into the house. This includes wiping them with alcohol or other cleaning agents, shaking them, or washing them in any manner.

4. Do not use gloves or tissues to touch contaminated objects. The only exception is for any activities that make you feel decontaminated. For example, if cleaning dishes feels as good as a handwash, you would first contaminate your hands by touching the dirty dishes, put on gloves to wash them, and then take the gloves off and recontaminate the dishes.

5. Take a single ten-minute shower daily. Critical to taking a ten-minute shower is the idea of doing it "wrong." It is unlikely that you would be able to take a fast shower that is satisfying to you. On the other hand, a shower that is done "wrong," that is, one that doesn't completely wash you, is easier to complete. There are a few steps to follow when taking a "wrong" shower: Do not wash your hands in the shower; take the shower in the wrong order, such as washing your feet or genitals first; and wash incompletely by rubbing the soap or washcloth quickly and incompletely over your body. Ideally, use a timer and leave the shower when ten minutes are up, even if you haven't washed yourself completely, even if you still have soap on you. Don't forget, as soon as you leave the shower, your first task will be to recontaminate yourself with whatever the exposure of the day is. The *goal of showering and washing is not to be clean, but to be cleaner than when you started.*

6. Do not seek reassurance from your family, and instruct them as to how to respond if you slip and ask them. Rather than reassuring you, they should, with your permission, say things such as "We might die from this, but I'm glad you are working hard in your treatment." "That's great, I'm so glad you are letting 'x' stay dirty."

7. Any "illegal" handwashing or washing of any kind is to be responded to

with immediate exposure to whatever led to your ritualizing. You are not to wipe your hands with water-free soaps or pre-soaped towelettes. Throw these away to remove the temptation.

8. Cease other cleaning rituals. For example, do your laundry without wiping down the machines prior to putting clothes in. Clothes are only to be washed for one normal cycle, and combine compatible colors—so white underwear can be done with other whites.

9. Stop all rituals that are part of cleaning, such as counting the number of times you do something (do it just once, and as part of exposure, do it wrong) or trying to be distraction-free when decontaminating so that you can concentrate (play music while you are engaged in the activity).

The first item, complete cessation of handwashing, is the one that many of you will find the most difficult. You might tell me that there are some situations in which everyone washes. However, many people don't wash after going to the bathroom. People who say they wash before meals will eat popcorn in movie theaters without washing. People put trash into Dumpsters on their way to work without washing. You will find that most of what I'm suggesting does take place in the "normal" world, and the only difference is that you are doing these things on purpose in order to recover.

When it comes to contamination, you are constantly a victim of "normal" people who lie. You're their victim, because they constantly claim to follow standards that they unknowingly violate, but you hear their words and think they are consistent like you.

I was recently giving a lecture about OCD to a college class that my wife was teaching. I asked the class how many of them would rub their hands on the floor and then eat. No one raised their hands, and many of them appeared to be grossed out by the idea. Later in the lecture, I asked them if they ever sat on the floor during a party. Most of them raised their hands. I then asked how many of them might lean back and rest on their hands when sitting on the floor. Again, almost all of them raised their hands. Finally, I asked how many of them eat at the party without first washing their hands. They raised their hands and for the first time realized what they had been doing. Despite this, only a few of them would touch the floor and then eat the snacks I had brought with me. Even stranger will be what they do the next time they are at a party. They may or may not remember my lecture, but either way they will sit on the floor as usual and eat with contaminated hands.

My favorite version of this discussion took place between me and the wife of one of my clients. Upon hearing about treatment, she responded that there were times when one *had* to wash. Rising to the challenge, I asked her for an example. She reiterated that she did not suffer from OCD and went on to tell me that when she and her children would go to the children's zoo, she would make them wash their hands before they ate lunch, because the animals really were dirty—there really were feces on the ground and on their fur. It almost sounds reasonable, doesn't it? I asked her if she made them wash their hands as soon as they left the children's zoo. She answered no with a look on her face that said, "Of course not, I don't have OCD." I asked if they ate lunch as soon as they left the children's zoo. Again, she answered no. I asked how old her children were. She responded that they were three and five years old. Armed with this critical piece of information, I asked, "Do they put their hands in their mouths?" Her face fell as she replied yes, realizing, with as much certainty as an individual can have, that her children's hands went into their mouths while they were at the children's zoo and that her making them wash their hands before eating didn't really serve a purpose.

Hand sanitizers are very popular and you may believe they are necessary, because so many non-sufferers use them. As usual, the non-sufferers have no idea what they are doing. For example, do they believe in civilized germs? Civilized germs are the ones that children at recess come into contact with when they are handling balls, falling down, climbing. Their hands probably rub their eyes, go into their mouths—maybe even their noses. After recess, many teachers will have them use a hand sanitizer, because the civilized germs provide a post-recess grace period before attacking the children. Of course, the problem with this is that there are no civilized germs. In fact, consider the 1960s when hand sanitizers weren't used. Mothers went food shopping and didn't clean the shopping carts before they used them. Children weren't sanitized after recess. I'm sure you remember the old newspaper stories from those times reporting the rampant loss of children in school and mothers from shopping.

Hopefully you don't remember these articles, because there were none. I'm not suggesting this means everything is safe, but it is also true it isn't as dangerous as the advertisers who sell these products would have us believe. In fact, current research has found that you can be too clean. Researchers have found that bacteria and parasites in our bodies actually outnumber our own cells by a factor of 10 of them for every cell of us. These organisms have evolved with us and it turns out that we need them to live. It is thought that rates of asthma, celiac's disease, and other autoimmune diseases are the result of us eliminating too many germs, since third world countries don't have these problems. In hospitals, the use of antibiotics can eliminate necessary bacteria in your stomach that prevent C-Diff, an infection not affected by antibiotics. C-Diff has been very difficult to cure until recently. It turns out that the most effective treatment for C-Diff is the reintroduction of bacteria into the gastrointestinal system via a fecal implant. There is such a thing as being unsanitary, but, again, it is also true that you can be too clean.

Are there any exceptions to the no-handwashing rule? Yes. For example, sometimes allowances have been made for people cleaning their contact lenses. However, for them the rules permit a time-limited "wrong" handwashing, so that their hands aren't as clean as they would like. After they are finished caring for their contacts, they are to recontaminate their hands with whatever exposures they were working on.

In our intensive treatment, sufferers follow rules like the ones above. There are a few basic principles for you to use when designing your program. Stop your rituals, even if many non-sufferers engage in similar behaviors. For behaviors that you do engage in, such as cleaning dishes, brushing your teeth, or cleaning your house, make sure that these are done "wrong." To do them wrong, you should do them incompletely, do them quickly, and do them less frequently than non-sufferers do.

I don't recommend modifying the rules, but if you do choose to institute a partial program of response prevention, then do so in an organized manner. Any decontamination rituals, such as handwashing, are not to be engaged in whenever you feel too anxious, but only in previously defined situations, and within this structure, there are still rules to follow as to how you may wash. Many of you might like the sound of a modified response prevention that allows some washing, but it is actually harder, for two reasons. First, it is easier to avoid rituals completely than to engage in them partially, just like it is easier for an alcoholic to stop drinking than to drink in a controlled manner. The second reason is that even engaging in a modified ritual is practicing ritualizing—you are still giving airtime to the enemy, the pro-OCD advertising campaign. However, by religiously following the rules below, you can institute a modified response prevention and still succeed in treatment.

WASHING RULES FOR MODIFIED RESPONSE PREVENTION PROGRAMS

1. Only wash your hands or decontaminate in your "legal" situations. If handling the mail was an item on your hierarchy that you have completed, then you can't wash your hands after handling the mail or clean anything that the mail has touched. But if the mail is an item on your hierarchy that you haven't reached, modified decontamination following handling of the mail is permissible. You and your house cannot be less contaminated than wherever you are in your hierarchy. There can be no "safe places." Maintaining areas that are uncontaminated is not modified response prevention; it is sabotaging your treatment.

2. Handwashing and decontamination are to be quick and done incorrectly by your standards. Although this will feel incomplete, your goal is not comfort but gradual normalization of your behavior.

3. Recontaminate following washing with whatever exposure materials you are currently working with. If you have conquered the mail, but not the bathroom, you would wash your hands after going to the bathroom, but you would immediately recontaminate your hands with mail after washing. With this approach, you are controlling the level of exposure, but you still are never completely decontaminated, and there are still no places that are 100 percent "safe."

4. Secondary contamination—for example, contaminating the faucet because you turned it on with your dirty hand—is not to be avoided. If you wash your hands after going to the bathroom, turn the faucet on with your contaminated hands and turn it off with your clean hands. *Washing doesn't make you clean—just cleaner than when you started.*

5. Don't conveniently time "legal" handwashing to decontaminate your hands for some other activity. If you properly recontaminate following handwashing, this won't be an issue.

As you prepare to go to the next chapter, ask yourself the following about your OCD concerns and your rituals: *Do I ever check anything more than once to make sure it looks the way I want it to look—that the pavement is clean, that the stove is off, or that food items haven't been tampered with? Do I ask others for reassurance? Do I try to be extra careful that I understand what I read? That I make no mistakes in my writing? Do I check anything?* If checking compulsions are not the core of your OCD rituals, they are still likely to play some role. The next chapter, Checking: the Pervasive Compulsion, will help you to design exposure-and-response-prevention exercises and scripts to get unnecessary checking out of your life.

Chapter 10

Checking: The Pervasive Compulsion

ontamination obsessions may be the most common concern for OCD sufferers, but the next largest group centers on checking—a class of compulsions rather than obsessions. Recall from Chapter 3 that obsessions refer to what you fear, and compulsions are what you do to try to neutralize your fear. Almost all of you, regardless of the type of obsessions that plague you, are likely to have some form of checking rituals as a part of your OCD repertoire. With a multitude of forms, you may wonder exactly what constitutes checking.

For the purposes of this chapter, *checking* refers to rituals that are direct attempts to affect the environment or to perceive the environment correctly. This would include making sure a stove was off by repeatedly turning it on and off, replaying a conversation in your head to make sure you didn't say anything wrong to your friend, or protecting children by constantly scanning the ground and picking up any small objects that they might put into their mouths. This definition excludes obsessions and rituals focusing on internal bodily processes, such as constantly feeling your pulse to make sure you are okay; internal mental processes, such as trying to make violent thoughts go away; and internally focused rituals indirectly related to external concerns, such as repeatedly saying "no fire" to make sure your house won't burn down.

Within these constraints, checking rituals can be used to neutralize almost any obsession. For illustrative purposes, this program will focus on seven different but common obsessive fears that rely primarily on checking rituals:

1. Damage and injury in the home
2. Hit-and-run—injury to others with your car
3. Protecting the world—injury to others in public places
4. Problems with reading and understanding
5. Problems with conversation
6. Indecision
7. Forgetting and/or loss

Don't despair if your fear isn't listed here. These examples are varied and detailed enough for you to be able to adapt the materials to your needs. At this time, gather your materials—your fear hierarchy, your Cost-Benefit Analysis, etc.—so you will be able to work on them as you read through the chapter.

Damage and Injury in the Home

For all of us, much of our lives revolve around our homes. Our homes are our refuge from the world, filled with our possessions and often with those we love. This central role makes the home a natural target of obsessive fears. The focus of most obsessions pertaining to the home involves fears of possible harm coming to yourself, others, or your property through fires, floods, and break-ins. The primary function of neutralizing rituals for these obsessions are preventive— you try to make sure that neither you, your house, nor others are injured.

Consider the case of Sharon. You can see by examining her hierarchy that she was frightened of fire. Her worst feared consequence concerned her cat, Rugrat. She was afraid that if a fire started, there would be nothing to save him from perishing in the blaze. Sharon had extensive checking rituals for turning off appliances and unplugging all of them except for the refrigerator and the electric stove. She did use her microwave, but she hadn't used her stove or oven for more than two years. All her clocks were battery-operated so she wouldn't have to unplug them.

Her method of making sure the stove was off was similar to the way she turned off all the appliances and lights. She'd stand in front of the stove, intently staring at the knob and repeatedly turning it on and off. The apartment had to be absolutely silent so that she could concentrate on the stove. Sometimes she would just stop and stare at the knob, trying to see that it was off, which might

Sharon's Hierarchy

Item	SUDs
Leaving home without checking the stove	98
Going to bed without checking the stove	97
Cooking on the stove	97
Leaving home without checking the microwave	95
Going to bed without checking the microwave	94
Leaving home with the toaster plugged in	94
Leaving home without checking the toaster	92
Going to bed without checking the toaster	91
Leaving home with the dryer running	89
Leaving home with items on top of plugged-in wires	83
Going to bed with items on top of plugged-in wires	80
Leaving home with the lights on	79
Leaving home with the washer running	75
Leaving home with the TV on	71
Leaving home with appliances plugged in	70

Sharon's list continued. Lower items were similar to the above, but in situations when she was at home and awake.

be followed by turning it on and off again. Finally she'd stop, because she either did her rituals "right" or because she was exhausted. But her ordeal would continue. While walking away, she tried to think about something else, or she would try to hold the image of the stove being off in her mind, mentally trying to convince herself that she did turn it off and that she last saw it in the off position. If friends were visiting, she would short-circuit the process by asking them to check the stove for her. She would still obsess that maybe her friends misunderstood her, or didn't do it right, or that she misunderstood their answers.

Of course, this pain, effort, and time were multiplied, because she checked everything in the apartment the same way. Leaving the apartment or going to bed for the evening was a three-hour process.

One of the scripts Sharon found especially useful in her therapy was a "My Rituals Are Useless Anyway" script. With my help, she used Socratic Questioning to examine her ritual behaviors for inconsistencies: In which ways was she really not doing enough? Her initial response to such flaws was similar to that of non-sufferers when caught in their inconsistencies—it would be too much work to be more careful. I had to remind her that there was a point in time when she would have said that about her current ritualizing. More to the point, I noted that the flaws in her rituals were real—if her current rituals were truly necessary, then the flaws were real ones that needed to be taken care of. If she wasn't going to start ritualizing more, then what she was doing was a waste of time. From the information provided about Sharon, can you detect the instances in which she violated her own rules? There are three.

The first is that she leaves the refrigerator plugged in while she is away. By unplugging all appliances and lights to protect Rugrat from perishing in a fire, why was she willing to make this compromise? Was the food in the refrigerator worth more than Rugrat's life? Her second "mistake" was leaving the stove plugged in. Her reason for this was that it was too hard to get behind the stove to unplug it. Also, she lived in an apartment building, so this meant that everyone else in the building who didn't take her precautions put her at risk. What did she do about that? She did worry about this, but she did nothing because her greatest concern was not to be personally responsible for a fire and because it would be too embarrassing to confront her neighbors. I asked her why it wasn't her responsibility to try to make sure the neighbors unplugged their appliances. Why shouldn't she spend the time it would take trying to convince her neighbors to do as she does? Isn't Rugrat's life worth the embarrassment?

Obviously, I wasn't trying to convince her to increase her rituals. We were working together to help her see that her rituals were futile, not because the risk of fire was small but because they didn't reduce the odds of her worst fears enough. Out of this came the material for her "My Rituals Are Useless Anyway" script.

SCRIPT

For all the effort I put into my rituals, my cat Rugrat is still at risk. A fire could start in the building at any time, because of all the other tenants. On top of this, even I don't check everything I can. I leave my refrigerator plugged in. I leave the stove plugged in, and I think that's the most dangerous appliance I have. I don't go into the storage room in the basement every night to check, and that place always makes me nervous about fire. I'm already taking these risks. I need to do these exposures to get better. I know that increasing my rituals isn't going to make the building any safer, so I need to learn to live with the uncertainty of fire and to live by the Three-House Rule.

The Three-House Rule concerns the importance and necessity of living with risk—even if you might be responsible for disaster.

SCRIPT

No one can assure you that there won't ever be a fire in your home. Nor can anyone promise you that it won't be your fault. A fire could even take place while you are in therapy. At my center, I tell sufferers that if this happens, I want them to continue doing exposure, even if the fire was caused by the exposure—that somehow leaving the lights on caused the fire, or the one time you didn't check the stove, not only was it on, but something was near enough to the stove for it to catch fire and burn the house down. I ask you to do this because fires can happen, and we have to find a way to continue. If I was driving and accidentally hit someone because I was changing the radio station at the critical moment when they walked into traffic, what would I do? I would feel horribly guilty. But I would have to find a way to cope with the guilt, and I would have to drive again. So if you burn your home down, I would ask you to continue with treatment. Now, let's suppose you follow my directions and burn down a second house. You are incredibly unlucky, but I would still urge you to stay in treatment. Finally, what if you burn down a third house? If you burn down three houses, then I think it is reasonable and important to discuss what you need to do to check and be more careful. Remember, this is three houses on three separate occasions. If you burn down a city block, that still counts as just one! This is the Three-House Rule.

If you have prepared all your materials, then you can start planning your response prevention. For checking in the home, sometimes the line between response prevention and exposure appears to be blurred, because leaving home without checking is response prevention, but for this problem it is also exposure. With this in mind, the rules for a total response prevention are slightly modified.

RESPONSE PREVENTION RULES FOR DAMAGE AND INJURY IN THE HOME OBSESSIONS

1. You are not to seek reassurance from family or friends. Ideally, they should be instructed to answer requests for reassurance with statements like: *Yes, the stove is probably still on, and I think there is a good chance that we'll die tonight because of you.* Family members may respond this way only if you have given them permission.
2. Family members should stop engaging in any checking rituals done for your benefit.
3. You are not to check any items that you have begun to address in exposure.

One of the difficulties of instituting response prevention for this problem is that checking often involves looking at a stove, light switch, or door lock, and you may do this out of habit, before you catch yourself. To get around this, use reminders and aids to support your response prevention.

Some sufferers argue that some checking is necessary and the issue is quantity—how much time are they spending. There is some truth to this, but this argument is similar to what alcoholics might say about drinking—drinking isn't the problem, it's the amount of drinking. A better measure of whether or not checking is useful and necessary is how often you catch a mistake. For example, whenever I leave my house, I try to spend a moment to make sure I have everything I think I will need with me. I consider this useful checking, because at least once a week I do forget something. But I don't check the front door to see if I have locked it when I leave. You should note that about once a year I accidentally leave home with the front door wide open. Shouldn't I check?

A few years ago, I began working with a woman who engaged in extensive lock-checking rituals before leaving home for work. She told me she felt these were very important to do because one day before coming to treatment, despite her rituals, she somehow left home without locking her back door. She came home to find that her house had been broken into. However, upon further questioning by me, she did admit that the thief had broken her kitchen window to come into her house—he didn't know the back door was unlocked.

Suggestions for Response Prevention Aids

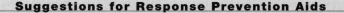

① Use big pieces of paper to cover locks and light switches so that you can't see the position they are in. You can also use this as a reminder to think about your reasons for working on your OCD.

② For stoves, a piece of masking tape over the labels will make it impossible to determine exactly where *off* is.

③ Keep bathroom doors opened, and put a sign on them to remember not to close them.

④ Put masking tape on switches, faucets, and locks you are supposed to leave in the "wrong" position, so if you forget, the different feel of the switch will remind you.

With your response prevention program in place, you are ready to begin your exposure. Compare your hierarchy to Sharon's. Are there enough details in yours to plan a program? Do you have a full range of high and low items? If not, take the time to fix this now.

In planning exposure, remember that you want to be active, and that means doing things that a dead person can't do. Dead people are great at not checking, but they are terrible at turning lights on and leaving them this way. If you look at Sharon's list, some items are easy to be active with: turning all the house lights on when leaving home (if faucets are your problem, then you can leave them dripping), plugging everything in, or putting books on top of cords. Other items seem like they would have to be passive, such as leaving home without checking the stove. One possibility would be leaving the stove on, but this is on our short list of exposures I don't have people do because of the certain risk. Fortunately, there is a way to work on these issues—you can turn things off or lock doors the wrong way.

TURNING APPLIANCES AND SWITCHES OFF "WRONG" FOR EXPOSURE

1. Turn your back to the knob, switch, or lock you are concerned with.
2. Turn it on or unlock it without looking (for some reason, you should note that most of you will have no doubts about this action).
3. Then still without looking, turn it off or lock it quickly. Do not turn it

hard so that you can feel it is in the right position or be especially conscious of a click. Make noise to make hearing a click harder.

4. Quickly remove your hand and walk away without looking.

This can be easier to accomplish if you are leaving the house, since it will be easier to resist giving in to the temptation to recheck if you aren't home. If you are doing this at bedtime, then the assignment should be completed while listening to your therapy script, and you should play it throughout the night both to add to your exposure and to support it. You might notice how this differs from contamination. For contamination issues, I might suggest continuing to contaminate the house if you are anxious. For this kind of checking, repeatedly turning the stove on and off wrong would be more akin to ritualizing than exposure, since each repetition feels like the process is starting over. For this reason, using therapy scripts becomes more important.

If you are finding it too hard to complete an exposure such as leaving the lights on in the house all day, this can be modified as long as you remember to use all your exposure time to complete the safe steps and use delay. For example, rather than doing your homework in the morning, when you will have to leave all day, do it at night and on the weekend. Following an exposure in which either the lights are on or the stove has been turned off wrong, leave the house. Decide beforehand how much you are initially willing to tolerate, whether it be one minute or one hour. When you go back inside, don't check. Stand in the entrance, listening to your therapy scripts. If you can, step out again. When your exposure time is completed, continue to work on not checking. Gradually you can work your way up to longer time periods and greater distances from your home. If this is too easy, consider leaving the house after exposure and driving away for a short time—whatever you are willing to tolerate to get better.

Turning off the ignition and locking the car doors is often another part of this problem. When you are ready to tackle this problem, while you're driving, listen to an imaginal exposure script about allowing your car to be stolen or rolling down the hill and hurting someone. This is to help remind you to be in an exposure frame of mind when you leave the car. Ultimately, anything that can be in the on position when you get out of the car should be. This includes windshield wipers, the fan, and the radio. If your neighborhood is relatively safe, plan to leave your car unlocked with the alarm off. When you pull into your driveway, prepare to race. Your goal is to move quickly and be unsure—to turn off the ignition and lights and perhaps hit the lock button on your keys once if your neighborhood isn't safe. Make noise while doing this, so as to further interfere with your concentration. Run into the house. Needless to say, walking around the car and examining the locks is on the list of behaviors forbidden by your response prevention. The blinds or curtains in your house should already be down with a reminder, either a Post-it note or a paste-on red dot, so that you won't forget that you are not to look out the window to check on the car.

Hit-and-Run—Injury to Others with Your Car

Hit-and-run is a common obsession in which the feared consequence is that you may have accidentally hit someone with your car. Sometimes being responsible for hitting someone is the worst part of the fear. For others, that fear may be secondary to being caught, publicly humiliated, and/or going to prison for hit-and-run.

Every car ride has the potential to be a nightmare. Every glance in the rearview mirror, bump in the road, or pedestrian you pass provides possible evidence of having hit someone without awareness. In response to this, you check the rearview mirror more and possibly drive around the block to retrace your path to make sure there are no bodies lying in the road. Unfortunately, in driving around the block, you may have had more possible hit-and-runs, requiring you to retrace those steps. Getting home can be a very long process.

But the nightmare doesn't end at home. Now you may check the car from top to bottom for dents and scratches that might be evidence of a hit-and-run. You may have a mental catalogue of old dents and scratches in the hope of limiting your concern to only new ones. But this can fail, because there is the possibility that you forgot or that the impression made by someone you hit was in exactly the same place where an old dent was. So you also need to establish whether or not old dents look different. As with all OCD problems, the anxiety and frustration experienced during this process are unbearable, even though you may appear calm to outsiders.

Once the external car check is over, the nightmare continues. You find a quiet place in your house and try to mentally retrace your driving to prove to yourself that you didn't really hit someone. You argue with yourself that you would know if you hit someone, only to counter with, *Maybe I wouldn't.* Finally, you watch the news to catch any reports of a hit-and-run where you had driven. And if there was a hit-and-run that took place fifteen miles from where you had been, you may feel the need to mentally retrace your path again to reassure yourself that you weren't there.

Your pain can be so great that you give up driving or restrict it to "easy" situations. This kind of passive avoidance is a perfect example of why I find the term *passive* misleading. By giving up driving, your world and possibilities become smaller, especially if you are not living in the middle of a town or city. Look at your Cost-Benefit Analysis: What are you losing because of your hit-and-run OCD?

Gather your program materials and consider the feared consequences you will have to cope with. What is *the question* for you—the uncertainty you have to accept to free yourself of OCD? For hit-and-run, the most frequent answer needs to be: "I want to learn to live with the possibility that I have unknowingly hit someone, left them there to possibly die, and now have to hope that I won't get caught."

Combined with your other materials, this answer can directly lead to an Imaginal Exposure Script of Your Feared Consequences.

SCRIPT

When I'm driving on the road, I know there is a possibility that I have hit someone. I always try to convince myself that I would know if I hit someone, but I know my attention to driving can't be perfect. Even though I don't like the idea, there is no way for me to be sure I would know if I hit someone. To fight my OCD, I'm going to have to risk leaving someone on the road, slowly dying, and not go back for them. Even if this means I'm identified later and have to stand trial for hit-and-run. That would be awful to go through, everyone knowing I irresponsibly ran over someone and left, my guilt that maybe I could have saved them if I had only checked, and the horror of maybe spending some time in prison. But I'm only allowed to check if I am 100 percent sure I hit someone. If I have the slightest doubt, I have to do exposure by continuing to drive without checking and hoping that if I'm wrong, no one catches me. If that is the case, I will also have to live with never knowing how many people I may have hit and if I've escaped being caught. . . .

Hit-and-run hierarchies tend to be straightforward. There are usually three variables that determine whether you rank an item as high or low. The first has to do with the kind of street the individual is driving on. Generally congested city streets crowded with pedestrians are scarier than expressways or country roads. Nighttime driving on poorly lit streets is usually scarier, because there is a greater chance of not seeing someone. Finally, having a passenger can make driving easier, since the sufferer assumes that the passenger will notice a hit-and-run. As always, your problem with hit-and-run may follow its own rules. For example, some hit-and-run sufferers prefer late-night driving, because they feel there will be fewer people for them to hit.

In planning response prevention for hit-and-run, unlike checking to prevent injuries or damage to the home, complete response prevention isn't always synonymous with exposure. Not watching the TV for news of hit-and-runs after driving is just one example of hit-and-run response prevention that is not simultaneously an exposure.

Response Prevention Rules for Hit-And-Run

1. You are not to drive around the block or retrace your path while driving.
2. Do not unnecessarily stop the car to look in the rearview mirror or to get out to see what you might have hit.
3. Rules 1 and 2 may only be violated if you have no doubt that you hit someone—if you have the slightest doubt, continue driving.
4. Try to limit rearview mirror checking to lane changes and when necessary. This may be so habitual that you will sometimes make a mistake. Paste a small red-dot label in the middle of the mirror to remind you to turn away. This will be small enough not to interfere with your vision. Also use these for sideview mirrors.
5. Do not drive slower than the posted speed.
6. Do not examine the car when you park it. If this feels too difficult, use the delay technique. However, delay by going into your home. Even if you plan to wait only five minutes, there is no reason other than convenience not to go in.

7. Do not watch or listen to the news if you do this to find out about hit-and-runs.
8. Interfere with mental retracing by staying active—do not isolate yourself to try and concentrate. Ways to interfere include talking to people, reading, engaging in other activities, writing a script to interfere with retracing your path, or listening to a therapy script.
9. Do not seek reassurance.

Your active exposures will primarily involve driving. Ideally, plan to drive for at least an hour every day. Initially, this may not be a part of your normal driving routine, because the roads you use may be too high on your hierarchy.

Start on roads that are easier for you and plan a route that doesn't retrace itself. Do this daily. If you plan to do an incomplete response prevention, this should never occur during active exposure. This means that the only checking that is permitted in your partial response prevention will take place when your driving isn't a part of your exposure program, and when you are on roads that are more difficult than wherever you are on your hierarchy. During your recovery program, you should not check your car after parking, whether you're doing partial or complete response prevention protocols. Therapy scripts should be played constantly while driving, whether the driving is part of your formal homework or is taking place during your normal routine.

Protecting the World—Injury to Others in Public Places

Concern for the safety of others doesn't have to stop in the home or the car. There are an endless number of ways for obsessions of this nature to manifest themselves. For Paul, a forty-two-year-old social worker, these obsessions made him feel responsible for any harm that might come to others, either directly from his own actions or from not taking steps to prevent other "dangers" that he noticed. As soon as he walked out of his house, he was bombarded with endless triggers for his obsessions. He wrote:

> *Even food shopping is torture for me. I constantly scan the floors for any small objects—such as paper clips, small pieces of paper, pebbles, or (God forbid)*

glass. I pick up everything I see, because what if a little kid was to pick it up and put it in his mouth? He could choke or bleed internally or something. Or maybe someone could trip on it. I worry that people will notice me doing this.

I have some ways of trying to cover up, like pretending to tie my shoe, but some days there is just so much on the floor that I'm sure they must see me and think I'm a nut. And I'm not just worried about stuff on the floor. I have to worry about damage I could do. I try to keep my shopping cart in the dead center of the aisle to make sure I don't knock something off the shelf without realizing it. I have to. I mean, what if I did and someone tripped because of me? You don't know how bad it is. Every time someone passes me, I have to turn around to make sure I didn't accidentally bump them or knock them down. The kids in the supermarket drive me nuts. I'm constantly looking this way and that. Sometimes I just want to run out and leave my cart where it is, but then I worry about that, too. . . .

—PAUL

Despite the fact that his desperation was so great that he felt unable to control himself enough to avoid periodic public humiliation, Paul was able to function at his job. He felt he was an effective social worker when he was actually working with people. However, paperwork was a problem. Just as he was afraid of physically hurting someone in the food store by bumping into them or leaving something on the floor, at work he was concerned that improperly completed paperwork might result in an individual losing important benefits. As a result, he was months behind in turning in his paperwork. The only reason he wasn't reprimanded for this was that many of his peers were also behind—though not as much as he was.

As you work on your program, take a moment to consider the partial list of Paul's rituals and avoidances. His list was quite long, in part because of his attention to detail, but mainly because there were so many triggers for his obsession in the environment. You may have noticed that some of his rituals conflict with one another—that is, he can't do more than one at a time. He described trying to simultaneously scan the ground for danger and at the same time stay aware of people both next to him and in front of him as an absolute agony.

For Paul to benefit in treatment, he had to decide to be willing to learn to live with the possibility of being responsible for seriously hurting someone. If you share Paul's concerns, have you taken this goal? If not, do you really do everything you can to protect others? Do you ever give up, in which case you may be hurting others? Do you have conflicting rituals? Consider creating a "My Rituals Are Useless Anyway" script like Sharon's (see page 172) to help yourself accept the impossibility of your self-imposed OCD demands.

In designing Paul's intensive recovery program, there were some situations that could be addressed with response prevention or exposure. Whenever such choices are available, choose exposure. Making exposure an active process in which you are directly attacking your fears will be more effective in helping you recover.

Items not covered in response prevention included where he walked, his scanning the environment in front of him, and his attempts to write slowly and neatly. These were incorporated into his exposure program. Below is the portion of his exposure homework for situations addressed in his hierarchy.

PARTIAL LIST OF PAUL'S DAILY EXPOSURE HOMEWORK

1. Go to the supermarket every day, whether or not you need to. As you walk down the aisles, don't allow your eyes to go lower than the shelf above your eyes. (This way, Paul looked as if he was shopping. On actual shopping days, you are allowed to look at lower shelves for items you need, but on homework days, this isn't necessary.)

2. Listen to your exposure script with headphones while shopping, and follow its directions. (At intervals of two to four minutes, the script should signal you to hit the shelves with your shopping cart. Listening to therapy scripts will also interfere with your ability to listen for cries of help or pain.)

3. Bump into one cart during each exposure session.

4. Drop eight or more paper clips on the floor while shopping.

5. At work, misspell some words on purpose.

6. At work, make sure some words are difficult to read.

7. In reports, put in one extra comma or remove a comma after the fourth word on the sixth line of every page. This was randomly chosen to prevent Paul from spending any time trying to plan to put in or remove a comma from the most innocuous place he could find.

Paul's List of Rituals and Avoidances

For Dangerous Ground Situations

1. Constantly scanning the ground for such objects
2. Picking up anything suspicious
3. Reporting any wet spots on floors to authorities
4. Keeping as far away from anything I might knock down or break as possible
5. Retracing my steps to make sure I don't miss anything
6. Staying inside on "bad days"

For Potential Bumping into People

1. Staying in the least populated spots, against walls or in the middle of walkways
2. Turning around to make sure others haven't fallen down
3. Retracing steps
4. Listening for cries of help or pain
5. Staying inside on "bad days"

For Paperwork at the Office

1. Writing very slowly and neatly
2. Check information until I'm sure it is right
3. Adding any figures until I'm sure they are correct
4. Checking and rechecking spelling
5. Checking grammar and punctuation to make sure the meaning is clear
6. When finished, doing one more final check

In designing your own program, remember the active nature of exposure. Paul didn't simply go to the supermarket when it was crowded and then act "normal" for his exposure. Instead, he bumped shelves with his cart and dropped litter in the form of paper clips on the ground. Just as the sufferer with contamination obsessions contaminates the environment and puts everyone else at risk, you should also actively take the risk of having your fears come true. To

Paul's Hierarchy

Item	SUDs
Navigating a stairwell crowded with children at my daughter's school	95
Passing a small child with a shopping cart in a crowded supermarket	94
Having my shopping cart by the shelves when another cart goes by	94
Dangerous objects, such as paper clips or glass, on the floor when children are around	90
Walking on a crowded sidewalk	83
Seeing dangerous objects on the sidewalk	80
Seeing dangerous objects on the floor at work	78
Seeing paper on the floor in a supermarket	73
On Client Forms at Work	
Writing in financial information	70
Getting names correct	68
Getting addresses correct	65
Misspelling words	60

decide whether or not you are going too far, use the Survey Method as your standard: Are there any non-sufferers who might engage in the same behaviors either accidentally or on purpose? Non-sufferers may periodically throw objects like paper clips on the ground purposely or by inattention—we know this, because you can find them. Given this fact, such an exposure is a reasonable part of your program. On the other hand, although bottles fall off the shelf and break, it is an infrequent event, so Paul wasn't asked to purposely knock bottles off the shelf. Similarly, the mistakes he was making on his paperwork were like those made by his coworkers. To his knowledge, no one had been fired for such mistakes.

However, if he did accidentally knock a bottle off the shelf, leaving it there without reporting it was part of his response prevention. Below are his response prevention rules.

Response Prevention Rules for Paul

1. Do not retrace your steps.
2. Do not turn around to check for injuries.
3. Do not pick up objects from the ground.
4. Do not look down.
5. Do not report "danger spots" on floors to authorities.
6. Do not use spellcheck or grammar check for reports.
7. Do not double-check information.
8. Do not recalculate figures.
9. Do not do a final check of paperwork.

Paul wanted to argue about the last five items. He was particularly adamant that the fifth rule in the list, which means not reporting a broken bottle on the ground in the supermarket, seemed terribly wrong. Although I did agree that such behavior was thoughtless, I did tell him that I didn't find it as outrageous as he did. I also noted that he is not alone in the supermarket, so someone else might report the problem. If not, then yes, he would be irresponsible. In this discussion, an important elaboration of his feared consequences was revealed. To take no action was not only irresponsible, but it was also bad. I had no difficulty agreeing with him. I would feel guilty if a child slipped on ketchup and then severely injured himself on the broken glass that I had seen and not reported. Despite this, I assured him that there is a good possibility I wouldn't report it, because there have been times in the past when I haven't. I also noted a potential dilemma to consider if he came across a broken ketchup bottle: Which is more important, reporting it or staying by the broken bottle and pointing it out to everyone to make sure no one slips? You can't do both. For Paul to overcome his OCD, he not only has to risk being responsible for causing injury to others, but he also has to decide to live with being as "bad" as most non-sufferers.

The response prevention for his paperwork may seem extreme; however, this was based on his own self-report that his checking was rarely useful. If he had reported finding a fair number of errors, a timed and structured single check would have been devised. If this had been the case, the structured check would only be used for work in which errors might result in job loss. If his writing problem had included all writing, then the structured check would not be used for any work that didn't put his job at risk, such as e-mails and memos at work, writing checks at home, and personal correspondence.

Problems with Reading and Understanding

This is one of the most insidious OCD problems you can have. In children, this problem is often misdiagnosed as a learning disability or as a part of attention deficit disorder. Misdiagnosis results from the way children describe the problem: "I can't understand what I am reading," or "The words don't make sense," or "I'll read a sentence over and over and still not get it."

Its effect on life ranges from OCD sufferers' tremendous struggles to make it through school to dropping out of school or college and trying to find a career with a minimal amount of reading. Those sufferers who have found a way to be successful usually have given up reading for pleasure. This is a tragedy that can be avoided with correct diagnosis and treatment.

Below are two paragraphs. The first is how a non-OCD sufferer would read and understand the paragraph. The second is written in the same way a person with a reading-checking problem might read it. Before reading the normal paragraph, try reading the problem paragraph first to see how rereading affects understanding. When you do this, make sure that you do not skip any words or phrases. You may have to read it aloud to successfully not skip any words. Following my suggestion will give you a small taste of what it is like to have this problem.

What Reading without Checking Looks Like

> *The core of this problem is having the feeling that you didn't understand what you read. As a result, you reread a sentence or a word over and over before going on to the next sentence. Unfortunately, this contributes to destroying the flow of what you are reading, so the feeling of understanding becomes even more unattainable. Generally, the more important the material, the greater the anxiety. Schoolwork becomes torture.*

WHAT READING WITH CHECKING LOOKS LIKE

> *The core of this problem is having the feeling, the feeling, the feeling, the feeling. The core of this problem is having the feeling that you didn't understand what you read. As a result, you reread a sentence or a word over and over, you reread a sentence or a word, you reread a sentence or a word, you reread, you reread. The core of the problem is having the feeling that you didn't understand what you read, what you read. As a result you reread a sentence or a word, you reread a sentence or a word, you reread a sentence or a word before going on to the next sentence. As a result you reread a sentence or a word before going on to the next sentence. Unfortunately, this contributes to destroying the flow of what you are reading, so the feeling of understanding becomes even more unattainable, so the feeling of understanding, so the feeling of understanding becomes more unattainable. So the feeling of understanding becomes even more unattainable. Generally, the more important the material, the greater the anxiety, the more important the material, the greater the anxiety, the more important the material, the more important the material, the greater the anxiety. Schoolwork becomes torture. The core of this problem is having the feeling . . .*

Did you have difficulty understanding the paragraph when you read the repeating version in the box? Imagine trying to read an entire chapter this way. Whatever difficulty you had would be multiplied and no matter how much or how little you understood, it's quite likely that you wouldn't read for pleasure. For sufferers with this problem, the feelings of discomfort and of not under-standing are intensified by the fact that this is the focus of their OCD feelings of uncertainty and by the anxiety accompanying the reading.

In actuality, understanding is not as compromised as the sufferer feels. When I have sufferers read something in my office without repeating, they often report that they didn't understand what they read. Upon questioning them about the material they just read, I find that they usually have grasped the main points. However, when this obsession is left untreated, perception is everything. If you have this reading problem, it feels as if the feared consequence has taken place: Your ability to understand what you read has been compromised.

Reading obsessions can be complicated by additional obsessive concerns that the individual might have. Such complications usually focus on "good" and "bad" numbers or words. If this is your problem, you may feel as though you can't go to the next page before looking at a "good" number or word, or you may have to find a "good" word whenever you come across a "bad" one. Needless to say, this kind of attention further erodes the feeling of understanding.

To overcome the reading rituals, you have to be willing to not understand portions of what was read or perhaps miss material that might be important. Of course, the result of your current behavior may very well be limiting your reading, so you are already missing information or you're taking so long to read that you have to give up other activities. At worst, the end result of treatment would be like tuning in to a TV show or movie in the middle—you may miss important information, but quite often you still can understand enough to figure out what is going on.

For this problem, exposure and response prevention are merged: Reading without ritualizing is exposure. The difficulty in attacking this issue, however, comes from another source. The act of ritualizing requires only the slightest movement of the eyes to the beginning of the sentence or word that was being read. The ease of this combined with the anxiety driving the rituals makes it very hard to resist the rituals. Fortunately, there are a number of techniques you can use to attack this difficulty.

Starting with the hierarchy, the key variable tends to be the importance of the material. For some, reading unimportant material—material having nothing to do with school or work—is less anxiety provoking, perhaps to the point where there is no difficulty reading it. The other common controlling variable is the length of the material, so short articles in a newspaper would be easier to read than a novel.

Almost all the suggested aids work by making response prevention easier so that exposure becomes the act of reading without rituals. There are a few techniques we use that add to exposure by interfering with the meaning of the material. All of them share the common goal of reading a text to the end without rereading.

READING EXPOSURE AIDS

1. The simplest technique to use is reading aloud. Because it is more active than silent reading, it makes accidental "drifting" back to what you have

read more difficult. Because you are not used to this, it may increase the feeling of not being sure what you have read. Combine this with the next aid.

2. Take an index card and, as you read, use it to cover the lines you have just read. This interferes with accidental automatic checks. To look back, you have to decide to cheat on your exposures.

3. For noncritical materials, which includes everything that is not work or school-related, take a black Magic Marker and randomly cross out words—one or two words per paragraph. This ensures that you will miss some material.

4. If during exposure you find that you go back to the previous page in books or magazines, then tear out the pages as you complete reading them.

This leaves the question of what to do about important material that you don't really understand. The definition of *important* is school-related material you have to learn or work-related material concerning procedures that you believe your peers would have difficulty understanding. For this material, you may reread it, but not until you come to the end of the chapter or document.

Problems with Conversation

This obsession focuses on whether or not you've correctly understood others, were correctly understood by others, or both. When the focus is on misunderstanding others, the feared consequences generally range from not wanting to make a mistake from mishearing, which may have secondary consequences, such as your being fired from work, causing injury, or getting lost from misheard directions to simply not wanting to tolerate the anxiety of being unsure that your perceptions or understanding were correct.

When the focus is on others understanding what you have said, the potential feared consequences are a broader list. They may include: others making a mistake in carrying out your directions from not hearing you, having accidentally insulted or hurt another person, or otherwise making a bad impression, that others will not be able to give you proper feedback as a result of misunderstanding you, being misunderstood as a person, and simply not wanting to tolerate the anxiety of being uncertain about whether you were understood.

For all of these, mental retracing, reassurance seeking, and repeating/ explaining what you said are the rituals most commonly relied on. For problems of understanding, mental retracing involves going over the conversation as carefully as you can to try to get the feeling that you either understood others or were understood by others. When the focus is on being understood, you may also imagine what you should have said differently to have effected a better or surer outcome.

Seeking reassurance to neutralize fears of misunderstanding often means requesting others to repeat or clarify what they've just said. Sometimes you may try to replay the conversation mentally before it is over. The result of this is potentially being less sure of what the speaker was saying during your rumination. Then you feel more anxious, and the possibility that you didn't hear something increases, making the ritual cycle even more unstoppable. Many sufferers have developed ways of trying to make such requests sound natural, somewhat masking the severity of their problem. This works particularly well on occasions when their anxiety level is low, since only one or two requests are made.

Finally, when being misunderstood is the issue, you tend to repeat and clarify what you've said. Many sufferers know that others are aware of this behavior in them. This results in trying to say everything perfectly, with enough detail to make sure everything you think is important was said—but not so much that the listener will lose interest or think that you have a problem, either of which would lead the listener not to pay sufficient attention. One sufferer I worked with always had the feeling that there were more details I needed to know about a situation, so each story had multiple tangents that he presented. There were many times when he forgot his original point.

The ideal response prevention program would be very straightforward: no repeating yourself, no requests made of others to clarify or repeat, and no mental replays of conversations. However, this is very difficult to achieve. To simply stop mentally retracing, you would have to stop thinking, and since thought stopping doesn't work, mental retracing can be disrupted only by action on your part. One of the most effective ways to do this is to have created a therapy script that you learned by heart. The easiest way to do this is to record it and listen to it until you know it. Don't rewind the script while it is playing. After you have heard the script a number of times, you will be able to recite the therapy script aloud when you are alone and tempted to mentally replay conversations, or under your breath when in public. When you use such self-talk, it is not important that you follow your therapy script exactly—doing so would become another ritual.

Following these instructions will not make the mental retracing stop, but it will, along with any other interfering activities you use, help you move the retracing from the center of your attention to the background. Sometimes the idea of this sounds intolerable: How can you possibly function with such thoughts anywhere in your head? But the fact is that you do function with them in your head, and the ultimate goal is not to eradicate them but to allow them to be there and not care about them. In the ACT (Acceptance and Commitment Therapy) discussed in Chapter 7, this assignment is the beginning work of cognitive defusion and mindfulness.

Below are two sample scripts for interfering with mental retracing. The first addresses "Mental Retracing for Concerns About Being Misunderstood," in which the sufferer's feared consequence is having possibly said something insulting.

SCRIPT

Going over today's conversation with Mary can only hurt me. I need to teach myself to accept that I can't know whether or not I hurt her. I can't call her to apologize or clarify what happened, because that will just make me look weird, and that's one of my reasons for getting over my OCD. If I hurt her feelings, it is going to have to be her responsibility to tell me. All the things we said and all her actions since then are not going to tell me for sure what happened. I would hate to have hurt her, but I have to remember that I also hate this OCD and what it has done to me. I can't forget that people notice it—probably more than I realize. How many times have people told me that I'm always saying "I'm sorry"? Maybe they aren't just being nice. They probably think that something is wrong with me for doing this. This is one of the reasons I'm talking to myself now, working on putting the retracing in the background, like noise.

Here is a sample script for "Interfering with Mental Retracing for Misunderstanding Others."

SCRIPT

As much as I want to go over the details of the conversation I had with Sam today, it is important for me to interfere with that temptation by listening to what I am saying now. I know I have OCD, and no matter how important the conversation might have been, I'm going to have to risk any disaster that might come from my not understanding what he said. I have to work on accepting the possibility of "x" in order to get over the hell of living with OCD forever. I should know by now that there is a good chance that all my retracing will do is create more anxiety and more questions. After all, I can't even know if I'm remembering the conversation correctly, let alone if I have a perfect understanding of it.

Add your own feared consequences to these scripts.

Instituting response prevention for reassurance seeking has its own challenges, particularly the fact that every social interaction is a potential trigger to ritualize. It's difficult to constantly be on guard. Situations will arise that seem so important at the moment or that give rise to such intense anxiety that they feel as though they must be exceptions to the response prevention rules you are following. But true exceptions are rare. Following through with your response prevention will involve using as much help as you can from trusted friends and aids that can serve as reminders.

RESPONSE PREVENTION AIDS FOR REASSURANCE SEEKING

1. Instruct trusted friends and family to interrupt repetitive questioning, refuse to give reassurance, and give "wrong" answers (such as "You will just have to guess," "You are probably going to get this wrong now," "I don't know what I/you said," or "Remember, you told me I shouldn't enable you at times like this").
2. Place reminders in the form of notes and red-dot labels wherever you can as reminders. Placing one in the center of your watch is a very good place. If anyone asks you why it is there, you can tell them one of your children put it there or it is there as a reminder.
3. In the morning, take time to think about any situations you will be in that day that are predictably problematic—by doing this, you are reminding yourself to try to be prepared so that you won't be caught off guard.

4. Instituting total response prevention would mean never asking for reassurance in any situation—including the highest items on your hierarchy. However, for reassurance seeking, this kind of response prevention is the same as exposure. Therefore, response prevention for reassurance seeking may be gradually introduced, starting with the lower items on your hierarchy. Remember, only permit yourself to seek reassurance for situations that you haven't yet addressed.

If you don't want to involve friends and family, ask yourself what kind of TIB (Treatment Interfering Behavior) this is. If your primary reason for not asking is that you truly have no one who understands your OCD enough and you believe that you wouldn't be able to explain yourself to the people you know, then don't consider this a TIB to be worked on. If your reason for not inviting help is embarrassment, I understand how hard it would be to approach anyone. However, ask yourself this question: *Is the degree of embarrassment I'll feel really worth doing anything that might interfere with my recovery?* Turn to your ERP Motivators and your Cost-Benefit Analysis to further think this through. If you didn't complete these, that's another TIB to record and work on. Finally, if you are excluding them because you would rather be reassured than have to cope with not being reassured, you are seriously considering undermining your treatment. But that doesn't mean your choice is to invite them in or fail. Asking others for serious help can become one of your hierarchy items. This way when you create your hierarchy below, the question changes from will this ever be a part of treatment to a planned time when it will become a part of treatment.

DEVELOPING YOUR EXPOSURE hierarchy is relatively straightforward and, most likely, item difficulty will depend on some measure of the importance of the different situations. The greater difficulty will be controlling exposure. For example, if listening to instructions from your superiors at work is a problem, there may not be a way to get them to delay giving you instructions until you are ready for this exposure. There is little to be done about such situations, except waiting for them to occur. But if you have been avoiding certain people or situations out of obsessive fear, then you will have some control over the times you want to do exposure with them. For example, you can decide when you will contact a person you have been avoiding. This allows you to be mentally prepared for the exposure, which will make it easier for you to be successful.

Indecision

Every day all of us make more decisions than we can imagine. Some decisions seem effortless, and others can be torturous. As noted earlier, regardless of how we make decisions, we can never truly know if we have made the right ones. Even a decision that seems perfect at the moment can later turn out to be disastrous. All that any of us can do is guess, because only when it is too late will we find out whether our guess was right or wrong. Of course this doesn't mean all our decisions amount to a random flip of a coin—some of our guesses are educated.

Indecision plays a role in many other obsessive concerns, but it can also be a primary OCD problem. In its most severe form, sufferers literally feel paralyzed with indecision, unable to make even the simplest decisions. Decisions can focus on any aspect of life—how you will choose the words you will say or write, what you will buy, whom you will date, where you will go today, which job you will apply for, and so on. The more common feared consequences for making a wrong decision include never being happy with your decisions, feeling as though something better may come along, feeling you haven't chosen the best (for example, the safest, cheapest, best-looking, ideal, most moral, etc.), or being responsible for having made a mistake and the consequences that follow.

Reassurance seeking, analyzing/figuring out, and seeking out additional information and facts are the prime rituals used by anyone afflicted with indecision. When indecision focuses on buying items, sufferers may also frequently return what they buy and exchange it for an item that's possibly better. Alternatively, they may never make important purchases because they can't obtain that feeling of certainty. Uncertainty about the best decision is only part of the problem. Besides the many possible feared consequences that those with obsessive indecision worry about, there is the additional concern about how much they will ruminate about their decision afterward. Without realizing it, sufferers assume that if they make the right decision, they will feel comfortable or satisfied with it—they will feel it is "right." While it is true that all of us do make some decisions that we accept effortlessly, there are many decisions for which we have mixed emotions. There is a phenomenon, known as *buyer's remorse,* that almost everyone has experienced at one time or another. This regret is felt whenever a buyer has to make a decision among two or more items for which the advantages of one don't overwhelmingly outweigh the advantages of the others.

For almost everyone, the following takes place. You finally make your decision to buy "A," and this is followed by ongoing mental comparisons with "B" and thoughts such as *"A" is better because . . .* (a list you go through) followed by *But "B" did have . . ."* (another list of the advantages of "B" and feelings of regret). And if something is wrong with "A," then the feelings of regret and thinking about what you should have done are tremendous. And this is normal. When I'm in this situation, I remind myself that it is too late—I'm stuck with whatever I've bought until it wears out, whether I like it or not, and that these feelings of regret are going to continue for some time before they fade.

If you suffer from obsessions revolving around decision, your assumptions about what a good decision should feel like are simply wrong. If your problem is severe, it means that over time your threshold for tolerating your version of buyer's remorse is lower, so even decisions that are unimportant become monumentally difficult. (Buyer's remorse doesn't have to be related to a purchase; you can experience it for any decision you must make.)

Overcoming indecision means accepting that you may make imperfect decisions and that you want to learn to live with the regret, the risk that whenever you are in "x" situation, you will be reminded that you made a wrong decision. The alternative is anxiety and paralysis.

Response prevention means limiting the time spent on the decision-making process. The question that arises is how much time, because there are some decisions that everyone would agree should take some time, such as buying a house or a new car. There are other decisions that most people would agree take little time to make, such as which brand of cereal to buy, whether you should brush your teeth or take a shower, or on which wall a picture should be hung. To help you, you can rely on the Survey Method. Using this method, you make guesses as to how long you believe it would take the average person to make such a decision. There is probably a range for many decisions, and for the purposes of treatment, choosing the shorter times will be better for you than choosing the longer times.

With this in mind, the rules for response prevention would look like the following:

Response Prevention Rules for Indecision

1. When problem decisions come up, I will only have "x" amount of time to make them. Depending on the situation, this may range from a few weeks to a few seconds. If I'm buying a car, a few weeks may be reasonable, but for buying a brand of cereal, a minute is more than reasonable.

2. Limits on how much information to collect for decisions need to be instituted. For important decisions—such as large purchases or deciding where to go to college or where to move—a limit will be needed with regard to how much information to collect per option and how many options will be allowed. Internet time needs to be strictly monitored. If possible, have a helper set these boundaries and agree to whatever he or she says without argument.

3. Advice may be asked for only when making important decisions, and this can only be asked once. Whomever you are asking for advice shall determine what information they need to give to help you. This means you have to depend on them to ask questions about your decision—if they don't ask questions, then you have to accept that they feel they don't need to know more. Not knowing whether or not they actually need to know more is part of your exposure.

4. No advice may be requested for less important decisions.

5. Limit the number of people you ask for advice, and you may not ask anyone whose advice you are unwilling to follow. This is a critical rule and will eliminate many people.

6. Special environmental conditions for making a decision, such as demanding complete silence so that you can concentrate, are to be violated.

Exposure begins as soon as the time limit for deciding is over, and it involves simply making a decision. If you are willing and have some idea which decision is "wrong," it would be useful for you to knowingly make the wrong decision. If you do this, you are choosing to risk living with regret to overcome your OCD. Most sufferers aren't willing to do this, but there is another approach. At the moment of decision, if you have any awareness of leaning toward one choice over the other, then make the preferred choice. If you don't know or you feel paralyzed, then we will rely on some very special, high-tech, binary decision-making aids to help you.

The first binary decision—making aid is the coin toss. Your initial response to flipping a coin to make a decision may be protest and horror, but if the decision between two choices is so close, then given that no decision is truly "right," let the coin choose for you. You will accomplish more with quick random decisions like this than with the paralysis of OCD. What if the coin chooses the wrong option? So be it. The goal of recovery is not and cannot be making "right" decisions. In real life, the goal is to make a good-enough guess (I know I said "best" guess earlier, but your interpretation of best may be too high a standard to meet) and then live with the consequences—if and when you discover that the decision is wrong, then that is the time to cope with it. Coping may mean making a new decision or simply working on accepting that you will have to live with your wrong decision.

Flipping a coin can be a very public behavior. If you are concerned about embarrassment, then here is a more subtle binary decision-making aid. If you have a digital watch, quickly glance at it and make your decision based on whether the seconds were an even or odd number. If your watch isn't digital or if you obsess over whether or not the number you saw was odd or even, then when the second hand or seconds is between 1 and 30, choose "A," and when it is between 31 and 60, choose "B." If you don't usually wear a watch, then you may want to buy one.

If your indecision problem occurs even with the very simplest of choices, then, in addition to the above, put aside an hour for "speed decisions," during which you will be deciding things very quickly, using the coin or watch to guide your behavior. If you have someone who can serve as a helper, then they can guide your behavior for the hour. If you do allow a helper to do this, you must agree to do whatever they say without argument.

Playing an "Indecision Exposure Support" script while you are doing this can be very helpful in reminding you of your goals.

SCRIPT

My exposure means making decisions the "wrong" way and risking them being wrong. It feels wrong to do this, and I really could make wrong decisions doing this. If this happens, I'm going to have to find a way to live with my wrong decisions, because there is no way to make a "right" decision, and even no decision is a decision. Up until now, I have often been choosing "no decision" by default, and look where that has gotten me. . . . (Include material from your Cost-Benefit Analysis and ERP Motivators here.) *I need to remember that if the decision turns out to be wrong, it doesn't mean the other decision was right. I always compare my current situation to the one that could have been, but I cheat; I always make that situation better. In reality, there are a million ways the other decision could have turned out and many could be worse. I have to work on the goal of what is next as opposed to what could have been.*

Forgetting and/or Loss

What will happen if you don't get everything done that you planned to do today? What will happen if you leave something behind as you travel from one place to another? These related concerns form the core of what I am calling *forgetting*. The potential consequences of each range from the practical (forgetting an important chore) to the unlikely (leaving a note with something embarrassing written on it) to simply not wanting to cope with the possibility of forgetting or losing something.

The main rituals to prevent forgetting include list-making, both mental and written, and rehearsing mental lists. Most often, sufferers are concerned with activities that they want to accomplish or with personal items that they don't want to leave behind. When the concern is an object, searching yourself and areas you are leaving to make sure you have everything is an additional ritual that is often performed.

With these obsessions, your goal is to learn how to cope with potentially forgetting or losing something. This reminds me of an interaction I had with Dave, a sufferer with this problem. His session was over, and he was searching under the cushions of the chair that he was sitting in to make sure nothing was left behind. He found a penny.

"See," he told me triumphantly, "you wouldn't have found this if I hadn't checked."

He gave me the penny. I smiled and handed it back to him, saying, "I want you to keep this, because I don't want you to forget all the pain your checking has caused you and what its true worth is: a penny. With the jobs you have lost and the distress it has caused in your marriage, to say nothing of your anxiety, a penny may even be too much. And what is the value of being freed from these chains? More than this penny. Keep this penny with you so you don't forget."

RESPONSE PREVENTION RULES FOR FORGETTING AND/OR LOSS

1. You are not to check to see if anything was left behind.
2. You are not to make lists, but under certain circumstances you can make limited lists for events that you might really forget. Ideally, you can use a helper to assist you in making these judgments.
3. For mental rehearsal, use therapy scripts or other methods, such as singing songs to yourself or reading, to force such rehearsal into the background.

As always, reminders in the form of colored-dot stickers and Post-its can be useful to help you remember what you are supposed to be doing.

You may wonder what can be done for exposure. There are many circumstances in which you can leave objects behind. Obviously, this can't be done with important possessions, such as your glasses, car keys, or purse. But you can leave behind things like money or pens. This may seem crazy, but leaving a few dollar bills behind is still less money than a single therapy session with a professional, so "wasting" money in this fashion is a therapeutic bargain.

Some sufferers are concerned that they may leave behind papers on which they have written embarrassing words or secrets about themselves. If you have this problem, consider taking small scraps of paper and writing words on them—either mildly embarrassing or neutral words. Do not check them after they are written. Instead, put them in your pocket, and when you are in public, randomly drop them on the ground. No matter what you wrote, if your obsessive fear is that you've written something wrong, the fact that you haven't checked the paper will accomplish your goal of feeling uncertain about what you have dropped.

THIS BRINGS US to the end of this chapter. Obviously, I haven't and wouldn't be able to cover every form of checking. By highlighting some of the more common forms of checking and providing specific suggestions for scripts and response prevention and exposure, you will be able to adapt the material here to your special concerns. However, you may find your concerns addressed in the next chapter, which focuses on problems in which ordering, symmetry, counting, and movement rituals are used to neutralize obsessions.

Chapter 11

Ordering, Symmetry, Counting, and Movement: Rituals of Perfection and Magic

As in the last chapter, this chapter also focuses on rituals used to neutralize obsessions rather than on the obsessions themselves. This chapter's compulsions are loosely connected to one another in two ways. First, they tend to focus on form, whether it be how objects are arranged, how words are grouped, or how your body moves. Often, these rituals occur in combination with one another. For example, I could have all of the items on my desk in a special order, or I could have them in a special symmetrical order, so that everything on the right side would have a counterpart on its left. Or I might tap my left foot on the floor in just the right way to prevent a disaster, or I might have to tap it fifty times to prevent disaster.

They are also connected to one another in how they often function to neutralize fears—by avoiding or preventing your feared consequences through "magic." Rituals described as working through magic or superstition are those for which the action does not have an obvious connection to the feared consequences. For example, avoiding a disease by handwashing after "contamination" sounds like a logical method of decontaminating. But if you decontaminate by going in and out of a doorway the "right" way four times, the logical connection between your obsessive fear and your ritual is not obvious. Engaging in rituals that function "magically" does not make your OCD problem worse or more difficult to work with. In a sense, all rituals work through "magic," in that almost all sufferers are aware that their actions don't need to be performed in the manner that they perform them. Like all rituals, magic rituals are not performed because they work or because the connection between the fear and the ritual is real. The connection between obsession and compulsion is your fear of uncertainty. Simply because you have the idea that there *might* be a connection between your fears and your rituals, no matter how slim that possibility may be, you decide against taking the risk of resisting them. Or, in other words, you do them because they might work. The major difference between the magic and nonmagic rituals is that the irrational nature of ritualizing is more obvious in the former. The rituals to be covered in this chapter are:

1. Ordering/Symmetry Rituals
2. Counting Rituals
3. Movement Rituals

Ordering/Symmetry Rituals

Rituals relying on ordering and symmetry can neutralize obsessions through "magic," or, when the goal of ordering/symmetry is to impose order on the external environment, perfectionism tends to be the goal. As is true of many OCD presentations, ordering can sound reasonable on the surface. Perhaps my kitchen cabinet is arranged so that the cans are in order of size, with the larger cans in the back, and the labels are all facing forward, and maybe older cans of the same size are closer to the front than newer cans. Such an arrangement makes sense, and with such a system, it is obviously easier to find everything. Laundry is perfectly folded and put into perfect piles in drawers and closets, the piles precisely spaced the proper amount of distance from one another. The clothes in the closet are arranged by season, outfit, and color, with a perfect one-half-inch spacing between each hanger.

Although all of the above may take some time, they don't sound terrible. Remember, OCD is a problem when it interferes with your life or the lives of those around you. It is probably obvious to you if your ordering is disrupting your life, but what about your family's life? Do you think your ordering behaviors are a problem for them? If not, does your family agree, or do you feel it isn't a problem because you feel you are right? If this last question describes your reasons, difficult as it may be, consider reexamining your demands—OCD may be in control of more of your life than you realize. If you filled out the ERP Motivators form, go back to it, then consider the effect your ordering has on your family—do you want your children to have your anxiety? Or alternatively, do you want to be seen by your children as a person whom they can't understand or relate to?

One way to avoid interfering with others is by living alone. If you have chosen to live alone because you don't want to make changes to accommodate others, you may want to consider what you are giving up to appease your habits.

Your intolerance of what you consider "disorder" can be a major cause of family conflict. When the focus is on the house, many sufferers are constantly cleaning up so that pillows are never out of place, ashtrays are emptied before cigarettes are finished, and so on. If you do this, then having company visit—especially for a party—tends to be torture, since the cleanup is constant, and trying to make sure everything stays in its place is impossible.

But the apparent rationality of this kind of ordering makes it very hard for you to give it up. There is a feeling that most of this is not your OCD—after all, what is wrong with wanting your house to be in order? The fact that you spend more time ordering than you want to is ignored in the midst of your discomfort with disorder and your arguing that your way of housekeeping is the right way. You might wish that the treatment goal would be doing everything you want to do, but more quickly. If I have just described your thinking, consider what that means. The two possibilities are that I am right and you do have a problem, or I understand your thinking but have the same misguided standards that everyone around you has. If the latter is true, I am still suggesting that you take the risk of joining us.

How can you change your mind and feelings about a neat and orderly home? Your desire to continue keeping your house the same way but doing it quicker is the same desire of many other sufferers. But it won't work. This solution would still mean giving in to impossible OCD demands. Your own experience has shown you that there is always something else to do or something that can be done just a tad better. You rarely, if ever, reach that magic moment in which everything is done, and if you do, there is the problem that as soon as anyone goes into the room, your attention focuses on the growing list of what you will have to fix. Go back to your self-assessment. What kind of cognitive distortions most characterize your thinking on this issue? All-or-none thinking is the most likely answer, because if anything among your concerns isn't perfect, you'll feel driven to correct it. Did you use any of the cognitive techniques to analyze your behavior? What are the worst consequences of imperfect ordering revealed by the Downward Arrow Technique? Are you afraid something bad will happen, or that people will judge you or is it simply that it feels like your mind won't be free if the house isn't the way you want? If the latter consequence is yours, you will also want to make sure you read the section concerning obsessing about obsessing that is in the next chapter, the Primarily Mental Obsessions. What does the Survey Method tell you about the behavior of others? And finally, what does your Cost-Benefit Analysis tell you about the advantages and disadvantages of changing?

IF YOU HAVEN'T followed through with any of the above steps, I would urge you to do so now. Do you need to turn to the TIBs form on page 150? Because you need to understand why you won't take every step you can to become free of this problem. Everyone has a hard time changing their behavior. The more effort you put into it, the more likely you are to change. All the suggestions in the preceding paragraph were safe steps—that is, none of them creates the actual disorder that makes you uncomfortable. You have nothing to lose and possibly everything to gain by following through with the safe step suggestions.

If you have done the above, your next safe step is to begin to create a "Confronting My Ordering" script to support your need for change.

SCRIPT

As much as I like a neat and clean house, I have to admit that the amount of time it takes to keep it that way is too much, even if I allow others to help. Imagine what I could do with that time that might be fun. I know my family would appreciate it. But what about my feelings and what I like? I know all my answers, but look at my Cost-Benefit Analysis. Look at what I lose: (insert your losses here). *Now I know what it feels like to be an alcoholic who has to give up drinking. Except alcoholics aren't ever supposed to drink. My ordering may be ruined, but my house won't be a total wreck. Changing may feel like complete chaos, but it really won't be. It just won't be my black-and-white way. And if I work to overcome this my life will be better because of* (insert your potential gains here).

Valery's Hierarchy: Family Room

Item	SUDs
Smudges on the glass coffee table	90
Vacuum cleaner lines on rug going in the right direction	88
Food or drinks left on the coffee table	83
Books perfectly lined up in bookcase	82
Videotapes in entertainment center	82
Knickknacks on bookcase	75
Knickknacks on coffee table	75
Magazines in rack	72
Three pillows on sofa	70
TV controller on the right side of the TV	60
TV Guide on the left side of the TV	60
Pictures on the wall	55
Fireplace tools	40

Listen to this script throughout the day and spend time adding to it, especially if you haven't decided to tackle your ordering.

The perfection imposed by ordering rituals can go beyond the seemingly sensible. If symmetry is involved, you may also require a special balance that feels right to you for the arrangement of everything. Note that in this example of ordering and symmetry, symmetry becomes a special type of ordering. In a similar way, both ordering and symmetry are part of a broader category of ways to make your environment look perfect. Obviously, the rules for this perfection can go beyond simple ordering.

An example of this can be seen in the portion of Valery's hierarchy presented here. In her hierarchy, you'll notice that her idea of visual imperfection included smudges on the glass coffee table as well as the ordering of her books, magazines, videos, and knickknacks. Her rules for ordering were quite complex. For example, fixing the books on the shelf took into account the size and color of each book, which was perfectly lined up along the shelf edge.

Within this broader category of visual perfectionism, the problem can extend beyond the order of the house. Some of you may find that owning anything new, whether it be clothing, a TV, or a car, to be terribly anxiety provoking, because of the effort involved in making sure it is flawless when you get it and then in trying to maintain that perfection.

Another illustration of this is provided by Melanie, whom you met in the introduction. In addition to her body dysmorphic disorder, she had perfection compulsions about her schoolwork—it had to look perfect. For her, this meant that notes from class were not allowed to have cross-outs or erasures nor could the paper have any creases or smudges on it. Sometimes she would throw away the page she was taking notes on as soon as such an imperfection occurred, leaving her without notes for that class. At other times, she would bring the notes home and spend hours recopying them to make them look perfect. She had the same rules about textbooks, which meant as soon as they didn't look perfect, she wouldn't read from them or use them. The suggestions found here for ordering will also be applicable to any other perfection concerns you may have.

In designing exposures for ordering and appearance-based perfection issues, the guiding principle is simply to make sure everything is wrong. This does not mean that Valery had to dump her bookcases onto the floor and put the room in complete chaos. On the other hand, for every item on her hierarchy, something had to be done wrong. After cleaning the coffee table, she would purposely smudge it. Vacuuming was done incompletely, so the lines didn't all go in the same direction. One drinking cup was always left on the coffee table. The books, magazines, knickknacks, and pillows were all set up wrong enough to bother her. The TV remote and *TV Guide* were both on the same side of the TV, imperfectly arranged. Similarly, the pictures and fireplace tools were imperfectly in place.

When she was doing homework, Valery would have to walk through the house, listening to her therapy script, lightly knocking everything that wasn't nailed down, so that everything was randomly and slightly out of place. The little red-dot reminders were placed throughout her house and served two purposes. First, their very presence was an exposure for her, because little red dots obviously had no place in a properly maintained home. Second, they were to remind her not only to keep everything imperfect but also to spend a few moments going over her therapy scripts in her mind to help reinforce why she was changing. If you think of the advertising campaign metaphor, the red dots functioned as mini-billboards in her anti-OCD, pro-recovery campaign.

Valery had engaged in numerous maintenance rituals to keep her house looking perfect. Below is a partial list of her response prevention rules.

PARTIAL LIST OF VALERY'S RESPONSE PREVENTION RULES

1. Major housecleaning is to take place only every other week. This includes vacuuming (except as described below), all dusting, arranging, or positioning anything on any shelves or tables, except for the family room coffee table and the kitchen table, and mopping the kitchen.
2. Wipe down the kitchen table at the day's end, but you must do so imperfectly and must have items on it arranged wrong.
3. The kitchen may be swept once daily.
4. Food, plates, and drinks may be removed from the coffee table once a day. One drinking cup is to remain on the table. The coffee table should be wiped down incorrectly, and knickknacks need to be placed incorrectly on the table.
5. Children's rooms are off-limits to you.
6. You may vacuum the hall and family room every other day, but you must do so incorrectly, making sure you miss spots and that the vacuum lines are crooked and unpleasing.
7. Magazines that are out are to remain out if anyone is not finished looking at them. They may be placed sloppily in the rack only once per day.

When perfecting appearance relies on factors other than ordering, such as Melanie's school problem, the rules for exposure and response prevention will be similar. For Melanie's exposures, she was to make sure that her notebook pages were "ruined" in advance by putting small random marks on pages or folding down the corners of pages. When taking notes, she made sure to cross out words on purpose as well as allow natural erasures and cross-outs to occur. Even for papers she handed in, small minor marks that would bother her were put on the pages.

You should also know that ordering does not have to involve manipulating objects. One client I worked with would mentally make every room symmetrical by picking three points in the room that seemed equidistant from one another. These points could be parts of the room or items in the room. What was important for her was the distances between them. If an item was moved, she would instantly reestablish this mental symmetry by choosing different points. She spent her every moment doing this. She felt compelled to create such symmetry and then to continuously check it. On those occasions when she tried to stop it, she found that her eyes almost automatically found symmetry. To help her break this habit, we found that having her walk very rapidly, turning her head too quickly to focus, and blinking her eyes helped her break this ritual. When I last spoke to her, she said that the symmetry still occurs, but she no longer cares about it, nor does she spend any time trying to create it.

Another client mentally reordered all the letters for every sentence that she heard. For any sentence she heard, she would almost instantly extract the letters, making up the words in the sentence, and then put them in alphabetical order. So for the sentence, "I can't believe she could do that," she would feel compelled to extract the letters and silently think to herself, *A, B, C, D, E, H, I, L, N, O, S, T, U, V.*

If you are like most sufferers, you probably want to know when you can return to your old habits without it being an issue. In other words, you wonder: When can things go back to normal? Never. There are a few reasons. First, your version of normal isn't normal. Second, why would you want to; your freedom from these habits needs to be more important than whatever it was that you may have pursued (such as a perfect order). As long as you long for the world that you one lived in where you gave in to your habit or rituals, you are at risk. You are like that alcoholic who wants just one drink. The question we pose to the alcoholic is the following: *It's true you might be able to get away with having a single drink without slipping, but given what you might lose, why is it so important to you to have one drink and take the risk? However, there is a time you can put your house in better order: when you truly no longer care about doing so.*

Counting Rituals

The category of counting rituals is a broad one. In its pure form, the focus of counting rituals is any set of items you feel an urge to count. Sufferers have reported counting road signs, highway divider lines, words in sentences, and tiles on a bathroom wall. Like my patients who engaged in mental ordering, counting feels both compelled and automatic. Often, the feared consequences are discomfort about not ritualizing or the fear that the counting will never stop, so that its presence will ruin your life. This latter fear is maintained by a "wishing" ritual, in which you constantly compare life with counting to how much better life would be if only the counting would stop. By wishing in this way, your anxiety and depression can dramatically increase as soon as you begin to count, because you are now sure that whatever you are doing will be ruined, and that is "proof" that your entire life will be ruined by this inescapable counting. It is as if your feared consequence is always coming true—you fear life will be ruined, and it is.

The goal of therapy is to stop conscious counting, but if automatic counting takes place, the goal is to allow it to go on in the background, the same way you might have a conversation with someone in a restaurant with music playing in the background. You will recognize this as the mindfulness discussed earlier in ACT. You need to remember that mindfulness is not a simple decision, but a goal that requires hard work. Sometimes sufferers become confused as to what would constitute exposure in this situation. Should you sit and stare at the tiles that you normally count, but without counting them? No, that would be like asking someone who checks to see if the stove is on or off to stare at the stove and not think about the position of the knobs. Ideally, I have them not look at the stove. Not looking at the tiles may be possible; however, if you count road signs while driving, not looking at the road is not a viable option. When counting has no feared consequences other than the anxiety its presence arouses, most of the exposure you will do will be in the form of listening to a therapy script.

Scripts for counting can take a few different forms. Some people find that listening to random numbers interferes with their counting. Or rapidly counting aloud is helpful for some people, because their eyes can't keep up with the count, which is too quick to count anything in the environment. You may have to experiment to see what works best for you. For others, the wishing ritual—wishing for the counting to stop—is so ingrained that it is hard to have counting occurring in the background without slipping into wishing. If this describes you, then you need to listen to a therapy script whenever you are in a potential counting situation. Do this whenever possible. Below is a script for "Wishing Away Counting."

SCRIPT

This is to remind me of my task in my "high-risk" situations. Am I counting on purpose? If so, I should pay more attention to this script. If I'm in a private place, I can even speak along with this script, because eventually I'll know it by heart. I can hate the counting, but when it is in the background,

I don't have to let it rule me. Maybe it will interfere with my concentration or enjoyment right now. I want to learn to say "So what?" to such interference. After all, many things can interfere. I could have a headache. I could be next to a loud, obnoxious person who is playing music that I can't stand. Life is full of imperfect times, and this is one of them. It doesn't matter if my life would be better without counting, because this is my life now. My job is to enjoy whatever I can at this moment—no matter how small the crumbs are. Gradually I will learn to allow counting to occur in the background without caring. But that isn't going to happen today.

The above can be combined with rapid counting or a list of random numbers to be played at the beginning or end of your therapy script. If there are any other feared consequences associated with your counting, make sure you have taken these into account when preparing "feared consequences," therapy scripts to listen to, and script cards to carry with you. Also it is important to pay attention to the line in the script reminding you to focus on whatever crumbs of enjoyment you can. The wishing ritual tells you that you would enjoy this moment so much more if it weren't for counting. In the middle of working on your OCD, it isn't reasonable to expect to have an 80 percent level of enjoyment (100 percent may be a nice wish, but no one gets that). You always focus on what you are missing, so whatever small joys there are you miss. Part of becoming free is learning to experience whatever moments of pleasure there are, even if it is only a brief moment every now and then. By practicing this, you are beginning to learn to live in the "here and now," but as I noted above, none of us will ever be perfect in this.

The core of your response prevention for pure counting is very simple. The more important issue is what you can do to support your response prevention, remembering that you are not trying to control automatic counting.

RESPONSE PREVENTION GUIDELINES FOR PURE COUNTING

1. Delay no activities because of feeling the need to count.
2. Do not engage in conscious counting.
3. Use Distraction and Refocusing if you feel you won't do step 1 or 2. Make sure that you listen to your therapy scripts during this time.
4. When possible, do not look directly at what you are trying to count. For example, counting tiles on a ceiling or floor requires you to look up or

down. Counting tiles on a wall could pose a greater problem, but if you aren't moving, you may be able to focus your attention elsewhere, such as on a book or another person. If you are walking, you could look at the people in front of you rather than at the ground or a wall.

5. Where else can you direct your attention? Sing aloud to yourself, talk to the people around you, or listen to music, an audiobook, or a script recording or CD. These latter options become especially important if you aren't in a position to avoid looking at what you count.

6. You can also try rapidly counting or reciting random numbers (you could also do this with the alphabet, either in order, or randomly) aloud. This will probably interfere with both conscious and automatic counting, and it will only become a problem if such counting becomes a driven ritual. If this happens, don't despair. The fact that your ritual has transformed doesn't mean you did something to make yourself worse. You will just have to modify your exposure and response prevention.

Counting can play a secondary role for those rituals that you feel must be repeated a certain number of times to be done correctly. The goal of doing this may be nothing other than reaching a specified number, such as going in and out of a doorway four times to prevent harm coming to your family. Or it may be in the service of another goal, such as feeling sure the stove is off if you look at it four times. In some cases, the number chosen is random in that it has no other meaning for the sufferer. For others, there are "lucky" numbers: either specific, such as 3 or 7, or a category, such as all even numbers or numbers divisible by 3, or numbers whose digits add up to the right number (for example, for 21, the digits 2 plus 1 equals 3). You may also have "unlucky" numbers that you feel you need to avoid.

When it comes to lucky and unlucky numbers, counting can become a part of ordering. For example, if 4 is your lucky number and 3 is unlucky, you will try to make sure that none of your belongings is grouped in threes, whether that means a pile of three shirts in a drawer, three pictures on the wall, or three place settings at a table. You may or may not be able to tolerate seeing or hearing the actual number 3. With regard to your lucky number, you will try to turn all 3's into 4's. So you would hang a fourth picture on the wall or set a fourth place at the table. Combined this way, counting and ordering neutralize bad luck through magic.

For some people, such counting interferes with reading and conversation. When engaged in either, they may be counting words, syllables, or letters in a sentence. The goal of this may have no purpose other than counting, or it may be to avoid or to find a way to "fix" a sentence with a bad number in it. Anyone without this problem would think that this would make communication or reading impossible, but as sufferers with this know, they may be tortured, but they are able to hide it.

Having lucky and unlucky numbers is part of a larger obsessional set in the same way that ordering and symmetry for the sake of "perfect" appearance were part of a larger set of obsessive rules for perfect appearance. In this case, the obsessional set is lucky or unlucky things. I knew a man with a checking problem who wouldn't lock his front door when leaving home until there were no red cars in sight. Some of you may not turn a page in a book until you find a "good" word to look at first. As with OCD, anything you can imagine can be part of this set.

Exposure to lucky or unlucky numbers is straightforward. The overriding principle for exposure is to find ways to arrange your life around the "wrong" numbers. Below are some specific suggestions for doing this.

Exposure Suggestions for Counting and "Lucky" or "Unlucky" Numbers

1. If seeing sets of objects is part of your OCD, group objects in the wrong way—for example, if 2 is lucky and 3 is unlucky, group items in threes rather than twos.

2. If seeing your unlucky number is a problem, use red dots to put it as many places as you can. For example, if 3 is unlucky, put a Post-it on your TV that says 3. On your wristwatch, place a small red-dot label with 3 written on it. For some sufferers, just knowing that an unlucky number is on them is disturbing. You can write 3 or put three dots on your skin where no one will see it.

3. Do activities on the "wrong" number, whether this is an unlucky number or simply not your lucky number. For example, if you won't turn off your TV until someone has said a sentence with an even number of words, turn it off at the first word of a sentence.

4. Use the random technique to time when to engage in activities. In the above example, rather than making turning off the TV dependent on a

speaker, do the following: When you decide to turn off the TV, put your hand on the off switch of the TV or controller. Look at your watch and turn off the TV when the second number or second hand is at a previously decided upon "wrong" place. This could be an unlucky number. If odd numbers have no special meaning, you could turn it off as soon as the seconds are on an odd number. This way, turning off the TV becomes independent of the speaker. While doing this, start talking aloud to interfere with being able to count the speaker's words. If by chance you are aware that the TV was turned off at what would be a ritually "right" time, do not repeat the exposure.

5. Put wrong groups of dots around your house, such as three dots on the corner of your TV screen.

6. Make an MP3 recording or CD that simply repeats your unlucky number every ten to forty seconds.

7. If you are counting spoken or written syllables, words, or letters, have a therapy script playing either random numbers or one that repeatedly counts to the wrong number. Again, if 3 is your unlucky number, the therapy script would keep rapidly repeating "one, two, three, one, two, three . . ."

8. Have script materials for any feared consequences that you have for imaginal exposures.

The response prevention guidelines for counting when lucky or unlucky numbers are involved are a little different than those provided for pure counting. The major difference is that some of the exposure suggestions will preempt response prevention guidelines. For example, rather than preventing yourself from engaging in an activity before you count, now you would be working on trying to engage in the activity when the count is wrong.

Movement Rituals

In turning to movement rituals, you will find that ordering in the form of symmetry and counting in the form of lucky or unlucky numbers often play a role. These are all part of a broader category of what makes a movement "right." First, there will be the actual form of the movement, whether it be foot tapping, head movements, or winking. The "just right" feeling usually determines whether or not a movement was carried out correctly. For many of you, carrying out movements correctly means moving symmetrically (for example, tapping your left hand followed by tapping your right hand) or repeating a movement a set number of times or even a set number of sets (for example, four groups of four). Of course, as you know from experience, even when a ritual requires symmetry or a certain number of repetitions, the "just right" feeling often comes into play. You may want to tap both your left and right foot three times each, but if one of those taps doesn't feel "just right," then you will feel compelled to start the set over from the beginning.

In its most severe form, every action you take becomes part of a ritual. So as you get ready to get out of a chair, you say to yourself, *if my right foot touches the floor first, it means I want my mother to die.* So you stand up, making sure to put your left foot down first, but now there is the problem of which foot you will make your first step with, which foot will be the first to cross the threshold of the door, which hand will turn the light off, what the first words out of your mouth will be, and so on. With every moment comes another torturous decision, sometimes complicated by the idea that you didn't put your left foot down "just right" when you left the chair, so you have to start over.

Movement rituals usually "magically" ward off some disaster of concern, as specific as harm to your loved ones or as vague as "things won't be right." If the latter describes you, it is worth spending some extra time to further explore any potential meanings that making wrong movements might have for you. Often, there are consequences that just aren't the more common, obvious ones. Using Downward Arrow, ask yourself what would happen or what would it mean if, for the rest of your life, you never felt that your movements were "right." Some of the more subtle feared consequences reported by others include not feeling like themselves or not being natural. If one of these is yours or if you have discovered a different one, what would happen or what would it mean if it were true? What if you never felt like yourself? Is there another disaster underlying these, or is this as far as you can go? Wherever Downward Arrow ends for you, the result should be included in your feared consequences script.

Exposure and response prevention for movement rituals should be implemented the usual way, starting with the items that are lower on your hierarchy. During your exposure sessions, it is important to do as many different exposures as you can—this is more important than how difficult each one is. The reason for this is that you can remember only so many "mistaken" movements. Creating an immersive environment of exposure for movement becomes a function of performing too many exposures to remember. Even if you remember the last five or six out of thirty, you still forgot the others. This means that you are learning to let go of rituals, even though you may feel the same amount of anxiety and urges to ritualize that you felt in the past. The difference is that in the past, you may have avoided so much of life that you only engaged in two or three activities, which made remembering any "mistakes" easy opposed to now, engaging in many activities and learning to forget. Perhaps you are uneasy about what you have forgotten. This is normal, but try to remind yourself that this is your goal in the long run.

When movement rituals are pervasively present every second, exposure and response prevention needs to be modified. For you, response prevention would simultaneously be exposure and constant. To move "wrong" every moment of the day takes an incredible effort, more effort than is possible. A more achievable exposure-and-response-prevention goal is choosing to do up to two hours of intensive exposure daily and breaking these down into half-hour sessions throughout the day. During the half hour, your goal is to move as rapidly and as "wrong" as possible. Using your hierarchy, choose the places your exposure is to occur and prepare therapy scripts to listen to for each situation.

Your therapy script should include general instructions of what you are supposed to be doing during your exposure. It is important to speak quickly, because during your exposures you want to move quickly. Having a helper who can encourage you by being a live therapy script can be very helpful, as long as the helper doesn't deviate from your general script by asking you to do more than you planned.

Ideally, your feared consequences should be included in your script. However, if you feel this would be too hard to listen to when you are first starting, then they can be included in a watered-down form. For example, saying "I might be causing my mother to die with this next step" would be replaced with "I have to take these risks to get better, even though I don't know what will happen."

The following "Exposure for Pervasive Movement Rituals" script is from Mark, who questioned the potential of every movement to cause harm to his family. His rules are too complicated to detail here, but you will be able to understand the instructions he used for his exposure session. His planned exposure was a half hour of walking from his home to a nearby park. This script was used early in his treatment. It contains exposure instructions to move "wrong" ("look for cracks, and step on these"), but his feared consequences aren't directly stated.

> *Make sure I always lead off with my left foot. This includes going through doors, stepping off and onto curbs, and going up steps. Look for cracks, and step on these with my left foot. When I pass poles or street signs, look to the right and pass them on the left. Anything may happen, but I need to get over this problem. It doesn't matter if I want everything to be safe—this is what I need to do now. Make sure I don't touch things twice with my right hand when I pass them. And sing. Listen to this script and sing. I'm not supposed to do any of those word rituals to undo anything. I need to learn to live with risk. And at the park, touch all swings with my left hand first. Sit in each swing, lift my feet, and then get off the swing with my left foot first. Always left, no matter what might happen.*

The script continued for another few minutes. Did you notice how the references to his feared consequences were indirect and mild? You know that he feared harm coming to his family only because I told you. As therapy progressed, he allowed himself to listen to more difficult scripts. Below is a later version of the Pervasive Movement Rituals script, which included more details of his feared consequences.

> *When I leave home, I have to make sure that I start with my left foot, so Mom might die. Always do this, whether going through doors or stepping off and onto curbs—use my left foot to risk my mom's life. I have to let her have a stroke so I can have a life. This problem has tortured me for too long. If I'm terrible for doing this, then I'll have to let myself be terrible. Look right when I come to street signs and poles, even if it causes Dad to have a car accident. Pass them on the left, even though the car accident may leave him a bloody mess. And sing. I'm supposed to sing quiet songs about Dad and Mom dying while I'm doing this, so I don't sneak in any of those word rituals.*
>
> *Mom and Dad may die because of me, and then it will be my fault. And I have to do this and live with it to overcome my OCD. At the park, risk their deaths by touching the swings with my left hand. . . .*

Although total response prevention is very difficult to implement for such pervasive rituals, the ideal goal is still to attempt as total a response prevention as possible. While accepting that the ideal won't be realized, you can still increase the amount of exposure and response prevention that takes place through the use of red-dot labels placed strategically throughout the house and on your person (such as the center of your watch or your thumbnail). These will serve as reminders to do a quick exposure whenever you notice a dot. Having a general therapy script playing constantly that reminds you to engage in exposure and why you want to do this, despite the consequences you will be risking, will be a tremendous help.

CONTAMINATION, checking for fires, reading rituals, ordering, and movement—with a few exceptions, the obsessive-compulsive symptoms discussed in the last three chapters have focused on events that take place in the external world. But, as you know, for almost every OCD presentation, much of the "action" takes place in your own mind. In the next chapter, the focus will be on obsessions that arise almost purely from your own thoughts. There you will find advice for coping with some of the mental ritualizing you have been engaging in. For those of you tormented by violent thoughts or questions about your sexuality or religion, the chapters you have read thus far have likely provided you with some ideas about how to design the behavioral components of your exposures, but the next chapter will address the core of your OCD concerns.

Chapter 12

The Primary Mental Obsessions:
It Really Is All in Your Mind

All obsessive fears originate within your mind. In my work with OCD, I have noticed that there are three traits that characterize almost all of you: creativity, imagination, and above-average intelligence. Creativity, because the core of creativity is asking "What if?" You are experts at asking "What if?" Imagination is the ability to think about a subject so vividly that it feels real. You scare yourselves to death. As for intelligence, if one accepts the basic premise of your OCD fears, the complex systems you devise are logical.

These traits serve you in many ways that you probably appreciate. Many of you are the ones to whom friends come for advice. They do this because you understand. And you understand because, when you listen to others, you can suspend your own reality and judgment to creatively imagine what it would be like to be in your friend's position.

But creativity is not something you can turn on and off or use only for fun. The evolutionary purpose of creativity is not for art. The evolutionary purpose of creativity is survival: *Where's the tiger and how can I make sure it doesn't get me? Where's the tiger and how can I get it?* In the modern world, survival isn't simply physical, it's also psychological. For a moment imagine that there were tigers loose in your neighborhood. If for some reason you left your house, you would be constantly searching for tiger signs. The same happens with your psychological survival. If you are questioning your morality, then you will be constantly scanning your mind for dangers, for seemingly immoral thoughts. The what-ifs of creativity will focus on anything important to you; creativity is your personal danger detector, whether it be illness, the death of family members, the nature of God, or your capacity for violence. Your creativity will lead you to be bombarded with all kinds of thoughts. And this is normal, that is, to think any thought is normal, no matter how bizarre or perverse you judge it to be. It is these kinds of thoughts that become the obsessive concern of the primary mental obsessions.

But having such thoughts is not the problem. Thoughts of killing your baby, blasphemy, and the nature of your sexuality are all normal thoughts. What makes this an OCD problem isn't having the thoughts, but what you do about them. For those without OCD, one of these "terrible" what-if thoughts will occur, and the non-sufferer will either think about it or dismiss it. And you do the same for what-if thoughts that are not the focus of your obsessional fears. For those that are, you think to yourself, *What if "x" were true? Oh no! That's terrible! I don't want to think that! What does that mean?*

Your thoughts become the focus of your OCD if you try to stop thinking them, if you try to control them, or if you decide you must know what they mean about you. Some of you may want to argue that the nature of your thoughts can't be normal and that you must be wrong about the problem, because you know you have these thoughts more often than "normal" people.

Actually, studies examining the thoughts of OCD sufferers and non-sufferers have found no difference in the content of the thoughts. As for the frequency of your thoughts, that is accounted for by your attempts not to have them. For example, if you were out in your car today, were you aware of how many red cars you saw? Do you know if you saw any? Unless this is the focus of your OCD, you would answer that you probably saw red cars but weren't really aware of it. Now imagine that I ask you to go driving tomorrow but to make sure that you don't notice any of the red cars on the road. If you try to do that, you know that you will notice almost every red car on the road. It is the same with your thoughts. You desperately don't want to think about something, but to do this you have to be on guard for it—you have to look for it. *I have to make sure I don't think about . . .* and before the sentence is done, the thought is back in your mind.

Asking non-sufferers if they have such thoughts isn't always helpful. Because they aren't trying to avoid such thoughts, they very well might not notice them, the same way you usually don't notice the red cars on the road.

In treating the primary mental obsessions, the goal is *not* to stop the thoughts or ever know what they mean about you. The goal is to learn to be mindful about the thoughts; to let them be there without overwhelming anxiety. That is normal.

The category of primary mental obsessions has also been referred to as *pure-O,* meaning pure obsession, suggesting that both obsession and compulsion are entirely mental, with no behavioral rituals or avoidances. Many sufferers with primary mental obsessions are concerned that there is no treatment for pure-O for two reasons. First, believing that they have no behavioral components to their OCD, they assume that there aren't any exposures they can do.

If you are worried about this, you'll be happy to know that you are wrong. There is exposure for the primary mental obsessions: imaginal exposure. In addition, although there may be some of you who truly suffer from pure-O, most of you will have some behavioral components that you have hopefully identified in your self-assessment. There are probably situations that you avoid for fear of bringing out your obsessions. You may also "freeze" yourself and refuse to engage in any activity whenever you are trying to "work out" your obsessional concern.

The second reason many of you may despair is that you have read elsewhere that the primary mental obsessions can be harder to treat. They can be more difficult to treat, but far less so than what you have read suggests. The key to overcoming the primary mental obsessions is understanding *why* they are harder to treat. Recall that the more totally immersive and inescapable you can make your recovery program, the more effective treatment will be. This is why those of you with contamination obsessions do best in treatment—your environment can be totally contaminated, leaving you with no choice but to stay with treatment.

The potential problem with mental obsessions is that they are portable— since most of the compulsions are mental, they can go wherever you go. This means that you have the potential to slip into your obsessive-compulsive nightmare anytime and anyplace. The way exposure and response prevention was instituted in the past, the amount of daily time you spent working on your obsessions had difficulty competing with the urges to ritualize during the rest of the day. Recalling the advertising campaign metaphor, the pro-OCD group has the budget of Pepsi. However, through extensive use of recorded therapy scripts that you can listen to constantly, you can win this competition. Implemented this way, treatment of the primary mental obsessions can almost be made as pervasive and immersive as the treatment of contamination.

Of course there are others, and mental rituals play a role in almost every form of OCD. By the time you come to this chapter's end, you will be able to adapt the information here to any of your mental rituals.

In designing your recovery program, you will find that the hardest part of overcoming your primary obsessive concerns is answering *the question,* because it will feel like the risks involved are too great to dare. I hope you will take the risk; I believe it is worth it. Although I can't promise you that your worst nightmare won't come true, I can say that you are not at any greater risk than the rest of humanity.

Finally, many of you are conflicted about involving your family in your treatment. If you have already told your family about the nature of your OCD, enlisting their help means letting them know what they can do. Families have the potential to play a very supportive role in your treatment. Guidelines for how they can help are provided in Chapter 14, Building Supports for Recovery: Beyond Exposure and Response Prevention. If you are married and want your family to help, you should consult with your spouse before involving your children in your treatment. If you are living at home with your parents and want to involve your family, consult with your parents before involving your younger brothers and sisters.

On the other hand, some of you may find the content of your obsessions so embarrassing or shameful that you've completely hidden your problems from your family, or they only know that you have some kind of OCD problem. If this describes you, should you involve them? This is a very individual question. Do you believe they are capable of understanding your problem? Do you think reading this book or having some joint sessions with a therapist would help them understand, or are you too embarrassed to let that happen? There is no right answer. You will have to decide (or make your best guess about) what you think will work best for you. If you want to exclude some or all of your family members from your recovery program, then your greatest problem will be figuring out a way to keep your recovery materials private.

The primary mental obsessions discussed in this chapter are:

1. Violent Obsessions
2. Sexual Obsessions
3. Relationship Obsessions
4. Religious Obsessions
5. Neutral Obsessions
6. Obsessions About Obsessing

Violent Obsessions

Most violent obsessions take the form of thoughts such as: *What if I were to stab my wife?* or *What if I threw my baby out the window?* There are generally three major feared consequences that accompany these thoughts, either separately or in combination:

1. These are terrible, depraved thoughts, and I want them to stop.
2. Only a terrible, depraved person would have these thoughts. Am I such a person?
3. Does having these thoughts mean that I will act on them?

The main ritual used for these thoughts is analyzing and figuring out in an attempt to prove to yourself that these thoughts don't mean anything. You can endlessly obsess: *Maybe I'll kill my wife. But I don't want to do that; I'm not that kind of person. But then why did I have the thought? Do I have a secret urge to hurt her? How do I know I won't hurt her? But I love her.* Your efforts to know this answer are endless.

You may come up with other rituals to "protect" those around you, such as saying certain phrases to somehow counteract your thoughts. Having read that people with OCD rarely act on their obsessive fears, you begin to obsess whether your thoughts are really OCD—if they are, you feel relieved, because now you know that you won't hurt another person; if they aren't, then you have to worry. And what if they are OCD thoughts, but you are the exception to the rule? And still you ask yourself, *Why do I have these horrible thoughts?*

Someone once asked Stephen King why he wrote about such terrible subjects. His answer was simply, "What makes you think I have a choice?" He was not implying that he has OCD. His answer was his way of saying that issues of good and evil, and the nature of the evil that dwells within all of us, are interesting to him. He writes stories about these because they are important questions to him. To give his stories a reality, he has to put himself inside the most evil of characters and try to be them. He would do this whether or not he was a writer. And we know that these issues are of interest to everyone. How? Because his books are bestsellers and are read by millions.

We think about the nature of good and evil and our capacity for it in an effort to understand evil. In part, we do this in hopes of being able to recognize evil and then to either feel safe or to protect ourselves from it. We also do this because none of us are pure and because our feelings in most situations are mixed. Everyone experiences thoughts, urges, and feelings that they find unacceptable. This is part of being human.

Each of the three feared consequences on the previous page dictates a recovery goal you need to embrace if you are ever to cope with your violent obsessions. The first is one I cannot repeat too often in this chapter: The goal of recovery is not to stop the obsessions from happening or to make them less frequent. It is true that they may become less frequent when you stop caring about them, but this isn't the same as the thoughts never occurring. You need to decide that you want to learn to live with them.

What do the thoughts mean about you? It is true that these thoughts are common to everyone. For example, when holding a small baby, it is normal to notice how small and helpless it is, and how easy it would be for you to hurt it. The person without OCD accepts this and may even have the thought *I could throw this baby against the wall.* But you won't hear them say this for one of two reasons. First, because non-sufferers aren't concerned by such thoughts—their occurrence is a minor event that is easily forgotten. The other reason they keep such thoughts secret is because of their concern about what others would think of them, even though they themselves have no fears about having such thoughts. If you believe that having such thoughts is evil, then your recovery goal is to accept being as evil as the rest of us. Do you have a real urge to follow through with the violent act? The answer is yes, your urge is probably as strong as it is for the rest of us. Remember, we all have mixed feelings, so urges not to follow through are also present and probably greater. If you begin to obsess about whether or not your violent urges are greater, then for the sake of your recovery, you will have to accept the possibility that they are greater.

Does having the thoughts mean you might act on them? You and I will never know. For example, how can I know whether or not I'll go crazy tonight—that I'll lose my mind, get my hunting knife, and then slice and dice my wife? I don't have a conscious plan to follow through with this now, but by definition, going crazy isn't something one plans for. What can I do to prevent this? Nothing. Just like you, I can do nothing. I'm stuck going to bed and just hoping I won't kill her. If I do kill her, I will have to cope with it in the morning. It will be terrible, my life will be ruined, I'll be consumed by guilt, I'll probably go to prison, and you will definitely not want to follow any of the advice in this book. But I have to accept that I might kill her, even if it isn't likely, because there is no way to guarantee with 100 percent certainty that I won't. My feelings of not wanting to kill her at this moment may make such action on my part improbable, but never certain. What would happen if I murdered her tonight? In the morning, one of two situations would be true. I've come back to my senses and will feel horribly guilty. I will need to be locked up, preferably in a good mental health facility, because I don't know what happened. At some point I would even need to forgive myself, since I apparently went crazy. Forgiving myself wouldn't mean that I no longer felt guilty or sad about the loss, but coming to an understanding that my behavior had been out of my control. It would mean finding a way to continue to make the best of my life, whether it be within an institution or when I was set free.

The other possibility is that morning comes and I'm still crazy and have no regrets. Guilt won't be a problem in this scenario. However, to make the best of my remaining life, I'll either have to find a good way to escape or, if and when I'm caught, find a way to make the best of my life in prison.

I don't think either of the above scenarios is likely, but not likely is not impossible. The fact that I don't worry about this doesn't mean I am less at risk than you. And if it were to happen that I engage in either of the above scenarios, I would urge you to continue to follow the advice in this book; I'm just one of many OCD experts, most of whom will give you the same advice I'm giving you. Your goal, like all of humanity's, is learning to accept that you will never know for sure whether or not you will act on your violent thoughts, even though you hope you won't.

Is there ever a real concern if you have violent thoughts? I would be more concerned about your potential for violence if you had no doubts that the violence that comes into your mind would be fun or exciting to do, that torturing people to see the terror in their eyes as you slice through them is something you wish to experience. A second cause for concern is if you are absolutely sure you hear voices or receive messages encouraging you to engage in any kind of violence. Finally, if you have a history of actually engaging in the same kind of behaviors that you are constantly thinking about, you are probably at risk to repeat this behavior. If you have any of the above and have no doubts, then you must seek professional help, and following the advice here would not be helpful and could be harmful. If you don't have the definite feelings or history described above, then your concerns fall within the OCD diagnosis. However, falling within the OCD diagnosis doesn't mean you won't engage in violence. Remember, the goal isn't to be reassured, but to take a risk. I am saying that without the above thoughts, the odds of your committing violence are lower and you are at the same level of risk as the rest of us, which is not zero.

Therapy scripts for imaginal exposure will be your main method of helping yourself to overcome the fear and anxiety caused by your violent obsessions. The material that needs to be recorded is the very material you are afraid to think about. Preparing your scripts will be the beginning of your exposure. To cope with this, you will probably be making a series of therapy scripts over time with later scripts containing more graphic descriptions of your feared consequences. Because of this, I would suggest that you have two hierarchies, one for behavioral exposures and the other for imaginal exposure material. As you progress through treatment, you will record new scripts, including more and more of the higher-level content.

Examine Sam's imaginal hierarchy on page 226. He had violent obsessions that mainly focused on hurting his family. He was less fearful about the possibility of him hurting people outside his family. Notice how the higher items tend to be more specific and graphic. Think about your own violent obsessions and what your hierarchy would look like. For some of you, graphic description of the violence is part of your OCD concerns. For others, such graphic details are repulsive and distasteful but not a part of what you obsess about. Finding lower-level items for the imaginal hierarchy may be very difficult for you. Sam, for example, had violent obsessions about killing his wife and son. In the portion of his hierarchy that appears here, harming his son is a lower-hierarchy item than murdering his son. However, when he used the word *harm,* he did not mean inflicting a lesser injury.

For him, harm still meant killing, but it was an easier word for him to use. Thus, the idea of kicking or punching his wife or son was not a part of his obsessions. If it had been, the hierarchy might have included a number of lower-level items in which he imagined himself inflicting lesser harm on them.

Three therapy scripts are provided on the next few pages to illustrate the difference between one you would use in the beginning of your recovery program and ones you would use later in your recovery. The very first script is one

Sam's Hierarchy of Violent Obsessions for Imaginal Exposure

Item	SUDs
Images of Me	
Stabbing my four-year-old son and hearing his screams	100
Stabbing my wife and hearing her screams	99
Stabbing my four-year-old son	97
Stabbing my wife	96
Standing over my sleeping four-year-old son with a big knife	92
Standing over my sleeping wife with a big knife	90
Thoughts of Me	
Killing my four-year-old son	88
Killing my wife	87
Harming my son	85
Harming my wife	84
Images of Me	
Stabbing a stranger	80
Harming a stranger	76
Thoughts of Me	
Stabbing a stranger	72
Harming a stranger	70

you would use if you haven't yet decided that you are willing to confront your violent obsessions. Using this script would be your way of trying to help yourself decide to design and follow through with a recovery program. If you choose to do so, you may find that you don't need to use the following script, "Preparing Yourself for Treatment of Violent Obsessions."

I find it so hard to imagine that I am supposed to allow these horrible ideas to stay in my head and never know what they will mean or if I will do them. It really doesn't seem possible to live with such thoughts in my head. But I have been suffering with this for so long. Look at all that I've lost while having this problem (include some facts from your Cost-Benefit Analysis). *It's not like I get to enjoy anything with this problem haunting me. This book says I might do the exposures and live with only 40 percent enjoyment. That's more than I get now, especially when I avoid things like* (include same or more facts from your Cost-Benefit Analysis here). *The worst of it is, the book is right. I don't know a way to ever be certain. There is some truth in the idea that all certainty is an illusion. I hate that. But reality doesn't care what I hate. Everyone hates uncertainty. I live with it in other parts of my life. I accept the possibility that "x"* (include uncertainties you do live with, for example, if you don't have contamination concerns or fears of being attacked by others) *could happen. That is what I'm going to need to do with my violent obsessions. I'm going to have to learn how to let the thoughts be there. Treatment sounds horrible, but so is my life right now. Look how I am when I'm in my worst state. I really do want to live in the present, because that's all any of us can have.*

If you need to use the script above, I would urge you to read it out loud onto a recording device and then let it play throughout the day as a constant reminder that there is hope and help. If you haven't yet decided to learn to accept the uncertainties that go along with recovering from violent obsessions, you may want to skip past the two scripts below, because they will provoke anxiety.

The first is a therapy script that you might use earlier in your exposure program. Notice how the references to the violent obsessions are vague and general. This script could be used for almost anyone with violent obsessions, since neither the type of violence feared nor the target(s) is specified.

SCRIPT

Lower-Exposure Hierarchy Imaginal Therapy Script for Violent Obsessions

There is nothing I can do to make sure that I won't harm anyone I love. It could happen at any of the times I'm concerned about, and the best strategy I can come up with is to hope it doesn't happen, knowing full well that hope won't prevent anything. If I do any of the things I'm concerned about, that's when I will have to cope with the consequences. I hate the thoughts, but I have to learn to let them be there. That's why I'm listening to this now and following through with all the exposures. I'm making them inescapable. If this pushes me over the edge, then I'll have to let that happen, because my way felt like I was going over the edge anyway. I have to remember why I'm doing this. I want to be able to enjoy life and my family. The way my life is now, I have nothing but pain. If I'm a terrible person for having these awful thoughts, then I have no choice but to be a terrible person. I don't know how, but I'm going to have to learn to be a happy terrible person, keeping my fingers crossed that I don't act on my fears. If I reject treatment, I am harming my relationships with my kids and my spouse. Against that definite harm, I will have to risk having them hurt by whatever I do.

You also may have noted that the therapy script didn't say that the sufferer would commit any harm. Your potential actions and feared consequences should always be put in the form of "maybe" happening as opposed to "definitely" happening. There are two reasons for this. First, your fear is not that you will definitely harm anyone, but that you might harm someone. Therefore, statements of what you *might* do are closer to what you actually fear. The second reason is related to the first and to all of OCD: Your goal in treatment is learning to live with uncertainty. You should make sure not to include any statement of reassurance in the script that might undermine your exposure. Among statements to be avoided are: "I know I don't really want to hurt anyone" and "This is just OCD."

Notice how, in the higher-hierarchy script on the next page, the worst feared consequences can be included in the script while still maintaining the position that the violence is a possibility, not a definite.

Higher-Hierarchy Imaginal Therapy Script for Violent Obsessions

There is no way for me to truly protect my wife and son from myself. I just have to live with the possibility that, just like everyone else, I could lose control and kill both of them tonight. If I do lose control, I might get my sheath knife and stab my little son in his sleep and then go to my wife and stab her before she has a chance to defend herself. Living with myself afterward would be so hard—I don't know how I would be able to take it. Going through a trial, knowing I had done the most horrible thing I could think of, and then languishing in a prison with nothing to do but be tortured by what I had done. But this is the possibility I have to accept to get better. If I lose control and stab them to death, then I'll have to cope with it. For all my ritualizing, I never feel 100 percent safe. The rituals never really prove that I won't be responsible for choking the life out of my son. So I have to keep doing these exposures and listening to this script. And when I start to worry that I might really do these things, because the scripts are beginning to bore rather than horrify me, well, that's another chance that I have to take. I want to be able to live in the present and enjoy my life rather than worry about what might happen. There are so many things I want to enjoy (insert items from your Cost-Benefit Analysis), *and I'm sick of this stupid OCD having its way with me.*

Although the bulk of your work will be with imaginal exposure, there are likely behavioral components to your obsessive fears, usually in the form of situations or cues you avoid because they remind you of your violent obsessions. On page 230 there is a list of cues that sufferers have reported to me over the years. Do any of these belong in your hierarchy?

As you prepare for treatment, prepare a collection of items you'll need. Rent or buy both violent films and books. Probably there is, within your own mind, a hierarchy of such material, in which *The Silence of the Lambs* with its intense graphic violence is going to be more fearful to you than *There's Something About Mary,* a film in which the minor violence that occurs is not memorable to most people. Some violent books you may find useful are *Mind Hunter* by John Douglas and Mark Olshaker, a book about real-life serial killers; *The Silence of*

Sample Hierarchy Items for Violent Obsessions

Newspapers
Television news
Police shows
Violent pictures
Looking at a violent book
Reading a violent book
Looking at a violent movie (for example, in its case)
Watching a violent movie
Anything red (like blood)
Police
Children (as potential victims)
Potential weapons, including knives, scissors, screwdrivers, hammers,
    guns, and rope
Words associated with violence or violent images, including *death, kill,
    blood, sharp, stab, bombs, poison, children, victims*
Places associated with violence or where violence might occur, including
    malls, playgrounds, and police stations

the Lambs by Thomas Harris; and most Stephen King books. Collect pictures and newspaper headlines, and put disturbing words on cards—during treatment, these can be placed around your house. For places where reminders need to be subtle, use red-dot labels.

In the beginning of your treatment, the lower-hierarchy reminders should be placed around your environment as pervasively as possible. Obviously you can't leave guns and knives around if there are children in the house. On the other hand, you can carry a penknife. You can use big scissors to cut coupons while watching TV with your children. Violent books, such as *The Silence of the Lambs,* can be left out in plain sight.

If posting violent words—such as *death, guns,* and *murder*—is too awkward, you can use the trusty red-dot labels as a reminder to think of five such items whenever you see one. Alternatively, you could put a single letter on different ones, such as a *G* to remind you of guns. As your treatment progresses, you will move up the hierarchy by exposing yourself to items such as watching and reading the news, watching violent movies, and going to places that you've previously avoided. Play your therapy scripts while engaging in these exposures. You can also make a recording that simply says whatever words you usually avoid hearing, such as *kill, maim, death, knives, dead bodies, stabbing my family, blood.*

If you are the kind of person who has never liked violent movies or books, even before you had OCD, you still need to do these exposures. The goal of treatment isn't to change your taste in entertainment (although it's okay if that happens), but to help you overcome a problem, and it is not unlike taking a bad-tasting medicine.

Usually analyzing and figuring out is the main ritual used with violent obsessions. You may have other mental rituals that function as distractions to try to force the thoughts out of your mind or to reassure you that the thoughts don't mean anything. These might include rituals such as thinking a "good" word or counting. Implementing response prevention for mental rituals is not the same as using it for behavioral rituals. Just as I can't tell you to stop thinking about your fears, I can't tell you to stop rituals that have likely become automatic. Instead, the goal is to put the mental rituals in the background. You may not be able to stop mental ritualizing, but you don't have to actively work to try to fulfill its OCD demands. Response prevention of mental rituals is really exposure. This is one of the reasons for suggesting that you listen to your therapy scripts as often as possible. If you are not in a public place, start reciting your therapy script material or forbidden words aloud. Doing so aloud will further interfere with your automatic mental rituals. Have a script card with you to read if you aren't in a position to listen to your scripts.

Behavioral rituals to ward off the feared consequences of violent thoughts may also be a part of your neutralizing repertoire. You may confess your thoughts to others or ask for reassurance that you won't engage in any violence. To support your response prevention, you can instruct them to give you the wrong answers, such as "Yes, I think you will kill me tonight—you're a very violent person." You may have other rituals that function magically, such as movement rituals. Ideally, your response prevention to these should be total. If you have difficulty doing this, try to use the Distraction and Refocusing techniques discussed earlier to delay your rituals. If you design a partial response prevention program, make sure that rituals occur only in response to hierarchy situations for which you have not yet started exposure.

Sexual Obsessions

Unlike violence, sexuality is a part of all our lives in some form or another. How we think about our sexuality and how we experience it are central parts of how we define who we are. These definitions, though not necessarily conscious, include our ideas of what it is to be a man or a woman, what we believe is moral or immoral, and whether or not we live up to our own moral standards. Having sexual obsessions often leads to questioning the very nature of who and what you are. Questions and issues of such import are natural targets for your creativity. These feared consequences tend to be the same as those for violent obsessions:

1. These are terrible, depraved thoughts, and I want them to stop.
2. Only a terrible, depraved person would have these thoughts. Am I such a person?
3. Does having these thoughts mean that I will act on them?

As with all the primary mental obsessions, it is probably hard for you to believe that the content of your thoughts is normal and that the real problem is your attempt to stop thinking the thoughts or to prove that they aren't true. Just as violent images are not socially acceptable to discuss, neither are certain thoughts regarding sexuality—perhaps more so. After all, you might hear someone say about their child, "He made me so angry, I could kill him." But you would be shocked if someone said, "My son is just so cute, I could have sex with him." However, the fact that people don't say such things is quite different from them never having such thoughts.

Sexual obsessions tend to fall into one of three categories:

1. *Thoughts of sexually molesting others.* The usual targets of sexual obsessions about molestation are children. For men, it may also include thoughts of raping or molesting women. Much of what was written about violent obsessions will also apply to obsessions about sexual molestation. This includes the recommendations for when you should not delay seeking professional help. The guidelines for when you must seek professional help are (1) if you have no doubts that molesting others or engaging in

any kind of said violence would be fun and arousing and you wish you could fulfill these fantasies; (2) you hear voices or receive messages encouraging you to carry out such acts; or (3) you have a history of engaging in any of these behaviors. If any of these descriptions fit you, this part of the book is not for you, and it could be harmful to you and others.

2. *Thoughts of sexual desires that you consider perverted or unacceptable.* These differ from the above in that the imagined sexual behavior is consensual. The most common of these is the obsession of possibly having homosexual desires, although you consider yourself to be and want to be heterosexual. If this problem is yours, the main obsession and feared consequence is the same: *Am I gay?* The inclusion of homosexuality in this category should not be taken to imply that there is anything wrong with homosexuality—the issue is the unacceptability of the behavior to you. Conversely, I worked with a young gay woman who had obsessions that she might be straight and was worried about how this would ruin her life. Her obsessions also belong in this category, since she found heterosexual behavior unacceptable to her.

Also falling within this category are obsessions about sexual desire toward other unacceptable objects, such as animals. Such thoughts can be considered obsessions if you don't want to have them, as opposed to having no doubts that you would find such acts arousing.

3. *Thoughts about others who might be acceptable in different circumstances but seem morally wrong in your current situation.* An example of this would be a married woman who finds she is attracted to men other than her husband and believes that she isn't supposed to have such feelings.

These categories form a kind of hierarchy of acceptability, in that most people would find sexually molesting others to be worse than the sexual behaviors of the third category. Regardless of which category your obsessions fall into, you probably feel as though your thoughts are repulsive or morally unacceptable to you and that having them can't possibly be normal. Analyzing and figuring out is the main ritual most of you rely on to uncover the truth of your worst fears. But figuring out what these thoughts mean about your sexuality is contrary to the treatment goal of learning to live with uncertainty. Before you can decide to go through a recovery program, there are some facts about sexuality that you need to know. You are mistaken in believing that having these kinds of sexual thoughts must mean something about you is not right. Nancy Friday, in her groundbreaking book *My Secret Garden* examined the kinds of fantasies women have. What she found, and what we know to be true of both men and women, is that people have fantasies of every kind, which they find arousing, even though they have no intention or desire to act on them in real life. Thus, your thoughts are not evidence of what you may or may not do in your life.

This raises the question of arousal. For some of you, you simply can't stand having these thoughts, but you find comfort in having no arousal from them. But there are some of you who monitor your body for signs of arousal under the assumption that such arousal will provide you with comforting or damning proof. As you have discovered, the result of monitoring is feeling some kind of genital sensation, which leads to new mental rituals during which you try to determine whether or not the sensation you feel is sexual arousal.

The problem with your method is that thinking about sex or focusing on a part of your body is likely to lead to a sensation. You can see this with other thoughts. If you think about food and eating and focus on your mouth, you will notice salivation. If you spend time thinking about ants crawling over your body, you will begin to notice that different parts of your body feel itchy, as if there really were ants crawling on you. There are female rape victims who may lubricate and sometimes even experience orgasm. These responses are horrifying to the victims, because they in no way have any pleasure in being molested. The fact that a body responds to something is not evidence that the individual actively desires the experience.

Finally, for those in the third category, it is normal to look at other people and find them attractive. Whether you are married or single, you will notice that others are attractive. To make matters worse, as you age, there may be younger people who will look better to you than your spouse. And whether you like it or not, your body may respond with arousal. Your ability to control this is no greater than your ability not to be startled if I sneak up behind you and then grab you and scream. If your body experiences sexual arousal, then sexual thoughts will follow.

All of these facts lead to the same conclusions about sexual thoughts: You can't control your thoughts or stop them; you can't control your feelings or stop them; and you can't ever know what they mean about you or whether or not you will act on them. Choosing any of the above is choosing to continue to suffer from OCD, and, worst of all, for all of the time you spend ritualizing, you still know nothing for sure about yourself, and you still have no more protection from your worst fears coming true. The only thing you know is that there are often times when you don't act on the feelings. You don't kiss random strangers you find good-looking. You haven't killed anyone when you are enraged. All you can do is hope that you don't engage in any of the behaviors you fear, while knowing that your future is unknown.

Answering *the question* is slightly different for each of the categories. If you obsess about molesting others, then overcoming your obsessions means accepting that you can never know whether or not you will act on them. If you aren't convinced that such thoughts are normal, then you can add learning to live happily with the knowledge that you are somewhat morally depraved, and using what you have learned about all-or-none thinking to work on accepting that there are also good parts of you.

If your fears are of being gay (or of being straight if you are gay), then your goal is to accept the possibility that you may be. This form of OCD is so common that it is often referred to as H-OCD (Homosexual OCD). Although, if you are in a heterosexual relationship, then you might want to amend this to the possibility that you are bisexual. You also need to consider what this would mean. If you are married, do you have to leave your spouse if you wake up tomorrow and realize that you are gay? No, if you choose, you can continue to live a heterosexual life—it will just be second best. Some of you may be concerned about the possibility of waking up tomorrow, feeling gay, and then choosing that lifestyle over heterosexuality. I can't guarantee that that won't happen, but presumably if you woke up this way, you would be happy with the decision—otherwise, why follow through with it?

After all, you still have some attraction to the opposite sex. Your focus on your sexual responsiveness can result in difficulties in your sexual relationships with your partners. It would be a mistake to automatically assume this is proof of your changing sexuality. Unfortunately anxiety and overattention to trying to feel/experience sexual arousal will interfere with arousal. Sexual arousal is dependent upon both mindfully experiencing the sensations and having sexual thoughts whether they be focused upon your partner or an enjoyable sexual fantasy. Worrying about my sexual responsiveness and being concerned over whether or not I'm having any gay thoughts/images/fantasies will obviously interfere with my response. As with all OCD, the fact that your H-OCD may be interfering with your arousal is no assurance that you aren't gay or won't become gay. In doing exposure, your answer to *the question* needs to be: It's better to risk being gay than to live with OCD.

If your sexual obsessions focus on objects you find unacceptable, or if homosexuality is morally unacceptable to you, then your answer to *the question* will be the same as the answer for those who suffer with sexual molestation obsessions.

For those of you in the last category, the feared consequences are usually one of two: that you are an immoral person for having such thoughts or that you don't really love your significant other. This latter concern will be discussed in greater detail below in relationship obsessions. If you don't want to accept the normalcy of sexual thoughts and feelings toward others, then your treatment goal is to accept that you are morally imperfect. Either way, it is important to learn to let the thoughts and feelings be there, so that over time you'll become comfortable having such morally imperfect thoughts and feelings. If your concern is trying to figure out whether or not you love your significant other, the goal of treatment is to be uncertain. You may feel that this is unfair to your lover. I would suggest staying with your lover without confessing these feelings, unless you are 100 percent sure you want to leave the relationship now.

The imaginal exposure you do for your sexual obsessions needs to be as detailed as possible. To the extent that graphic sexual details are disturbing, they should be included. As with the violent obsessions, you can moderate the intensity of the scenes with the kinds of details you include. In addition, you can moderate the scenes' intensity with the kinds of activities and situations you imagine yourself in.

Following are a number of sample scripts illustrating this. If you haven't decided to follow through with treatment, you may find these more graphic than you are currently willing to cope with, so you should consider not reading them at this point in time. Instead, you need to write a "Script for Preparing Yourself for Treatment of Sexual Obsessions" similar to the analogous script for violent obsessions that appears on page 227.

Lower-Hierarchy Imaginal Script for Sexual Molestation

I see my son riding his bicycle, and the thoughts pop into my mind. I have to let them stay there without reassuring myself. I'll hate myself if anything happens, but that's the risk I'll have to take. I can't tell if I'm feeling anything, but it doesn't matter. If the feelings mean I'm aroused by him, then I'll just have to live being the kind of person that I am. I'm going to work at getting used to these feelings, so at least OCD won't interfere with our relationship. As it is now, I avoid being alone with my son, and it's becoming a problem between my husband and me. I have so much to lose if I don't overcome my OCD. As for what I might lose if my feelings aren't OCD, I'll have to cope with that if it happens.

Higher-Hierarchy Imaginal Script for Sexual Molestation

What if I was giving my son a bath and suddenly was overwhelmed by sexual feelings? Suppose this happened just when I was getting ready to wash his penis. If this happened, just the idea of soaping it up would excite me. I might think that because he is three, he won't know what I'm doing. But even though all of this might happen, I still have to confront my OCD and give him baths. Even though when I'm drying him off, I could start blowing raspberries on his belly and, while he is laughing, work my way down to his penis and then take it into my mouth. The sexual arousal running through me might be so overwhelming that all of this could happen. But he and I are going to have to take the risk that I'm really this kind of evil person. I'm already evil enough to have these kinds of thoughts, and I have to learn to live with this (include material from your Cost-Benefit Analysis as to why you should keep listening to this).

Lower-Hierarchy Imaginal Script for "Am I Gay?" Obsessions

I'm in Starbucks, noticing the other men getting coffee. Some of them look gay to me. I'm not sure how this makes me feel. If I'm really gay, I'll have to decide whether or not to stay married and accept second best. I really would like to leave Starbucks, but I have to stay here with these feelings and let them be here.

Higher-Hierarchy Imaginal Script for "Am I Gay?" Obsessions

I'm going to start using public restrooms again. I know that if someone is using the urinal next to me, I will notice his penis. I may even get those feelings in my penis that might be sexual arousal. If I'm really gay, the man next to me may notice. I might suddenly realize I'm gay and try to find a way to let him know. If we're both gay, we could go into the stall and I could finally feel what it is like to hold another penis. All of this may happen if I start using public restrooms again, but I'm tired of OCD ruling my life, telling me where I should or shouldn't go to be safe. I'm sick of it. If I'm going to become gay from public restrooms, then so be it. Better gay than this hell. If I end up giving strange men oral sex in restrooms, then I'll just have to learn to cope with it when it happens.

Lower-Hierarchy Imaginal Script for Sexual Feelings for Others

I find that man behind the counter attractive. These feelings might mean that I don't really love my husband. I have to stay here with these feelings, noticing that he is attractive. I'm not as good a person as I would like to be because of these feelings, but I have to accept my faults. As for my husband, I only know that I'm not leaving him today. I am not allowed to confess this to him, so that probably makes me even worse. But this is my exposure. The way my OCD was going, he would have left me if I didn't get better. At least this way it will be my choice if it comes to that.

Higher-Hierarchy Imaginal Script for Sexual Feelings for Others

I have to start going out in public again, no matter what kinds of feelings I get in my body. If I start getting sexually aroused by other men, I'm going to have to let that mean whatever it means. If I suddenly wake up and realize that I don't love my husband, then I'll have to decide what to do about our marriage and the children. If I decide to leave, then that's what will happen. Maybe I'm evil for having these thoughts, and maybe going out in public will just provide too much temptation. Men seem to want to sleep with anyone, so maybe if I find myself attracted to a man, he'll be willing to sleep with me if my arousal becomes too great to handle. We could go to a hotel somewhere, and I would get to experience the feel of a strange man's hands on my breasts (continue on with explicit details). *I don't know what I would tell my husband afterward, but I won't have to deal with it unless all this happens. All I know is that I have to start living again and not follow my OCD rules. They may feel like they keep me safe, but all they really do is keep me in prison.*

In constructing the scenes, the details of your worst fears are stated in a what-if fashion to emphasize that your goal is to take the risk of living normally. The places where the scenes take place can be items from your hierarchy. This way, listening to your script during exposure helps to interfere with any automatic mental rituals and provides support for continuing to keep up with the exposure.

The in vivo exposures can be very active for sexual obsessions. If you had difficulty coming up with items for your hierarchy, examine the sample hierarchy items provided on page 240. At this point in the book, much of what you will have to do should be obvious, including the posting of forbidden words or red-dot labels; if there are realistic reasons for not posting the words (for example, with a seven-year-old in the house, you could post words like *bath, child,* or *playground,* but you wouldn't want to post words like *rape* or *pedophile*). If there are places or situations you have avoided, then as you work your way up the hierarchy, you should go to these places. If your obsession focuses on "Am I Gay?" you can include going to gay bars and looking through the gay literature section of your local bookstore.

As part of your exposures, you can obtain pornographic literature, pictures, and movies. These can be easily found in bookstores, video stores, and on the Internet. The one exception to this is any child pornography. It is illegal to obtain this, so do not do so.

If there are no children in the home, pornographic pictures should be posted where you can see them. I have also found that some sufferers find carrying such pictures to be an exposure.

Sample Hierarchy Items for Sexual Molestation Obsessions

Giving my children a bath
Seeing my children naked
Seeing children in public
Seeing certain words, including *child, molesting, playground, pedophile,* and *rape*
Going to children's clothing stores and handling the clothing as if I was going to buy some
News stories about pedophiles
TV shows about pedophiles
TV shows with pretty children
Seeing pictures of children

The behavioral rituals you rely on are likely to be very similar to those used for violent obsessions, such as reassurance seeking, confession of your feelings, and an array of magic rituals in the form of "If I do 'x,' it means I'm gay or a child molester."

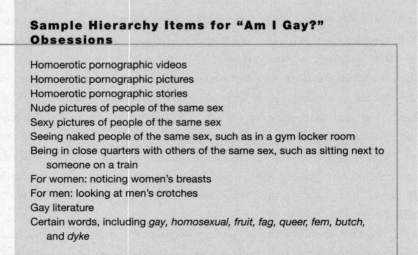

Sample Hierarchy Items for "Am I Gay?" Obsessions

Homoerotic pornographic videos
Homoerotic pornographic pictures
Homoerotic pornographic stories
Nude pictures of people of the same sex
Sexy pictures of people of the same sex
Seeing naked people of the same sex, such as in a gym locker room
Being in close quarters with others of the same sex, such as sitting next to someone on a train
For women: noticing women's breasts
For men: looking at men's crotches
Gay literature
Certain words, including *gay, homosexual, fruit, fag, queer, fem, butch,* and *dyke*

Sample Hierarchy Items for Bestiality Obsessions

Reading bestiality pornography
Pictures of bestiality
Petting animals
Looking at animals' genitals
Being licked by an animal
Hearing people mention sex with animals
Seeing animals

Sample Hierarchy Items for Sexual Feelings for Others Obsessions

All of the items below refer to members of the opposite sex who aren't your significant other.

Being sexually aroused by attractive people
Talking to attractive people
Being near attractive people
Seeing nude pictures of attractive people
Seeing pictures of attractive people
Stories of affairs
Certain words, including *sex, kissing, petting,* sexual parts of the body, *affairs,* and *divorce*

Relationship Obsessions

It would be hard to calculate how much our culture and personal lives revolve about being in a long-term intimate relationship, maintaining one, or finding someone to love. Being in a healthy, loving relationship adds so much to our lives that we often feel that this kind of relationship is something we need rather than want. Many OCD sufferers and non-sufferers often make the mistake of defining their self-worth by whether or not they are in a relationship. With so much at stake, it is no surprise that your creativity, your danger detector, would focus upon your relationship with your significant other.

There are two primary forms of what has come to be referred to as relationship obsessions. In the first, obsessive jealousy, the sufferer is obsessed with the possibility that their loved one will leave them, have an affair, or simply be attracted to others. The other form has come to be known as R-OCD for relationship OCD. In this form sufferers are not sure they love their significant other and are constantly testing themselves to try to figure this out. These two relationship obsessions are very different in how they present and how they are treated.

If you suffer from obsessive jealousy, you are constantly trying to ascertain how faithful your significant other is to you. Your concerns may focus on present and possible future actions, thoughts, and feelings you fear your lover may have toward others or even over the existence of past relationships and feelings. You will find yourself checking on your partner every way possible, from relentless questioning as to where they were/are at any given moment to going through their e-mail and cell phone to stalking them.

In addition, sufferers may put numerous restrictions upon their partner as to where he or she may go, how long they are allowed out of contact, and so on. Their partner may be accused or questioned for simply looking at a member of the opposite sex. Often when I speak to these sufferers, they feel they have evidence for their beliefs. For example, they will have caught their partner in a small lie and conclude that if they will lie about small things, obviously they will lie about big ones. In actuality, this is frequently not true. The reality is that the partner lied about something they considered small in order to avoid a huge fight—they gambled. I'm not suggesting that lying is justified, but noting that it isn't evidence that greater lies are occurring or will be concealed.

There are some critical caveats to be considered when evaluating this form of OCD that revolve around the partner's behavior. The most important of these is: Has the partner had a known recent affair? The definition of *known* is both partners agreeing that the unfaithful behavior occurred. If cheating occurred within the past year, more information is necessary to label the betrayed person's behavior as obsessive jealousy. Most betrayed partners initially will behave in ways similar to someone with obsessive jealousy. This makes perfect sense; they have been betrayed and lied to. If they are trying to stay in the relationship, their concern that they are making the right choice for themselves, that the risk is worth it, that the cheating partner won't betray them again is very scary. They want answers that they often can't have, such as why did this happen and how can I know this won't happen again.

If this is your situation, you may or may not suffer from obsessive jealousy; some of the goals of treatment would be the same as for an obsessive jealousy sufferer, but the steps you would take are different. The anxiety and depression you feel is understandable, but this doesn't mean that you wouldn't find it helpful to see a professional to help you through this trauma.

As the time between a known affair (a known affair is one in which you and your partner agree that the behavior occurred) and the present increases, the level and frequency of such questioning should begin to decrease. As more time passes, a normal response to betrayal might turn into obsessive jealousy. Again, it doesn't matter if you feel your suffering is justified, seeking professional help to find a better way to cope is still a very sensible way to take care of yourself.

A less severe offense by a significant other could be overt behavior such as overtly flirting with the opposite sex (as judged by the standards of others, without prompting from you) or openly sexual comments about others (either about their appearance or wanting to be sexually involved with them). Such behavior by a partner doesn't mean you don't have obsessive jealousy, but having that partner change his/her behavior under the guidance of a therapist would be a reasonable demand. I say "with a therapist" because no matter how accurate you may feel about your partner's behavior, potentially having this form of OCD means your perception may be distorted.

No matter what you think you have for evidence, obsessive questioning regarding your partner's fidelity will ultimately end your relationship. Your first step in recovery is answering your version of the uncertainty question: Are you willing to learn how to live with a partner where you can never be 100 percent sure that they love you the way you want them to? Trust in all relationships is never a fact, it is an educated guess and a hope. If this isn't your goal, then the only believable statement your partner can make would be admitting to an affair—any other statement is potentially suspect.

For the sake of simplicity, the exposure and response prevention we'll address will assume that a known affair has not occurred. Collect data about your rituals and avoidances and create your hierarchy. Except in rare circumstances, exposure will not involve your being with your partner and purposely asking him/her to stare at potential rivals, comment on their appearance, suggest they look better than you, or spend time speaking to them. It would involve the two of you going out in public and your learning to tolerate the fact that it is impossible for your partner to not see or to never notice someone. In your response prevention you would not chastise them for possibly looking at another; nor would you question what they were doing, or ask if they found another individual more attractive than you. As always, you can take your time going up the hierarchy; going out to dinner in public may be too high to start with.

If you have been forcing your partner to check in with you at regular intervals or you call whenever your anxiety over your partner's fidelity is high, you will use exposure to restructure this. Intervals between check-ins can gradually increase; these would include scheduled or unscheduled check-ins. If you have been having contact every thirty to forty minutes, then your initial goal might be fifty minutes. Response prevention would ultimately eliminate all questioning regarding your partner's whereabouts or level of interest in you. Remember, I am talking about obsessive jealousy when a known affair has not taken place. If a known affair has taken place, obtaining professional help should be a part of the treatment plan to help you negotiate the path between the rebuilding of trust and your obsessive jealousy.

This may seem very hard, but your goal is to learn to rely on the same data all couples do—we assume our partners want and love us, because they have apparently chosen to be with us and not someone else. We don't look for evi-

Sample Hierarchy Items for Obsessional Jealousy

Imagining my partner engaging in intercourse with someone else
Imagining my partner engaging in intercourse with a former lover
Seeing my partner speak to someone of the opposite sex
Watching a movie with my partner and the actor/actress is good-looking
Not knowing where my partner is for more than one hour
Wondering if I'm loved as much as my partner's former lover/s
Thinking about my partner's former romantic lover/s

dence that we can trust them; we wait for blatant evidence that we can't. At the top of your hierarchy is most likely imagining your partner with someone else. If the someone else is from your partner's past, it is acceptable to imagine them in the act of making love. I know this would be aversive for most people, but it is important for you to learn to live with your partner's history, with your only reassurance being that your partner is with you. If your fear is of your partner being with someone in the future, it probably makes more sense to focus on how you would cope with the situation after your discovery.

Imaginal Script for Obsessive Jealousy

I can just imagine Y in bed with his old girlfriend X (insert details of what you imagine). *Whenever I think about her, it makes me so insecure—I wonder if he wishes he was with her and if he fantasizes about being with her. Maybe I'm only second best. It's so painful to think this, but I know I can't question him, because no matter what he says, I can't have the certainty I want. I'm going to have to stay with him and hope I'm number one in his heart without ever knowing for sure. All I can do with my questions and rules is drive him away and then I'd have the same problem with whomever I met next. And if I'm really second best and he is looking for someone else, so that one day I come home to find him in bed with another woman, that is when I will have to deal with it. I don't worry about having cancer right now even though I may one day be threatened with it. This will have to be the same. I'll have to deal with it if it ever happens—I know it would be devastating for me, but my rituals don't protect me. I have him for now, he says he loves me, and I love the moments that aren't stolen from us by the real enemy—OCD* (insert material from your Cost-Benefit Analysis and what you love and enjoy about your relationship).

On the opposite end of the relationship obsessions is R-OCD; how can you be sure you love your partner? Sufferers find themselves plagued with trying to figure out whether or not they love their partner. R-OCD is particularly destructive. In an effort to be "honest," sufferers frequently confess their concern to lovers and spouses with statements like *I'm not sure I love you anymore. I don't know if I'm sexually attracted to you. I saw someone in the street and thought she was really pretty*. It is not surprising that many relationships are destroyed by such statements. Sometimes R-OCD sufferers will end their relationship; however, they do so not because they realize they don't love their partner, but in order to put an end to the interminable obsessing and anxiety. Amazingly—and thankfully—there are many R-OCD sufferers with partners who are able to recognize that this is a form of OCD.

Every relationship has ups and downs and couples who stay together do not constantly have feelings of passion and love. There will always be times when couples will aggravate one another or have an argument. If I don't have R-OCD, these feelings are not a threat to me or my relationship. But with R-OCD, you have an expectation of how you should feel and wrongly believe you should be feeling it all the time. It seems to you that everyone else knows they love their partner. You are forgetting that "normal" people use words like *certainty* and *knowing*, but that doesn't mean what they are saying is accurate. Think of a presidential election; many Republicans and Democrats are certain and feel like they know that their candidate is good for the country and that their opponent would be a disaster. Feelings of certainty and knowing don't really prove anything, so the fact that non-sufferers are so free with these words does suggest they are less anxious than you, but less anxiety doesn't necessarily reflect objectivity.

On the other hand, you are so torn about what to do—after all, this is the rest of your life and you feel so unhappy about possibly spending it with the wrong person. If the goal of treatment isn't to find out whether or not you love your partner enough to stay committed to the relationship, then what does treatment offer? There are two major steps involved in working on your R-OCD. The first is looking at the relationship and identifying any behavioral issues/conflicts that you feel are problems separate from your R-OCD; if you were sure of your love, what would you still wish for your partner to change? Behavioral issues would include constant arguing about non-OCD issues, a very controlling partner with numerous demands, one who never helps around the house, and others. There is a possibility that these issues are playing a role in your R-OCD. If necessary, seek couples counseling to resolve them. If the therapist is not familiar with R-OCD, show her this chapter, so she can use her judgment to distinguish between OCD and non-OCD problems.

Working on any real issues will probably not resolve your R-OCD, but it will improve the quality of your relationship. For some sufferers, these other issues may lead the two of you to separate because of irreconcilable differences even though your R-OCD has not been resolved. Remember, there are couples who feel love for each other but find they can't live or be together. If your differences lead to a breakup like this, you may still have to learn to cope with R-OCD in your next relationship. If the issues the two of you have are resolvable and your R-OCD remains, or if your R-OCD prevents you from being able to identify issues separate from your OCD, or if you feel there are only minor "normal" relationship issues other than your R-OCD, then it is time to turn to step 2 of working on R-OCD: designing yourself a self-help program of exposure and response prevention.

As always, your first step is answering your version of what uncertainty you need to live with. In the case of R-OCD, your goal would be learning to be in a relationship in which you were never sure if you love your partner enough or at all. For most R-OCD sufferers, the immediate response to this is "Why would I stay in a loveless relationship?" However, it is not a loveless relationship— if you are sure that you don't love your partner, then you don't suffer from R-OCD. What is true is: You might not love your partner. If you are like most sufferers, at this moment the only reason you want to leave your partner is to escape the anxiety of your R-OCD, but you don't feel 100 percent ready to leave. The recommendation for what to do about your relationship is to stay in it as long as you are not 100 percent ready to leave or not 100 percent sure you don't love your partner.

How can I be with someone I might not love is still the question that haunts you; what if there is someone better out there? For everyone in every relationship, there may be someone better out there. It is possible that all of us may be with the person who is second best or not the One—no matter how much a non-sufferer would claim to feel otherwise. Attempting to perfectly feel an emotion generally interferes with experiencing that emotion. Remember Elise's problem in Chapter 3 where she was wanting to feel natural and connected to the environment. Like you, her desire to feel a certain way assured she wouldn't experience what she wanted. Working on the goal of treatment may not answer the question you most want answered, but it will allow you to enjoy the relationship you have. As you should expect by now, accepting uncertainty means that you can't guarantee that you will want to stay in the relationship forever or that, at some point, you won't decide that you don't love your partner. Staying is your decision to work on your OCD, to learn to enjoy your relationship, and to hope this is the best guess for you to make.

But isn't this unfair to your partner? Don't they have a right to know that you might not love them? That someday you might hurt them by leaving? Shouldn't you confess your feelings and doubts so that they can be prepared? R-OCD sufferers frequently tell me that they are constantly confessing to their partners in an effort to be honest, telling them not only about their doubts but also if they see someone else who is attractive or appealing in any way and perhaps even comparing them to their partner. I could argue that your confessions are unfair, because you might love your partner, because there is always someone who may have a trait we desire that our partner does not. If your partner does not understand that you have R-OCD, your confessions will torture them rather than inform them.

It is important to realize that for everyone in a relationship, the feeling of love is not ever-constant; that there is always going to be another individual who is more attractive; and that even during lovemaking, fantasies about another are common. You don't differ from others in having these feelings. You differ in two ways. First, non-sufferers always know not to tell their partner, "Honey, that woman over there is more attractive to me than you," or "When we were making love last night I was pretending you were Georgio." The second way is the one that you find most disturbing: Non-sufferers believe they know they love their partner. Earlier in the book I noted that non-sufferers are very inconsistent in their behavior and often don't know what they are doing. They might say they would never eat off the floor but may put their pen in their mouth. In the same way, non-sufferers may always feel like they love their partner, but if you ask them how do they know or if the feeling is always as strong, they won't be able to tell you. Furthermore, for people in bad relationships, where most of their "love" for the partner is a fantasy, the feeling you want is there, but it is leading that individual to suffer. We can agree it is very comfortable to feel like you know you love your partner, but even that feeling isn't proof. In the end, you and the non-sufferer have decided you don't want to leave the relationship you are in at present.

As with all of the primary mental obsessions, almost all of your exposure will be through therapy scripts. To create your script/s you will need some information that you haven't already collected. Besides the forms you have filled out, you need to make a list of what you do enjoy or like about your partner. The purpose of this list is not to convince you that you love your partner; it is to help you focus on what is pleasant about your relationship. When creating this list, it is important to not purposely focus your attention on judging the quality of what you enjoy.

Your response prevention will focus upon all of the ways you are constantly trying to test your feelings and any ways in which your OCD involves confession rituals. R-OCD sufferers have numerous ways to evaluate and "test" their feelings, and as you have discovered, none of them work. The simplest is just trying to see if you feel love. As noted above, as soon as your OCD focuses upon trying to experience a feeling a certain way, it won't happen. You may counter that you aren't trying to experience a feeling a certain way; instead, you are trying to figure out if you have a feeling of love. There is no difference between the two; your attempt to be sure about how you feel ensures that you won't feel what you wish.

R-OCD sufferers may also try to make lists of pros and cons about their partner to help them decide what their feelings are. There may be times when such a list could inform you that you need to leave, but it won't result in clarifying your feelings.

R-OCD sufferers may start comparing their partner to others to try to measure their feelings. Do they find others more attractive or sexually arousing? Do others have traits they like? Or are you concerned that you notice other potential partners because you believe that if you are truly in love, you would never do this. Perhaps during lovemaking, pleasurable fantasies of others pop into your head. These comparisons are meaningless and will not help you. As already noted, feeling attracted to others, or even thinking about others while making love, is normal and not a positive or negative sign about your "true" feelings toward your partner.

If one of your love "tests" is noticing your arousal and passion during lovemaking, this will have the effect of interfering with your arousal. Again, it won't be possible to ascertain whether decreased arousal is due to the anxiety over your concerns or to a lack of love.

If your R-OCD rituals involve confession of any kind, whether it be the uncertainty of your feelings or thoughts of others, these have to stop immediately and totally. Your "honesty" is hurtful to your partner and your relationship. I put *honesty* in quotes, because your OCD is interfering with your making the guess that non-sufferers make. Although it is impossible to distinguish between your OCD and truly being uncertain about your relationship feelings, you are potentially lying if all of your uncertainty is OCD-based. The result could be destroying a potentially good relationship because of your OCD. It is true that whichever you choose is a risk; however, because of your constant anxiety and constant obsessing, it is highly probable you have OCD, so I'm suggesting working on that problem. Treatment is asking you to risk living forever with a partner who is not "the One." Think of the following situation: You have found the One and are married and after seven years s/he has a terrible accident and is crippled, disfigured, and can't walk. S/he is no longer the perfect One and yet most people will stay with that person, even though they are technically no longer the best, nor is your life as rosy as it was. Or a more likely example, after thirty years of marriage, your spouse will no longer be as attractive as when you were married. You will notice this and presumably you won't leave for this reason. In both these examples, your partner is no longer perfect. Your life with them is no longer perfect. Is this second best? Is this like staying with a partner you like, but no longer love, for the sake of your children? What is love? Is it simply a feeling? Is it a feeling combined with a good working relationship? I have my thoughts as to what makes up love, but I have no proof I'm right. I feel sure I love my wife and that is very comfortable, but I have no proof I'm not deluding myself. If, like you, I was to try to search for proof, I would stop living in the present and live in a fantasy world comparing what I had to an impossible template of perfect feeling. There is not a template of how you should feel all of the time. Relationships take work, and though they can be wonderful, it is also true that there are times when they will be stressful. So what can you do? Like all of life's decisions, this is another guess and the best any of us can do is to hope we find a way to make the best of our lives if the guess was wrong. Examine the following script for R-OCD and be sure you personalize it to your situation.

SCRIPT

Even though I long to feel certain about my feelings for Y, I know my OCD will only torture the both of us. Because of R-OCD (your ERP Motivators Form—page 118—should have details of specific times when your R-OCD led to painful scenes. These should be inserted here with the most painful details you can recall). *I know I'm not ready to leave Y now, so the best I can do is work on my plan for coping with never knowing. I know this may mean that Y may not be the best person for me. My only solace can be that people without this problem may believe they are with "The One," but that doesn't make it true. If I knew I was in love and Y had a debilitating accident or a long-term devastating disease, I like to believe I would stay and make the best of the situation, even though they would no longer be the same person. Certainly as we both age, neither of us will be as good-looking as younger people and yet I would not expect us to part. My ritualizing has only resulted in pain for us. My goal is to learn to focus on what I enjoy about our relationship* (insert the specifics of what you enjoy from the list you created). *I am trying to learn to do this because even in the best of relationships, couples don't feel constant romantic passion and at times will find some of their partner's behaviors aggravating. As much as I want to confess my feelings, I'm trying to behave like non-sufferers. They don't tell each other if they have a thought of what it would be like to live with another. Besides, I don't know if I'd be confessing truths or obsessions. I may never get to know whether or not I'm settling for second best or less, but I can learn to enjoy what I have. And should it occur that I someday decide to leave, it will be sad for both of us, but this wouldn't make us different from any other couple. I have to work on living and enjoying the present instead of comparing my life to the one in which I'm sure. At this time, learning to do this is the best for me and, hopefully, my partner.*

Religious Obsessions

Religion plays a major role in both our inner and outer worlds. On the international scene, religious differences still cause wars. In our inner world, questions about the nature of God, our souls, and our existence are important to countless people. It is natural for our creative curiosity to focus on the nature of our beliefs and the ways we succeed and fail to live up to the rules we claim to follow. Religious obsessions, also known as *scrupulosity,* arise from your awareness of unanswerable questions and inconsistencies in your behavior. The questions and ambiguities that are the basis of countless philosophical tracts become your enemy. For most religious obsessions, the feared consequence is usually that you are evil. It may be evil arising from the nature of your thoughts or the inconsistencies of your actions. For some of you, a variation of being evil is the possibility that you have accidentally sold your soul to the devil.

One might think that anyone suffering from scrupulosity would be a very religious individual. Surprisingly, this is not the case. Among those I have treated for scrupulosity are the most devoutly religious of their faith and those who aren't sure they believe in God. Hard as it may be to imagine, I have even worked with an atheist who had religious obsessions.

The kinds of situations that serve as triggers for these fears tend to fall into one of the following five categories: (1) blasphemous images or thoughts; (2) "immoral" thoughts or desires; (3) concerns about perfectly following religious rituals; (4) potentially sinful behaviors; and/or (5) concerns about the morality of past actions. The sample hierarchy on the following page provides representative items for each category. The source of your own obsessions may involve any or all of these categories, or you may have come up with different religious concerns. The common thread running through these is a perfectionistic demand to control your thoughts, feelings, and behavior in an effort to rigidly follow religious doctrines.

Two of the five categories—blasphemous images or thoughts and "immoral" thoughts or desires—are the most pure-O. I have put "immoral" in quotations to emphasize the impossibility of achieving the standards you've set for yourself. Controlling thoughts and feelings is always impossible. With religious obsessions, all-or-none thinking creates sin out of the most normal behaviors. Noticing that someone looks good today can become the equivalent of sexual desire, which becomes the equivalent of an illicit sexual encounter.

The attempt to perfectly follow religious doctrine turns religious rituals into triggers for both obsessions and neutralizing compulsions. For example, when reciting a prayer, your concern turns to saying the words perfectly, with perfect attention. The slightest stutter or wandering thought can be a cause to repeat a prayer. The anxious pressure exerted by your OCD just adds to the likelihood

Sample Hierarchy Items for Religious Obsessions

Blasphemous Images or Thoughts
Having sexual intercourse with God
Images of a nude Virgin Mary
Cursing at God or other religious figures
Anger at God
Thoughts of possibly praying to the devil
Destroying holy objects

"Immoral" Thoughts or Desires
Sexual thoughts in church
Sexual thoughts anytime
Anger at others
Wishing harm or death to others
Not paying enough attention during religious services
Doubts or questions about religious doctrine

Concerns About Perfectly Following Religious Rituals
Keeping kosher
Confessing
Praying

Potentially sinful behaviors
Possible praying to the devil
Possible "soul selling"
Possible lying
Possible feelings of "immoral" arousal

Concerns About Morality of Past Actions
Sexual encounters
Shoplifting
Abortions
Lies
Masturbation

of this happening. And, of course, in an attempt to feel certain, you may decide to repeat the prayer, simply because you might have made a mistake. If you are a Catholic going to confession, uncertainty makes you question whether or not you really confessed everything or explained your confession well enough for the priest to understand. As for your penance, you can turn a normal penance into a burden. For Jews, keeping meat and dairy separate in an effort to follow the normal rules of keeping kosher becomes an ordeal of worry and ritual. Perhaps you worry that the ice cream cone you ate this afternoon may have dripped onto your clothing. You may feel compelled to change your clothes before eating dinner, just to make sure you don't touch the dairy spot and contaminate your meat dishes.

If your religious obsessions include acting with perfect morality, life does become hell. The commandment "Thou shalt not kill" may be extended to insects. Consider the intense vigilance required to walk down a street and avoid hurting both real and possible bugs and to be sure that if there is a dead bug, you weren't the culprit. If you are asked if you like your friend's outfit, what do you answer if you don't like it or have mixed feelings about it? Other actions may represent potentially hidden evil desires. For example, you may worry that eating a devil's food cake is really your secret way of praying to the devil. Finally, there is the possibility that if you wish evil to come to others, you are engaging in a double sin of having "wrong" thoughts and perhaps enlisting the aid of the devil.

There is a wide array of both mental and behavioral compulsions that sufferers use to neutralize religious obsessions. The mental compulsions start with analyzing and figuring out in an effort to convince yourself that a possible "sin" is either forgivable or not a "sin" in the first place. Then there are the mental prayers and phrases, which may be said in a formulaic way that is your own, such as repeating a prayer three times, trying to hold on to a mental image of the Virgin Mary, or performing some mental penance. Each of the mental rituals can have behavioral analogues. Analyzing and figuring out becomes reassurance seeking from family members and authority figures as you try to determine whether a thought or behavior was wrong. Prayers and certain words or actions may have to be repeated until you get a "just right" feeling. Being perfectly honest may require confessions to religious authorities or to everyone close to you, so that they will know the "truth" of your thoughts.

In your effort to control thoughts or feelings, anything that might be a trigger for your obsessions might be avoided. I worked with one woman who tried to avoid seeing churches, because this would give rise to her blasphemous thoughts. Halloween is often a time of torture for many of you, with its pervasive decorations portraying devils and witches everywhere.

Although your recovery program will involve exposure and response prevention, there is no reason for any of your religious beliefs to be violated. The goal of treatment is not to undermine your faith. I will be suggesting a number of ideas that you can feel free to incorporate into your approach to your religious beliefs. For those of you who are not extremely religious, despite your religious obsessions, you may find these helpful when thinking about your faith.

If you are a very strong follower of a particular faith, you may want to consult a religious authority about the ideas I will be presenting and about your recovery program. It would be helpful if your authority is knowledgeable about OCD or is willing to read parts of this book in order to have a better understanding of the disorder. In my experience, most understanding religious authorities are easy to work with.

The most frightening aspect of your religious obsessions is the possibility that you could be dooming your soul for eternity, and the goal of treatment is to have you take that risk. To help you do this, I am going to suggest that you will be able to rely on your faith to get you through treatment, so before describing exposure and response prevention for religious obsessions, I would like you to consider the nature of your religious beliefs and the nature of God. Most of what I say refers to Judaism and Christianity, but when I have worked with Muslims and Hindus, they can find support for many of my suggestions with their religious authorities and within their religious texts. Many of you have focused so much on following rules that you have forgotten to think about the nature of your faith. If this is important to you, treatment will not only help you overcome OCD but also may help you strengthen your faith.

I often suggest to clients with scrupulosity that they believe in two Gods. Needless to say, their initial response is confusion. So I continue and note that, on the one hand, they have a loving and forgiving God who cares about their souls and well-being, and, on the other hand, they have a stern and exacting God who will damn them for the slightest misstep. Most sufferers agree with this analysis. Do you?

If you do, my first suggestion is that you need to decide which of the two Gods to believe in. In this matter, the Bible is a double-edged sword, as you can find support for either view. Consider Jacob, who lies to his father to steal his brother's birthright. Not only is he not punished, he becomes one of the Patriarchs of Judaism. David is another person beloved by God despite a great deal of immoral behavior, including sending one of his generals off to war to die so that he could have the general's wife. Which version of God is the accurate one?

Without the miracle of a personal revelation from God, you are stuck guessing. And, like all guesses, you don't get to find out if your guess is correct until it is too late.

For myself, I choose to believe in the forgiving God, even though I may be wrong. One reason for doing so is that if God is very demanding, then which demanding God should I believe in? Most of us choose our religion because we are born into it. For me, the demanding God would feel irrational. How can I pick the right religion without revelation? Should I be Hindu, Christian, or Jew? What if I guess wrong? In these circumstances I don't worry, because I believe there is nothing I can do to obtain an answer. If God is this irrational, and if His plan for me is eternal damnation, then I hope He explains it to me before casting me into the pits.

Because I have to guess, I choose to believe in the forgiving God, because it makes sense to me. I realize that this is just a guess, and I may be wrong. I may be making the whole thing up just to comfort myself. I cannot prove that I am right, but then again, there is no proof that I am wrong. I am completely willing to change if there's any definite proof that I'm wrong. If the heavens open and tell me to be a Buddhist, I'm ready.

You will find support for imperfect behavior within your religion. For example, one of Christianity's main principles is forgiveness of your sins. Although you may try to be good, the belief is that only God is perfect and that, as a human, you will make mistakes. If this weren't the case, there wouldn't be the need for so many prayers of repentance asking for forgiveness. If you are Catholic, you would expect to go to confession only once in your life if such perfection were possible. In a sense, striving for perfection the way you do is not accepting your imperfection nor is it trusting the forgiveness of God that you claim to believe in. Deciding to take the risk of trusting God is an act of faith. It does not guarantee your salvation, but neither does your lack of faith in God's mercy.

In Orthodox Judaism, with all of its rules that seem to govern every aspect of life, uncertainty is built into the system, because perfection is impossible. This can be seen in three principles. The first is K'zayit. K'zayit is a measurement of food that is very small. To keep kosher, meat and dairy products are never mixed, but should a K'zayit of accidental intermingling occur, e.g., if only a drop of milk should touch meat, you don't have to worry. The second is Rove, a principle also used for keeping kosher. Consider the following situation: You find a butchered chicken in the street, and you want to know if it was butchered according to the kosher rules, which would allow you to eat it. Obviously, the only way to be sure is not to eat it. However, the law says that if the majority of the butchers on the street are kosher, then you may consider the chicken to be kosher—even though this is only a probability. And last, there is the principle of B'dieved. The ideal is to totally concentrate on the prayer in a perfect communion with God. B'dieved, which roughly translates to *second best,* says that if your mind wanders while praying, keep going and don't repeat the prayer. It is actually wrong to repeat.

Where does all this leave you? Making a decision of blind faith. Most people like to think of faith as a feeling that gives strength, but it can also simply be a decision you choose to follow. In choosing a forgiving deity, you might also view your treatment as trusting God. You probably make the assumption that God always knows what is in your heart, whether or not you do. This means that if your intentions are evil, God knows it, whether or not you do. So if you repeat a prayer because you feel you said it wrong, is this for God or for you? In a sense, your rituals show a lack of faith in God, as if He can be fooled by your words, so that if you accidentally mispronounce something in a prayer, He won't know what is really in your heart. It means that rituals you follow that go beyond the normal rules of your religion are not for God but for you.

I would go further and suggest that in doing some of the exposures that seem wrong, God will know your true intentions. That if you are simply doing treatment, He will understand. On the other hand, if treatment is really a cover for your evil, He will know. In either case, you should still go through treatment, accepting that you will never know, because if you are so evil that treatment is simply a cover, that evil will be there unrepentantly, with or without treatment. You can decide that you want your faith to be so strong that you will put yourself in God's hands—that if He deems you should be punished, you will accept it. Remember, as horrible as this sounds, you have little choice—your current state has already shown you that ritualizing and not trusting haven't brought you any peace.

You may be wondering if there is a positive way to use your faith. The answer is yes. However, rather than ask for relief, I would suggest something different. I'm reminded of Terry Anderson, a reporter who was held captive by Iranians during the years Carter was president. He was held captive for months.

He hadn't been a religious man prior to his captivity. During his imprisonment, his captors gave him a Bible. He read it and over time developed a deep faith and prayed every day. In his prayers, he never asked for freedom. Instead, he simply prayed for the strength to keep his newfound faith. If religion is important to you, then I would suggest that you pray for the strength to cope with the anxiety that is part of your treatment.

With this in mind, you can make an "I'm Not Going to Let the OCDemon Win" Script with a Religious Twist.

I'm not going to listen to your false promises anymore. If anything were ever a devil, it's OCD. You always make promises to me that you will make my fear go away if I listen to you. But whenever I listen, I find myself deeper in hell, with you telling me that you want just a little more. My religious rituals are all my ways of giving in to fear, and that isn't the kind of religion I want. So you can do your worst, but I'm not going to follow your lies anymore. I have lost too much of my life listening to you (include details of losses from your Cost-Benefit Analysis). *I'm going to turn to my real faith and ask God for the determination to stay with my recovery program. Even though I may be wrong, I'm going to believe God is nice and forgiving, and going through this treatment that seems so blasphemous is actually an act of faith on my part. If I'm wrong in what I'm doing, then so be it. I trust God's will, even if it means I'm to be punished by Him.*

Hopefully this brings you to answering your version of *the question* with a yes, that you will risk treatment and risk being as evil as the rest of us. With the uncertainty of religion, guessing is the only option. You might be damned for not engaging in your rituals. Or you might be damned for engaging in them, since they show a lack of faith in God's understanding. At least you won't be praying to the OCDemon.

You will use imaginal exposure for blasphemous images and thoughts. You don't have to do anything that your religious advisor forbids. Hopefully, your religious advisor understands your OCD and the spirit of why we are engaging in exposure as an act of faith that God can be trusted to know your heart, even if you don't. Anything that your religious advisor allows should be included without further question. You will need to tell your advisor that you may ask questions over and over, and that he or she needs to give you ambiguous answers after telling you once, even if you legitimately forgot the answer. Many sufferers often find it helpful to use the following rule: If they think they might know what the authority would answer, then they will choose to go with that guess rather than ask. You may be able to use the Gun Test described on page 12 to establish whether all answers seem equally probable to you or there is a guess you would make given requirements of the gun test.

For imaginal exposure, there are a variety of recordings you can make. The simplest is the repetition of forbidden words and phrases—either continuously or with a minute or so in between phrases. These might include: "devils, evil, hell, damned," "God and the Virgin Mary having intercourse," or "I give myself to Satan."

You can control the intensity of the exposure by choosing words or ideas that are more or less frightening to you. You can also use longer therapy scripts that include supportive—not reassuring and neutralizing—statements. Below are two short scripts for blasphemous images, one for use early in treatment and one for later in treatment.

SCRIPT

Lower-Hierarchy Imaginal Therapy Script for Religious Obsessions

I have to let that scene stay in my head, no matter what it means. I hope this doesn't send me to hell, but I will accept whatever God wants to do, including damning me. It's important for me to prevent myself from all my undoing rituals. Whenever thoughts come to my mind that have to do with that scene, I have to let them be there for my exposure. If I can't explain this on Judgment Day, then I'll spend time suffering in eternal damnation, but this is what I have to risk to overcome OCD. It may seem crazy to me, but my rituals weren't working, and maybe they are as evil as what I'm doing now, so I already may be damned.

Notice how supportive statements are embedded in the script. Accepting God's will in the second line is a proclamation of faith. The last line reminds you that the very ritual you engage in might be the real sin. This provides you with more reasons to stop ritualizing.

Later in treatment, the script would include many more upsetting details and content. Your religious obsessions may be exacerbated by the presence of sexual or violent obsessions. Include in your imaginal exposures any feared consequences that these might add to your scrupulosity.

Higher-Hierarchy Imaginal Therapy Script for Religious Obsessions

I see the Virgin Mary doing a striptease in a club. I'm in the crowd, cheering her on. I'm letting this scene stay in my mind, because I need to do exposure to overcome my fear of my own thoughts. She keeps dancing to the music, and the crowd is going wild. I will let these thoughts stay in my head no matter what the consequences. I can hear Satan in the background, laughing and cheering all of us on. I will accept whatever God wants to do with me for doing this exposure. I won't be happy if He throws me into hell, but I trust His judgment. If that's what has to happen to me for trying to overcome my OCD, so be it. Accepting God's will is an act of faith. I hope He gives me the strength to keep doing this exposure without ritualizing. I will hold on to the image of a sexy Virgin Mary dancing nude in the background. I'm tired of making God into a demanding monster. I'm tired of praying to the OCDemon. If I'm wrong, I'm willing to pay the price. OCD has already put me in hell, and I'm going to beat it. I'm going to hold on to the image of me and a crowd of screaming men, with a happy Satan. I will hold on to the image of Mother Mary bumping and grinding until I don't care whether or not it's there.

There are many behavioral exposures that you can include with your imaginal obsessions. Martin was twenty-five when he first came to my center. His obsessions focused on fears that he was praying to the devil and may have sold his soul to the devil. Any negative or angry thoughts he had toward anyone were triggers for his soul-selling concerns. He would worry that in his anger he may have sold his soul to harm someone. After any of these incidents, he would argue with himself that he hadn't really done this, and he would engage in compulsive praying, saying a series of prayers seven times. Often he felt he hadn't done this properly, and he would have to start over. The feeling that he wasn't perfectly saying his prayers frequently occurred during his sixth repetition. Martin liked to avoid 6s, because 666 is the devil's number. What kind of exposures can you think of for this kind of problem?

In addition to imaginal exposure, Martin pasted the number 666 throughout his house and on most of his belongings. All of his computer passwords were modified to include *666, Satan,* or *devil* in them. As he progressed up his hierarchy, exposure time was spent trying to wish me and my staff dead with the help of Satan. He obtained a copy of the *Satanic Bible* and performed the rituals in my offices and at home. Finally, he signed numerous soul-selling contracts. As part of his response prevention, all his praying was reduced to a single prayer that he was allowed to say at the beginning or end of every day. The prayer was: "Thank you, God." He agreed to do the latter, because he did agree that God knew what was in his heart better than he did, so the obsessive clarifying of his hopes and wishes would be for himself and the OCDemon, but not for God.

Although Martin believed in God and was a practicing Lutheran, he was not an ardent member of his church, so he felt no need to work with a religious consultant. If you are an observant member of your faith, you may be wondering if it's really possible to do exposure and response prevention without violating the articles of your faith. The answer is yes. For example, Orthodox Jews with religious obsessions about keeping kosher do not have to mix meat and dairy. For these sufferers, the normal activities of their friends, such as putting a carton of milk in the same shopping cart with a steak, feels like an exposure.

Another client, Sara, was concerned about offending God if she didn't try her best to be perfect. She tried to never lie and to always be nice and considerate to others. These two desires were often in conflict, because she felt compelled to tell others anything she noticed about them that could be improved, such as recommending a different hairstyle or clothes that wouldn't emphasize an individual's weight problem or suggesting places where someone might have gotten a better deal on something they bought. This did not win her any popularity contests. In an effort to be nice and considerate, she never turned down a request for a favor or help, so she had little free time to herself. Her concerns about being good were pervasive. Among the standards she tried to maintain to avoid offending God were: being a perfect driver so as not to potentially be bad by contributing to an accident, never littering, always recycling and using recyclable materials, and conserving energy by keeping the house temperature low and taking showers as cold as she could tolerate.

Designing a program for Sara was relatively easy. There were so many ways in which her behavior was controlled by her fears of offending God that she quickly devised an extensive hierarchy. However, for the first six months that we met, I wouldn't let her start treatment, because she was unwilling to risk offending God and wanted to be reassured that her soul would not be at risk. Obviously I couldn't provide this for her. She had been sent to me by the minister of her church, who frequently had told her that her behavior was unnecessary. If she wasn't going to listen to him, then obviously she wasn't going to take my word. Her argument always boiled down to agreeing that she wasn't and couldn't be perfect, but that she had an obligation to do her best.

What finally helped her change her mind was a variation of the Double Standard Method. In the Double Standard Method, you examine your behavior in relation to others to determine whether you hold yourself to a different standard than everyone else. Sara had no difficulty recognizing that she held herself to a higher standard than others. However, she didn't care. She didn't feel that others were wrong—they could do whatever they wanted—but trying her best was right for her. The crack in this idea came after five months. I asked her to imagine that she had a daughter. Would she want her daughter to live up to her standards or not to try her best? Sara said she wouldn't want a daughter of hers to live the same way she was. Over the next month, examining why she wouldn't want her daughter to make the same sacrifices helped her to decide that her idea of always trying her best didn't really work. In the end, she agreed to risk offending God, and then her real journey could begin.

In the months that followed, she began to tell white lies, took comfortable showers, threw away recyclables, turned down requests to do favors she didn't want to do, and committed other "sins." What she found the hardest was simply having fun. She had always felt that fun must be earned, and in her world of trying to be best, she had never felt as if she had done enough to earn free time to engage in fun activities. So her most anxiety-provoking exposures were having unearned leisure and fun. As you might expect, habituation occurred, and fun exposures actually became enjoyable.

Neutral Obsessions

In my mind, neutral obsessions are the purest OCD experience. A thought, image, or sensation that has no negative meaning comes to your attention, and the feared consequence is that it will never leave you. This feared consequence is a part of almost every OCD experience. Often, there is no need to attend to it, because for non-neutral obsessions, other feared consequences play a greater role, and coping with them makes direct attention to this obsession unnecessary.

The neutral stimuli can be literally anything. Ellen, whom you met in Chapter 3, was tortured by the image of a billboard for two years. Other examples of neutral obsessions are: images of anything you might have seen, such as billboards, people, buildings, or cars; thoughts of certain words, phrases, advertising jingles, or music; and physical sensations, such as your heartbeat, breathing, or minor aches and pains.

Despite the fact that the focus of the obsession is neutral, this type of obsession can be among the most devastating. One of the reasons for this is that you feel as though your feared consequence has come to pass; that is, you fear the thoughts will never leave and as a result your life will be ruined, and, indeed, your life is misery whenever the thoughts are present. You are further upset that the focus of these obsessions is on pointless subjects/objects. After all, everyone has had the experience of a thought or jingle staying with them longer than they would have preferred. Therapists you have gone to may have tried to use Downward Arrow to discover what disaster was associated with the thoughts and you had trouble defining an exact disaster. If this has happened to you, it isn't evidence that you are doing something wrong or that your OCD is harder to treat. It is evidence that your therapist needs to learn more about this form of OCD. I identified the feared consequence for you above: It is simply that your life will be ruined or intolerable if these obsessions continue. The difference between sufferers and non-sufferers can be found in your OCD goal—desperately wanting the thoughts or images to go away. As you now realize, the harder you try to force your attention away from these, the more you actually notice them. People without obsessions may find the thoughts irritating, but they don't try to get rid of them. Your goal needs to be learning to live comfortably with these obsessions.

Upon hearing this, the initial response I have seen in most neutral obsession sufferers is hopeless depression. If you are like them, you are thinking, *Dr. Grayson, you are just telling me that there is no hope for me and I might as well get used to it.* But I'm not saying that there is no hope, and I'm not saying that you need to accept the misery you are living through. The goal is to achieve the "ten-minute" frame of mind discussed on page 130 in the Mindfulness section of Acceptance and Commitment Therapy. You may want to reread that section now to refresh your memory.

This brings us to the second reason that neutral obsessions are so painful. Whatever rituals you use to try to overcome neutral obsessions, wishing is almost certainly one of them. In this case, whenever the obsession is present, somewhere in your mind is the thought of how much better life would be if your obsessive thought wasn't present. You compare life to a fantasy, and as you may recall, we always make our fantasies better than real life. So for every moment that you are noticing your obsessive thoughts, you are also wishing for a better life, which has the effect of making this one seem worse and making the offending thought seem like the most exquisitely painful torture ever devised.

You may have even started to avoid engaging in certain activities, because you know you won't be able to enjoy them when you have obsessive thoughts. In so doing, you begin to strip your life of whatever enjoyment might be possible and have made more time and room for wishing your life would be better.

Some of you also make the mistake of blaming all your life's problems on your obsession. For example, if you are having any problems at work that stress you, you may be assuming that your OCD is the culprit—that if you didn't have this obsession, work would not have bothered you. Although it may be true that OCD contributes to your work stress, that isn't the same as saying it is the cause of it. To better understand your stresses, you should start to keep a daily record of two or three events that you believe were ruined by your OCD.

For each entry, I would like you to imagine that your experience was not the result of your OCD—that your feelings were due, in part, to what happened in the situation. Or, in other words, because of the event, you should be having the feelings you are having. With this thought in mind, what aspects of the event could have caused your feelings? After identifying some potential causes, write down the actions that you may need to take in the future if the same event reoccurs. This undermines some of the power of your wishing, in which your OCD, as torturous as it is, no longer is responsible for every bad experience that you have.

You have a twofold treatment goal: learning to allow your obsessive thoughts to be there and learning how to stop wishing. In an ideal world, this would mean that whenever you noticed the obsessive thought, you would remind yourself to let it be there, and that would be your entire treatment. But this doesn't work.

To understand why, consider someone with contamination rituals. If you suffered from contamination, you would find that the exposures you were prepared for were easier to cope with than ones for which you weren't. When surprised by a sudden exposure, you'd find yourself resorting to your old neutralizing rituals, even if you realized that you should be doing exposure and response prevention. Furthermore, once you start ritualizing, it's hard to stop. The same is true with mental rituals. What makes contamination easier is that you can irrevocably contaminate your environment, so that when a surprise contamination takes place, the fact that there is already no way to "fix" your environment, as well as the possibility that the surprise is lower on your hierarchy than what you have already done, combine to raise the odds you will respond with exposure rather than rituals. After all, if you are currently contaminated with public restroom toilets and you have touched a dirty ashtray, it might feel silly to wash. With a neutral obsession, if there have been any moments of freedom, the return of obsessions will automatically trigger old responses, the *I can't believe it's here again to ruin everything. This treatment isn't working. It's back . . .* The reappearance of your neutral obsession after moments of freedom will be met with your conditioned neutralizing response of wishing it had never come back. By accident, you have unconsciously redefined your treatment goal as getting rid of the obsessions rather than living with them. Their reappearance fills you with disappointment and despair.

The way out of this wishing dilemma is to totally immerse yourself in treatment, which is very simple for neutral obsessions. You will create a recorded Single Word Exposure Script that reminds you of your obsessive neutral thought, like the one on page 122 under Distraction and Refocusing. If, like Ellen, your obsession is a billboard, the word would be *billboard*. If you focus on your breathing, then the word would be *breath*. If a piece of music pops up relentlessly in your mind, you would record about fifteen seconds of it. Between each recitation, have a quiet period that varies between thirty and eighty seconds. The reason for the silence is to have the experience of having the word pop into your mind unexpectedly. Play this script constantly.

Because the script makes it impossible to stop thinking about your obsession, you eventually give up trying. It is important to engage in as many activities as you can while listening to the script. Remember, you can go to the movies, because you can use headphones and turn down the script's volume. You may not hear every recitation, but you will periodically hear some. You may not enjoy the movie as much as you normally would, but that is part of your goal. Rather than expecting to get the maximum enjoyment possible out of life, your goal is to settle for less. The reason for this is that in response to your own demand for ideal enjoyment—another part of wishing—you have been choosing to have none. Imagine two different people in a multiplex movie theater where they can hear the sound from the theater next to them. Most people will find this aggravating, but will enjoy the movie they are watching. Person A is able to focus on the movie, albeit with only 60 percent enjoyment rather than 80 percent (I assume 100 percent is too rare to expect or hope for). However, Person B focuses her entire attention upon the sounds coming from the other theater and spends the movie wishing they would stop or, perhaps, that she and whoever she is with can leave the theater. Her wishing will reduce whatever enjoyment she could have felt. If she leaves, then she has gotten no movie enjoyment and can spend the day lamenting her decision to go to a terrible movie theater and her bad luck. This is what you are doing. Either you remove yourself from anything your obsessive thoughts might ruin, or you do go, but you focus more on the obsessive thoughts and how much they are interfering rather than getting the 60 to 80 percent enjoyment that you could.

You might protest and, semi-accurately, tell me that you have no choice and that you wish you could achieve what I'm suggesting. I say "semi-accurate" because directing your attention the way I'm suggesting is a skill you can learn, not a simple decision to make. This may sound impossibly hard, but you already possess the core skills to do it. I'd like you to imagine another situation. This time imagine you are in an electronics store facing a wall of TVs, when you suddenly notice that just one of them is showing a program you are interested in. You stand in front of that TV and listen, despite all of the other TVs. Suddenly a number of TVs alarmingly say, "Important announcement!" You turn your head and decide you are more interested in what is on the TV in front of you. You still hear the other TVs and they may even briefly grab your attention. I assume you believe you would be able to pay attention to the TV of your choice. It might also seem true to you that you would not be as upset as you would in the movie theater. Why? Is the movie theater more upsetting because a person is supposed to be able to enjoy the movie he paid for without interference from another movie? If this is your answer, you are only partially right. Your feelings about what *should* happen in the movie theater versus what you experienced at the electronics store led to two different unconscious decisions. In the electronics store, you decided to allow the other TVs to be on. Since your decision/desire was in line with reality, you were okay. In the movie theater, the decision/desire clashed with reality—the sound from the other theater "had" to be turned off or else. Unfortunately, the "or else" is proof of your engaging in the wishing ritual and enjoying the movie less than you might have.

This is what you are constantly doing by accident with your neutral obsessions. Your goal is learning to attain the "ten minute frame of mind" discussed on page 130 in the mindfulness section of ACT. By engaging in exposure and simultaneously focusing on whatever enjoyment you can glean from any situation, whether it be 2 percent or 70 percent, you are practicing the skill of making the best of any situation as opposed to wishing your life away.

Think about other ways you can make your treatment totally immersive. You can play the script throughout the night, so that it is among the first things you hear in the morning. Use red-dot labels as additional reminders of your obsession. Place them wherever you will notice them.

If you aren't willing to totally immerse yourself, then start by playing the script for shorter periods throughout the day. However, it is very important to play other scripts during the day that remind you of why you want to fight your OCD this way and what your treatment goals are.

There is another obsessive phenomenon that is closely related to neutral obsessions that should be mentioned—obsessions about not-so-neutral (or seemingly not neutral) stimuli. Not-so-neutral stimuli tend to be physical or sensory sensations that are mildly uncomfortable and/or unusual, and like all neutral obsessions, the sufferer feels they should not be present. This has also been labeled sensory-focused OCD (SF-OCD). The stimuli can be internal sensations, such as the ringing in the ears that characterizes tinnitus or external, such as chewing. In general, the sufferer's response to internal stimuli is very different from that of external stimuli.

The sufferer's response to internal stimuli straddles the line between hypochondriasis and neutral obsession. It shares with hypochondriasis the sufferer's demand that the problem has to be fixed. Also, in hypochondriasis, the feared consequence is that the physical symptoms might represent a dangerous underlying disease process. The main feared consequence for sufferers with internally driven SF-OCD is that the sensations will never stop. It is possible for you to have both, in which case you may find the section on hypochondriasis helpful.

Examples of internally driven SF-OCD symptoms are focusing on breathing, heart rate, muscular sensations, or the high-pitched ringing sound that accompanies tinnitus (tinnitus is a medical problem that should be checked out by a physician, since some forms of it are caused by infections that need to be treated. There are other forms of tinnitus for which there are no current cures).

From the examples you can see that the focus can be upon normal bodily functions or the result of a disorder. What they share is not only the sufferer's desire to be free of the obsession, but the severity of their response. Because these sensations are ever present, the greater your determination to avoid experiencing them, the more unavoidable they will become. Sufferers with this tend to report very high levels of anxiety and depression and frequently will disable themselves over time, because it feels like nothing is worth doing as long as their torture is present.

The first step of treatment is deciding that you want to learn to live with the possibility of noticing this sensation forever. This seems impossible to you, but if we look at people with tinnitus, we find that there are two groups. One group finds the tinnitus intolerable; their tinnitus seems to ruin everything in their life, and they often become suicidally depressed because of its presence. The other group may not like their tinnitus, but they enjoy life, and the tinnitus doesn't interfere. The difference between these two groups is wishing. The first group keeps comparing the tinnitus existence to the fantasy existence without tinnitus.

Treatment is no different for tinnitus sufferers than for those with neutral obsessions. They prepare a script as above and simply say "tinnitus" or "ringing"—some word to help them notice the presence of ringing. If you have tinnitus, you may feel unwilling to do this treatment. You would tell me that I don't understand, that the ringing is real and annoying. You are right that it is real and annoying, as are many problems, such as arthritis and back pain. The issue isn't whether or not it is real, but how much time you spend wishing it away while life is passing you by. You can learn to live comfortably with tinnitus and other not-so-neutral obsessions, whether they be strange muscle sensations, noticing your breathing, or any other sensation.

I should mention that I contracted tinnitus about eight years ago. I called my physician to ask whether I needed to have medical concerns over this and he replied no. It is strange to know that I will never hear silence again, and, of course, at times like these when I'm discussing it, the experience of the whine is much louder. Despite this, it truly doesn't bother me in any way and I don't wish it away. It would be nice to hear silence, but because I know that there is no need for my tinnitus to interfere with anything, it doesn't. I allow it to be there. You can learn to do this too!

For externally focused SF-OCD, the most common target is chewing sounds (with gum being the worse). Sufferers often report that there is one individual whose chewing is worse than everyone else's; however, even when this is the case, the sound of anyone chewing tends to be annoying. Although anxiety may be present, the most common emotional response is anger. Sufferers with this are still using the wishing ritual, but instead of simply saying "life would be better if 'x' wasn't occurring," they add: ". . . how can that person (those people) be so inconsiderate . . ." The sufferer may lash out at the "offending" parties, quietly stew, or avoid situations such as going to the movies in order to cope with the problem. In their histories, there is frequently a brother or sister whose chewing was hated and whom the sufferer relentlessly tortured with complaints about how gross they were to listen to. When sufferers marry, they will often become disturbed by a different member of their immediate family. Often SF-OCD sufferers also have OC Personality Disorder (OCPD, see page 278 in the OCD Spectrum Disorders).

Obviously, the external stimulus doesn't have to be chewing sounds. Any noise that elicits an anger response as part of your wishing ritual falls into this category. Your treatment will follow the same course as it does for all neutral obsessions. However, because the stimuli are external, there are extra exposures you can do. At our center, we have created a chewing recording, available on our website (www.FreedomFromOCD.com). Download this or have the person whose chewing you find intolerable make a recording of their chewing. It is essential that you listen to this constantly. Have your family chew gum as frequently as possible. Carry gum with you and offer it to office mates, people sitting next to you on public transportation, and anywhere you go. Remember, the more immersive a program is, the better your outcome. Your goal is to learn to live in a world of which whatever sensory-focused stimulus that you want to avoid is a permanent part—to achieve the "ten-minute frame of mind." After all, there is no real alternative to this other than wishing and anger.

Obsessions About Obsessing

Obsessing about obsessing occurs when the initial form of your OCD becomes less important than the fact that you are obsessing. Consider the case of Bill, a forty-three-year-old man who reported numerous checking rituals with seemingly obvious disasters. For example, whenever he used the microwave oven, he would be plagued by images of fire bursting from it that wouldn't stop unless he ritualized. Before going to bed at night, he would go through a set of extensive door locking and checking rituals so that he wouldn't worry about the door being locked. His concerns appeared to be obvious, and one would assume that exposures would focus on the risk of fire from microwave use and the possibility that the front door wasn't locked and, as a result, someone might break into his house. Exposures like this were done by his therapist, but they didn't work; Bill's anxiety continued relentlessly.

The problem was the focus of the exposures. Although there had been a point in time when Bill's feared consequences were these disasters, this was no longer true. Now his main feared consequence was that his obsessions would continue forever. So while his therapist was trying to treat his fear of disaster, Bill kept trying to make the obsessions stop. For Bill, treatment became another one of his rituals to try to make the obsessions stop. The purpose of his old rituals was no longer to prevent disaster but to stop his obsessing. Whenever he was confronted by an obsession, he would obsess about which method he should use to try to stop his obsessions—his old rituals or exposure? Neither worked, so whichever one he tried, his failure was a trigger to obsess that he should have tried the other technique.

Of course, you now recognize that the goal of treatment is not to stop the obsessions. Initially, to help him stop escaping from his obsessions, he made loop tapes in the manner described in this book, but he quickly ran into a problem. He was making a loop tape for every obsession, so the number of tapes he needed was threatening to become unmanageable. To overcome this problem, I had him make a generic loop tape that simply said, "Here it is," like the one on page 122 under Distraction and Refocusing. "Here it is" now stood for whatever obsession was currently on his mind. If he changed obsessions in the middle of the day, that was fine. "Here it is" stood for the current one. As with the neutral obsessions, the goal of treatment is to learn to mindfully ("the ten minute frame of mind," page 130) have the obsessions in the background, as if you were in that electronics store and the obsessions were those other TVs, but your primary focus is upon the life you want to have.

The tape freed him from ritualizing, because while listening to it, he knew it was impossible to banish the obsessions from his mind, so he allowed them to be there. He was happy about this, but it took some time for us to find a way to reduce his dependence on the tape. We found two methods to be useful in helping him to continue to progress. The first was using the little red-dot labels, pasted in numerous places. The second was gradually lengthening the silences in the tape. Initially, the silent intervals were thirty to forty-five seconds between recitations of "Here it is." This length of silent intervals was increased to forty-five to ninety seconds. As the intervals became longer, we also introduced short periods in which he stopped listening to the tape. At present, he is still working on this problem, but he is now more active than he has been for years, and he is able to enjoy himself.

Obsessive Staring

Obsessing staring is one of the most frustrating forms of OCD to have. It is not a rare manifestation, but it is rarely written about by professionals. I don't have an answer as to why it is so hard to find anything written about it. The core symptom is a feeling that you are staring at the genitals/breasts of other people. I have found that some sufferers don't actually do this, but fear doing so. Other sufferers find that their eyes really do keep ending up focused upon the genitals/breasts of others. As with all OCDs, symptoms include every variation you can imagine. Some sufferers will only have this problem with the opposite sex, for others it may be the same sex, and for others it can be anyone.

Getting caught blatantly and/or repeatedly staring at the genitals/breasts of another would be, at the very least, embarrassing and humiliating. This is usually the primary feared consequence for most sufferers and many sufferers who actually do stare have experienced their feared consequence. Sufferers may also have feared consequences concerning the meaning of their staring (e.g., *Am I a pervert?*). For feared consequences about meaning, the goal is still learning to live with uncertainty; in this case, never knowing what their symptom means.

Earlier in this book, I used an example about noticing red cars while driving. I noted that when you drive you probably pass red cars without consciously being aware of them. However, if I gave you the assignment of trying not to see red cars while driving, the end result would be noticing every red car. This is why sufferers cannot avoid thoughts, because to avoid a thought is to think about it. Whether you actually stare or not, the desire and attempt to not stare guarantees that you will be conscious of what you want to avoid, you will notice what you are avoiding and finally, for some of you, you will actually stare more.

Sufferers of obsessive staring live in dread of public meetings with people. The interference in their lives may be as simple as constant anxiety and concerted efforts to always be looking down or, in some way, away from what they fear. Eye contact feels very risky, since looking down is more likely to occur. In more severe cases, the sufferer avoids going out and misses out on living.

If this is one of your OCD problems, you are probably wondering what exposure and response prevention would look like. If response prevention means not staring, you feel you are constantly trying this without success. If you've been reading this book carefully, you realize that response prevention doesn't mean avoiding behaviors that might lead to your feared consequence. On the other hand, having you blatantly staring at genitals/breasts in public will get you into trouble. We call the exposure solution used at my center for obsessive staring *sneak peeks exposure*.

Behaviorally your goal is to try to surreptitiously sneak peeks without getting caught at whatever you are trying to avoid looking at. In this case, uncertainty about getting caught still exists, but you are actively trying to do *something*, which is usually easier than trying to do nothing. The purpose of your Obsessive Staring Therapy Script is to help remind yourself why sneak peeking is your new goal rather than not having this problem.

SCRIPT

I know I don't want to be caught staring at someone's privates, but I'm going to have to risk it with sneak peeking. I don't know why the normal urge to do this is so strong with me—part of it probably comes from how scared I am of being caught and the pressure I put on myself to not do it. At this point in time, it makes perfect sense that whenever I'm in a problem situation I automatically respond with anxiety and urges. It would be wonderful if these just stopped, but that is a fantasy—I'm going to have to shoot for second best, sneak peeking rather than trying not to look at all. I still may be caught and embarrassed, and if that happens, I'll claim innocence and hope I get away with it.

AT THIS POINT, all the major manifestations and forms OCD can take have been presented. You may have found that your recovery program is made up of details found primarily in a single chapter or that you have needed to combine elements from all the chapters you've read in Part 3. The next chapter focuses on some disorders known as the *obsessive-compulsive spectrum disorders*. The ones I have chosen to discuss are generalized anxiety disorder (GAD), obsessive-compulsive personality disorder (OCPD), hypochondriasis, and body dysmorphic disorder (BDD). I believe these particular disorders are actually different manifestations of OCD. What they share with one another is overvalued ideation (OVI), that is, the sufferer believes that the feared consequences of their symptoms are real. This can occur in any form of OCD and may characterize your own. Or you may discover that some of your concerns are the very issues that define these disorders. If so, you will find it useful to adapt and include the recommendations for these problems into your own recovery program.

Chapter 13

Selected Obsessive-Compulsive Spectrum Disorders: OCD Problems with Another Name

The obsessive-compulsive spectrum disorders are thought to be neurobiologically related to OCD. The evidence researchers rely on to support this concept is threefold: (1) many sufferers of these spectrum disorders also have OCD; (2) the same SSRI medications that are used to treat OCD seem to be useful in the treatment of these spectrum disorders; and (3) they tend to be characterized by behaviors that the sufferer feels as though he or she can't control. Some of the disorders included in the spectrum are trichotillomania (hair pulling), hoarding, compulsive gambling, generalized anxiety disorder (GAD), hypochondriasis, obsessive-compulsive personality disorder (OCPD), and body dysmorphic disorder (BDD). For some of these problems, the sufferer's urges are experienced as appetitive, meaning that the symptoms are enjoyable and addictive even though the ultimate consequences may be very upsetting. Coming to terms with uncertainty plays little role in these disorders. From the list above, trichotillomania, hoarding, and compulsive gambling would fall into this category.

For other problems, the anxiety over the inability to be certain is central to the problem, and treatment will not be different from what you've read about so far. Generalized anxiety disorder, hypochondriasis, obsessive-compulsive personality disorder, and body dysmorphic disorder fall into this category, and in my opinion they are simply different presentations of OCD. They share in common with one another one characteristic: *overvalued ideation,* the belief that the concerns underlying the symptoms are entirely realistic. To understand what this means, consider two sufferers with contamination concerns, who differ only in the presence or absence of overvalued ideation.

Suppose you are the sufferer without overvalued ideation, which is the more common presentation. You may worry about the possibility of catching a disease from the door handle of a public restroom. However extensive the precautions you take following such an exposure, when questioned using the standards of the Gun Test (I have a gun pointed at your head and you need to give me your best guess as to whether you will catch disease "x" from the doorknob. If you guess wrong, I'll shoot), your answer will be the same answer that everyone else gives: "Probably not." Your anxiety is driven by the possibility that you might get sick.

Now suppose your OCD is complicated by overvalued ideation. When questioned about the possibility of catching a disease from the bathroom doorknob, the answer will be a definite yes. In addition, you may believe that many of the extensive rituals you use to wash your hands are necessary. Perhaps you would like to do them more quickly or be able to be certain that they were done correctly, but you don't doubt the necessity of whatever complicated rituals you've devised.

Both sufferers are tortured by all the possible contaminants in the environment and by their extensive washing rituals. The sufferer without overvalued ideation wishes to find a way to return to normal living without anxiety, rituals, and avoidance. The sufferer with overvalued ideation only wants to live without anxiety while continuing to follow the demands imposed by OCD—demands that they believe are reasonable.

Overvalued ideation can be a component of any manifestation of OCD. But for GAD, obsessive-compulsive personality disorder (OCPD), hypochondriasis, and BDD, it is one of the defining characteristics. If it is not addressed, treatment will fail because the individual has no reason to try to give up behaviors that make perfect sense to him or her. If you have overvalued ideation, notice how it is handled in each of these obsessive-compulsive spectrum disorders. If you have overvalued ideation in a different form of OCD, you will be able to adapt the guidelines here to your own issues.

Generalized Anxiety Disorder (GAD)

The prominent feature of GAD is excessive worry. This worry is usually differentiated from OCD issues in that it focuses on concerns that most people consider "normal"—normal in the sense that these worries are shared by everyone at some point in time, just not so excessively. Some examples would include performance, personal interactions, financial concerns, and the well-being of family.

A second differentiation is how sufferers of GAD cope with their worries. Their prime method of coping is using analyzing and figuring out or reassurance seeking to neutralize their concerns. In the eyes of the public, this makes sense. I'd like you to recall the discussion about rituals that work by "magic." The difference between magic and nonmagic rituals was simply that the connection between ritual and obsession was more obvious in nonmagic rituals. Washing your hands to get rid of contamination "makes sense," whereas the connection between counting and contamination is not obvious. However, with regard to severity of dysfunction, whether you use magic or nonmagic rituals tells us nothing. In the same way, to the public, spending hours worrying about your child's performance in school doesn't seem as unusual as washing your hands for hours. But the bottom line is that GAD sufferers attempt to use their rituals to achieve certainty and thus neutralize their anxiety.

A third differentiation between GAD and OCD is that GAD sufferers generally have many concerns as opposed to a single focus. When you read this, you probably immediately realize that this difference is also artificial—many of you have more than one obsessive concern. In addition, if your OCD symptoms haven't completely taken over your life, many of you now realize that you probably have GAD or did have it before the severity of your OCD intensified.

If this describes you, don't worry about having two diagnoses. You can take comfort in the fact that GAD is not really different than OCD and that the treatment is not different, except that with GAD, you must also treat overvalued ideation.

Examine the overvalued ideation associated with your GAD. For your OCD symptoms, it is likely that some part of you feels as though what you are doing makes no sense. You have that frustrating agony of knowing that your symptoms make no sense yet simultaneously feeling that they do. With GAD, the feeling that the concerns are real—*I might really lose my job; My son really isn't doing well in school; We paid the bills last month, but it was close*—makes it seem as though these are real issues that must be resolved *right now!*

But they can't be. In fact, all your worries are uncertainties that you want an immediate and definite answer for. All your worries are linked to potential catastrophes that you are afraid might happen and that you want to avoid. Is this different than OCD? No. And the goal of exposure is also the same: to help you cope with possibilities that may come true. If it is true that the catastrophic worries of GAD are more reasonable and thus have a greater probability of coming true, then answering *the question* with a yes, that you want to learn to live with uncertainty becomes more important, not less, because living with uncertainty, means choosing to cope with whatever may happen. There is no real alternative. like OCD, the rewards of succeeding at treatment are being able to live in the present and enjoying what you have as opposed to always having your mind on the future or past, trying to solve the unsolvable. Or to put it another way, learning to live with uncertainty is not simply something that OCD sufferers need to do, while so-called normals get to be certain. Living with uncertainty is better coping for everyone, so when you overcome your OCD, you still won't be normal. In fact, you will be better than normal, because the majority of non-sufferers won't cope with uncertainty as well as you!

Everything you have learned about designing and implementing an OCD recovery program is applicable to GAD with little modification. The one potential challenge some of you may run into is having worries that change so rapidly that designing an imaginal exposure to a specific concern isn't always possible, because something new is always bothering you by the time you get a chance to sit down to design your recovery program. If you are in this position, look at the kind of feared consequences underlying your concerns using Downward Arrow. You are likely to find a few major themes that keep reappearing in different forms. These more general themes can be the focus of your imaginal exposures. For example, if the themes revolve about finances, whether it be not having enough money to pay the bills or losing your job, your exposure scripts will always end at the same point: If the worst happens, what will you attempt to do next? If your worst fear is truly losing your home, then imagine how your family will cope on welfare. If you believe you will get a job someday—even if it isn't as good as your current one—what will that look like? This may not be a preferable situation, but if it happens your life will continue in some manner. Will it be hard on your children? Yes, but the reason to be determined to live with such adversity is that there is no choice. You don't have to look forward to it, but rather than panicking over what might happen, you want to learn to hope that you will be able to cope with whatever challenges arise.

Obsessive-Compulsive Personality Disorder (OCPD)

One of the most frustrating experiences for OCD sufferers is hearing a non-sufferer say, "I'm OCD about doing such-and-such." If you've experienced this, you know the feeling of wanting to tell that person how painful and crippling OCD really is. There are certainly sufferers, who, outside of their OCD, are organized, orderly, and dedicated workers. These behaviors are not part of their OCD and helping them to cope with their OCD will not result in these useful behaviors disappearing. This public image of OCD is actually a partial image of obsessive-compulsive personality disorder (OCPD).

People who have OCPD generally don't feel they have a problem. They believe there is a right and wrong way to do things and only an idiot wouldn't do things the right way. For example, if they believe that canned goods should be put away in order of date, from largest to smallest with the labels facing forward, then that is how it has to be. Unlike OCD, the person with OCPD can accomplish their goal in a normal amount of time, whereas an OCD sufferer with ordering concerns would take hours attempting to put the canned goods away correctly.

OCPD sufferers tend to be preoccupied with orderliness, perfectionism, and control. Again, for all of these they are able to follow their rules without excessive ritualizing. Rather than having difficulty coping with uncertainty, they seem absolutely certain that their way is the best and they can supply numerous arguments to support their view. Often their rules become more important than the activity they are engaging in. For example, on a family vacation, the sufferer's schedule may be more important than having fun, so the family is rushed along, never being allowed to linger and enjoy an activity or site or take a detour to a site or event that looks fun.

You may be wondering how this is related to OCD. As noted earlier, overvalued ideation is a core component of OCPD; its sufferers have no doubt they are right. Their primary ritual is the wishing ritual—they are constantly wanting the world to do everything right and compare their present reality to that fantasy. You'll recall that underlying the wishing is denial; comparing reality to fantasy. Their attempts to coerce the world into following them are constantly frustrating. However, rather than feeling anxiety, their emotional response is anger and with frustration they wonder why everyone around them is so stupid. As a result, OCPD sufferers are often very difficult to live with. They tend to badger and bully those around them into doing everything their way. Their expectations of their children will be very high and difficult to live up to. In their minds, they are just trying to help them learn the right way to live.

I remember one of my clients who had a mother who had OCPD telling me about a time in her twenties when her mother was yelling at her. The source of the problem was how my client was cutting onions for the spaghetti sauce she was making. My client was cutting them wrong and the pieces were too big for the spaghetti sauce. It was true that my patient wasn't cutting the onions the most efficient way, but she enjoyed doing it her way. Since this was her home—Mom was just visiting—and she wasn't a sous chef in a restaurant, why did the onions have to be cut efficiently? Was there really a reason she shouldn't do it the way she enjoyed? Furthermore, the spaghetti sauce was for herself, so was there any reason for my client not to have the onions the size she preferred? These are arguments that the OCPD sufferer simply rejects.

The primary difference between OCPD and OCD is that OCPD sufferers focus on a perfectionism they can achieve as opposed to trying to attain absolute certainty. However, having OCPD doesn't preclude also having OCD. If a major disruption occurs in their life—an unexpected illness, loss of a job, or a divorce, they may respond with overwhelming anxiety. When this happens, existing OCD will be exacerbated or the disruption might trigger the onset of OCD.

OCPD sufferers rarely come to treatment for help; after all, they are sure they are right. Most often they come in response to a major life disruption or a spouse who has finally delivered an ultimatum. The question that they have to answer is: "Are you willing to forever live in an imperfect world?" In their case, this also means letting family members do things "wrong," as well as changing their own behavior.

One of my OCPD clients, who had been forced by his wife to come to see me, commented during the course of treatment, "I've discovered that being right isn't always important." In his pursuit of right, he had almost lost his marriage and his teenage children were frightened of him. His values of doing everything right was conflicting with values of have a loving relationship with his family. The goal of treatment is to help the sufferer see that the issue isn't right or wrong, but that others have different opinions and reasons for their behavior. Living with them means making compromises, and although they may not like the compromise, they can continue to believe that they are right.

After getting their OCPD under control, continued work in ACT can help the suffer to further give up control and to better appreciate the here and now.

Hypochondriasis

When most people hear the word *hypochondriac,* they get the image of a person who runs from doctor to doctor, looking for illnesses that really aren't there. This is a misconception; having hypochondriasis in no way means that an individual is not also suffering from an illness. Or, to put it another way, you can be sick *and* a hypochondriac. This misconception leads to a great deal of misunderstanding and mistreatment of hypochondriacal symptoms by professionals and families who try to reassure sufferers that they aren't physically sick or that the problem is all in their head.

If being a hypochondriac doesn't mean thinking you are sick when you aren't, what is it? Hypochondriasis is a form of OCD in which you spend most of your waking time worrying about having an illness. You may have real symptoms. You may or may not have a diagnosable illness. The defining feature is worrying and engaging in rituals to try to avoid your feared consequences. There are four major feared consequences. The first three may occur singly or in combination with one another, but the last can only occur in combination with one of the first three.

1. Which illness do I have?
2. What can be done to cure it?
3. What can be done to alleviate my symptoms?
4. It would be terrible if it was my fault that any of my other feared consequences took place.

The goal of treatment is not for you to believe that you are not sick, nor is it to have you give up seeking help from medical specialists. Each of the above feared consequences is a version of *the question* you must answer to recover, and each has its own set of implications.

In demanding to know which illness you have, you make the assumption that just because you have symptoms doctors will find an answer. There are many diseases for which a diagnosis is frequently not possible—connective tissue diseases, for example. For some of these diseases, there may come a time later when your symptoms progress to the point where they will be diagnosable. Or they may never progress or turn into anything serious. If you have seen doctors numerous times and they have failed to find anything wrong with you, the goal of your therapy isn't to accept that you are well but to accept that medical science at this time can't diagnose you, leaving you uncertain about what might happen with your symptoms in the future. In this situation, use the following "I May Be Undiagnosable" Script.

> *No matter how much I want to know what is wrong with me, there may be no answer. I have to limit my going to doctors, because it consumes all my time and I'm so miserable that I never enjoy life. It feels like it would be easier if I knew what was wrong, but after all this time, that's a fantasy. As for all my checking at home, this serves no purpose. I'm not a doctor. And I know that whatever I checked last time is going to be there with or without checking again. I really don't believe it will magically have disappeared.*

Obviously you would like to prevent an illness from getting worse. For many illnesses, whether diagnosed or not, prevention is not possible. Again, there are many connective tissue diseases that are going to progress regardless of what you attempt. It is difficult to accept your helplessness. Luckily, for most of you, progression is not definite, because not all diseases do progress, and you probably don't have a firm diagnosis. In this scenario, the following "I May Have an Illness That Will Get Worse" Script will support your exposure work.

> *I may be terrified that I might have a horrible progressive illness that I don't want to live with, but medical science obviously isn't at a point to explain my symptoms. My feeling that the symptoms must mean something isn't nec-*

essarily true. I need to live with the risk that it may be something awful.
For certain diagnoses, I may feel as though I would commit suicide because
of how disabling they would eventually be. But I'm not that disabled now,
so even if I found out I had something awful, I could let myself live and not
deal with how intolerable it would become until later.

No one likes to suffer, so it is natural that you would want any disturbing symptoms to subside. But doctors are limited in what they can do. You may feel that you would receive better treatment with the right diagnosis, but the truth is that this is no more than a hope and a maybe. Again, for many connective tissue diseases, you would be treated symptomatically prior to diagnosis. That is, doctors would try to treat each uncomfortable symptom rather than treat the underlying illness. If at some point you get a diagnosis, two things happen. You will be in heaven and hell: heaven, because the diagnosis proves you weren't crazy and that something really was wrong; hell, because now you really do have a serious medical condition. With most diseases of this nature, once you have been diagnosed, your treatment won't change. You will still be treated symptomatically. The "I May Not Get Further Relief from My Symptoms" Script would apply here.

SCRIPT

The discomfort I suffer with may not be able to be treated. Right now I focus
on it so much that however bad it is, I make it worse. There are aches I have
that have nothing to do with my fears, and I cope with them. Sometimes I
may not notice them for a short period of time, even though they still hurt.
I need to learn to manage my discomfort differently, since there may be no
other relief.

Doctors make mistakes. Occasionally you do hear stories, especially on the Internet, of people who suffered needlessly for years until a brilliant doctor correctly diagnosed them. How could you live with yourself if you suffered for years or became needlessly disabled because you didn't do everything you could to help yourself? You will have to find a way to live with yourself, because it's impossible to do absolutely everything you can to get a diagnosis. This is where overvalued ideation comes into play. To you, this isn't some "crazy" contamination problem—this is about real illness and real symptoms, and no one seems to understand. You are right about many of the people around you, but you are wrong in your own understanding. The overvalued ideation isn't necessarily referring to whether or not you are sick, but to your belief that, because this is a "real" problem, there must be a way to have answers. The "I Can't Do Enough" Script will strengthen your recovery in this area.

SCRIPT

I find myself endlessly checking and constantly looking for reassurance. I have to find a reasonable way to pursue my medical concerns, which means accepting many ideas that I don't like. I'm stuck accepting that there might always be another test or a test that came out wrong, but my choices are living in hell like I have been or learning to live with risk. The sad thing is, for all my checking, I don't feel better either mentally or physically. No matter how much it seems to me that someone should have an answer, they haven't to date. And rather than setting up appointments and living my life in between, I spend every second suffering with worry. If nothing really is wrong, look at the time I've wasted and lost. And if something is wrong, look at the time I've wasted, lost, and will never have a chance to recover.

The final script you will need to prepare is for a scenario in which your medical fears come true. In creating this script of your gradual deterioration, you need to include three categories of content. The first is obvious: Describe the medical symptoms that will overcome you and provide a detailed description of what they would feel like if your worst fears came true. State this hypothetically: "If it turns out that I really do have MS, then I will . . ." Add to this ways that you would cope with such symptoms if you were going to try to make the best of your situation. Coping with the illnesses you fear may be very difficult, so your imaginal coping should reflect the amount of effort this would take, how hard it will be to bear the difficulties of what you will have to go through starting with the beginning: "What do I do when I leave the doctor's office after being diagnosed?" Many of you would say that you would fall apart. Obviously you would be upset, but would you fall apart in the street or go home? Would you call someone to take you home? What would you do when you arrived at home? Would you eat dinner that night? Would you ignore your children or try to set a good example? Would you try to go to sleep that night? Would you eat breakfast in the morning—you have to eat sooner or later. I want you to think about all of the specific details, because life doesn't really stop. Like everyone else, you imagine that horrible moment of discovery when the whole world stops and then you stop imagining. Just like everyone else. But the reality is that something comes next and I want you to imagine trying to cope. A very wise client of mine once said, "You can't do what you won't imagine." Imagining how to cope doesn't mean you will cope, but it raises the odds in your favor.

So think about all of the details. If you are worried about becoming wheelchair bound, then it would be useful for you to be thinking: "When I can't walk anymore, I hope I can find the strength to find a way to get around in a wheelchair. I know it will feel embarrassing to have people look at me, but I want to learn to make every possible moment count. If I'm in a movie theater, the movie is just as good whether I'm in a theater seat or my wheelchair." Last but not least, include reminders of the reasons you need to do exposure: "I have to keep up with this exposure, even though all of this might happen, because I have been losing my life to these worries. I want to make the best of the present (*include data from your Cost-Benefit Analysis*)."

Much of your current anxiety and misery is not the result of medical symptoms; the culprit is your worrying—your OCD. I'm reminded of my client Susie, who had had an almost lifelong fear of going blind. She reported constantly trying to stare at things to see if her vision was going. She would close her eyes and touch her eyelids to see if the eyeball was okay, and then, after doing this, would be concerned that she had damaged her eyes. There were hours spent staring in mirrors to check both her eyes and her vision. Of course there were numerous calls and visits to doctors. About fifteen years ago, prior to seeking treatment with me, she came down with a very serious disease that was diagnosed as hereditary spastic paraplegia (HSP), a rare genetic disorder that is very disabling and will eventually lead to her dying. In addition, in some cases of HSP, blindness can occur. Needless to say, her OCD went through the roof, not over the physically disabling aspects of the disease, but over the fear of blindness. A few years later Susie came to me. And at this time, many years later, she would tell you that despite being unable to work, being divorced, living in assisted living, and having to get around in a scooter because walking is too difficult, she is the happiest she has ever been in her life. Because she has beaten her OCD and has her mind back, because she is willing to go blind if her disease should progress to that, and because she isn't blind today.

It is not the disease you have that is ruining your life, it is trying to submit to the demands of your OCD. You rely on numerous rituals to try to neutralize your concerns. You make multiple visits and/or calls to either a single doctor or a variety of specialists. Of all your rituals, these are the ones for which your overvalued ideation provides you with feelings that they are necessary and justified. However, for some of these visits, especially the ones that are not for new tests, you know what the doctor will say based on past conversations. When this is the case, the purpose of the contacts is not really diagnosis, but either to seek reassurance or because you hope that the doctor will say something new. You refuse to accept the possibility that the doctor doesn't have answers and keep asking, wishing for a change as much as the gambler wishes that the slot machine will pay off the next time.

Seeking reassurance from others is another ritual that you probably abuse. I say abuse because you will ask people for reassurance and then won't believe them. And why should you believe them? They aren't medical specialists—a good reason to discount their reassurance, but also a good reason not to have asked your questions in the first place. Your overvalued ideation can't justify this ritual, since it has nothing to do with truly fixing your possible medical problems. This kind of reassurance is, at best, like an addict's crack cocaine—it works briefly, but then you need another hit.

You may have a variety of medical self-checking rituals: for example, visual examination of your body, feeling for lumps, testing sensations (*Does it still hurt? Does the limb move correctly?* or *How is my eyesight?*), or taking your blood pressure or pulse. Your overvalued ideation attempts to justify this, but much of it is for self-reassurance, not true medical monitoring. There is no reason to expect a lump that you feel to be any different in one hour. The frequency of your checks simply feeds into your mental ruminations, during which you worry where the symptoms will lead, and then you try to accept what doctors have told you, only to counter with all the reasons they might be wrong.

Finally, you may have a number of rituals that you feel are necessary to cope with your symptoms, although they may have no medical basis. Some of these may be harmless, such as taking certain vitamins. Others may not have helped your symptoms but are nevertheless good health habits. These might include exercising regularly or following a healthy diet. Your recovery program can allow these to continue if your way of using them is safe according to medical authorities, and you are not compulsively ritualistic about them. For example, if you exercise regularly, missing a day is not likely to be a real problem, but if you feel as though you can't miss a day and unbendingly structure your life around your exercise, then it is a problem. You may also have ritualistic practices that aren't safe—such as using multiple enemas for a bowel problem. Realistically, whatever relief is provided by such rituals is not worth the long-run risk of the damage they will cause. Your overvalued ideation may try to justify these because of how you feel after doing them. You need to identify what you are attempting to accomplish with these behaviors and prepare scripts for why you want to give them up.

Much of your exposure will be imaginal. Plan to listen to therapy scripts every day, and perhaps almost constantly. Your hierarchy items may reflect different levels of the medical severity of your potential condition. The other items on your hierarchy will reflect the gradual institution of response prevention. Like some of the other OCD checking problems, response prevention and exposure are almost inseparable. Not checking is a part of your exposure. It is critical that you don't allow response prevention to be a passive activity, simply not doing something. Every response prevention should be accompanied by active listening, reading, or thinking about the scripts you have created. I prefer listening or reading to help focus your mind and to help keep it from wandering into mental rituals.

In planning your program, divide your rituals into two categories: (1) those involving medical personnel, such as visits and calls to doctors and hospitals; and (2) those that don't involve medical personnel, such as self-checks, reassurance seeking from family and friends, and mental analyzing and figuring out. You may feel the need to break the second category into two parts: those that you believe are medically necessary for yourself, and those that you admit are only attempts to reduce anxiety. These two or three categories will be your hierarchy of response preventions to implement.

The hardest will be the first category, doctor contacts. Am I suggesting that you may no longer call doctors or that you should stop seeking answers to your medical concerns? No, but if you want to be freed from the torture of your worrying, rules will have to be instituted for doctor contacts and any medical self-checking you believe to be necessary.

RESPONSE PREVENTION RULES FOR HYPOCHONDRIASIS

1. You are not to call doctors about symptoms that haven't significantly changed, unless otherwise directed by your physician.

2. If you have a history of getting second opinions and there is frequent agreement among physicians, then pursue no second opinions unless very different testing techniques are to be used.

3. Self-checking of symptoms should not occur more frequently than a doctor has ordered. This would include daily or more frequent checking of lumps, functions, vital signs, etc. Such checking may occur under two circumstances: You notice a change in feeling or size when you weren't looking for one, or a doctor has given you a checking schedule. You may find a checking schedule easier to follow, as it can be gradually instituted, although you should be aware that it is easier not to check than to check a little bit. Because of this, to successfully keep to a schedule, perform the checks when you don't have time to get lost in checking, such as before dinner or going out, whatever would force you to check quickest. Such checks should always be preceded by listening to your therapy scripts for a few minutes before, as well as during and after, your check.

4. Although the ideal goal is to find a physician who you are willing to risk trusting, initially you may pursue new tests for symptoms or treatments. The lesser goal is to learn to cope with worry between such tests. Eventually you should introduce a standard of no new tests without the okay of your physician.

5. Stay off the Internet if you cannot resist looking up medical issues or seeking further information about your possible condition from others. When you are first diagnosed with a problem, the Internet can be a wealth of information. If your problem has been going on for a long time, your searching is likely to be fruitless or will generate new, endless possibilities to worry about. You may miss something important, but consider the amount of time you have spent searching. Taking the risk of missing something in order to have a life might be worth it. If you refuse to do this, consider scheduling Internet searching to take place only once a month.

Overcoming hypochondriasis is a scary process; you will feel as though you are risking your life. Your overvalued ideation and your anxiety will combine to tell you that every step is a critically important and reasonable one. If you implement a recovery program according to the above guidelines and the other suggestions in this book, you won't be giving up access to all physicians or attempts to find relief from your medical problems. But you will be limiting such contacts, which is not risk-free, but it will leave you time to enjoy life.

Body Dysmorphic Disorder (BDD)

To those who don't suffer from BDD, it seems to be a mystery, because they don't see the ugliness or imperfections that sufferers see, or if they notice some imperfection it seems minor and insignificant. To some extent, this is even true of BDD sufferers. Anytime I have introduced two BDD sufferers, they always say the same thing to each other: "You have BDD; I'm ugly."

In the introduction you met Melanie, whose pretreatment history is a testament to the ruin BDD can bring to a life. She spent hours trying to get her hair to look good enough to go out and often failed to satisfy herself. She spent hours in front of the mirror, staring at her hair, or as many hours hiding in bed, wishing she was dead. She lost fifteen years of her life. Her major feared consequence was being ugly. Her main concern was her hair. For most BDD sufferers, the perceived imperfection that is the focus of their attention is often on their face or head, although it can be anywhere. Like Melanie, there are numerous secondary feared consequences that follow from the belief in their ugliness; most of these revolve around social rejection. If you suffer from BDD, you may feel that your imperfections mean that no one would want to marry you, no one would seriously want to be your friend, or even that you are so hideous that everyone notices you and perhaps is pained by your very presence.

I remember my first session with Melanie. She had been released from the hospital just two weeks earlier, after a serious suicide attempt that she survived only because her mother found her. She sat before me, feeling hopeless and crying uncontrollably:

MELANIE: (*sobbing*) I know you can't help me. No one can. I'm ugly and nothing you can say is going to change that or make me think otherwise.

DR. GRAYSON: If that's what it would take to get you better, you'd be right. Fortunately, that isn't how it works. I'm not going to try to change your opinion
about how you look—not because I agree with you, but because that's not
how you're going to get over this.

Because overvalued ideation is part of BDD, I knew that Melanie believed
she was ugly with all her heart. There was no uncertainty about her belief. Like
hypochondriasis, the treatment focuses on how much appearance rules her
thoughts. I told her the goal was to learn to live, regardless of how she looked.
She didn't like this idea, but it was different than anything she had heard for the
last fifteen years. Still, she wasn't convinced.

MELANIE: You don't understand. How can I live life looking like this? It's impossible; it's with me every moment of the day.
DR. GRAYSON: Do you like movies?
MELANIE: (*confused by the question*) Yes.
DR. GRAYSON: Then explain to me what your looks have to do with seeing a
movie. Once the lights are out, a good movie is good whether you're beautiful or ugly.

Melanie understood the point immediately—her appearance didn't have to
rule every moment. But she still had a long way to go, because it did seem to
her that her appearance was going to deprive her of most of life's important joys.
However, this was a beginning in which she could concede that her being wrong
might mean there was hope, even if it was slim.

The goal in treatment of BDD is to learn to live a full life, regardless of how
you actually look or think you look. You may feel as though you are ugly, but
the idea of knowing you are ugly and functioning sounds impossible. What you
don't realize is that liking the way you look isn't normal. Most people are dis-
satisfied with their appearance and can tell you exactly what their defects are.
When they say they look good, they mean they look better than how they usually look. Men and women take extra time to prepare for first dates, despite the
fact that in two hours their hair won't be perfectly in place and their clothes
won't be wrinkle-free. Many women who don't have BDD won't go out of the
house without makeup. They are living with what we might think of as the socially acceptable level of BDD.

There is a reason most of us aren't satisfied with our appearances: We don't look at ourselves the same way we look at others. When we look at other people, we see a whole—that is, we look at their whole face. When we look at ourselves, we focus on parts. That's why a pimple on one's own face seems more noticeable than a pimple on someone else's. Staring at the details of your face makes them stand out in your own mind. You can make anyone look ugly if you deconstruct their face or appearance this way. In fact, I have seen OCD sufferers with a kind of reverse BDD. They find imperfections in their lovers or spouses and then they obsess constantly about the imperfections and their inability to get it out of their minds. This will be discussed further later.

Another false belief you have that is shared by everyone is that you can trust your eyes, that you know what you see. It turns out that vision is no different than hearing. Think about a song you like to listen to. Do you like to listen to it endlessly, or are there days when you aren't in the mood for it? Like everyone else, sometimes you aren't in the mood for it. But how can that be? The song is exactly the same. What changed was your mood. The same is true for vision: We can like something one day and not like it the next. Fashions that looked great ten years ago look silly today. The actors and actresses designated as the sexiest of the year weren't the sexiest the year before. Did they dramatically change, or did the public's view of them change?

Finally, there is the issue of individual taste. If one hundred people are asked to judge you, it is likely that some of them will like the way you look and others won't. I don't know anyone who is considered universally beautiful by everyone. Suppose for a moment that if you're a man, you look like Ben Affleck, and if you're a woman, you look like Gwyneth Paltrow. What if you find both of them ugly—and that your ideals are Tom Cruise and Cameron Diaz? Your opinion of yourself will be quite different from everyone else's.

You may be sure how you feel about your appearance, but you can't be sure what others will think. I once worked with a woman who was a model for Bloomingdale's and was a long-distance runner. She was sitting before me, explaining how fat her legs were. I could see her legs, and, as you might imagine, Bloomingdale's is not known for hiring heavy models. Presumably, you would have agreed with my assessment of her legs. I knew I wasn't going to convince her that she was wrong, so I didn't try. Nor am I trying to convince you that you are wrong about your appearance. However, perhaps you may agree that it is possible that not everyone will agree with your self-assessment. If you have an opportunity to meet with other BDD sufferers, do so. This will allow you to have the experience of being on the other side of the argument. Accepting this possibility gives you two goals for your recovery program: to learn to enjoy life no matter how you look and, no matter how inexplicable it may seem to you, to accept that others may have a different opinion about your appearance.

Some of you might think this is a fine treatment goal for someone with BDD, but you may think it's not for someone like you—someone who really is hideous. You are wrong. If you came to me, disfigured and deformed by an accident, I would still urge you to get out of the house and live. If, in my opinion, you were disfigured, I would agree that people will stare and that there will be fewer people who would be willing to date you, but I would tell you that you still need to learn to cope with this by getting out and enjoying life.

This idea of enjoying life even if you are disfigured had a powerful effect on Melanie, because she had a friend who had lost her leg. This friend was happily married and would wear shorts in the summer and bathing suits at the beach— she had chosen to have the best life she could with one leg rather than give up and hide from life. This was another reason for Melanie to hope that what I was suggesting was possible for her.

And it is also possible for you. Like all OCD, BDD steals your life through avoidance and rituals. Your rituals probably include extensive preparations to go out, frequent mirror checking, and reassurance seeking. Uncertainty plays a role not in your belief about your imperfections but in your hope to successfully hide them. There may even be times when you feel you can do this. Trying to prepare yourself to go out quickly and perfectly is not an option. You will keep finding imperfections. Your goal isn't to look perfect but to look better than when you started. But that is after treatment. During treatment, you would do better by allowing your appearance to be imperfect. There are three levels of doing this: preparing quickly and imperfectly, not preparing at all, and making your appearance worse. Consider how this would apply to makeup. The first would be a quick job with some possible mistakes. The second would be going out with no makeup or, if you were going to institute this gradually, imperfectly applied makeup minus one product. And most difficult would be applying makeup "wrong."

You will find that mirrors are your enemy. The urges to look in the mirror can be overwhelming. Sometimes it is to see if you look "right." At other times, you might be hard-pressed to tell me what you hope to accomplish. For example, suppose you have been looking at your imperfection throughout the day. You are at home and haven't tried to hide it or fix it for the day. Why do you check? You know you don't like how it looks, and if you thought it was horrible at eleven in the morning, then you know you don't believe it will look any better later in the day. Remind yourself of this when you have urges to look in the mirror.

The best way to deal with mirrors is to cover all the mirrors in your house. You can use newspaper to do this. If you aren't ready to completely give up all of your mirror rituals, leave a one-inch square exposed on one mirror. The mirror should be one that you don't usually use. The inconvenience of this will make it a little easier not to get involved in your preparation rituals. This will allow you to put yourself together imperfectly, but it won't allow you to get an exact sense of how you look. During your preparations to go out, play your therapy and exposure scripts to help support yourself through your temptations.

The exposure scripts should include the possibility of all of your feared consequences coming true. By *possibility*, I mean that the scripts should be worded hypothetically: "If I'm as ugly as I think, then everyone will probably be staring at me when I go by, noticing how huge my nose must be." I believe this is more helpful than saying, "I'm ugly, with a huge nose that everyone must be pointing at."

To overcome reassurance seeking, inform those around you who know about your BDD that they should not comment on your appearance at all, nor should they respond to any questions you have about your appearance.

Your behavioral exposures will be made up primarily of going out in public in the imperfect states discussed earlier: imperfect, without preparing, and "wrong." Your hierarchy may also include the kinds of places you go. Walking down an empty suburban street is likely to be easier than being in a well-lit mall.

Treatment won't be easy to go through. Melanie found that on days when she properly prepared herself mentally, she could go out without looking "right" and not care. Sometimes after a run of such carefree days, she would feel as though she would be able to fix her hair in a normal way, without trying to make it perfect. Early in treatment she found that as soon as she would try to

Possible BDD Hierarchy Items

Not Going out in Public Without Hiding Imperfections by Wearing:
A hat
Certain clothing
Sunglasses
Makeup

Refusing to Leave the House with Imperfect:
Clothing
Hair
Makeup
Nails/nail polish

Avoiding the Following Places:
Places where you will see members of the opposite sex
Well-lit places crowded with people
Well-lit places where you will be close to people
Crowds

do this, she would slip into her old thinking and get stuck in front of the mirror, afraid to go out.

Now, about two years later, she can quickly fix her hair. And being out in the rain fills her with joy, because her hair is a mess and she doesn't care. At her worst, she would have never gone out if the skies merely threatened rain. During a recent session, when she was thinking about how far she has come, she summed up her progress and her feelings of freedom by saying, "It's great to be an American."

Not all forms of BDD are focused upon one's own looks. Earlier in this chapter I mentioned Reverse BDD. In reverse BDD, the sufferer focuses upon some imperfection in their partner's appearance—it can be anything from the person's weight, a mole or freckle, a perceived asymmetry of the body to a true disfigurement. Generally the sufferer will report that all they can think about is the imperfection and that it interferes with everything. Notice how this is similar to obsessing about obsessing. It may feel like the issue is the "imperfection," and the feared consequence is how attention to the "imperfection" will ruin everything. The goal of treatment is learning to live with the imperfection. Exposure involves working on making it impossible to avoid the source of the reverse BDD with recorded scripts and other reminders.

BDD can focus upon other aspects of your body besides your looks. For example, there are those among you who feel sure that your body emits some horrible stench, whether it be your armpits, your breath, or wherever. Because overvalued ideation is part of the symptom picture, you feel absolutely certain the odor is there; and yet, despite this belief, you still check to see if it is present. Like BDD, the goal is not to be convinced that you don't have an odor. If no one has directly complained (perceptions that people are subtly turning their heads, covering their mouths, and so on don't count. The complainer has to say it directly in clear words, as opposed to offering you a mint), and you believe they are just being nice, I will agree that it is a possibility. And as long as they don't complain, you have to act normal. You can't constantly deodorize and you can't try to avoid being near other people and whatever else you do to try to hide the odor. Examine your ERP Motivators (page 117) and your Cost-Benefit Analysis (page 120). How much have you lost as a direct result of the odor you think you emit versus what you lost by giving in to your OCD fears.

You might ask what do you do if someone does tell you that you smell. If this were to occur, you can explain that it is a problem you've had for a long time and, unfortunately, there are no treatments for it. You may apologize if you like, but you still have to continue to live as if there were no odor, because in the long run that is much easier and more satisfying that being ruled by your OCD.

IF OVERVALUED IDEATION is part of your OCD, the goal of treatment is not to convince you that you are wrong. Instead, the goal is for you to decide which risks you will take in life. You saw how this worked for the four different disorders presented in this chapter. For GAD, the idea that the worries are real only reinforces the necessity of accepting the treatment goal that disaster might really happen. For OCPD, a sufferer learns to accept living in an imperfect world and purposely doing things "wrong." For hypochondriasis, a sufferer has to accept possibly having an illness that doctors can't fix. For BDD, a sufferer learns to accept that they may always find themselves ugly. What do you have to accept? After acceptance, the real goal of treatment can be pursued: learning to live without being obsessed.

This brings you to the end of Part 3. You have the understanding and the tools to design your recovery program. If you have just been reading, it's time to go back and begin to work. You may be tempted to skip some steps or to try to take shortcuts. Listening to a therapy script as often as I have urged you to is a pain in the neck. You may feel sure that you will be able to remind yourself of everything you need to know. Maybe you are right. But if your way doesn't work, please reconsider for your own sake, rather than incorrectly assuming that you can't recover or that this is the wrong treatment for you. OCD has probably had control over you for some time. Although treatment can be relatively quick, it does require work. If it were easy to get better, you would have done so long ago. Go back over the text and try completely working the program. If you aren't on any medication, consider asking your doctor to add it to the work you need to do.

The process of recovery is one of rebuilding and restructuring your life. Part 4 is devoted to enhancing the recovery process. Chapter 14, Building Supports for Recovery: Beyond Exposure and Response Prevention, focuses on the use of helpers and self-help groups to support your treatment. The final chapter, In Recovery for Life, is devoted to what happens after recovery. In that chapter, you will find the tools needed to maintain your treatment gains.

PART **4**

Recovery and Beyond

Chapter 14

Building Supports for Recovery:
Beyond Exposure and Response Prevention

No matter how much time and effort you devote to your recovery program, you won't be able to do it perfectly. You have other obligations and stresses in your life that will demand your attention. There will be times when working your program will feel too hard and you will be tempted to give in to urges—and sometimes you will. You need to have more than one way to help you through these times. Having more than one way to help means that if one way fails, you have another avenue to try. Your therapy scripts are one method you can use to cope with hard times. Another is having a support system that you can rely on when you need extra help.

The most obvious support system to develop is one made up of family and friends whom you trust. They see you frequently and, for many of you, are available whenever you need them. Another potential support system would be an OCD self-help group. There may be one in your area that you can find out about by contacting the International Obsessive-Compulsive Disorder Foundation (see page 347), or you may want to start your own. There are advantages and disadvantages to families, friends, and support groups.

In thinking about your family and friends as potential supports, I would like you to consider a question: How many times have they accused you of engaging in OCD behavior when you were innocent? If you are like most of the sufferers I have known, the answer is often. Their failure to understand you is a frustrating experience. You are going to have to help them understand both your OCD and what they can do to help. I would like you to consider another question: How many times have they correctly accused you of engaging in OCD behavior but you lied and claimed you were not? In my experience, your answer is the same as it was to the first question: often.

If you are really going to let them help, you will have to change this behavior. Your dishonesty is one of the reasons they don't trust you when you claim you aren't engaging in OCD behavior. Being honest will not only regain their trust, but you won't be able to get away with OCD behavior—which is bad if you want to get away with ritualizing and good for your recovery.

If your OCD is obvious to your family and friends, watching you has been a painful experience above and beyond whatever you have been forcing them to do. I remember the daughter of one of my patients with OCD telling me about a heated argument she had had with her mother. At one point, her mother screamed at her, "You don't know what it is like to be me!" The daughter responded, also in a raised voice, "You're right, we don't know what it is like to be you. But you don't know what it is like to be us!" This response surprised both of them, and they were able to calm down and have a real discussion.

Your family loves you and can see the pain you are in. They are desperate to help, and helpless because they don't know how. Giving in to your symptoms is enabling, but the pain you are in if they try to resist seems too great to force you to bear it. You and they want the same thing—recovery, so that you can be with them. They are probably one of the reasons you want to recover.

To help you, your friends and family will need to understand OCD, what you need them to do and not to do, and how they should act while helping you. For understanding, you can have them read the early chapters of this book, and you can discuss how your own feelings match those that they read about. If they won't read the book, that is okay; you aren't trying to turn them into OCD treatment specialists. Explain your OCD to them as best you can. There is an exercise presented in the box below that often helps non-sufferers to get a better understanding of what it is like to have OCD.

What they need to understand most is the second part: what they should do and not do to help.

Their first job is to be a cheerleader. Too often families, and to a lesser extent friends, expect improvement to be rapid. Rather than noticing successes, they are quick to point out failures or how much work remains to be done. When

Exercise in Understanding the OCD Experience

If you are a family member or friend, stop reading and come back with a pen and paper. You may feel tempted to read on, but given all you are asking of your loved one, isn't it worth the effort of a few minutes on your part? If you have a paper and pencil, do step 1 without reading further.

Step 1: On the piece of paper write: "*I want*" and then after that insert the name of someone you dearly love. Do this before reading further!

Step 2: Complete this step before reading step 3. Go back to your piece of paper and after the name of your loved one write: "*to die a horrible, painful death.*" Again, complete this before reading further.

Step 3: Did you write it? If you did, do you want to cross it out? Do you feel uncomfortable about this? My question for you is why? These are just words on a piece of paper. You may say that they are horrible, but does writing them or seeing them make them more real? Are you suggesting that writing it may make it happen? If not, then why is it worse seeing it on paper? I've put the thought in your head, whether it is written or not. If you didn't write it, I don't understand—don't you want to understand your loved one? Proceed to step 4.

Step 4: If you've written it, are you willing to carry the piece of paper in your wallet? If you aren't, why? You may say that someone might find it, but then I would ask, "How often does someone go in your wallet?"

Step 5: If this exercise made you uncomfortable, you've had a taste of OCD in which you treated the words of a horrible thought as if they were more than words. The difference between you and your loved one is that you won't be bothered by this in the next few hours. For your loved one, this is their life, 24/7. If this didn't bother you, I'm afraid I won't be able to help you to better understand how overwhelming OCD feels. But you can still go back to the chapter and follow the guidelines for being a loving support.

they do this, it makes you feel like your efforts are useless, so why bother trying? If they really want to help, they need to stop being negative. Their role is to notice successes, no matter how small, and to applaud you.

Your helpers need to be supportive. *This means helping you cope with anxiety during exposure without offering reassurance that your feared consequences won't happen.* Tell them what you would like to hear: "I know it's really hard, honey, but you can do this. Think about all of the reasons you want to get better. I'm right here with you."

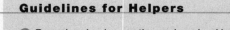

Guidelines for Helpers

1. Be a cheerleader—notice and applaud improvement. Don't dwell on failures or what still needs to be done.

2. Be supportive but not reassuring.

3. Don't undermine exposures by questioning them.

4. When possible, do the exposure yourself. However, do this only with permission, and don't do more.

5. Encourage completing planned exposure goals, but don't nag or push for more to be done.

6. Point out the slips you notice. Be gentle, not aggressive, when encouraging the sufferer to keep doing the program.

7. Don't try to become the "anti-OCD police." It won't work.

If reassurance seeking is one of your problems, tell them how to respond to you. For example, if you suffer from hit-and-run obsessions and you often try to get your spouse to reassure you that you probably didn't hit anyone, instruct them to answer your requests for reassurance with a statement like: "It's really sad. I think you probably did leave a trail of dead babies between the store and here." If this feels reassuring, because you believe that they wouldn't really permit this, then they should answer your question with a reply that doesn't make sense with a statement like: "I wonder if it's going to rain today." This won't be reassuring, because you won't be sure enough that they heard you correctly.

If they don't like the exposures you are doing, they should not try to talk you out of them or suggest that you are going too far or don't have to do them. If they do this, you won't be able to use them. Ideally, they should do what my staff and I do whenever we work with OCD patients. We do whatever exposures we have you do. So for more than twenty-five years, a few times a week, a sufferer and I do exposure together, rubbing our hands on toilets, touching garbage in Dumpsters, and then eating without washing our hands. If your helper is willing to do your exposures with you, that would be very therapeutic. However, they shouldn't do the exposure by themselves without your permission, nor should they do more than you permit.

At the beginning of an exposure session, let them know the minimum you hope to accomplish. This way, they know how far you wish to go. They should encourage you to meet your goal, but they shouldn't do so by nagging or belittling you. They also shouldn't push you to do more than you were planning to do—that is your decision. If you don't succeed in meeting your goal, their role is to be supportive that you tried and to urge you to try again with them tomorrow.

Helpers can be especially important at those times when you are having difficulty maintaining your response prevention. Ideally, you will let them know when you are having difficulty, so they can help you. Unfortunately, there will be those occasions when they catch you in the middle of cheating on your program. When this happens, they should gently remind you of your own goals. They can offer to help you with some on-the-spot exposures or suggest that you try using your delay techniques or therapy scripts to resist ritualizing. You will both be disappointed if you refuse, but rather than continuing to nag you or becoming angry, they should leave you alone. Before they become involved in your recovery program, all of you need to agree that their role is not to become the "anti-OCD police."

If your family and friends can follow these guidelines, they will be able to help you through the rough spots. You may feel that OCD is your problem and that your family shouldn't be burdened by having to support you through your recovery. You are wrong. When you suffer from OCD, so does your family. At one extreme, you may be pressuring them to accommodate your OCD by having them engage in rituals. At the very least, they have to watch you suffer and be lost in the rituals of your mind rather than being with them. Helping you helps the family, so accept their help if they are willing to offer it.

Sometimes, no matter how helpful your family is, you will feel alone because they don't really understand. You will find yourself wishing that there were someone you could talk to who really understands what you are going through. Depending on where you live, you may discover that your wish has come true. There may be an OCD support group within traveling distance of your home.

Across the country, support groups for OCD have multiplied. You can contact the International Obsessive-Compulsive Disorder Foundation by phone or the Internet to find out if there are any support groups near you. If you decide to attend, you may find yourself freed from the isolation of feeling that no one, neither friends nor family, understands. At our support group, new members are filled with wonder when they finally meet people who understand exactly how they feel. They are filled with relief that the people they see are just individuals who they might see anywhere—there is nothing about them that screams, "Look at me, I have OCD." Support groups draw their power from the sharing and camaraderie that develop between members.

Many support groups do not go beyond this sharing. Some may just meet monthly and listen to a speaker discuss topics that are relevant to OCD. Others may discuss the trials and tribulations of having OCD. Some actually become very negative and turn into what one of our group members calls a "pity party," in which the conversation focuses on how terrible it is to have OCD and the side effects of their medications.

If you are really lucky, there may be a GOAL group near you. I started GOAL (*G*iving *O*bsessive-Compulsives *A*nother *L*ifestyle) in 1981 with Gayle Frankel (an OCD sufferer and former president of the Philadelphia Affiliate of the International Obsessive-Compulsive Disorder Foundation). The idea behind GOAL was to develop a format that would provide sufferers with more than a place to meet. Our goal was to create a group that would help sufferers to begin to take control of their OCD. Now, thirty-three years later, a number of OCD support groups across the country have adapted GOAL to their own use, and the International Obsessive-Compulsive Disorder Foundation supports GOAL through dissemination of the GOAL Manual on their website (go to www.ocfoundation.org and type in "goal manual" in the search box or go to this book's site at www.FreedomFromOCD.com) we developed for them.

If there are no OCD support groups near you, you may be interested in trying to form a GOAL group to help you and other sufferers. If there is a local group near you that doesn't use GOAL, you may be able to interest them in converting their format to that of GOAL. What follows is a brief description of how to successfully run a GOAL group.

The GOAL meetings at my center are a joint project of the Philadelphia Affiliate of the International Obsessive-Compulsive Disorder Foundation and my center. We meet every other week, which is frequent enough to allow members to provide steady support for one another. We have found it useful to formally break the meetings into three parts: topic discussion, goal planning, and socializing. As you will see, each of these fulfills a different function to meet the needs of everyone attending.

After providing newcomers with information about how our meetings are run, we move on to discussing the question of the night. Prior to the meeting, the group's leaders choose a topic relevant to OCD for everyone to discuss. At the end of this chapter, you can find a list of questions we have used in the past. Having a question to focus on allows everyone to share their thoughts about different aspects of OCD. Without a question, the group's attention will often end up focusing on the problems of a single member, leaving little time for others.

After the topic discussion, the meeting turns to its main business: goal planning. The idea behind this is deceptively simple: Members are asked to choose a behavioral goal that can be accomplished between meetings. This simple idea transforms meetings into a place of hope, where every individual's success becomes a celebration and inspiration to the other members.

To make your goals work, there are a few rules you need to follow. First, it is critically important that the goal be behavioral and not impossibly huge. Everyone, especially new members, has a tendency to pick something too vague ("I'll cut down on my washing") or too big ("I won't obsess this week"). The problem with the first is how would you know if you were successful. Suppose you had one good day followed by six bad ones. Is that failure or success? The second goal is not only vague, it is impossibly huge. If you can stop obsessing for a week by making a simple decision, you don't have OCD.

Making a goal behavioral requires you to be very specific. A more appropriate goal for washing might be: "On Tuesday and Thursday this week between 2:30 p.m. and 3:00 p.m., I'll do my household chores without washing," or "On Tuesday and Thursday, I will touch the trash can, contaminate my kitchen, not wash for a half hour, and leave the kitchen contaminated for the rest of the day." Being specific makes it easier for you to know when you have succeeded. Before you started your recovery program, you probably attempted to confront and control your symptoms. Most sufferers I have met have tried to face up to their OCD outside a program. Usually they were briefly successful for a few minutes to a few days. If you are like them, this success was followed by slipping back to your symptoms. Then you made the mistake of considering yourself a

Guidelines for Choosing Goals

1. Goals should be behavioral and specific.
2. Don't pick impossibly huge goals.
3. Success should be clearly defined.
4. Goals should be active. Pick something a dead person can't do.
5. Pick something you will do, not something you will try.

failure, wrongly concluding that your failure to forever control your behavior or to reduce your anxiety proves that you are helpless against OCD. In fact, not noticing that there was a period of success was your greatest failure. When you carefully define your goal, you know when to give yourself credit for success.

You will have greater success if the goals you choose are active—or, to put it another way, pick something a dead person can't do. Dead people are notoriously good at not obsessing and not washing. On the other hand, they are terrible at confronting their fears. Passive goals are harder to accomplish and are less effective in producing behavioral change.

The last and most important guideline is to choose a goal that you *will* do, not one that you want to *try* to do. Success is far more important than size. No matter how severe your OCD, a completed goal is a step on the road to success. Over time, using the support of the group, you will build on your goals and move through your recovery program.

GOAL planning is a two-part process for each member. First, each member will report their success or problems they had with the goal they chose at the last meeting. After this, they will choose new goals or find a different way to work on the goals that they didn't achieve. It should be a different way, because if you didn't succeed last time, then why would you expect to succeed if no changes are made in how you approach the goal?

The most obvious way to make a goal different is to make it smaller; perhaps too much was attempted for a first effort. Maybe a newcomer who planned to touch a public restroom toilet with the intention of going home and contaminating his home and everything in it tried to do too much for the first time. A

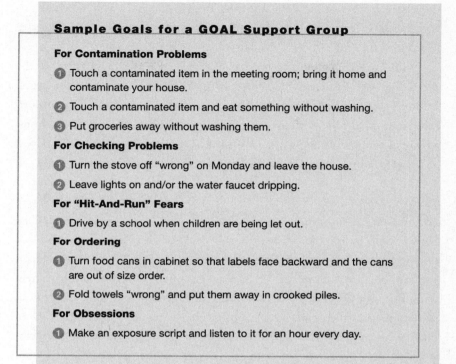

Sample Goals for a GOAL Support Group

For Contamination Problems

1. Touch a contaminated item in the meeting room; bring it home and contaminate your house.

2. Touch a contaminated item and eat something without washing.

3. Put groceries away without washing them.

For Checking Problems

1. Turn the stove off "wrong" on Monday and leave the house.

2. Leave lights on and/or the water faucet dripping.

For "Hit-And-Run" Fears

1. Drive by a school when children are being let out.

For Ordering

1. Turn food cans in cabinet so that labels face backward and the cans are out of size order.

2. Fold towels "wrong" and put them away in crooked piles.

For Obsessions

1. Make an exposure script and listen to it for an hour every day.

more reasonable goal might have been touching a light switch in the room and then contaminating everything at home.

A second possibility is arranging a situation so that you can't fail. There are many ways to do this, and they are limited only by the imagination of the group. In general, you will accomplish this using the support of the group. For example, you could call another member when you are having trouble. Or a member could either meet with you or call you when you are planning to work on your goal.

Some members are intent on trying to achieve their goals without support. They could make an agreement that if they don't achieve their goal by the next meeting, they will allow the group to support them.

Because GOAL is a support group and not intensive therapy or an individualized recovery program, there may be group members who are not as motivated as you are. Respect their feelings. You can encourage members to take goals, but don't pressure them. Over time, the more resistant members will hopefully notice that the members who are doing the best are those who are the most active in working on their recovery, just like you are trying to do.

With GOAL planning completed, everyone is ready to socialize. If the meeting is well organized, members can agree to bring snacks and beverages. Informal socializing allows friends to catch up with one another, to continue to informally discuss the evening's topic, or to just have fun, which will help foster a sense of community and trust. This is crucial for the group, because all of you will be depending on one another for support in accomplishing your goals.

IT IS POSSIBLE to implement your recovery program on your own, but it will be hard. If support from family, friends, and OCD self-help groups is available, I urge you to take advantage of it. In your battle against OCD, use every weapon you can, because you can stop OCD from controlling your life and have freedom. But your OCD is a relentless enemy, one that will look for opportunities to rise up and strike again. After you find freedom, you will have to work to maintain it. Support from others can be one of the weapons you use to defend yourself. But there is more you can do. The next chapter is devoted to life after recovery, and what you can and need to do to stay free from OCD.

SAMPLE QUESTIONS FOR GOAL GROUP DISCUSSIONS

1. What else are you as an individual, besides OCD?
2. Do you use denial in your life or recovery process, and if so, how and when do you find yourself doing so? Would your family agree with your evaluation? Would your therapist agree with your evaluation?
3. (A seasonal question) The holiday is upon us, and we all realize that it will bring with it additional stress. What problems do you ANTICI-PATE having at this time of year? How are you going to cope with them in order to help yourself?
4. When you have done exposure and response prevention and feel that you are contaminating the people around you without telling them, do you feel guilty? How do you handle your feelings?
5. **Series Slip 1:** When you slip, what techniques do you use to help yourself? Which techniques do you find difficult to apply?

6. **Series Slip 2:** Last week the question focused on the steps you may or may not have taken to prevent slips and maintain your gains. Did you do anything different this week as a result of the discussion? If not, why? If you did, what did you do?

7. Group discussion: What are your OCD triggers (for example, overtiredness and various stressors)?

8. Have you told anyone about your OCD; if so whom, and under what circumstances? Whom do you feel you would not choose to share this information with?

9. What one thing was the most difficult for you this week? How did you handle it? How would you handle it differently in the future?

10. How honest do you feel you have been with your therapist, your group, and yourself regarding your fears/obsessions/compulsions, and how would you rate yourself:

   a. Good (I talk about everything, and if something new arises or I slip I bring it up immediately.)
   b. Partially (I tell about most.)
   c. Selectively (I avoid talking about the things I don't want to work on yet.)
   d. Poor (I am guarded and do not talk about all of my OCD problems.)

11. How has the way you have been handling OCD helped or hurt you in your goal of living a symptom-free life?

12. Where would you like to be this time next year? What is your part and/or what do you plan to do to get there? Be specific!

13. David Bowie, at fifty years old, told *Total TV* magazine that he was "happy to resign myself to the knowledge that the search for certainty is the road to insanity. I'm quite content just being a shoveler of knowledge; it compensates for not having the certainty." What are your thoughts about his statement?

14. A few meetings ago, the issue of acceptance came up as an important part of overcoming/coping with OCD. This concept is very important, but in many ways is very hard to understand. If you are here, it's obvious that you know you have OCD, so:

a. What does acceptance mean to you?

b. How do you know if you accept it (that is, what are the signs of acceptance)?

c. How does one come to acceptance?

15. **Fantasy Series 1:** Do you have "fantasies" about the way things should be? In what ways does this affect your life? (See section on Wishing, page 40)

16. **Fantasy Series 2:** Two weeks ago we discussed fantasies and goals. We concluded that each can make us feel better or worse about ourselves. Continuing our discussion from two weeks ago:

a. What fantasies do you have about your OCD or life that make your life more difficult?

b. What realistic goals do you have that help to motivate you?

17. **Fantasy Series 3:** For the last 2 groups we have talked about how trying to make your life match a fantasy leads to misery. Do you know how to give up the fantasies that make you miserable? Have you given them up? If not, why?

18. Miracles come in many forms, but they are usually unexpected. The big ones are obvious, but sometimes the important ones aren't. Finding treatment can feel like a miracle. Finding that it can work for you can be a miracle. And that brings us to the question. Often to find a miracle, you may have to take a risk, a leap of faith. Have you taken any such leaps in the past two weeks and if so, what were the results? Did you experience a small miracle? If you haven't taken any leaps, why?

19. What do you get from coming to group? In what ways has group helped you? Would you miss it, if there were no group?

20. When did you first realize you had a problem? How did you find out that it had a name (OCD) and that there was help for it? What have you done with this knowledge?

21. If your OCD was a creature, an animal or person (real or mythical), what or who would it be and why? Can you think of a way to use this idea in your treatment?

22. A maze is an intricate and winding pattern of interconnecting passages in

which it is easy to get lost. Do you ever feel this way about your OCD? Describe your feelings. How do you cope with such feelings?

23. When dealing with the techniques of exposure, therapists often talk about letting your anxiety be there. What do you do to try to tolerate anxiety?

24. What question would you want answered about OCD? If this were tonight's question, what answer would you give?

25. Have you given in to your OCD this week? Before you gave in, did you think about what treatment would tell you to do? If yes, what could you do to make it more likely that you would listen? If no, would it be helpful to remember? How can you help yourself to remember?

26. Some people, when part of a group, focus on the other members who aren't doing well and use them as an excuse to feel hopeless and give up instead of being inspired by those who are doing well. What do you do? Does it work for you? Do you want to keep doing it?

27. When you have an OCD urge or you actually are about to give in to one, how much time do you spend thinking about what would be best to do treatment-wise? Talk about an occasion when you had difficulty and didn't take the time to consider the treatment steps you should take. Why do you think you didn't do this?

28. **Part 1 of A Different Person Series:** If you didn't have OCD you might be a different person. What would be different about your personality (do not include what different things you would be doing in your life)? Which differences would you like? Which changes would you not want to see?

29. **Part 2 of A Different Person Series:** If you didn't have OCD you might be a different person and as a result your life might be totally different from what it is now. What would be different about your life (do not include what would be different about you)? What would you miss from your current life? What would you have in your different life that you would like? For some of what you would like, is it really true that OCD prevents you from having them?

30. Which is stronger: your hatred of what OCD has stolen from you or your fear of what not giving in to OCD might do to you? Which feeling controls your behavior? Does your answer to the second question agree with your answer to the first?

31. If you could put yourself in your family's place, what would you have them do to help you with your OCD?

32. Has OCD hurt any of your close/important relationships? How? Can you use this as part of your motivation to recover?

33. What is your responsibility in treatment? Are you responsible in your treatment? What does this mean?

34. How do you feel when someone in the group accomplishes a particularly hard goal? Does it inspire you to try harder? Do you have an obligation to the group?

35. Helen Keller said, "Security is mostly a superstition. It does not exist in nature, nor do the children of men as a whole experience it. Avoiding danger is no safer in the long run than outright exposure. Life is either a daring adventure, or nothing." Do you believe this is true and what are your reasons? Given your answer, are you true to your beliefs?

36. We always talk about the advantages of overcoming your OCD, but there are also disadvantages. What would you lose if you didn't have OCD? Would it be worth it? If you have recovered from OCD, what did you lose? Was it worth it?

37. Thomas Edison had many failures before he invented a lightbulb that worked. When asked about this, he replied, "I haven't failed. I've found 10,000 ways that don't work." What does this mean to you?

38. Is there any way that love can help you in overcoming OCD? Why or why not? If you answered yes, how can love help you?

39. What part of your life is affected by OCD that you have chosen to not work on or ignore?

40. Should you share your OCD with non-sufferers? Is there anything to be gained from such sharing? Can you think of any guidelines to follow about sharing?

41. What do you feel is your single biggest success in your fight toward recovery? What has been or still remains your biggest struggle in working on your OCD and toward recovery? Why aren't you successful with both?

42. There probably have been times when you believed your symptoms, thoughts, feelings, and rituals had meaning and you believed they could be true. How have you motivated yourself under these circumstances?

43. Trust and treatment: How are these related? What is their connection to your recovery from OCD?

44. When, if ever, are decisions best left to chance? Why? Does your answer reflect OCD thinking or healthy thinking?

45. How do you handle a relative or person who thinks s/he understands OCD but doesn't, but nevertheless insists upon giving you advice? If this hasn't happened, how would you handle it if it did?

46. The GOAL part of this meeting is what makes our group special and it is the reason it has a national reputation. What do you see as the point of GOAL? Do you use the GOAL part of the meeting to its best advantage? If yes, what guidelines do you follow to choose your goals? If you don't use any of the guidelines, why not?

47. Knowing that you have OCD and that your children may have it, what can you do to help them?

48. Imagine that your worst feared consequence happened yesterday. There is nothing you can do to undo it. How would you cope? (Suicide is not an option.)

49. To overcome OCD you are stuck having to accept living with uncertainty, but acceptance involves the loss of something you want. What will you lose if you accept uncertainty, do ERP, and give up OCD? If you have gone through treatment, what did you lose besides OCD?

50. What would your OCD say to you if it could talk? How would you answer it? Who would be helped by your answer: you or OCD?

51. What do you love about uncertainty? Why?

52. Other than *not* having OCD, what other thing would make you happiest? Do you feel it's obtainable for you?

53. Exposure is an act of confronting your fears. Can exposure be an act of love? What else can it be? How so and how can this help you in treatment?

54. If you had to have a different set of OCD symptoms, what would you choose and why?

55. OCD robs so much from you and can leave you feeling you have lost so much. How do you cope with your losses?

56. What are the advantages of being a slave? What are the problems with having freedom? With regard to your OCD, which of these better reflects your coping?

57. Are you overly concerned with what others may or may not think about you? Does this play any role in your OCD?

58. We often say that it is good to talk back to your OCD, to be angry at it, to fight it, but this is a hard task. Pretend your OCD is a person standing in front of you and talk back to it the way you would want to.

59. No matter how hard you work at fighting your OCD, unexpected situations often arise that result in you giving in. Can you identify any situation(s) that would be especially hard for you to resist? What can you do to help yourself with this knowledge in mind?

60. What one reaction by an important family member or friend to your OCD or recovery most disturbs you? What have you done about it?

61. Although much of life can be uncontrollable and you can't have everything you want, it is also true that *you can't do what you won't imagine!* What does this mean to you?

62. Responsibility is not a matter of what you should do. Responsibility is taking the steps to accomplish the things you want to do. How does this relate to how you handle OCD in your life?

63. What are the characteristics of a good goal?

64. What does accepting uncertainty mean? Have you or haven't you accepted uncertainty? How has this affected your recovery?

65. Shakespeare's Hamlet says, "'Tis an unweeded garden that goes to seed; things rank and gross in nature possess it merely . . ." How is this like OCD in your life?

66. Since uncertainty in life is unavoidable, what is good about living with this fact besides overcoming your OCD?

67. Are you the person you want to be? Would fighting your OCD help you to be that person? How can you use this information in your treatment?

68. *Why me?* Have you ever asked yourself this question with regard to OCD? Is there any harm in asking it? If so, what is the harm?

69. OCD interferes with life in so many ways and often in the midst of giving in, you forget those painful experiences. With this in mind would you be willing to share one of the times your OCD embarrassed you? If not, can you recall an experience and describe how this recollection can help you fight OCD?

70. We are not crippled by our fears so much as we are crippled by our avoidance of fear. Is this true for you and, if so, how?

71. What major non-OCD uncertainties or tragedies have you had in your

life? How did you cope with them? Did you cope with them better or worse than you cope with OCD? Which would you rather face?

72. At one time or another, many of us have felt that we would rather die than live with OCD—so why wouldn't we rather do exposure than have OCD?

73. Research has shown that exposure and response prevention works. All of the people here who have successfully overcome their OCD have used ERP. Have you committed yourself to it? If not, what excuses do you use to avoid it?

74. No one can make us get better if we don't do our part. At the same time, the support and camaraderie of this group help us. How do you expect the group to help you and how are you going to make it possible for the group to help you?

75. When asked what he wanted for his birthday at age five, my son Josh said he wanted to be a movie star. We explained that he'd have to pick something more modest. With regard to your OCD, what gift would you like for this season? Like Josh, you will have to be more modest than wishing for a cure or to be certain.

76. How often do you give yourself credit for the achievements you've already accomplished in group or in treatment? Do you find it easy or hard to give yourself credit for past successes or do you dwell only on the work left to be completed?

77. What about having OCD, if anything, makes you angry? Does this help or hurt your recovery efforts?

78. OCD is often portrayed on talk shows, in movies, and on TV shows. What kind of feelings do you have about the way OCD is represented? What would you want the public to know or understand about OCD?

79. What disasters might happen if you didn't ritualize? What disasters might happen if you give in to OCD? Which would you prefer to live with and why? ("Neither" is not an acceptable answer.) If you preferred giving in to OCD, why are you here?

80. Is it fair that you have OCD? Why or why not? What role, if any, does your attitude play in how you approach treatment?

81. What frightens you most about having OCD besides its symptoms?

82. If someone could guarantee that at some unknown point in your recov-

ery all OCD thoughts and rituals would disappear, would you be willing to work on all of the behavioral goals suggested by a therapist? How much of a guarantee do you need?

83. What risks did you take this weekend? How did this affect your life and your OCD? If you didn't take any risks this past weekend, what risks will you take tomorrow?

84. Denial takes place whenever you compare reality to a fantasy. How does denial interfere with you overcoming OCD?

85. What emotion best portrays how your family reacts toward you and your OCD? What emotion best portrays how you feel about your family during an OCD episode?

86. OCD sucks! With this in mind, it is often said we learn from adversity. I disagree. I think we can learn from adversity and if we are going to be stuck with adversity, we might as well get something from it. What positive things has suffering from OCD taught you?

87. Overlooking how many things he was wrong about, Freud said that the three most important things in life were love, work, and play. Why is play important and can it have a role in fighting your OCD?

88. Faith can take many forms. You can have faith in yourself, in another person, in a higher power. Does faith have any role in your own recovery? How does it help you cope with the uncertainties you fear?

89. Why take risks? In what ways has taking risks helped you? Please note that we are asking how taking risks has helped, not harmed. What risks have you taken this week? If you've taken none, in what ways has avoiding risk harmed you?

90. In *Dune*, Frank Herbert writes, "Fear is the mind-killer. Fear is the little-death that brings total obliteration. I will face my fear. I will permit it to pass over me and through me. And when it has gone past I will turn the inner-eye to see its path. Where the fear has gone there will be nothing. Only I will remain." What are your thoughts about his statement?

91. Imagine you have been diagnosed with a noncontagious fatal illness that will kill you in two years. What changes will you make in how you cope with OCD? What other changes might you make in your life? If the changes are positive, why are you waiting? (Suicide is not an option.)

92. Many of you wish you could *feel* the certainty of knowing. So-called

normal people *feel* certainty when the actual odds are not 100 percent. Is your goal in treatment to eventually *feel* certain when the odds are not 100 percent or to actually *be* 100 percent certain? How much does your answer reflect reality and your odds of recovery?

93. Do you consider yourself an optimist or a pessimist? How does this influence the way you cope with your OCD?

Chapter 15

In Recovery for Life

hen my wife and I first moved into our house, its gardens were completely overgrown with weeds. It took us two or three days just to rip out all the weeds. Then we had to break up the ground, add fertilizers and topsoil, and plant the flowers and shrubs we wanted. The next year it looked wonderful, but we weren't finished. The new plants needed pruning and more fertilizer, and the weeds kept threatening to return in full force if we allowed them to. Your life is like a garden, and OCD is one of the weeds you will have to watch out for.

Overcoming OCD is not like taking care of strep throat, when once you have recovered, the problem is gone. After you complete your recovery, you will still have to cope with OCD. But don't despair. I am not saying that you will have to cope with the kind of devastation and anxiety that you went through before treatment. You can have long periods during which OCD is so completely out of your life that you will wonder how you ever could have been worried by the fears that used to rule you. And then you will slip.

You would think that after successfully battling your OCD, a slip could never bring you down. You are sure that at the first sign of a slip, you will immediately reinstate your recovery program, which is precisely what you are supposed to do. What makes this hard is that you aren't prepared for what a slip feels like. When it hits, it will feel as though you are back where you started. Old learning is reactivated because your anxiety serves as a cue to call up all the other feelings that were associated with your OCD—ritualizing urges, depression, and hopelessness. You will feel as if treatment didn't work, so you might as well give up.

In fact, ritualizing will feel like your best bet, because if exposure and response prevention didn't work, then all that is left is to desperately try to regain your balance through rituals. The hopelessness that drives this can send you spiraling back down into old OCD behavior with its never-ending anxiety and rituals. At my center, my staff and I always warn people about this, so that when it occurs, sufferers can say to themselves, *I didn't really believe Dr. Grayson when he said it would feel like this. Everything inside me is screaming that treatment doesn't work for me and I might as well give up. But he warned me of this. Maybe this is what he meant. Maybe there really is hope if I can get back to work, even though it doesn't feel possible.*

Like your OCD recovery program, a maintenance program is a three-step process of understanding the problem, assessing yourself, and then implementing a program. The first step is understanding how and why relapses occur and how you can cope with them.

Regarding your OCD, you've already learned that the factors that maintain a condition are not the same as those that may have initiated it. For your recovery program, this meant that any environmental or psychological factors that played a role in causing your initial OCD symptoms did not have to be addressed in order for you to overcome your OCD. By the time you came to treatment, your OCD had developed a life of its own. This is not to say that those initiating factors are unimportant. Dealing with them may be helpful to you in a variety of ways, but not in overcoming your OCD. This statement also applies to your recovery. You achieve your recovery by designing and implementing an OCD recovery program. Maintaining your recovery will require different steps.

The implication of the above is that slipping is normal. Research has found that any behavior that has developed and been maintained over a period of time will be resistant to permanent change. Consider how many people you know who have tried to lose weight, stop smoking, start an exercise program, stop drinking, or get organized and have never slipped. The problem is not in the slipping, but in the magnitude of the slip.

Imagine that Charlotte, a five-foot-two blonde, was a hundred pounds overweight before she went on a diet and successfully lost her excess weight.

Suppose she slips and gains five pounds. I would hope she would immediately go back to dieting, because losing five pounds would be easier than losing fifty. But either way, five or fifty, Charlotte can always go back on her diet to lose her extra pounds. How long she waits merely determines how much work it will take to lose the weight again. The same is true for you. Recovering from a small slip in which your handwashing has increased to five minutes per wash will be easier than recovering from handwashes that last five hours.

So you will slip. Slips occur because treatment doesn't replace or erase old learning—it competes with it. All your feelings and behaviors are going to be triggered by the cues and contexts they were learned in. Imagine an alcoholic who goes into an inpatient recovery program. While there, treatment removes all the triggers for his drinking. He goes through withdrawal, thus removing biological urges to drink, and he is away from all his environmental triggers to drink, such as bars, fights with his spouse, and the sight of a can of beer. By the end of his stay, he, like many alcoholics in this situation, will report that he has no urge to drink. But then what happens? He goes back into an environment of bars, a spouse to fight with, and readily available alcohol. Within the first three months of rehabilitation, 50 percent of these alcoholics will have returned to drinking.

The more ways in which the conditions of your life match your pre-recovery conditions, the greater the odds that you will be faced with urges and feelings that will make it hard for you to not slip. Never slipping isn't likely, but never permitting yourself to again become crippled by OCD is possible. At my center I have found that the sufferers who do best are those who accept slips. For them a slip is a red flag, a warning that they need to step up their maintenance work. For those sufferers who don't accept the idea of slips, their occurrence is experienced as a sign of failure and a reason to give up.

To recover from OCD, you had to accept the impossibility of ever being 100 percent certain. To maintain your gains, you have to accept the inevitability of slipping. You don't have to like the fact that you slip, you can hate it when it happens, but you have to find a way to make rapid recovery from slips a way of life. Your denial will translate into attitudes and excuses that you will use as reasons to give in to OCD, despite the hard work you have done.

Examine the excuses in the following box. These excuses have been reported and used by other sufferers to ritualize instead of returning to their recovery

Excuses for Giving in to Urges to Slip*

1 *I won't ever slip.* This overconfident denial will set you up for a terrible crash when you slip for the first time.

2 *I can do this ritual just this one time.* This is the ultimate denial—you are back to gambling at slot machines. How often do you really just do it once?

3 *It's not fair that I have this problem/I will have to work on this forever.* This is true, but refusing to work on slips because they aren't fair won't help.

4 *This is different mode.* You are trying to give yourself permission to slip. Are the consequences of slipping really worth it?

5 *I can't live my life this way/I can't do this anymore.* The work of fighting OCD feels overwhelming, but it is still less work than dealing with the pain of giving in to OCD's relentless demands.

6 *I feel too tired/stressed/rotten, etc.* No matter how overwhelmed you are feeling at the moment, giving in will be worse.

7 *Why should my family have to go through this again?* They'd rather go through exposure than live with all your old rules and demands.

8 *Please let me get away with murder.* You are trying to get your family to pretend that they don't notice that you are slipping, so that you can keep giving in. Would you let one of them fall by the wayside?

9 *I feel too good (also known as leaky roof syndrome).* When a roof is leaking, you can't fix it while it is raining. On the other hand, who wants to work on the roof when you can have fun in the sun? Neither feeling good nor bad is an acceptable excuse to delay doing exposure work after a slip.

*Adapted from Gayle Frankel's *13 Excuse Modes,* a handout she developed for identifying the sufferer's excuses for giving in to urges to slip.

program of exposure and response prevention. Do you recognize any of these excuses as your own?

When you do slip, try to remember the thoughts that were going through your mind at the time. Refer to the thoughts in the box if you are having trouble remembering. Write down the excuses you used, and find an answer that you can try to use in the future if your excuse is the same.

When you examine your slips, you will find that you tend to slip in one of two ways: insidiously slowly or suddenly. Insidiously slow slips start innocently. Imagine that you have contamination concerns and that you allowed yourself a single "illegal" handwash. You do it quickly and don't even have an urge to do another. Do you really have to do exposure in response to this? Before your recovery, you were washing your hands for three to six hours daily. Now, after three months of being almost symptom-free, you slipped with a one-minute handwash. A single one-minute handwash every three months is not a symptom of OCD, especially if there were no other urges or temptations. So you don't respond to the slip with exposure.

Suppose this happens again next week. One minute of rituals a week is hardly a problem. Even the so-called normal population must engage in more than one minute of rituals a week. The real question is: When do you call it a problem?

To understand what is really happening, think about and compare the triggers and cues that used to control your behavior in the past to the ones that do so now. Before treatment, you responded to feelings of contamination with anxiety and washing. Your recovery program taught you to respond to those feelings with exposure and response prevention. In *that one minute, washing your hands instead of relying on exposure increases the power of your old learning*. In addition, before your recovery program, engaging in a ritual was a cue for doing it again. Thus, your one-minute handwash should result in a slight urge to repeat. Neither of these may be enough to have you slip entirely, but what you are doing is setting the stage. Ultimately, the response that will be the strongest will be the one you practice most.

The second kind of slip is sudden and overwhelming. It usually occurs in response to an unexpected situation. If you have fire safety concerns, a major fire in the news or a neighbor's house burning down might trigger your obsessions. Your anxiety and urges to ritualize may hit you like a rushing flood. In this panicked state, another feeling is triggered, one that used to be associated with this onslaught of emotion: You feel hopeless. This experience feels like the old days before your recovery, when you were helpless in the face of your OCD. The fact that you successfully fought your way to health seems irrelevant. I am warning you about this so that in the midst of this nightmare, you will have a thread of hope to hang on to. Hopefully, you won't give up and turn a few bad hours—or even a few bad days—into a relapse lasting many months.

The purpose of your maintenance program is to reduce the frequency of these slips and to cope with them when they occur. To accomplish this, you will have to identify the triggers that lead to slips and then develop and implement alternative ways to cope with those triggers. Some of your triggers will be obvious and easy to identify. These will be situations that were difficult for you to cope with before your recovery and that still periodically result in urges. For example, if you used to suffer with violent thoughts, a particularly violent story on the news may sometimes affect you.

However, triggers also include other cues and situations that make ritualizing more likely. So, for many of you, being at home versus in public may have been more of a trigger for giving in to OCD urges in the past. When you start to include your emotional state and other life events, can you really tell what is causing you to be more responsive to your old OCD cues? Like everything else in life, the answer is not certain. But you can make some good guesses. Identifying these other triggers does not require a deep probing analysis of your psyche. Instead, you merely need to record events that were taking place near or around the time of the slip. Were you sick when the slip occurred? Was there something different about today when you gave in versus yesterday when you didn't?

To help you with this, at the end of this chapter there are two self-monitoring forms that have been modified for post-recovery use. The first one is blank and is for your use. The second has sample entries from a few different sufferers to illustrate how to complete it.

The trigger forms have seven columns. You are already familiar with the time and SUDs columns. The event column has been relabeled Red Flags to emphasize that you are trying to identify triggers that make your ritualizing more likely, whether these are directly or indirectly related to OCD. In place of the ritual column is a Coping Plan column where you can work on alternatives to ritualizing. The remaining three columns are for further categorizing your red flags. They represent three different dimensions that partially describe how the trigger functions in your life. The three dimensions are internal/external, controllable/uncontrollable, and predictable/unpredictable. Understanding how your red flags function will help you develop alternatives that better address your needs.

The internal/external dimension refers to whether the trigger is a function of psychological/biological factors or your environment. Psychological/biological triggers are most likely going to reflect how you are feeling and how you are responding to your own feelings. This kind of trigger usually requires you to take better care of yourself in some manner (for example, getting enough sleep, learning new coping stills, taking your medication, etc.).

Examples of Triggers

Internal/External Dimension

Internal

Emotions (for example, depression, anxiety, low self-esteem, or feeling good), PMS, being overly tired, injuries, chronic illnesses, needing medication for your OCD

External

New jobs, new marriages, new houses, promotions, graduations, divorces, arguments, financial problems, OCD hierarchy items

Controllable/Uncontrollable Dimension

Controllable

Being overly tired due to failing to take care of yourself, social anxiety, staying in a bad relationship, being unassertive

Uncontrollable

PMS, chronic illnesses, a spouse divorcing you, a death in the family

Predictable/Unpredictable Dimension

Predictable

PMS, visits from your in-laws, chronic illness, a new baby, being confronted with past high-risk situations (for example, a public restroom)

Unpredictable

Car accidents, illnesses, discovering that your spouse is having an affair, deaths

One internal feeling that often turns out to be a risk factor for slipping deserves special attention: good feelings. Given that one of your goals was to try to feel better, it may seem strange to you that such feelings may put you at risk. In my experience, it is not unusual for recovered sufferers to report that everything had been going great and then *bam*—they found themselves in the middle of a sudden onslaught of OCD urges. Why does this happen? The answer is deceptively simple: During good times, you will tend to stop practicing your relapse prevention measures. This means that when you are confronted by an urge, you are out of practice, leaving you vulnerable to a sudden slip.

External factors tend to be stressors in your environment. Although what is stressful to one person may not be stressful to another, research has found that all change, whether positive or negative, is stressful. Furthermore, all problems, whether medical or psychological, worsen under stress. Coping with stress may require you to make important life changes that, in turn, will create more stress.

The next dimension to consider is whether the red flags are controllable or uncontrollable events. Controllable situations will require you to take steps to "fix" the situation. Uncontrollable events are ones that you will have to find a way to cope with to minimize their effect on you.

Finally, there is the predictable/unpredictable dimension. Predictable events can be planned for, so that you can preemptively be prepared to cope with them. By analyzing your slips after they occur, you will discover that you can be more prepared for a variety of triggers that previously caught you off guard. But life is never 100 percent predictable, so surprises will happen. Unpredictable situations will be your greatest source of danger. Part of developing a plan of relapse prevention is increasing the odds that you will quickly use exposure to confront surprises rather than delaying and giving your fear a chance to gain a foothold.

It is important to realize that relapse prevention is a very individual process. Because maintaining your gains requires attention to your whole life, you need to carefully examine your life situation. The trigger sheets will help you identify OCD triggers that still need attention and other life problems that are in need of attention.

Maintaining your gains requires you to implement two kinds of interventions: those that make symptomatic behavior less likely to occur and those that make symptom-free life worthwhile. In many ways, the first will be an extension of what you have already done in your recovery program. It is part of creating a totally immersive environment of exposure and response prevention, so that there is little room for slipping. The second may be uncharted territory for you. *It means creating a new life that you will never want to leave.*

There are many ways for you to work on capturing even more territory from your OCD, so that there will be fewer parts of your life for which it can gain a foothold. At this point, you may be wondering if you will ever be able to forsake response prevention to live a "normal" life. Although you should expect that exposure and response prevention will always be a part of your new life, there will come a time when you will be doing it far less intensively. You will be ready to do this when you no longer care about it so much. For example, you can begin to wash your hands when you stop caring so much about washing them.

The purpose of keeping the trigger sheets is to be able to understand what your OCD triggers are, so that whenever possible you can prepare for them in advance. It is always easier to execute a preemptive strike against your OCD than to wait for it to come to you.

Consider the predictable triggers. If you know you always feel stressed when your in-laws come for a visit, then you should start working on your maintenance before they come, not after. If you have contamination fears, then start doing exposure a week before they come, even if you aren't currently suffering from any urges. This way, you will already be back in the habit of exposure when they arrive, so the stress that they bring with them will be less likely to increase your vulnerability to slipping.

If your body has a predictable biological cycle, such as PMS or seasonal patterns of depression, take steps before you find yourself in the middle of the cycle. If possible, consult with a doctor to see if you should raise your medication at vulnerable times or if there is some other medication that you could add during these higher-risk periods.

This kind of preparation is like dieting before you go on a cruise, not afterward. Before the risky event takes place, you will already know what kind of shape you are in, as opposed to figuring out how to recover later.

Every time you leave your home, you should make a habit of thinking about the situations you may find yourself in that could present a challenge. If you are going out to dinner, what will seem contaminated? If you are going to the movies, are you likely to see anything that may trigger your violent or sexual obsessions? The purpose of doing this is not to avoid these situations, but to create therapy scripts that will help you face whatever you come up against. You should keep these therapy scripts and periodically listen to them, just to keep your long-term goals in mind.

Continue to use red dots as reminders to do this. Put them in places that were high-risk areas for you. Over time, you will stop always noticing the red-dot labels. Whenever you see one, treat it as if you had slipped or were about to, and spend some time doing exposure and response prevention, even if you don't need to. This way, you are practicing using exposure when you hadn't been expecting to, which will make you more likely to use it when you really need it.

Don't completely forsake your exposure and response prevention. If you have violent obsessions, then at least one picture that depicts violence should always be in sight. If you have contamination fears, the house should always be a little bit contaminated. Keeping exposure and response prevention in your life will act as a barrier between you and OCD. In this case, your plight is like that of an alcoholic. If he has given up drinking, then going to a bar is a slip. If he permits himself two beers a day, a slip is that one extra drink, and that doesn't seem like a big deal, but he is three drinks closer to slipping than if he hadn't been drinking at all.

Don't lie to yourself. It is normal to try to minimize your problems, to let yourself get away with a slip. This is how you will slip insidiously slowly. Your family and friends will be a safeguard against this. When they catch you, your honesty with them will not only help keep you OCD-free, but it will also strengthen your relationship with them. If there is a GOAL group in your area, then attending meetings can be a great way to take the time every once or twice a month to make sure that you aren't slipping. Meetings can be a great help for coping with unpredictable triggers—those times that OCD sneaks up on you and yells *"Boo!"* Once at the group, you can get help to keep your OCD under control.

If you are confronted by that rare event that requires you to engage in ritualistic-type behavior, plan to do exposure afterward. For example, if you were exposed to radiation, following recommended washing instructions makes perfect sense. On the other hand, this should be followed with exposure, so this real situation doesn't become an OCD relapse.

Finally, have more than one plan to cope with slips. You may have reached the point where you can simply ignore urges and go on. If this works, then it is okay to take no further steps. If urges to ritualize start to become more frequent or intense, or if you ritualize, then you need to have a plan B. Talk to your supports or return to a support group. If necessary, re-implement your exposure program.

This brings us to the second part of recovery: making a symptom-free life better than one with OCD. You may find this goal confusing—how could a symptom-free life not be better? This is a very individual question. I have worked with people who suffered from OCD and had few other problems. For them, recovery meant being able to enjoy their family, being more productive at work, and finally having free time to enjoy long-neglected hobbies. If this describes you, then there may be some situations in which you need to improve your symptom-free life, but it probably won't be your biggest task.

If, on the other hand, your OCD has had you housebound for eight years, so that you have no solid career plans and few social relationships, you will now face a host of other problems. Overcoming your OCD didn't fix these—it merely put you in the position to start working on them. It may feel overwhelming and frightening to have to cope with these issues. In fact, in comparison, coping with your OCD may now seem to be the easier of the two, because I could tell you exactly what to do to achieve freedom from OCD, but not what to do with your career or social relationships.

A related problem for most sufferers is the newly available free time created by overcoming OCD. If all your pre-recovery time had been completely occupied by rituals, you will find that after a brief honeymoon of freedom, learning to cope with free time is a stressor. A void is created, and if you don't fill it, then OCD will. Learning to plan and pursue life goals rather than dreaming about them is work.

Building a meaningful and satisfying life is perhaps the most important maintenance strategy you can implement. If you have other issues, whether they be marital problems or low self-esteem, work on them. You lost too much time to OCD for you to settle now. You are trying to create a life that is so rewarding that a slip becomes a screaming red flag that terrifies you into exposure, because you know with all your heart that you don't ever want to go back to where you were.

Ideally, you will experience just the right amount of upset when an urge arises. You won't be so nonchalant that you simply ignore the slip, and you'll also want to avoid the other extreme in which you berate yourself as a failure to the point where it seems that you might as well give up. Finding the middle ground between denial and self-condemnation is the kind of balanced response you want to cultivate. Life with its stresses and surprises guarantees that urges will arise, and sometimes you will give in. That's okay, because no one can do a maintenance program perfectly. It probably isn't even desirable, let alone possible.

So HERE YOU are, in America at last. But that was only part of the goal. After all, what's the point of coming to America if you aren't going to take advantage of all that it has to offer. A good journey is one with more to see. I hope such a path is now yours to explore.

TRIGGER SHEET FOR IDENTIFYING AND PLANNING FOR RED FLAGS

TIME	RED FLAGS (events, stressors, etc.)	INTERNAL/ EXTERNAL	CONTROLLABLE/ UNCONTROLLABLE	PREDICTABLE/ UNPREDICTABLE	COPING PLAN (exposure, red dots, etc.)	SUDS

TRIGGER SHEET FOR IDENTIFYING AND PLANNING FOR RED FLAGS

TIME	RED FLAGS (events, stressors, etc.)	INTERNAL/EXTERNAL	CONTROLLABLE/UNCONTROLLABLE	PREDICTABLE/UNPREDICTABLE	COPING PLAN (exposure, red dots, etc.)	SUDS
8 A.M.	being caught off guard by the morning news	E	C	P	place a red dot on the TV, make sure to watch	
10:30	coworkers discussing a shooting on the news	E	U	U	make a point of bringing up the subject first	
5:15	violent thoughts while driving home	I	U	U	play exposure recording while driving this week	
—	violent thoughts	I	U	U	carry a pen knife all the time	
—	violent thoughts	I	U	U	use red dots to remind myself to do "mini" exposures	
8:00	hearing a man coughing behind me in a movie theater	E	C	U	next time, prepare myself before going out both mentally and behaviorally by pre-contaminating myself; have Jeff remind me to do exposure if he notices my discomfort	
—	having thoughts of the devil as Halloween approaches	E	U	P	decorate my house for Halloween, listen to exposure scripts, watch devil movies starting Oct. 1	
—	I'm tired and more vulnerable when I stay up late watching TV	I	C	P	don't watch the evening news; instead, listen to radio and/or read in bed	

SAMPLE

Appendix A

Therapy Script Starters

For your convenience, the scripts that have appeared throughout the book are reprinted with some modifications in this appendix. Rather than present them in the order in which they appeared in the text, they have been rearranged according to their purpose and theme. When you are creating scripts, incorporating more than one theme is preferable to using only one. The following script samples have been broken down into different themes and are written so that you can choose the numbered statements you like and string them together to make a sensible and coherent script for yourself. To help maintain the sense of the script between statements you may need to add words like *and, but,* and *because.*

Some items are starred (★). This indicates that the phrase can be used for problems other than the ones that are suggested with no change or a minor change. For example, the item might say, "I need to live with contamination." This one could easily be changed to "I need to live without checking" or "I need to live with the risks of not checking."

This organization should allow you to easily find the scripts and materials you will need for your ongoing recovery program. You will be able to find useful materials in scripts for OCD presentations other than your own. For example, the futility of trying to protect others from harm presented in the "I'm Not Going to Let OCD Win" script for contamination fears can easily be adapted to any presentation with this feared consequence. The page numbers where the original scripts can be found in the text are provided in parentheses after the script title to make it easier for you to review how the script was originally used. Statements from ERP Motivators Form (page 117) can be added to any of these or they can just be strung together as necessary. Finally, included in this section are subject headings and page numbers for various unscripted parts of the book that you may want to locate readily, such as the "marriage metaphor," for finding out whether a decision you made was right or wrong.

GENERAL SCRIPTS SUPPORTING YOUR SELF-HELP PROGRAM

On the Impossibility of Knowing, of Being Certain, or of Making a Good Decision

1. Logic won't change feelings, nor will it lead to certainty: the pizza metaphor (page 11)
2. Logic won't change feelings, nor will it lead to certainty: the scientific explanation (page 19)
3. Finding out whether your decision is right or wrong: the marriage metaphor (page 57)
4. Gun Test #1: how to make guesses (page 12)

On the Role of Medication in Your Recovery

1. The interplay of medication and learning: the Prozac side-effects example (page 42)
2. How medication helps: the alcoholic metaphor (page 43)

To Support Your Ability to Do the Work of Recovery

1. Your competence in everyday life (page 4)
2. Gun Test #2: ritualizing is a choice (page 23)
3. Your past attempts don't predict the future: my son biking up the hill metaphor (page 70)
4. Overcoming fears of confronting uncertainty: the *Fiddler on the Roof* metaphor (page 58)

I'm Not Going to Let OCD Win (Page 138)

1. ★*I'm sick of what you have been doing to my life.*
2. ★*You are there at every turn, trying to ruin everything that I do.*
3. ★*Look what listening to you has done to my life. I'm sitting here an anxious wreck.*
4. ★*I've lost too much to you already and I'm not letting you take any more from me.*
5. ★*You can do your worst, but I'm not going to listen.*
6. ★*I've been running from your threats, but look where that has gotten me. No more! I'm not giving in to you.*
7. ★*You think you can make my anxiety worse? Then do it, because I'm not going to let that work.*
8. ★*I will beat you and I'll learn to cope with whatever life throws at me, because after living with you, I know what hell is like. And after beating you, I'll know that I'll be able to handle anything life throws at me.*
9. ★*I have lost too much of life listening to you.*
10. ★*That's why I'm listening to this now and following through with all of the exposures. I'm making it inescapable. If this pushes me over the edge, then I'll have to let that happen, because my way felt like I was going over the edge anyway.*
11. ★*As it was, I was harming my relationships with my kids and spouse. Against that definite harm, I will have to risk having them hurt by whatever I do.*

Noticing My Successes (page 137)

1. ★*Today I succeeded by doing "x." If I'm not feeling like this is much of a step, I'm forgetting to follow through with one of the important rules for beating this: congratulating myself.*

2. ★*No matter what else happened today, I was being successful when I did "x." My big goal is to build on this, so that I am doing more—doing bigger exposures and more response prevention.*

3. ★*What I did today puts me on the road to where I want to go.*

Rules for Taking Risks: the Three-House Rule (page 173)

1. ★*No one can assure you that there won't ever be a fire in your home. Nor can anyone promise you that it won't be your fault. A fire could even take place while you are in therapy. At my center, I tell sufferers that if this happens, I want them to continue doing exposure, even if the fire was caused by the exposure—that somehow leaving the lights on caused the fire, or the one time you didn't check the stove, not only was it on, but something was near enough to the stove for it to catch fire and burn the house down. I ask you to do this because fires can happen, and we have to find a way to continue.*

2. ★*If I was driving and accidentally hit someone because I was changing the radio station at the critical moment when they walked into traffic, what would I do? I would feel horribly guilty. But I would have to find a way to cope with the guilt, and I would have to drive again. So if you burn your home down, I would ask you to continue with treatment.*

3. ★*Now let's suppose you follow my directions and burn down a second house. You are incredibly unlucky, but I would still urge you to stay in treatment. Finally, what if you burn down a third house? If you burn down three houses, then I think it is reasonable and important to discuss what you need to do to check and be more careful. Remember, this is three houses on three separate occasions. If you burn down a city block, that still counts as just one! This is the Three-House Rule.*

Reminders of How My OCD Affects My Family (page 161)

1. ★*As my children grow older, I will lose their respect and have to live with the thought that they may be telling their friends how crazy their mother (father) is.*

2. ★*And that assumes my husband (wife) stays with me. What if he/she leaves? And the worst of it, the way they live, they could still get hepatitis (insert your own feared consequences here) if they left and all my rituals would have accomplished was losing both their respect and their company.*

Accepting Less Satisfaction Now for a Better Life Tomorrow (page 145)

1. ★*Maybe I'm not going to totally enjoy doing "x." Maybe I will only get 60 percent of the enjoyment I could get if I were anxiety free. By delaying and continuing response prevention, I am fighting my OCD and working toward a time where I won't have to worry about ritualizing.*

2. ★ *Rather than focus on what I might miss now, I need to remember how much more I will miss in the future if I don't fight my OCD.*

Support for Contamination Exposure and Response Prevention (page 138)

1. ★*I'm not going to decontaminate (insert your obsession). In fact, I'm going to do more exposure. Maybe I'll get sick (insert your feared consequence) from this, but so what? At least I'll be free of you. Being sick (insert your feared consequence) in peace is better than the living hell you try to keep me in. Just watch me do exposure.*

2. *You think making my family sick will stop me. Then do it, because I'm not listening to threats anymore. At least I'll be able to enjoy my family, however long I'll have them.*

Religious Obsessions Exposure and Response Prevention (page 258)

1. ★*I'm not going to listen to your false promises anymore. If anything were ever a devil, it's OCD. You always make promises to me that you will make my fear go away if I listen to you. But whenever I listen, I find myself deeper in hell, with you telling me that you want just a little more.*
2. *My religious rituals are all my ways of giving in to fear and that isn't the kind of religion I want. So you can do your worst, but I'm not going to follow your lies anymore.*
3. *I'm going to turn to my real faith and ask God for the determination to stay with my recovery program. Even though I may be wrong, I'm going to believe God is nice and forgiving and that going through this seemingly blasphemous treatment is actually an act of faith on my part. If I'm wrong in what I'm doing, then so be it. I trust God's will, even if it means I'm to be punished by Him.*

SCRIPTS TO SUPPORT RESPONSE PREVENTION

1. How learning makes you want to ritualize: the gambling metaphor (page 22)

Supporting Response Prevention Script Using Delay (page 144)

1. ★*I can make myself hold out for just a few minutes, no matter how hard it is. There have been other times when I was forced to delay by circumstances, so even though this is hard, I can make myself do it.*
2. ★*It doesn't matter if I have always ended up ritualizing in the past, because any practice in delaying will build up my ability to delay in the future.*
3. ★*As for what I do after this delay, I will put off deciding either way until this delay is over. And the other reasons I'm going to do this are . . .*

Rituals Don't Really Work: Certainty Is Impossible (page 227)

1. ★*The worst of it is, the therapy rationale is right: I don't know a way to be certain. There is some truth in the idea that all certainty is an illusion. I hate that. But reality doesn't care what I hate. Everyone hates uncertainty. I live with it in other parts of my life. I accept the possibility that "x" (include uncertainties you do live with, for example if you don't have contamination concerns or fears of being attacked by others) could happen.*
2. ★*I accept the possibility that "x" (include uncertainties you do live with, for example if you don't have contamination concerns or fears of being attacked by others) could happen. That is what I'm going to need to do with my (include your obsessions).*
3. ★*There is nothing I can do to make sure that I won't harm anyone I love. It could happen at any of the times I'm concerned about and the best strategy I can come up with is hoping it doesn't happen, knowing full well that hope won't prevent anything.*

Rituals Don't Really Work: I Can't Truly Protect Anyone (page 141)

1. ★*Knowing that my loved ones could die from "x" is very painful and I hope it doesn't happen. However, I realize that death is not in my control. In fact, this fear—that they could die from "x"—is really covering up a more pervasive fear and truth: I can't really protect my loved ones and there are too many ways they might come to harm. There are even other ways I could make myself responsible for their well-being that aren't related to contamination (insert your own obsession here). Do I have our cars perfectly maintained? Do I check them thoroughly before driving them anywhere? Have I done everything pos-*

sible to protect my family from fire (insert an obsession that isn't yours here)? And although I try to make sure I don't contaminate (insert your own obsessions here) them, do I really do everything possible or are there ways I could protect them more? For example, why shouldn't I be responsible for making sure they don't come into contact with anything potentially dangerous in the environment when I'm not around?

2. ★ *The fact is, I only try to protect them from harm related to my OCD fears and even there, I don't do everything possible. I am inconsistent and this is good, because the more consistent I am, the worse my OCD would be. In learning to accept they could come to harm from my exposures, I am also trying to cope with the fact that I can't protect them as much as I would like. I need to do these exposures to reach the point where I accept that the only time I can have my family is when I am with them. When they aren't with me, they are just fond memories of the past and a hope to see them in the future. With my OCD, I don't even get to have them in the present.*

3. *I need to try to learn to accept the possibility of their loss if I am ever to enjoy them while I can. That's why I have to choose to put everyone at risk with these exposures.*

4. ★ *Because the saddest thing of all is that for all of the time and pain spent on my ritualizing, I don't even get the safety I crave.*

Rituals Don't Really Work: My Rituals Are Useless Anyway for Contamination (page 162)

1. ★*If I look at my rituals, do they accomplish what I want? Am I 100 percent consistent or are there areas that I allow to slide just like non-sufferers do? And what about my family members? I can't watch them twenty-four hours a day, so I don't know if they carry out the rituals that I ask. Even if I try to fall back and claim that I'm not responsible for things they might bring in the house, why aren't I? Couldn't I be more observant? Couldn't I do a better job of cleaning up after them?*

2. *The fact is, the contaminants I fear are probably already in the house, so I would actually have to engage in more rituals than I currently do to be safe and sure. And that's too much, even for me. Besides, I can never be 100 percent certain, so doing exposure to get used to the current level of contamination and risk is my only real choice.*

3. ★ *And what if my OCD drives my family to leave me? That would be my fault. And the worst of it, the way they live, they could still get hepatitis (insert your own feared consequences here) if they left and all my rituals would have accomplished was losing both their respect and their company*

Rituals Don't Really Work: My Rituals Are Useless Anyway for Checking (page 172)

1. *For all of the effort I put into my rituals, "x" is still at risk. A fire could start in the building at anytime because of all of the other tenants. On top of this, even I don't check everything I can. I leave my refrigerator plugged in. I leave the stove plugged in and I think that's the most dangerous appliance I have. I don't go into the storage room in the basement every night to check and that place always makes me nervous about fire. I'm already taking these risks. I need to do these exposures to get better. I know that increasing my rituals isn't going to make the building any safer, so I need to learn to live with the uncertainty of fire and to live by the "Three-House Rule."*

Rituals Don't Really Work: My Rituals Are Useless Anyway for Hypochondriasis (page 283)

1. ★*I find myself checking endlessly and looking for reassurance constantly. I have to find a reasonable way to pursue my medical concerns, which will mean accepting many ideas I don't like.*

2. *I'm stuck accepting that there might always be another test or a test that came out wrong, but that my alternative is living in hell like I do or learning to live with risk. Because the sad thing is, for all of my checking I don't feel better either mentally or physically.*

3. ★ *No matter how much it seems to me that someone should have an answer, they haven't to date.*

4. *Rather than setting up appointments and living my life in between, I spend every second suffering with worry.*

5. *If nothing really is wrong, look at the time I've wasted and lost. And if something is wrong, look at the time I've wasted, lost, and will never have a chance to ever recover.*

SCRIPTS TO SUPPORT THE HARD WORK OF EXPOSURE

Supporting Exposure to Decision-Making Obsessions (page 197)

1. *My exposure is to make decisions the wrong way and to risk them being wrong. It feels wrong to do this and I really may make wrong decisions doing this. If this happens, I'm going to have to find a way to live with wrong decisions, because there is no way to make a right decision and even no decision is a decision. Up to now, I have often been choosing the "no decision" by default and look where this has gotten me (include material from ERP Motivators, page 117).*

Supporting Exposure to Ordering (page 204)

1. *As much as I like a neat and clean house, I have to admit that the amount of time it takes to keep it that way is too much, even if I were to allow others to help. Imagine what I could do with that time that might be fun. I know my family would appreciate it.*

2. ★*But what about my feelings and what I like? I know all of my answers to this, but look at what I lose (include material from ERP Motivators, page 117).*

3. *Now I know what it feels like to be an alcoholic who has to give up drinking. Except alcoholics aren't supposed to ever drink. My ordering may be ruined, but my house won't be a total wreck.*

4. *Changing may feel like complete chaos, but it really won't be. It just won't be my black-and-white way.*

Supporting Exposure to Primarily Mental Obsessions (page 227)

1. *I find it so hard to imagine that I am supposed to allow these horrible ideas to stay in my head and never know what they will mean or if I will do them. It really doesn't seem possible to live with such thoughts in my head. But I have been suffering with this for so long. Look at all that I've lost while having this problem (include material from ERP Motivators, page 117).*

2. *It's not like I get to enjoy anything with this problem haunting me. Therapy says I might do the exposures and live with only 40 percent enjoyment. That's more than I get now, when I avoid things like . . . (include same or more facts from ERP Motivators, page 117).*

3. *The worst of it is, the therapy rationale is right. I don't know a way to ever be certain.*

There is some truth in the idea that all certainty is an illusion. I hate that. But reality doesn't care what I hate. Everyone hates uncertainty. I live with it in other parts of my life. I accept the possibility that "x" (include uncertainties you do live with, for example if you don't have contamination concerns or fears of being attacked by others) could happen. That is what I'm going to need to do with my violent/religious/sexual obsessions. I'm going to have to learn how to let the thoughts be there.

4. ★ *Treatment sounds horrible, but so is my life right now. Look how I am, when I'm in my worst state. I really do want to come to America.*

Scripts for Imaginal Exposure to Feared Consequences
Exposure Script with Supportive Statements for Contamination Fears (page 160)

1. *I need to contaminate my entire house, even if my family contracts hepatitis (insert your own feared consequences here) and everyone blames me and asks how could I have followed advice from this stupid book. I don't want this to happen, because if it did, I can see myself standing over the open caskets of my family, looking at my husband/wife and knowing it was my fault he/she died; and seeing my innocent little ones, knowing that I robbed them of their life and knowing that everyone in the church is staring at me and accusing me. But I still need to do this, because even though all of the above might happen, if I don't follow through with exposure, I won't have any family life, because I can't function this way.*

2. *As my children grow older, I will lose their respect and have to live with the thought that they may be telling their friends how crazy their mother (father) is. And that assumes my husband (wife) stays with me. What if he leaves? And the worst of it, the way they live, they could still get hepatitis if they left and all my rituals would have accomplished was losing both their respect and their company.*

Exposure Script for Hit-and-Run Obsessions (page 178)

1. *When I'm driving on "x" road, I know there is a possibility that I have hit someone. I always try to convince myself that I would know, but I know my attention to driving can't be perfect.*

2. *Even though I don't like the idea, there is no way for me to be sure I would know it if I hit someone without realizing it. To fight my OCD, I'm going to have to risk leaving someone in the road, slowly dying, and not go back for them. Even if this means I'm identified and have to stand trial for hit and run.*

3. *It would be awful to have everyone know I irresponsibly ran someone over and left. Especially if I could have saved them.*

4. *I'm only allowed to check if I am 100 percent sure I hit someone. If I have the slightest doubt, I have to do exposure by continuing to drive without checking and hoping that if I'm wrong, no one catches me. If that is the case, I will also have to live with never knowing how many people I may have hit and escaped being caught.*

Exposure Script to Interfere with Mental Retracing Obsessions of Being Misunderstood with the Feared Consequence Being Insulting Others (page 191)

1. *Going over today's conversation with X can only hurt me. I need to accept that I can't know whether or not I hurt her/him. I can't call her/him up to apologize or clarify what*

happened, because that will just make me look weird and this is one of the reasons for getting over my OCD.

2. *If I hurt X's feelings it is going to have to be his/her responsibility to tell me. All of the things we said, and all of his/her actions since then, are not going to tell me for sure what happened.*

3. *I would hate it if I hurt X, but I have to remember I hate this OCD and what is has done to me. I can't forget that people notice it, probably more than I realize. How many times have people told me that I'm always saying I'm sorry? Maybe they aren't just being nice. Probably they think that something is wrong with me for doing this. This is one of the reasons I'm talking to myself now, working on making the retracing something in the background, like noise.*

Exposure Script to Interfere with Mental Retracing Obsessions of Misunderstanding Others (page 192)

1. *As much as I want to go over the details of the conversation I had with X today, it is important for me to interfere with that temptation, by listening to what I am saying now. I know I have OCD and no matter how important the conversation might be, I'm going to have to risk any disaster that might come from me not understanding what he said.*

2. *I have to work on accepting the possibility of whatever disaster (insert your own feared consequences here) in order to get over the hell of living with this OCD forever. I should know by now that there is a good chance that all my retracing will do is create more anxiety and more questions. After all, I can't even know if I'm remembering the conversation correctly, let alone having a perfect understanding of it. (Add to this scripts of your own feared consequences).*

Exposure Script to Interfere with Both Counting and Compulsions of Wishing Problems Away (page 209)

1. ★*This is to remind me of my task in my "high-risk" situations. Am I counting (insert your own ritual here) on purpose? If so, I should pay more attention to this script. If I'm in a private place, I can even speak along with this script, because eventually I'll know it by heart.*

2. ★*I can hate the counting (insert your own ritual here), but when it is in the background, I don't have to let it rule me. Maybe it will interfere with my concentration or enjoyment right now. I want to learn to say "so what?" to such interference. After all, many things can interfere. I could have a headache. I could be next to a loud obnoxious person who is playing music I can't stand.*

3. ★*Life is full of imperfect times and this is one of them. It doesn't matter if it would be better without counting (insert your own ritual here), because this is my life now. My job is to enjoy whatever I can at this moment—no matter how small the crumbs are. Gradually I will learn to allow counting (insert your own ritual here) to occur in the background without caring. But that isn't going to happen today.*

Lower-Hierarchy Exposure Script for Symmetry/Movement Compulsions (page 216)

1. *Make sure I always lead off with my left foot. This includes going through doors, stepping off and on to curbs, and going up steps. Look for cracks and step on these with my left foot.*

When I pass poles or street signs, look to the right and pass them on the left. Anything may happen, but I need to get over this problem.

2. ★ It doesn't matter if I want everything to be safe, this is what I need to do now.

3. Make sure I don't touch things twice with my right hand when I pass them. And sing. Listen to this and sing. I'm not supposed to do any of those word rituals to undo anything. I need to learn to live with risk. And at the park, touch all swings with my left hand first. Sit in each swing, lift my feet and then get off the swing with my left foot first. Always left. No matter what might happen.

Higher-Hierarchy Exposure Script for Symmetry/Movement Compulsions (page 216)

1. When I leave home, I have to make sure that I start with my left foot, so Mom might die (insert your own feared consequences). Always do this, whether going through doors, stepping off and onto curbs, use my left foot to risk my mom's life. I have to let her have a stroke so I can have a life. This problem has tortured me too long.

2. ★ If I'm terrible for doing this, then I'll have to let myself be terrible.

3. Look right when I come to street signs and poles, even if it causes Dad to have a car accident. Pass them on the left, even though the car accident may leave him a bloody mess. And singing. I'm supposed to sing quiet songs about Dad and Mom dying while I'm doing this so that I don't sneak in any of those word rituals.

4. ★ Mom and Dad may die because of me and then it will be my fault. And I have to do this and live with it to overcome my OCD.

Lower-Hierarchy Exposure Script for Violent Obsessions (page 228)

1. ★There is nothing I can do to make sure that I won't harm anyone I love. It could happen at any of the times I'm concerned about and the best strategy I can come up with is hoping it doesn't happen, knowing full well that hope won't prevent anything.

2. ★That's why I'm listening to this now and following through with all of the exposures. I'm making it inescapable. If this pushes me over the edge, then I'll have to let that happen, because my way felt like I was going over the edge anyway.

3. ★If I do any of the things I'm concerned about, that's when I will have to cope with the consequences. I hate the thoughts, but have to learn to let them be there.

4. ★I have to remember why I'm doing this. I want to be able to enjoy life and my family. With OCD I have nothing.

5. ★If I'm a terrible person for having these awful thoughts, then I have no choice but to be a terrible person. I don't know how, but I'm going to have to learn to be a happy terrible person, keeping my fingers crossed that I don't act on my fears.

6. ★As it was, I was harming my relationships with my kids and spouse. Against that definite harm, I will have to risk having them hurt by whatever I do.

Higher-Hierarchy Exposure Script for Violent Obsessions (page 229)

1. There is no way for me to truly protect my wife and son from me. I just have to live with the possibility that, just like everyone else, I could lose control and kill both of them tonight. If I do lose control, I might get my sheath knife and stab my little son in his sleep and then go to my wife and stab her before she has a chance to defend herself.

2. Living with myself afterward would be so hard—I don't know how I would be able to take it. Going through a trial, knowing I had done the most horrible thing I could think of and

then languishing in a prison with nothing to do but be tortured by what I had done. But this is the possibility I have to accept to get better. If I lose control and stab them to death, then I'll have to cope with it.

3. *For all of my ritualizing, I never feel 100 percent safe. The rituals never really prove I won't be responsible for choking the life out of my son. So I have to keep doing these exposures and listening to this script.*

4. *And when I start to worry that I might really do these things, because the scripts are beginning to bore rather than horrify me, well, that's another chance that I have to take. I want to be able to live in the present and enjoy my life rather than worry about what might happen. There are so many things I want to enjoy (insert from your Cost-Benefit Analysis) and I'm sick of this stupid OCD having its way with me.*

Lower-Hierarchy Exposure Script for Sexual Molestation (page 237)

1. *I see my son riding his bicycle and the thoughts pop into my mind. I have to let them stay there without reassuring myself. I'll hate myself if anything happens, but that's the risk I'll have to take.*

2. *I can't tell if I'm feeling anything, but it doesn't matter. If the feelings mean I'm aroused by him, then I'll just have to live being the kind of person that I am.*

3. *I'm going to work at getting used to these feelings so at least OCD won't interfere with our relationship. As it is now, I avoid being alone with my son and it's beginning to be a problem between my husband and me. I have so much to lose if I don't overcome my OCD. As for what I might lose if my feelings aren't OCD, I'll have to cope with that if it happens.*

Higher-Hierarchy Exposure Script for Sexual Molestation (page 237)

1. *What if I were giving my son a bath and suddenly was overwhelmed by sexual feelings. Suppose this happened just when I was getting ready to wash his penis. If this happened, just the idea of soaping it up would excite me.*

2. *I might think that because he is three he won't know what I'm doing. But even though all of this might happen, I still have to confront my OCD and give him baths.*

3. *Even if this ends with me blowing raspberries on his belly and while he is laughing work my way down to his penis and then take it into my mouth. The sexual arousal running through me might be so overwhelming that all of this could happen. But he and I are going to have to take the risk that I'm really this kind of evil person.*

4. *I'm already evil enough to have these kinds of thoughts and I have to learn to live with this (include material from Cost-Benefit Analysis as to why you should keep listening to this).*

Lower-Hierarchy Exposure Script for "Am I Gay?" Obsessions (page 237)

1. *I'm in a Starbucks noticing the other men getting coffee. Some of them look gay to me. I'm not sure how this makes me feel. If I'm really gay, I'll have to decide whether or not to stay married and accept second best. I really would like to leave Starbucks, but I have to stay here with these feelings and let them be here.*

Higher-Hierarchy Script for "Am I Gay?" Obsessions (page 238)

1. *I'm going to start using public restrooms again. I know that if someone is using the urinal next to me, I will notice his penis.*

2. *I may even get those feelings in my penis that might be sexual arousal. If I'm really gay, the man next to me may notice. I might suddenly realize I'm gay and try to find a way to let*

him know. If we're both gay, we could go into the stall and I could finally feel what it is to hold another penis. All of this may happen if I stop avoiding situations that scare me, but I'm tired of OCD ruling my life, telling me where I should or should not go to be safe. I'm sick of it.

3. *If I'm going to become gay from public restrooms or going to Starbucks, then so be it. Better gay than this hell. If I end up giving strange men oral sex in bathrooms, then I just have to learn to cope with it when it happens.*

Lower-Hierarchy Exposure Script for Sexual Feelings for Others (page 238)

1. *I find that man behind the counter attractive. These feelings might mean I don't really love my husband. I have to stay here with these feelings noticing that he is attractive. I'm not as good a person as I would like to be because of these feelings, but I'll have to accept my faults. As for my husband, I only know that I'm not leaving him today.*

2. *★I am not allowed to confess this to him, so that probably makes me even worse. But this is my exposure. The way my OCD was going, he would have left me if I didn't get better. At least this way it will be my choice if it comes to that.*

Higher-Hierarchy Exposure Script for Sexual Feelings for Others (page 238)

1. *I have to start going out in public again, no matter what kinds of feelings I get in my body. If I start getting sexually aroused by other men, I'm going to have to let that mean whatever it means. If I suddenly wake up and realize that I don't love my husband, then I'll have to decide what to do about our marriage and the children. If I decide to leave, then that's what will happen.*

2. *Maybe I'm evil for having these thoughts, and maybe going out in public will just provide too much temptation. Men seem to want to sleep with anyone, so maybe if I find myself attracted to a man, he'll be willing to sleep with me if my arousal becomes too great to handle. We could go to a hotel somewhere, and I would get to experience the feel of a strange man's hands on my breasts (continue on with explicit details).*

3. *I don't know what I would tell my husband afterward, but I won't have to deal with it unless all this happens.*

4. *★All I know is that I have to start living again and not follow my OCD rules. They may feel like they keep me safe, but all they really do is keep me in prison.*

Exposure Script for Obsessive Jealousy (page 245)

1. *I can just imagine Y in bed with his old girlfriend X (insert details of what you imagine). Whenever I think about her, it makes me so insecure—I wonder if he wishes he was with her and if he fantasizes about being with her. Maybe I'm only second best.*

2. *It's so painful to think this, but I know I can't question him, because no matter what he says, I can't have the certainty I want. I'm going to have to stay with him and hope I'm number one in his heart without ever knowing for sure.*

3. *All I can do with my questions and rules is drive him away and then I'd have the same problem with whomever I met next. And if I'm really second best and he is looking for someone else, so that one day I come home to find him in bed with another woman, that is when I will have to deal with it.*

4. *★I don't worry about having cancer right now even though I may one day be threatened with it. This will have to be the same. I'll have to deal with it if it ever happens—I know it would be devastating for me, but my rituals don't protect me.*

5. *I have him for now, he says he loves me, and I love the moments that aren't stolen from us*

by the real enemy—OCD (insert material from your Cost-Benefit Analysis and what you love and enjoy about your relationship).

Exposure Script for R-OCD (page 251)

1. Even though I long to feel certain about my feelings for Y, I know my OCD will only torture the both of us. Because of R-OCD (your ERP Motivators Form—page 118— should have details of specific times when your R-OCD lead to painful scenes. These should be inserted here with the most painful details you can recall). I know I'm not ready to leave Y now, so the best I can do is work on my plan for coping with never knowing.

2. I know this may mean that Y may not be the best person for me. My only solace can be that people without this problem may believe they are with "The One," but that doesn't make it true. If I knew I was in love and Y had a debilitating accident or a long-term devastating disease, I like to believe I would stay and make the best of the situation, even though they would no longer be the same person. Certainly as we both age, neither of us will be as good-looking as younger people and yet I would not expect us to part.

3. My ritualizing has only resulted in pain for us. My goal is to learn to focus on what I enjoy about our relationship (insert the specifics of what you enjoy from the list you created). I am trying to learn to do this, because even in the best of relationships, couples don't feel constant romantic passion and at times will find some of their partner's behaviors aggravating.

4. As much as I want to confess my feelings, I'm trying to behave like non-sufferers. They don't tell each other if they have a thought of what it would be like to live with another. Besides, I don't know if I'd be confessing truths or obsessions. I may never get to know whether or not I'm settling for second best or less, but I can learn to enjoy what I have.

5. And should it occur that I someday decide to leave, it will be sad for both of us, but this wouldn't make us different from any other couple. I have to work on living and enjoying the present instead of comparing my life to the one in which I'm sure. At this time, learning to do this is the best for me and, hopefully, my partner.

Lower-Hierarchy Imaginal Exposure Script for Religious Obsessions (page 259)

1. ★I have to let that scene stay in my head, no matter what it means.
2. ★I hope this doesn't send me to hell, but I will accept whatever God wants to do, including damning me. It's important for me to prevent myself from all my undoing rituals. Whenever thoughts come to my mind that have to do with that scene, I have to let them be there for my exposure.
3. If I can't explain this on Judgment Day, then I'll spend time suffering in eternal damnation, but this is what I have to risk to overcome OCD.
4. ★It may seem crazy to me, but my rituals weren't working, and maybe they are as evil as what I'm doing now, so I already may be damned.

Higher-Hierarchy Imaginal Exposure Script for Religious Obsessions (page 260)

1. I see the Virgin Mary doing a striptease in a club. I'm in the crowd, cheering her on.
2. ★I'm letting this scene stay in my mind, because I need to do exposure to overcome my fear of my own thoughts. She keeps dancing to the music, and the crowd is going wild. I will let these thoughts stay in my head no matter what the consequences. I can hear Satan in the background, laughing and cheering all of us on. I will accept whatever God wants to do with me for doing this exposure. I won't be happy if He throws me into hell, but I trust His judgment.

3. ★*If that's what has to happen to me for trying to overcome my OCD, so be it. Accepting God's will is an act of faith. I hope He gives me the strength to keep doing this exposure without ritualizing.*

4. *I will hold on to the image of a sexy Virgin Mary dancing nude for me and a crowd of screaming men, with a happy Satan in the background. I'm tired of making God into a demanding monster.*

5. *If I'm wrong, I'm willing to pay the price. OCD has already put me in hell, and I'm going to beat it. I'm going to hold on to the image of Mother Mary bumping and grinding until I don't care whether or not it's there.*

Exposure Script for Obsessive Staring (page 273)

1. *I know I don't want to be caught staring at someone's privates, but I'm going to have to risk it with sneak peeking.*

2. ★*I don't know why the normal urge to do this is so strong with me—part of it probably comes from how scared I am of being caught and the pressure I put on myself to not do it. At this point in time, it makes perfect sense that whenever I'm in a problem situation that I automatically respond with anxiety and urges.*

3. *It would be wonderful if these just stopped, but that is a fantasy—I'm going to have to shoot for second best, sneak-peeking rather than trying not to look at all. I still may be caught and embarrassed, and if that happens, I'll claim innocence and hope I get away with it.*

Hypochondriasis Exposure Script for Having a Possibly Undiagnosable Illness (page 281)

1. *No matter how much I want to know what is wrong with me, there may be no answer. I have to limit my going to doctors, because it consumes all of my time and I'm so miserable, I never enjoy life.*

2. *If feels like it would be easier if I knew what was wrong, but after all this time, that's a fantasy. As for all of my checking at home, this serves no purpose. I'm not a doctor.*

3. *And I know that whatever I checked last time is going to be there with or without checking. I really don't believe it will magically have disappeared.*

Hypochondriasis Exposure Script for Having and an Illness That May Get Worse (page 281)

1. *I may be terrified that I might have a horrible progressive illness that I don't want to live with, but medical science obviously isn't at a point to explain my symptoms. My feeling that they must mean something isn't necessarily true. I need to live with the risk that it may be something awful.*

2. *For certain diagnoses I may feel like I would commit suicide because of how disabling they would eventually be. But I'm not that disabled now, so even if I found out I had something awful, I could let myself live and not deal with how intolerable it would be until later.*

Hypochondriasis Exposure Script for Possibly Never Getting Any Symptom Relief (page 282)

1. *The discomfort I suffer with may have no help for it. Right now I focus on it so much, that however bad it is, I make it worse. There are aches I have that have nothing to do with my fears, and I cope with them. Sometimes I may not notice them for a short period of time, even though they still hurt. I need to learn to manage my discomfort differently, since there may be no other relief.*

OCD Resources

Below is a brief list of some of the major OCD resources available to you. The list is not meant to be exhaustive, but it will provide you with a good start for obtaining further information and help.

ORGANIZATIONS

The International Obsessive-Compulsive Disorder Foundation

PO Box 961029, Boston, MA 02196

Phone: 617.973.5801

E-mail: info@ocfoundation.org

Website: www.ocfoundation.org

With more than 10,000 members, this international organization is your best resource. It is made up of professionals, sufferers, and their families and is an excellent resource for information about OCD and other anxiety disorders. Their annual convention for professionals, sufferers, and their families will provide you with information about current treatment approaches to OCD.

In addition to providing up-to-date information about the treatment of OCD, they maintain a nationwide (and the beginning of an international) list of treatment providers and OCD support groups.

The International OCD Foundation's annual convention for both consumers and professionals includes experiential and educational workshops. Attending it will not only provide you with information about current treatment practices, it will also offer you the opportunity to see what some of the treatments are like. If you can attend, it is an experience not to be missed.

This organization's website should be your prime source for OCD information and resources. Besides the aforementioned resources, it provides lists of therapists who treat OCD, of other organizations, websites, and online support groups. The site also provides a special

"Ask the Experts" section in which you can have your questions about OCD answered by nationally recognized OCD experts from the organization's Scientific Advisory Board.

Association of Cognitive and Behavioral Therapies (ABCT)

305 Seventh Avenue
New York, NY 10001-6008
Phone: 212.647.1890
Website: www.abct.org
This organization of cognitive behavioral professionals can refer you to doctors in your area who treat OCD. Their directory lists professionals by states, cities, and specialties.

Anxiety and Depression Association of America

8701 Georgia Avenue #412
Silver Spring, MD 20910
Phone: 240.485.1001
Website: www.adaa.org
This organization of mental health professionals and sufferers of a variety of anxiety/depressive disorders including OCD has information on different disorders, treatment options, and where to find therapists in your area.

National Institute of Mental Health (NIMH)

Website: www.nimh.nih.gov
Type *OCD* in the search field for a wealth of information, including the latest research findings and information about how to participate in one of their research protocols.

Index

Page numbers in **bold** indicate charts and tables; those in *italics* indicate checklists.

imperfection (fear), 29, 35

"Indecision Exposure Support" Script, 197–198, 338

indecision obsessions, 170, 194–198

individual taste and BDD, 290

Inflated Responsibility, **97,** 101, 110, 112

injury to others in public places, 170, 180–186, **183, 184**

injury to others with your car, 32, 38, 69, 73, 101, 103, 116, 136, 137, 139, 170, 177–180, 302, **307,** 339

insidiously slow slips, 322

intellectual uncertainty, 8, 10, 11, 12, 18

intelligence (above-average) trait, primary mental obsessions, 218

"Interfering with Mental Retracing for Misunderstanding Others" Script, 191–192, 340

internal/external dimension of triggers, 323, **324,** 324–325, **330, 331**

International Obsessive-Compulsive Disorder Foundation, 46, 127, 299, 303, 304

Intolerance of Uncertainty, **97,** 98, 99

Ira's story (contamination), 7–8, 37, 156–157, **157**

it really is all in your mind. *See* primary mental obsessions

Jack's story (hit-and-run), 32, 38

Jacob and God, 255

Jane's story (contamination), 23–24

jealousy obsessions, 242–245, **244,** 343–344

Jessica's story (foot tapping), 5, 36, 37–38, 44–45

Jewish people, 58

Judaism, 254, 255, 256–257, 261

"just right" feelings, 35, 39, 213–214, 254

keyboards, 72, 142

King, Stephen, 222–223, 230

knowing vs. guessing, 12–13

known affairs, 242–243, 244

K'zayit principle, Judaism, 256

learned component of OCD, xiii, 14, 15, 18, 19–27, 42–43

learning and medication side effects, 42, 46, **46,** 334

"letting go" of thoughts, ease of, 42

Lexapro, 46, **46**

lies, 33, 247

Lily's story (contamination), 127–128

list-making, 198

"Living with Reduced Satisfaction" Script, 145, 335

Liz's story (diabetes and insulin), 41–42

lock-checking rituals, 174

logic, 6, 10–11, 12, 18, 97, 101–102, 334

loss and acceptance of uncertainty, 54–56, 98, 103, 110

loss and/or forgetting obsessions, 29, 31, 170, 198–199

loss obsessions, *77–78*

Lost to OCD, Exposure and Response Prevention (ERP) Motivators, 115, 116, **117,** 139, 144, 145, 161, 193, 198, 203, 251, 294, 333

Loved Ones Hurt by OCD, Exposure and Response Prevention (ERP) Motivators, 115, 116, **118,** 139, 144, 145, 161, 193, 198, 203, 251, 294, 333, 335

Lower-Exposure Hierarchy Imaginal Therapy Script for Violent Obsessions, 228, 341

Lower-Hierarchy Imaginal Script for "Am I Gay?" Obsessions, 237, 342

Lower-Hierarchy Imaginal Script for Sexual Feelings for Others, 238, 343

Lower-Hierarchy Imaginal Script for Sexual Molestation, 237, 342

Lower-Hierarchy Imaginal Therapy Script for Religious Obsessions, 259, 344

low-probability events, 10

"lucky" numbers, 211, 212–213

Lutherans, 261

Luvox, 46, **46**

"magic," 201–202, 214, 276. *See also* perfection and magic rituals

magical compulsions, *85*

magical obsessions, *78*

Mark's story (movement), 215–216

marriage, 57, 333, 334

Martin's story (devil fear), 260–261

Mary's story (symptom-free periods), 14–15, 16

"master artist," xiii

medical fears coming true, 283–284, 345

medical personnel rituals, 285, 286, 287

medication role, 41–47. *See also* obsessive-compulsive disorder (OCD)

    antipsychotics, **46**

    anxiety as driving force behind OCD, 42

Jonathan B. Grayson, PhD is the director of the Anxiety and OCD Treatment Center of Philadelphia and a Clinical Associate in the Psychology Department of the University of Pennsylvania. A nationally recognized expert who has worked with OCD sufferers for more than three decades, Dr. Grayson was awarded the Patricia Perkins International OCD Foundation Lifetime Achievement Award in 2010 for his work with OCD. Dr. Grayson organized the first OCD support group in the country for OCD. He lives near Philadelphia.